Love

Vol. 1

by

andi watson

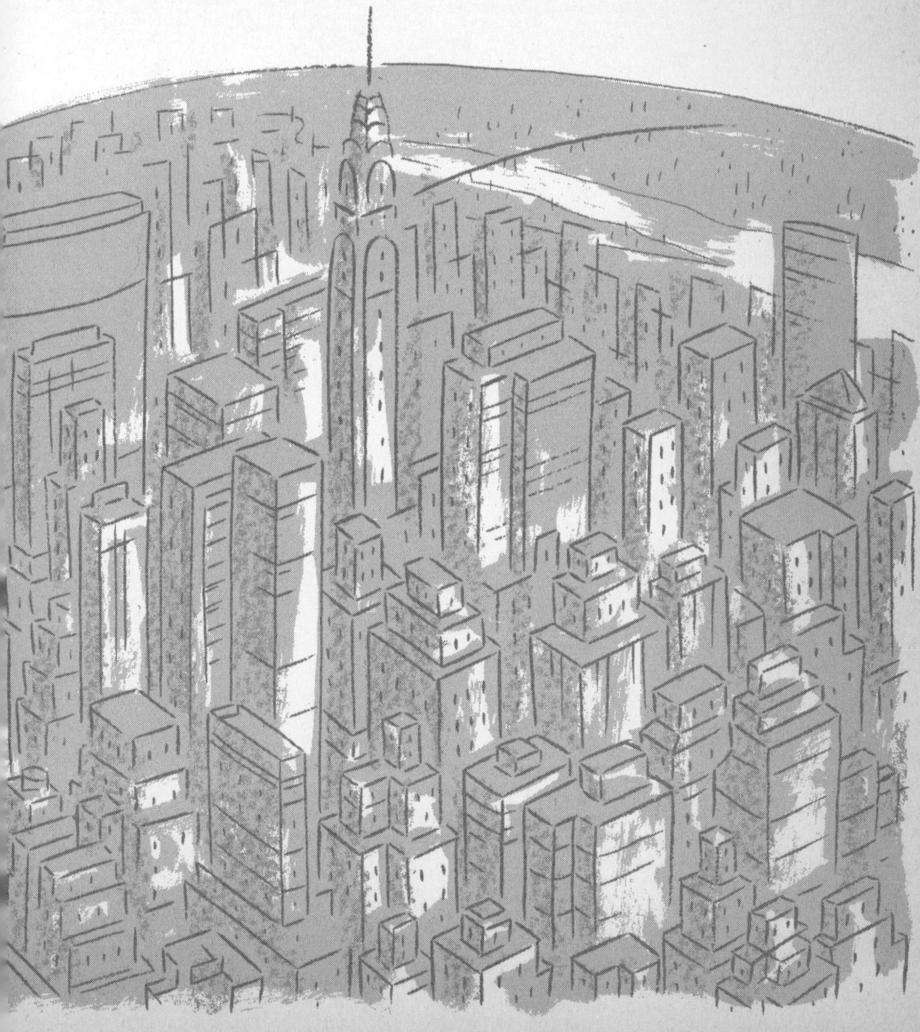

afterword by J. Torres & B. Clay Moore

book design by Keith Wood
edited by Jamie S. Rich

Woodercaps Font designed by Woodrow Phoenix

This book collects issues 1-6 of the Oni Press
comic book series *Love Fights*.

Published by Oni Press, Inc.
Joe Nozemack, publisher
James Lucas Jones, senior editor
Randal Jarrell, managing editor

ONI PRESS, INC.
6336 SE Milwaukie Avenue, PMB30
Portland, OR 97202
USA

www.onipress.com
www.andiwatson.com

First edition: April 2004
ISBN 1-929998-86-4

1 3 5 7 9 10 8 6 4 2
PRINTED IN CANADA

For Jamie

Love Fights ™

#1

andi watson

ONI PRESS

$2.99 U.S., $4.60 CAN.

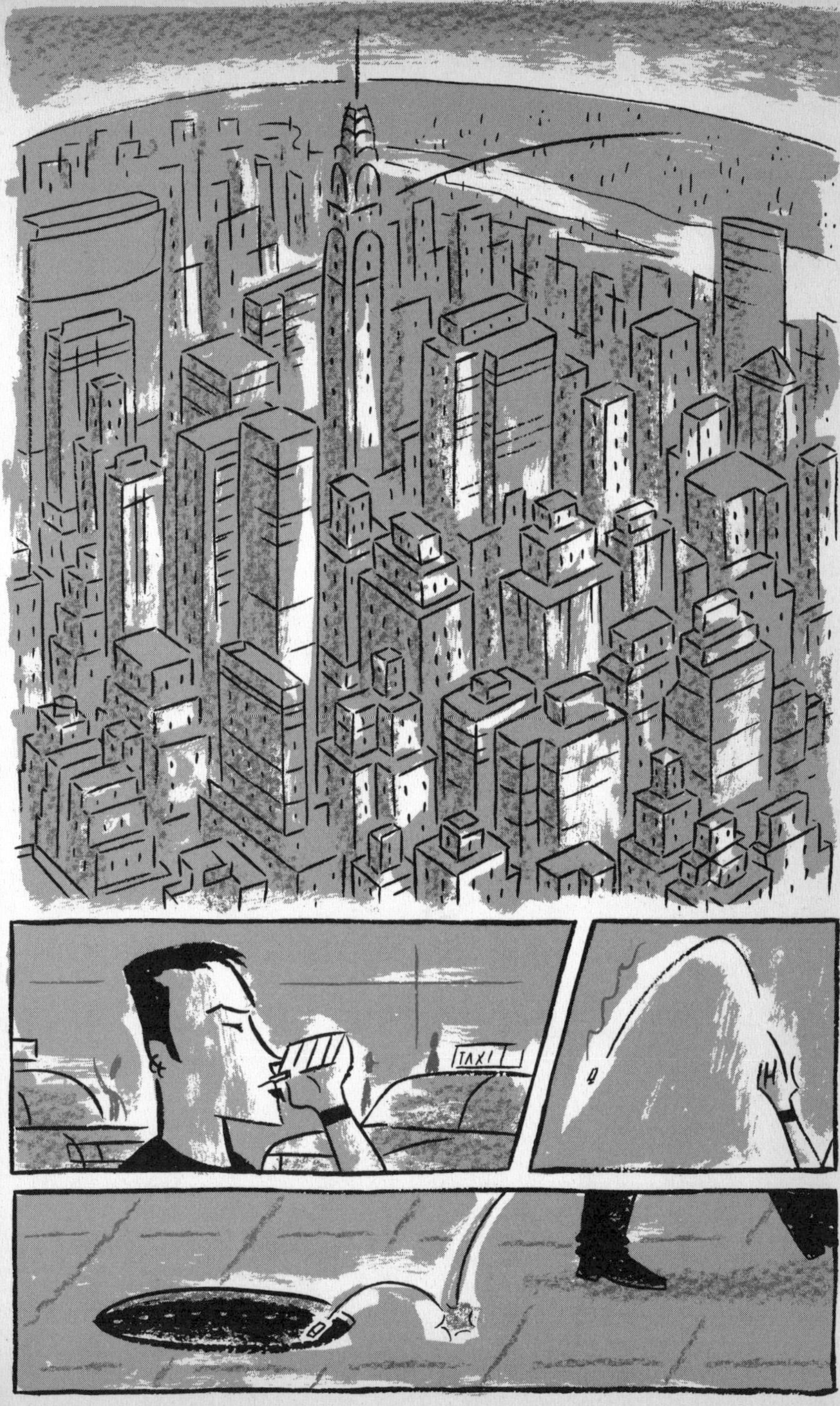
TAXI

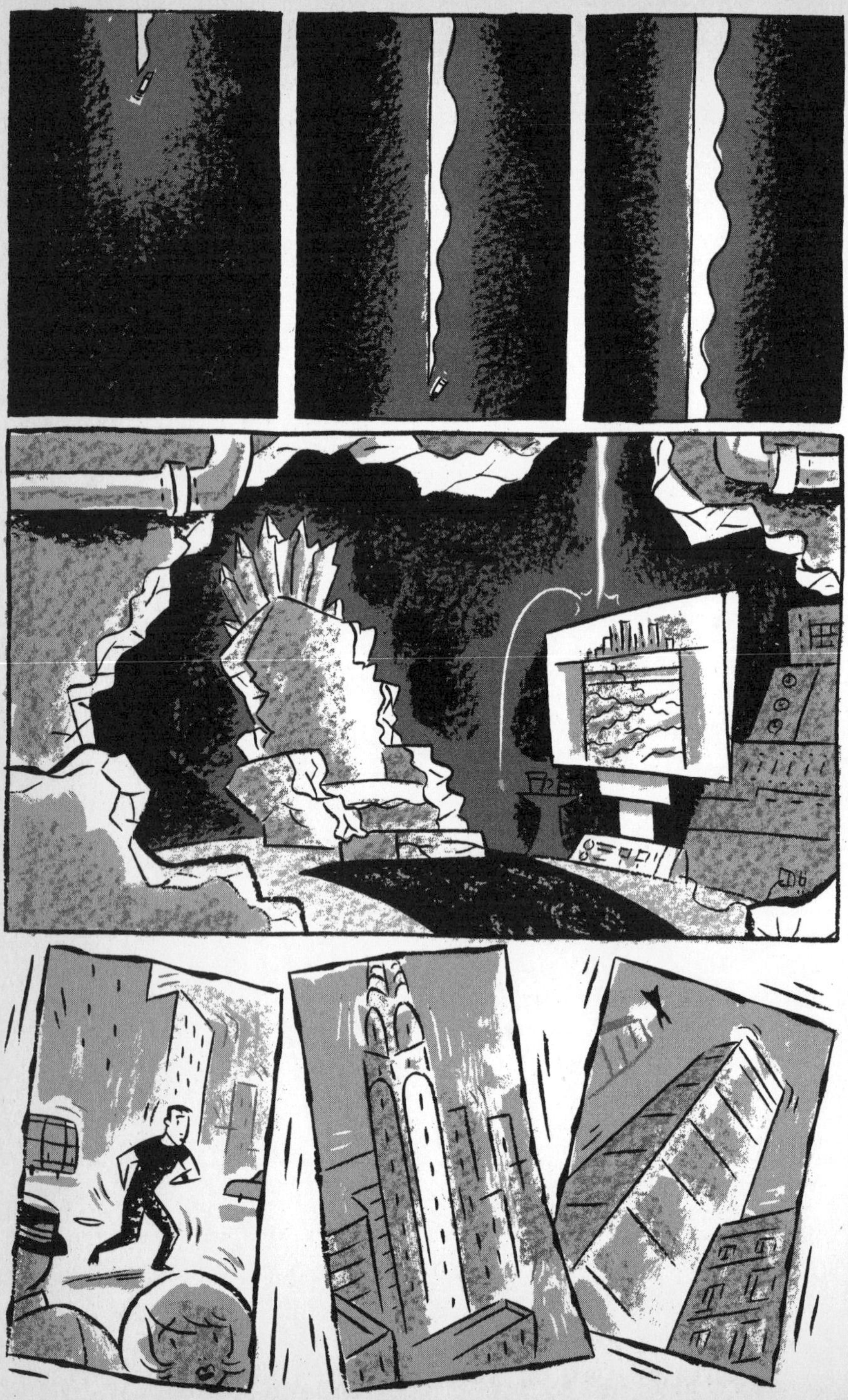

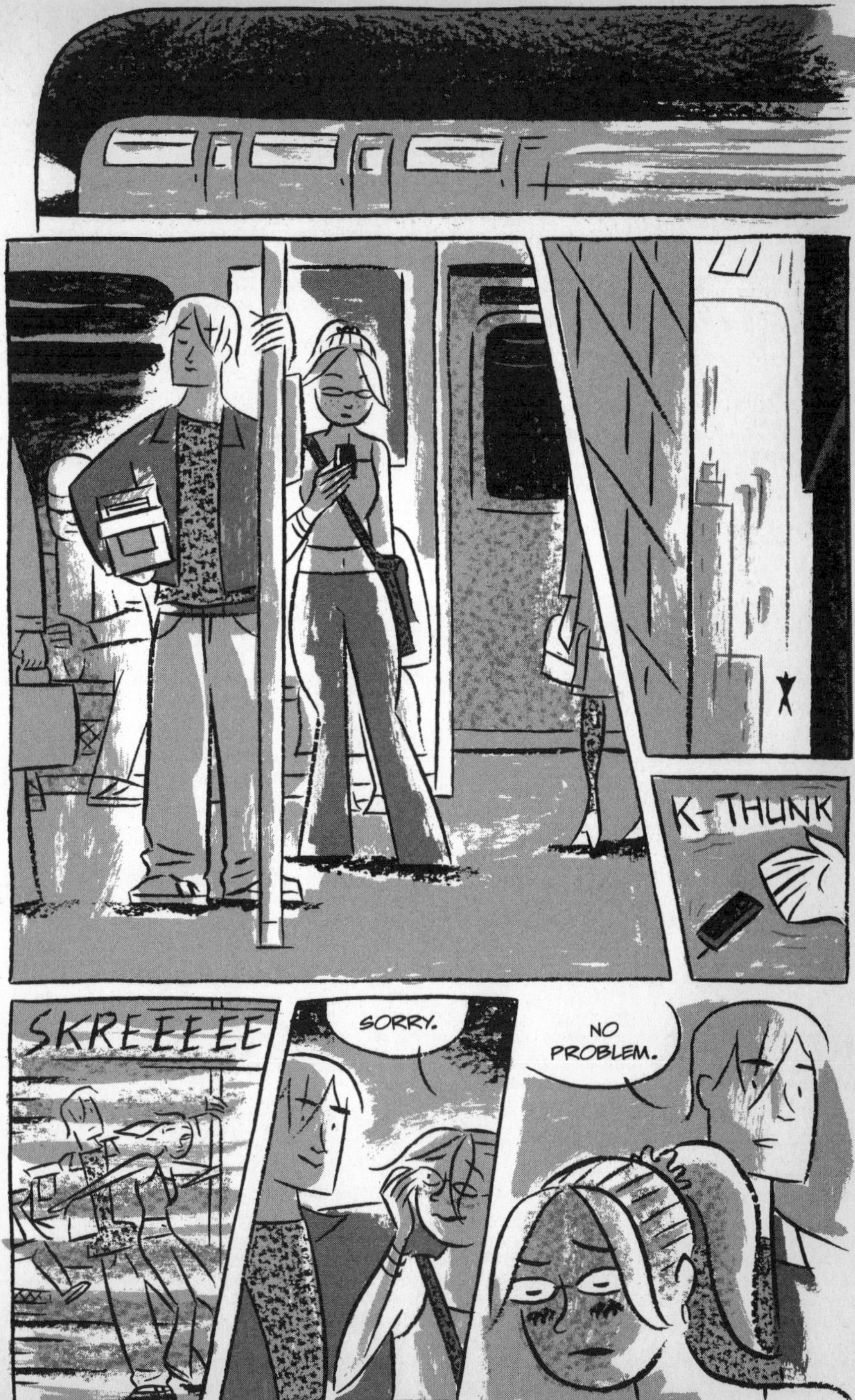
K-THUNK
SKREEEEEE
SORRY.
NO PROBLEM.

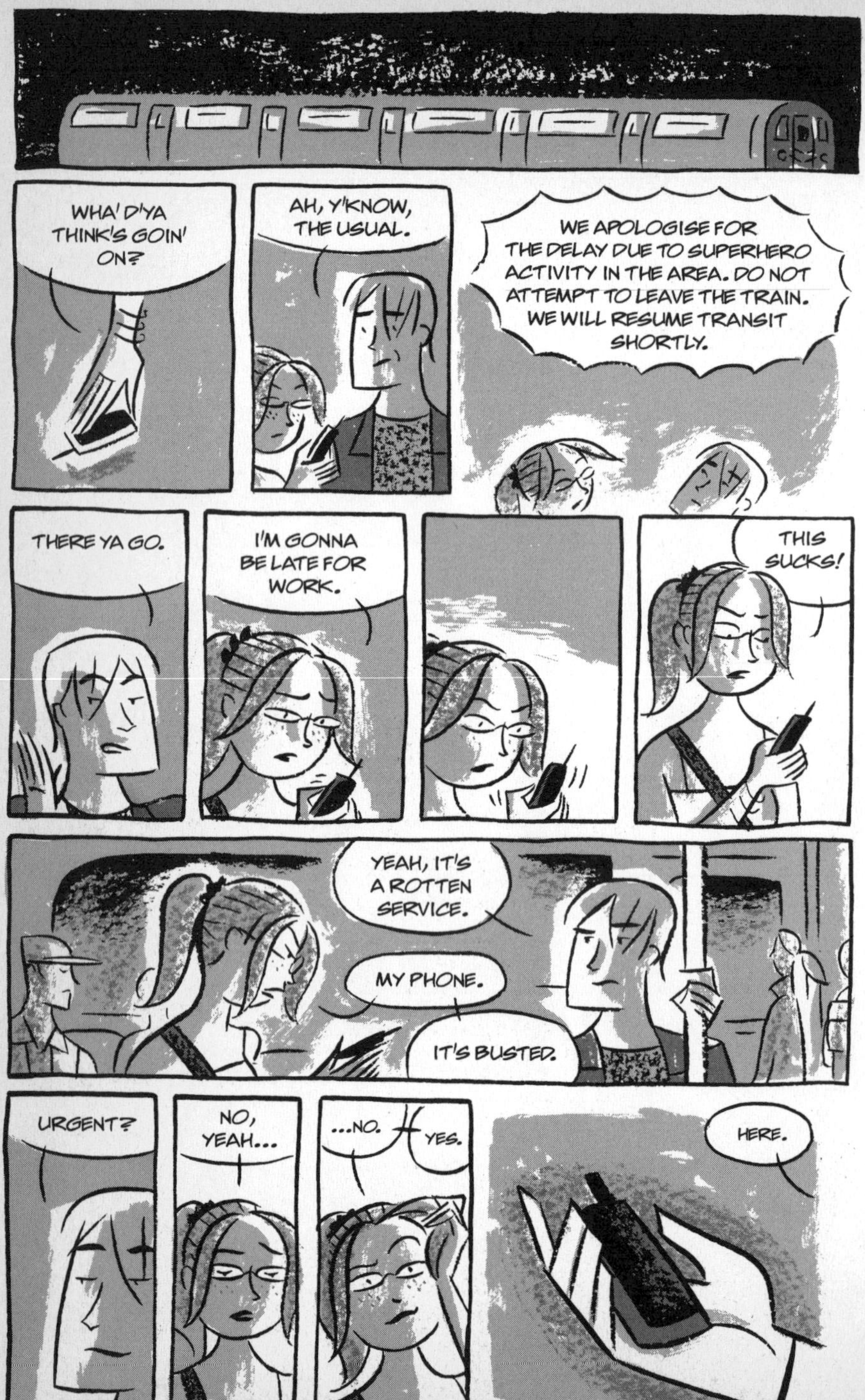
WHA' D'YA THINK'S GOIN' ON?
AH, Y'KNOW, THE USUAL.
WE APOLOGISE FOR THE DELAY DUE TO SUPERHERO ACTIVITY IN THE AREA. DO NOT ATTEMPT TO LEAVE THE TRAIN. WE WILL RESUME TRANSIT SHORTLY.
THERE YA GO.
I'M GONNA BE LATE FOR WORK.
THIS SUCKS!
YEAH, IT'S A ROTTEN SERVICE.
MY PHONE.
IT'S BUSTED.
URGENT?
NO, YEAH...
...NO.
YES.
HERE.

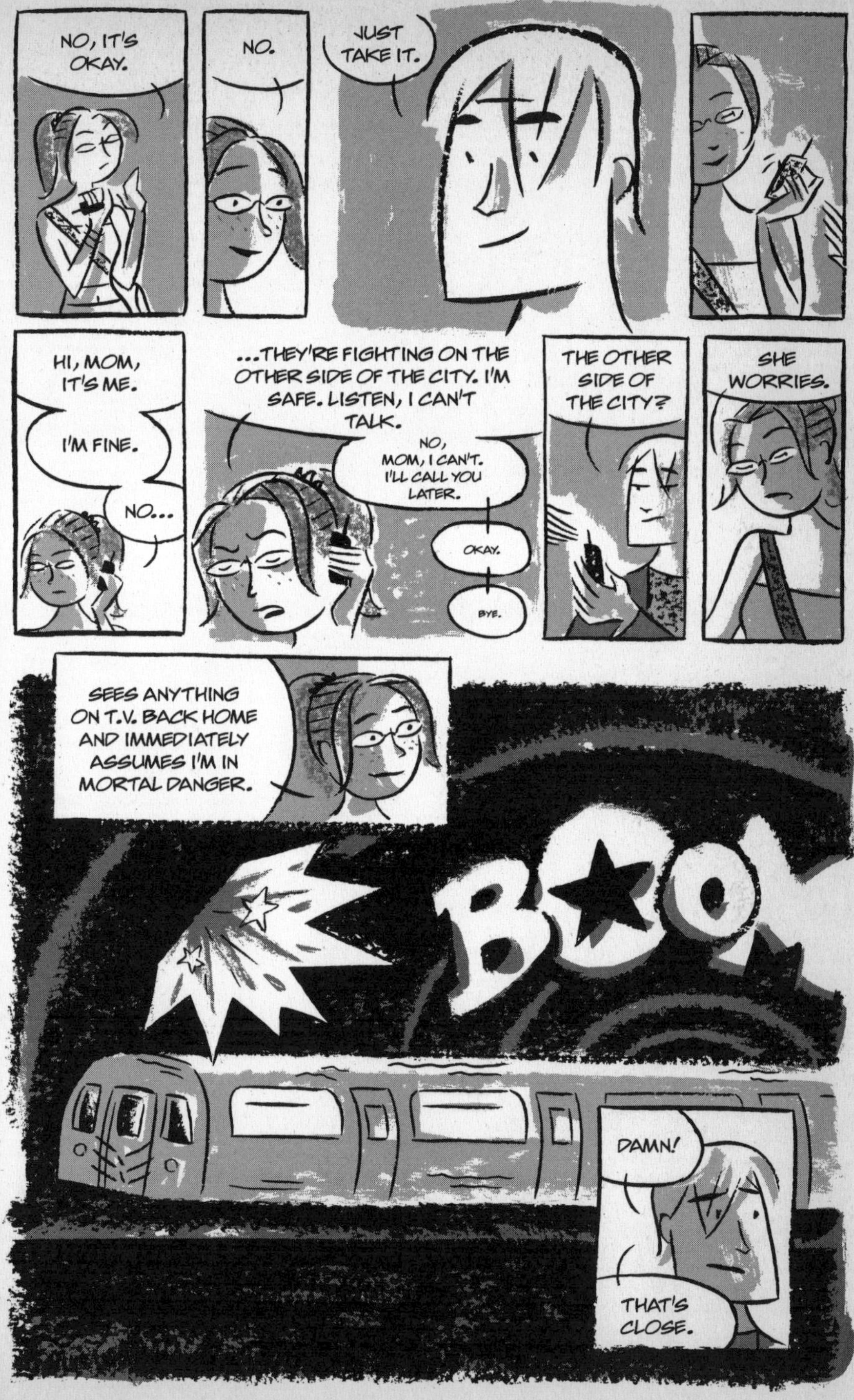
NO, IT'S OKAY.
NO.
JUST TAKE IT.
HI, MOM, IT'S ME.
I'M FINE.
NO...
...THEY'RE FIGHTING ON THE OTHER SIDE OF THE CITY. I'M SAFE. LISTEN, I CAN'T TALK.
NO, MOM, I CAN'T. I'LL CALL YOU LATER.
OKAY.
BYE.
THE OTHER SIDE OF THE CITY?
SHE WORRIES.
SEES ANYTHING ON T.V. BACK HOME AND IMMEDIATELY ASSUMES I'M IN MORTAL DANGER.
DAMN!
THAT'S CLOSE.

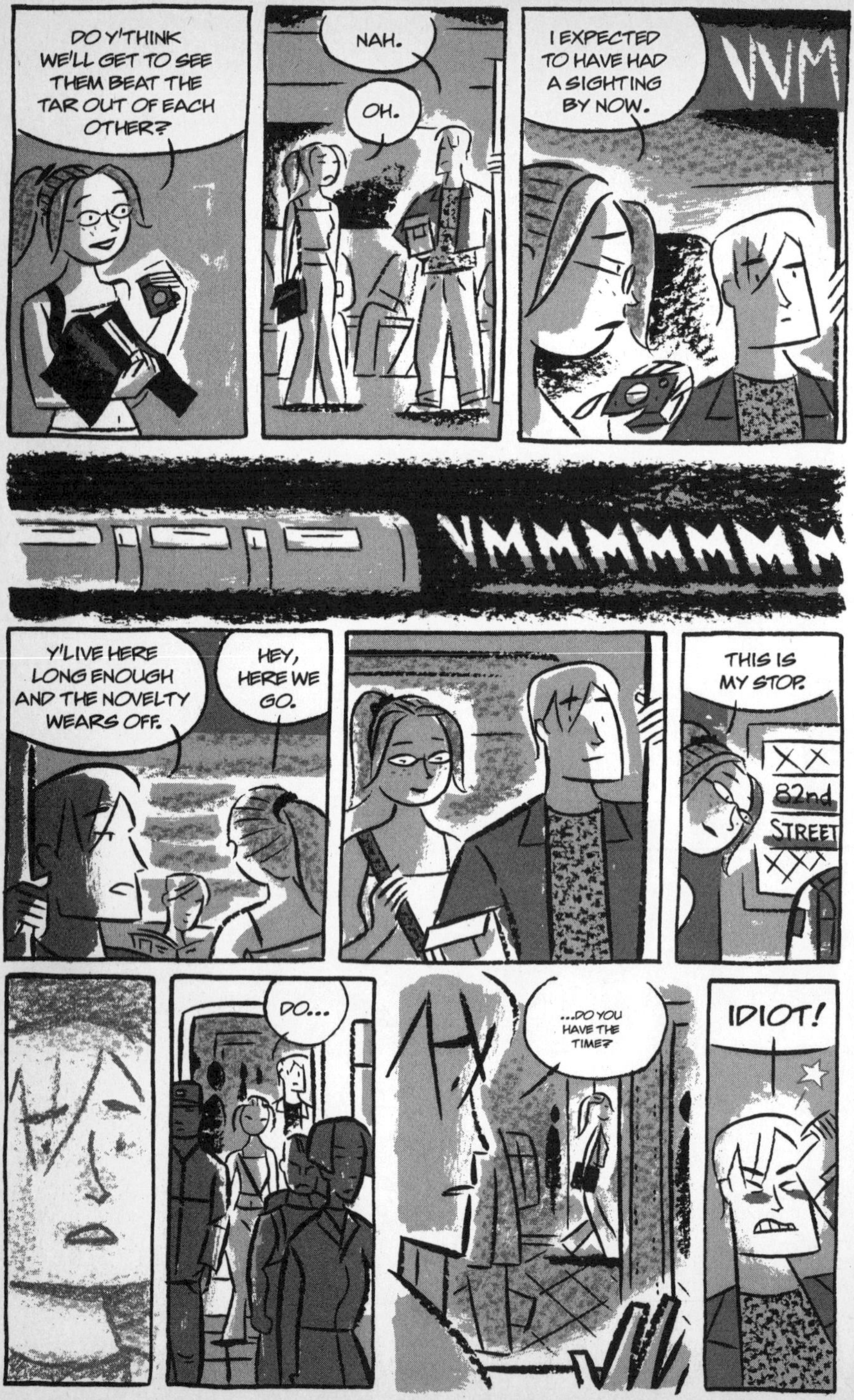
DO Y'THINK WE'LL GET TO SEE THEM BEAT THE TAR OUT OF EACH OTHER?
NAH.
OH.
I EXPECTED TO HAVE HAD A SIGHTING BY NOW.
VVM
VMMMMMMM
Y'LIVE HERE LONG ENOUGH AND THE NOVELTY WEARS OFF.
HEY, HERE WE GO.
THIS IS MY STOP.
82nd STREET
DO...
...DO YOU HAVE THE TIME?
IDIOT!

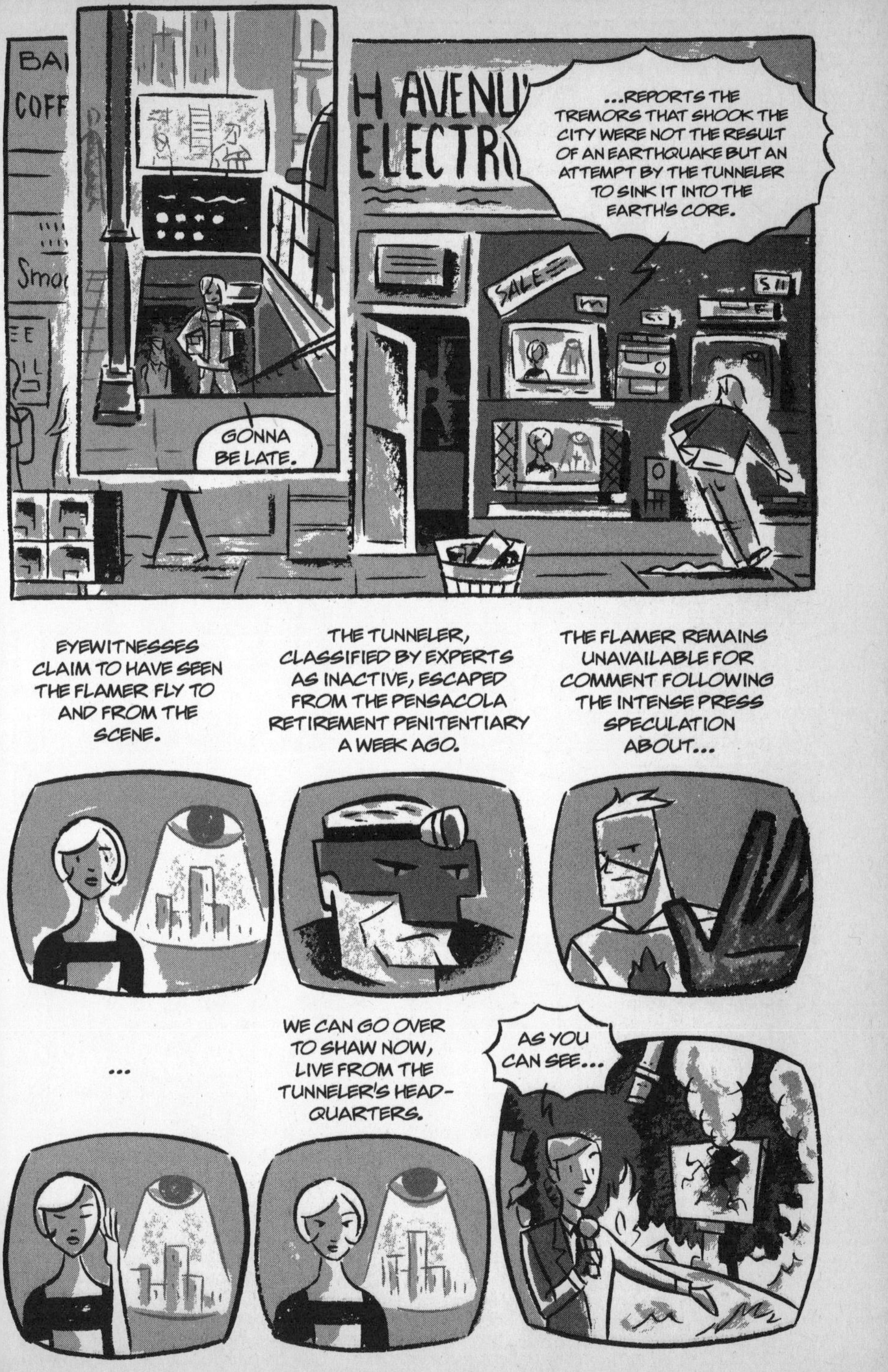

SALE
...REPORTS THE TREMORS THAT SHOOK THE CITY WERE NOT THE RESULT OF AN EARTHQUAKE BUT AN ATTEMPT BY THE TUNNELER TO SINK IT INTO THE EARTH'S CORE.
GONNA BE LATE.
EYEWITNESSES CLAIM TO HAVE SEEN THE FLAMER FLY TO AND FROM THE SCENE.
THE TUNNELER, CLASSIFIED BY EXPERTS AS INACTIVE, ESCAPED FROM THE PENSACOLA RETIREMENT PENITENTIARY A WEEK AGO.
THE FLAMER REMAINS UNAVAILABLE FOR COMMENT FOLLOWING THE INTENSE PRESS SPECULATION ABOUT...
...
WE CAN GO OVER TO SHAW NOW, LIVE FROM THE TUNNELER'S HEAD-QUARTERS.
AS YOU CAN SEE...

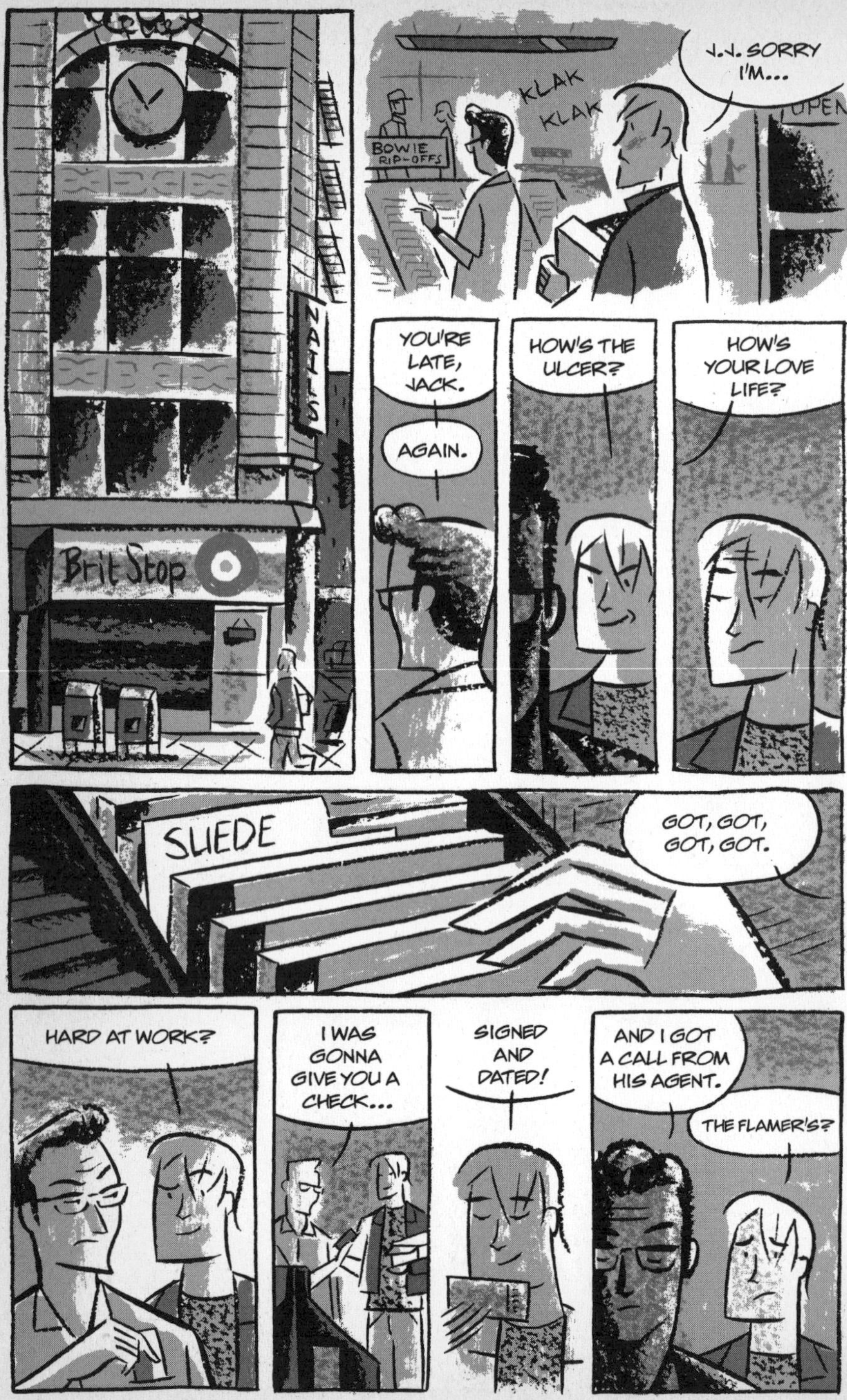
Brit Stop
NAILS
BOWIE RIP-OFFS
KLAK
KLAK
OPEN
J.J. SORRY I'M...
YOU'RE LATE, JACK.
AGAIN.
HOW'S THE ULCER?
HOW'S YOUR LOVE LIFE?
SUEDE
GOT, GOT, GOT, GOT.
HARD AT WORK?
I WAS GONNA GIVE YOU A CHECK...
SIGNED AND DATED!
AND I GOT A CALL FROM HIS AGENT.
THE FLAMER'S?

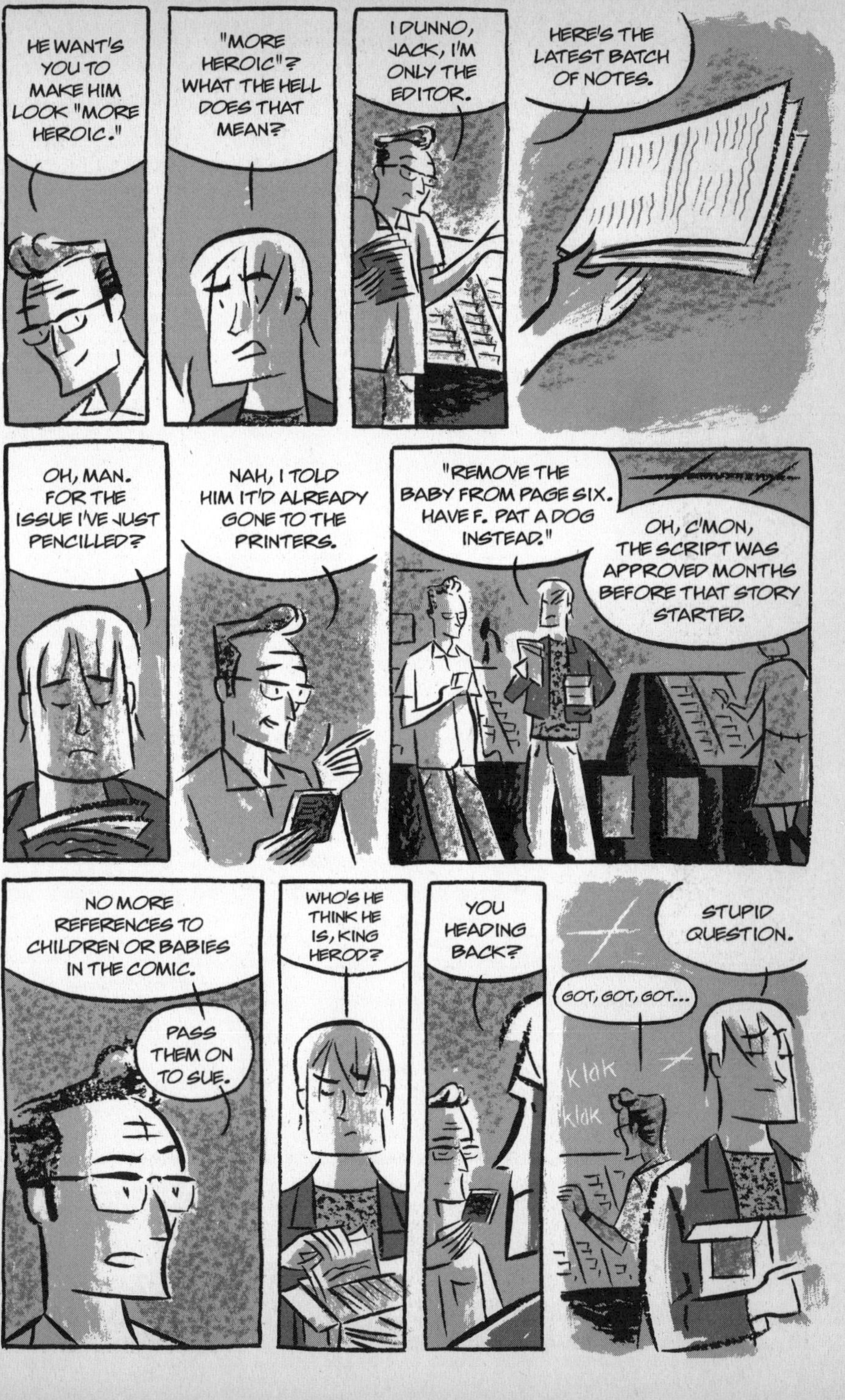
HE WANT'S YOU TO MAKE HIM LOOK "MORE HEROIC."
"MORE HEROIC"? WHAT THE HELL DOES THAT MEAN?
I DUNNO, JACK, I'M ONLY THE EDITOR.
HERE'S THE LATEST BATCH OF NOTES.
OH, MAN. FOR THE ISSUE I'VE JUST PENCILLED?
NAH, I TOLD HIM IT'D ALREADY GONE TO THE PRINTERS.
"REMOVE THE BABY FROM PAGE SIX. HAVE F. PAT A DOG INSTEAD."
OH, C'MON, THE SCRIPT WAS APPROVED MONTHS BEFORE THAT STORY STARTED.
NO MORE REFERENCES TO CHILDREN OR BABIES IN THE COMIC.
PASS THEM ON TO SUE.
WHO'S HE THINK HE IS, KING HEROD?
YOU HEADING BACK?
STUPID QUESTION.
GOT, GOT, GOT...
klak
klak

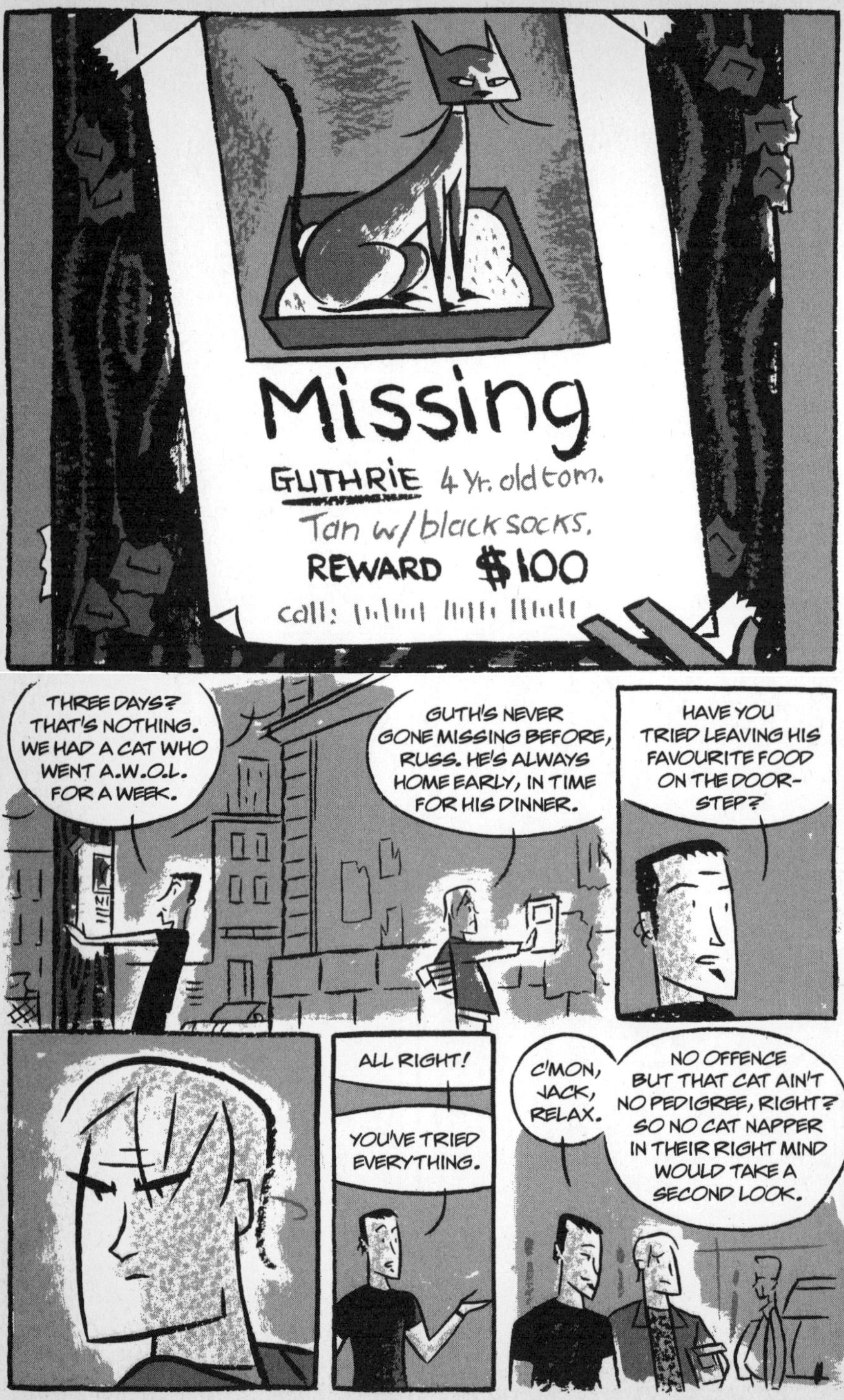
Missing
GUTHRIE 4 Yr. old tom.
Tan w/ black socks.
REWARD $100
call:
THREE DAYS? THAT'S NOTHING. WE HAD A CAT WHO WENT A.W.O.L. FOR A WEEK.
GUTH'S NEVER GONE MISSING BEFORE, RUSS. HE'S ALWAYS HOME EARLY, IN TIME FOR HIS DINNER.
HAVE YOU TRIED LEAVING HIS FAVOURITE FOOD ON THE DOOR-STEP?
ALL RIGHT!
YOU'VE TRIED EVERYTHING.
C'MON, JACK, RELAX.
NO OFFENCE BUT THAT CAT AIN'T NO PEDIGREE, RIGHT? SO NO CAT NAPPER IN THEIR RIGHT MIND WOULD TAKE A SECOND LOOK.

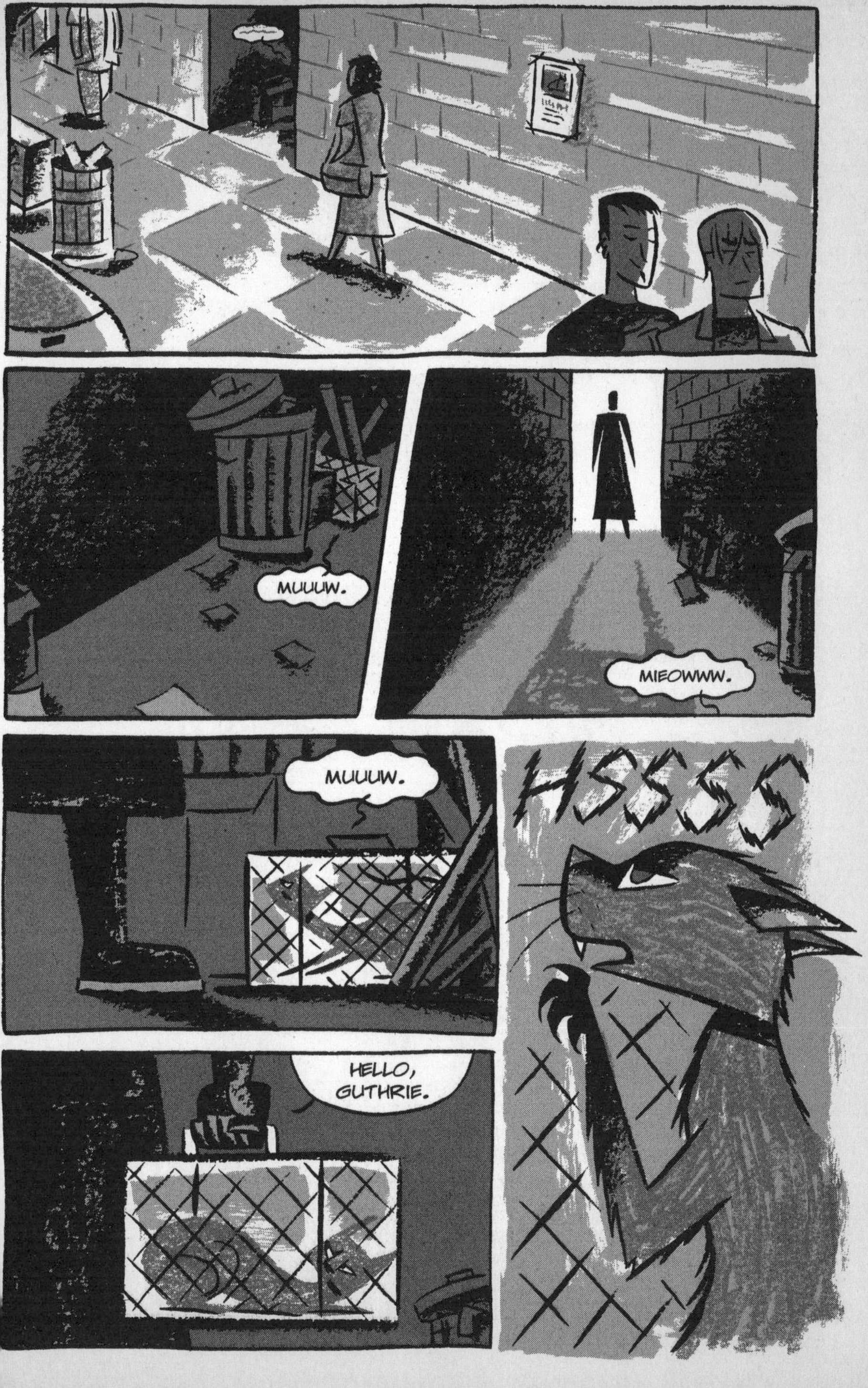
MUUUW.
MIEOWWW.
MUUUW.
HELLO, GUTHRIE.
HSSSS

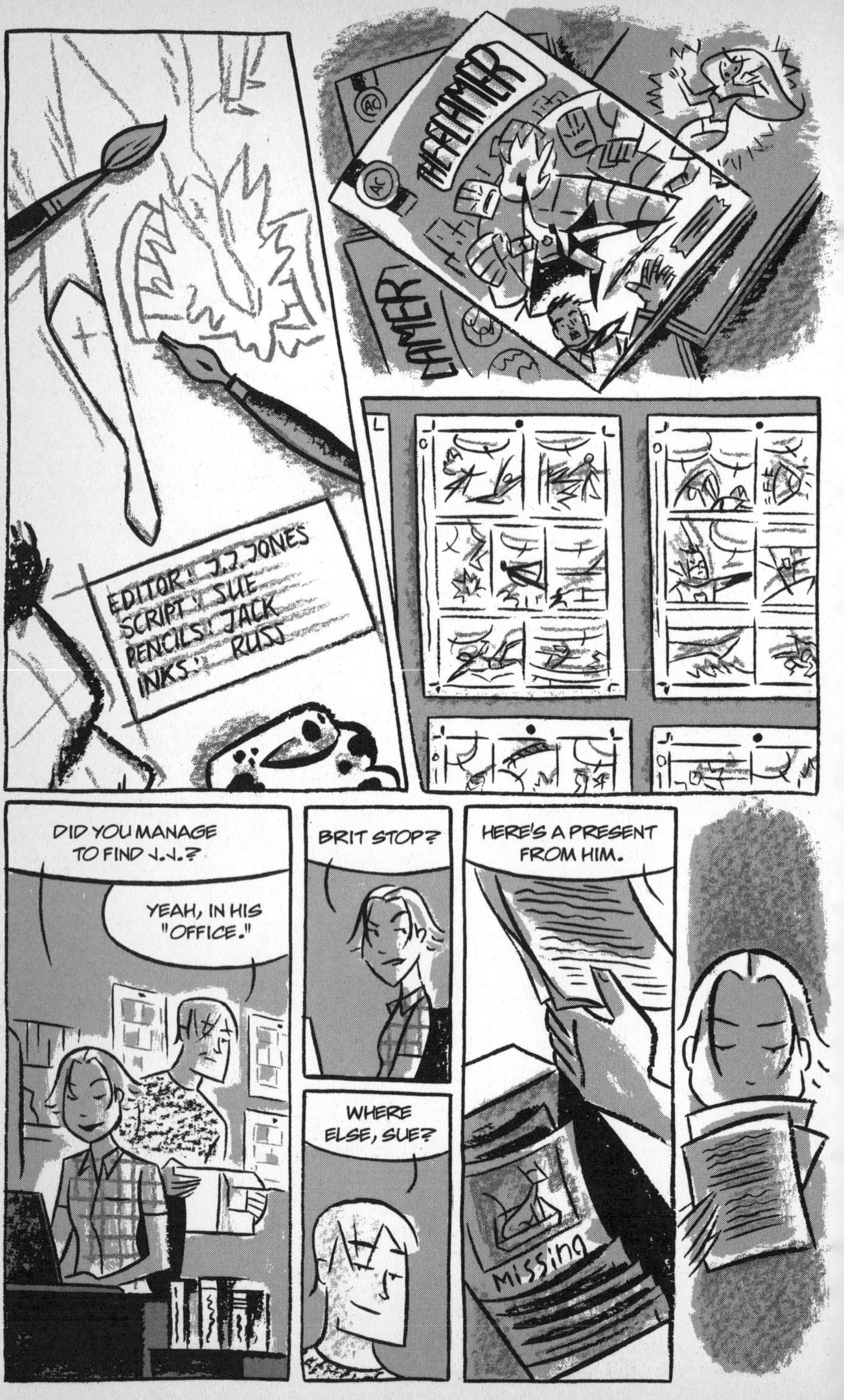
EDITOR: J.J. JONES
SCRIPT: SUE
PENCILS: JACK
INKS: RUSS
DID YOU MANAGE TO FIND J.J.?
YEAH, IN HIS "OFFICE."
BRIT STOP?
WHERE ELSE, SUE?
HERE'S A PRESENT FROM HIM.
Missing

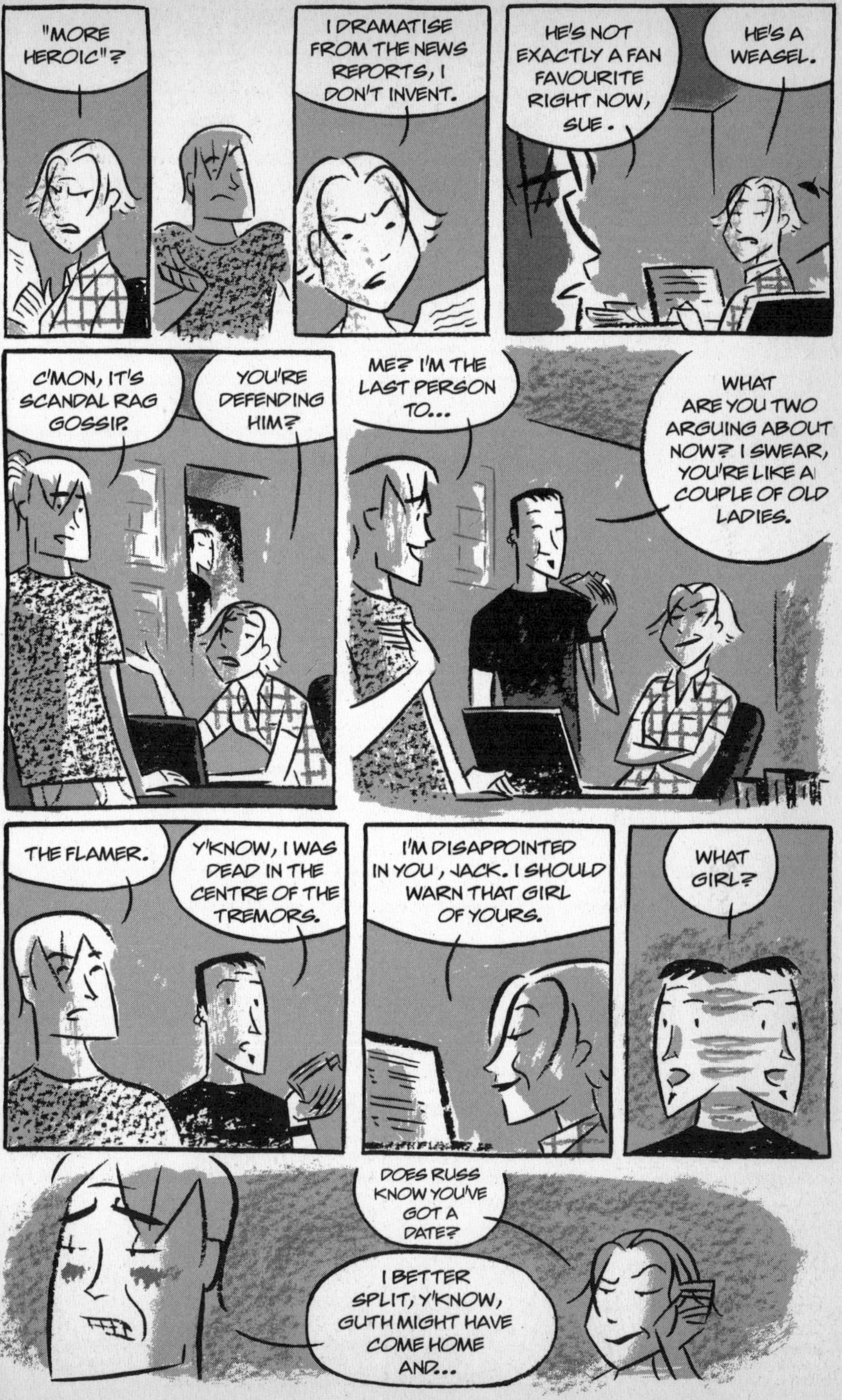
"MORE HEROIC"?
I DRAMATISE FROM THE NEWS REPORTS, I DON'T INVENT.
HE'S NOT EXACTLY A FAN FAVOURITE RIGHT NOW, SUE.
HE'S A WEASEL.
C'MON, IT'S SCANDAL RAG GOSSIP.
YOU'RE DEFENDING HIM?
ME? I'M THE LAST PERSON TO...
WHAT ARE YOU TWO ARGUING ABOUT NOW? I SWEAR, YOU'RE LIKE A COUPLE OF OLD LADIES.
THE FLAMER.
Y'KNOW, I WAS DEAD IN THE CENTRE OF THE TREMORS.
I'M DISAPPOINTED IN YOU, JACK. I SHOULD WARN THAT GIRL OF YOURS.
WHAT GIRL?
DOES RUSS KNOW YOU'VE GOT A DATE?
I BETTER SPLIT, Y'KNOW, GUTH MIGHT HAVE COME HOME AND...

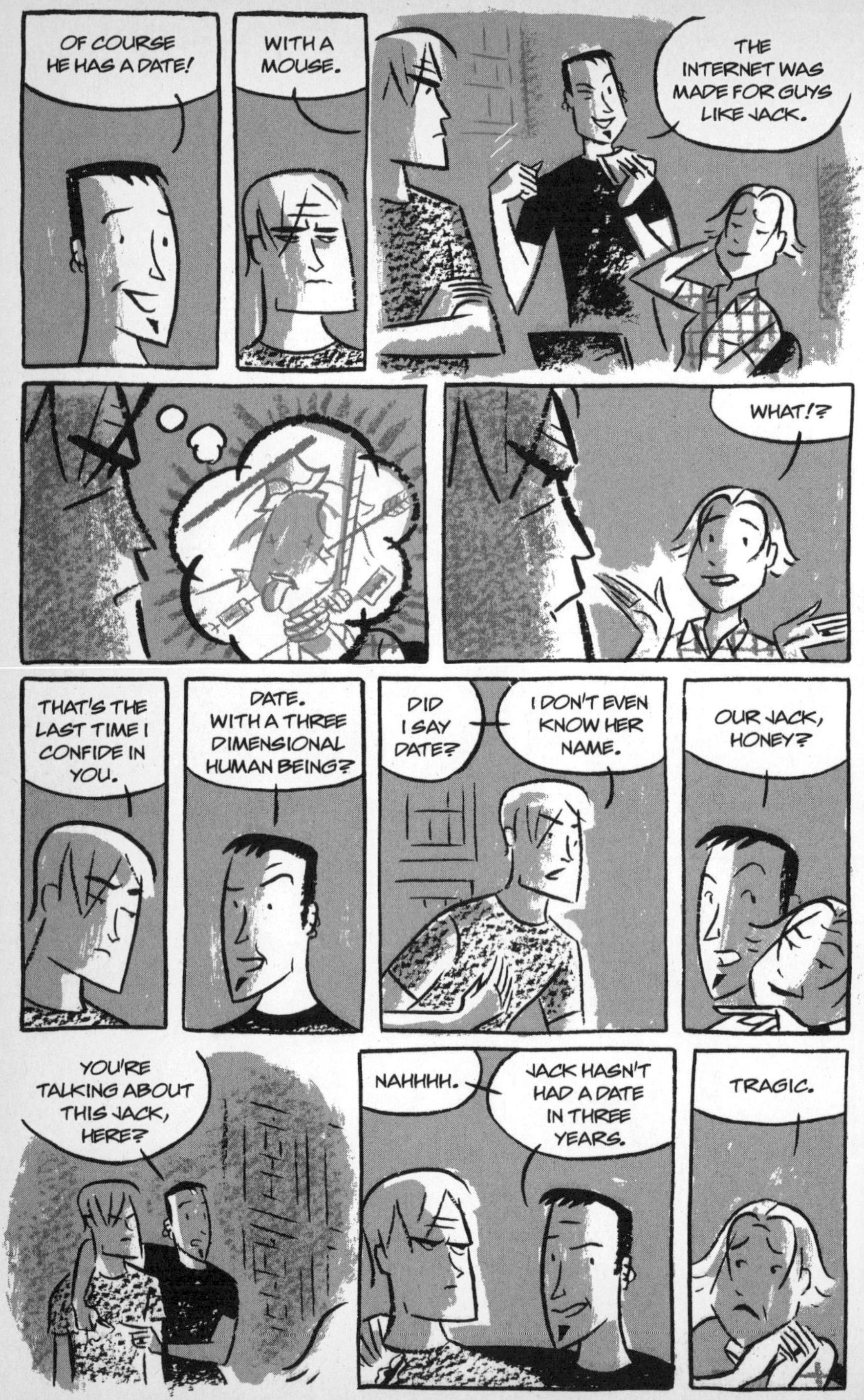
OF COURSE HE HAS A DATE!
WITH A MOUSE.
THE INTERNET WAS MADE FOR GUYS LIKE JACK.
WHAT!?
THAT'S THE LAST TIME I CONFIDE IN YOU.
DATE. WITH A THREE DIMENSIONAL HUMAN BEING?
DID I SAY DATE?
I DON'T EVEN KNOW HER NAME.
OUR JACK, HONEY?
YOU'RE TALKING ABOUT THIS JACK, HERE?
NAHHHH.
JACK HASN'T HAD A DATE IN THREE YEARS.
TRAGIC.

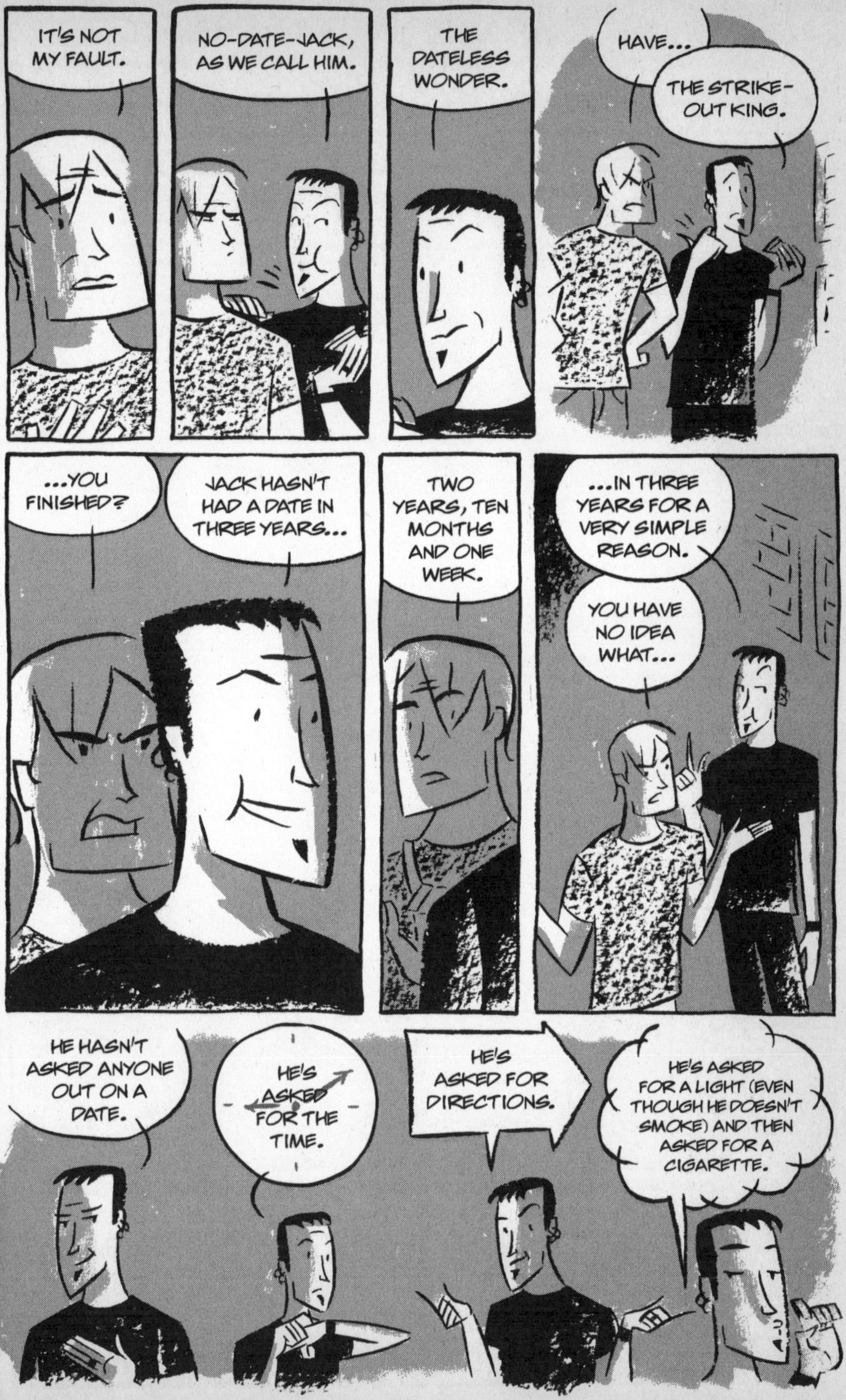
IT'S NOT MY FAULT.
NO-DATE-JACK, AS WE CALL HIM.
THE DATELESS WONDER.
HAVE...
THE STRIKE-OUT KING.
...YOU FINISHED?
JACK HASN'T HAD A DATE IN THREE YEARS...
TWO YEARS, TEN MONTHS AND ONE WEEK.
...IN THREE YEARS FOR A VERY SIMPLE REASON.
YOU HAVE NO IDEA WHAT...
HE HASN'T ASKED ANYONE OUT ON A DATE.
HE'S ASKED FOR THE TIME.
HE'S ASKED FOR DIRECTIONS.
HE'S ASKED FOR A LIGHT (EVEN THOUGH HE DOESN'T SMOKE) AND THEN ASKED FOR A CIGARETTE.

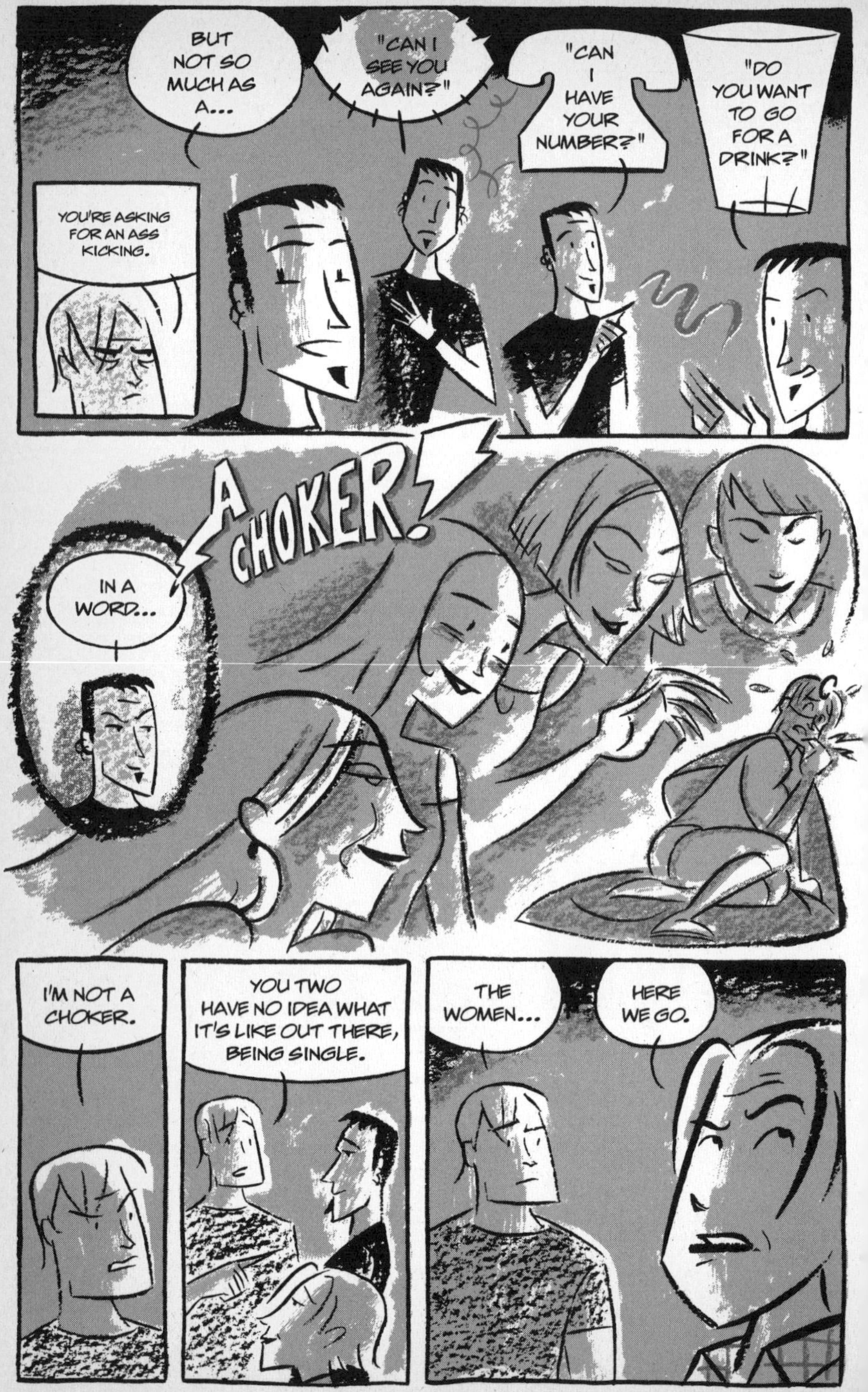
BUT NOT SO MUCH AS A...
"CAN I SEE YOU AGAIN?"
"CAN I HAVE YOUR NUMBER?"
"DO YOU WANT TO GO FOR A DRINK?"
YOU'RE ASKING FOR AN ASS KICKING.
IN A WORD...
A CHOKER!
I'M NOT A CHOKER.
YOU TWO HAVE NO IDEA WHAT IT'S LIKE OUT THERE, BEING SINGLE.
THE WOMEN...
HERE WE GO.

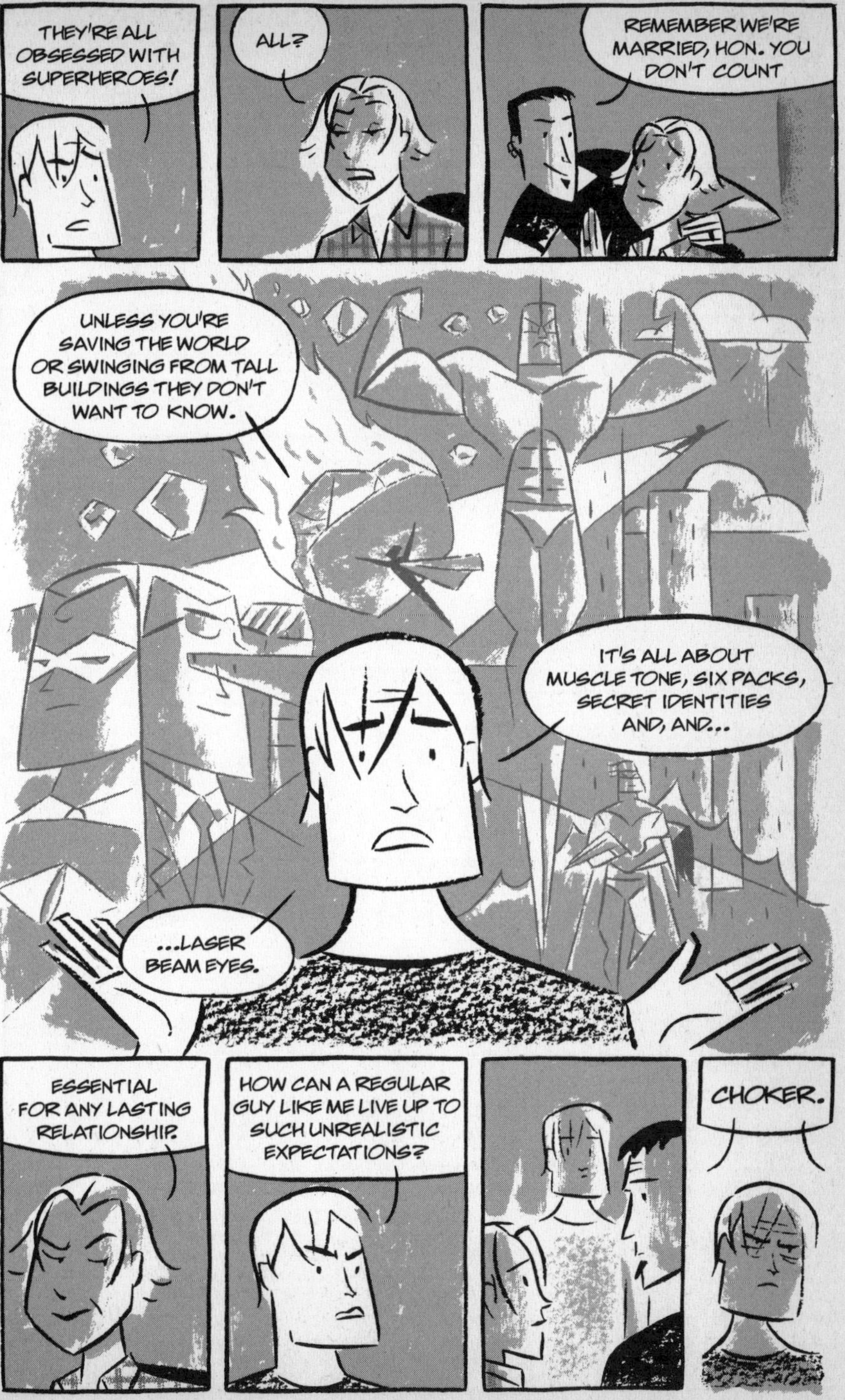
THEY'RE ALL OBSESSED WITH SUPERHEROES!
ALL?
REMEMBER WE'RE MARRIED, HON. YOU DON'T COUNT
UNLESS YOU'RE SAVING THE WORLD OR SWINGING FROM TALL BUILDINGS THEY DON'T WANT TO KNOW.
IT'S ALL ABOUT MUSCLE TONE, SIX PACKS, SECRET IDENTITIES AND, AND...
...LASER BEAM EYES.
ESSENTIAL FOR ANY LASTING RELATIONSHIP.
HOW CAN A REGULAR GUY LIKE ME LIVE UP TO SUCH UNREALISTIC EXPECTATIONS?
CHOKER.

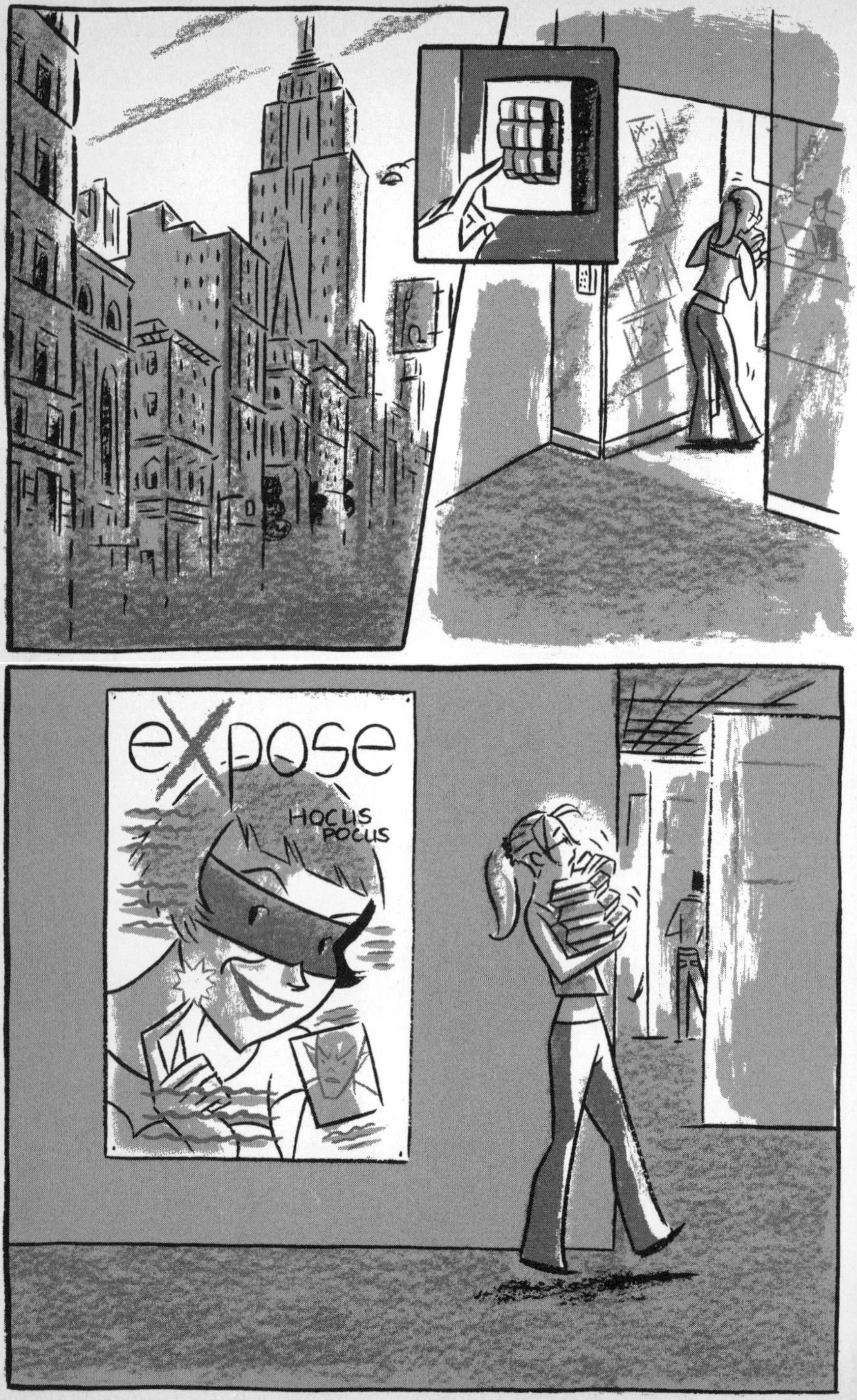
eXpose
HOCUS POCUS

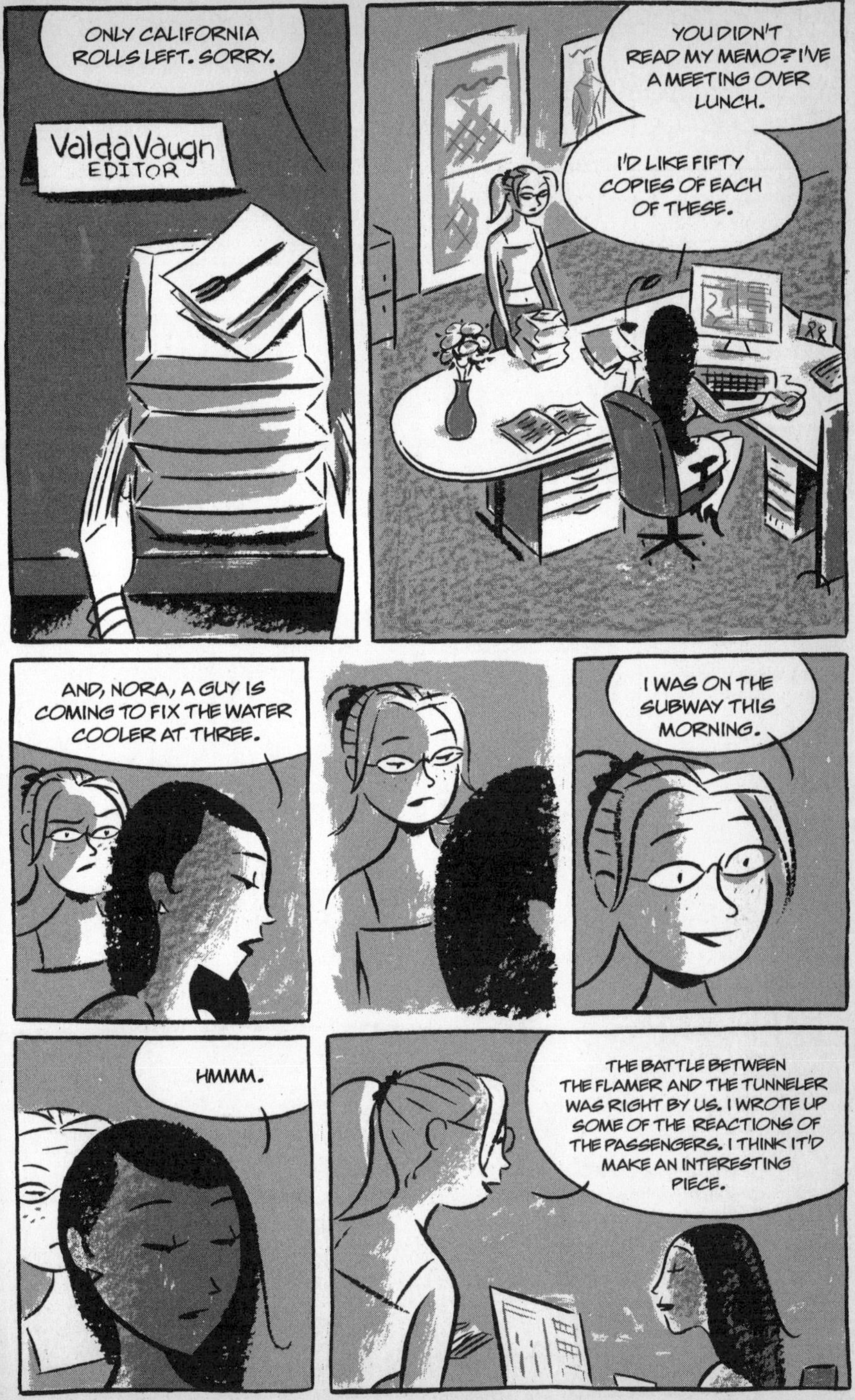
ONLY CALIFORNIA ROLLS LEFT. SORRY.
Valda Vaugn EDITOR
YOU DIDN'T READ MY MEMO? I'VE A MEETING OVER LUNCH.
I'D LIKE FIFTY COPIES OF EACH OF THESE.
AND, NORA, A GUY IS COMING TO FIX THE WATER COOLER AT THREE.
I WAS ON THE SUBWAY THIS MORNING.
HMMM.
THE BATTLE BETWEEN THE FLAMER AND THE TUNNELER WAS RIGHT BY US. I WROTE UP SOME OF THE REACTIONS OF THE PASSENGERS. I THINK IT'D MAKE AN INTERESTING PIECE.

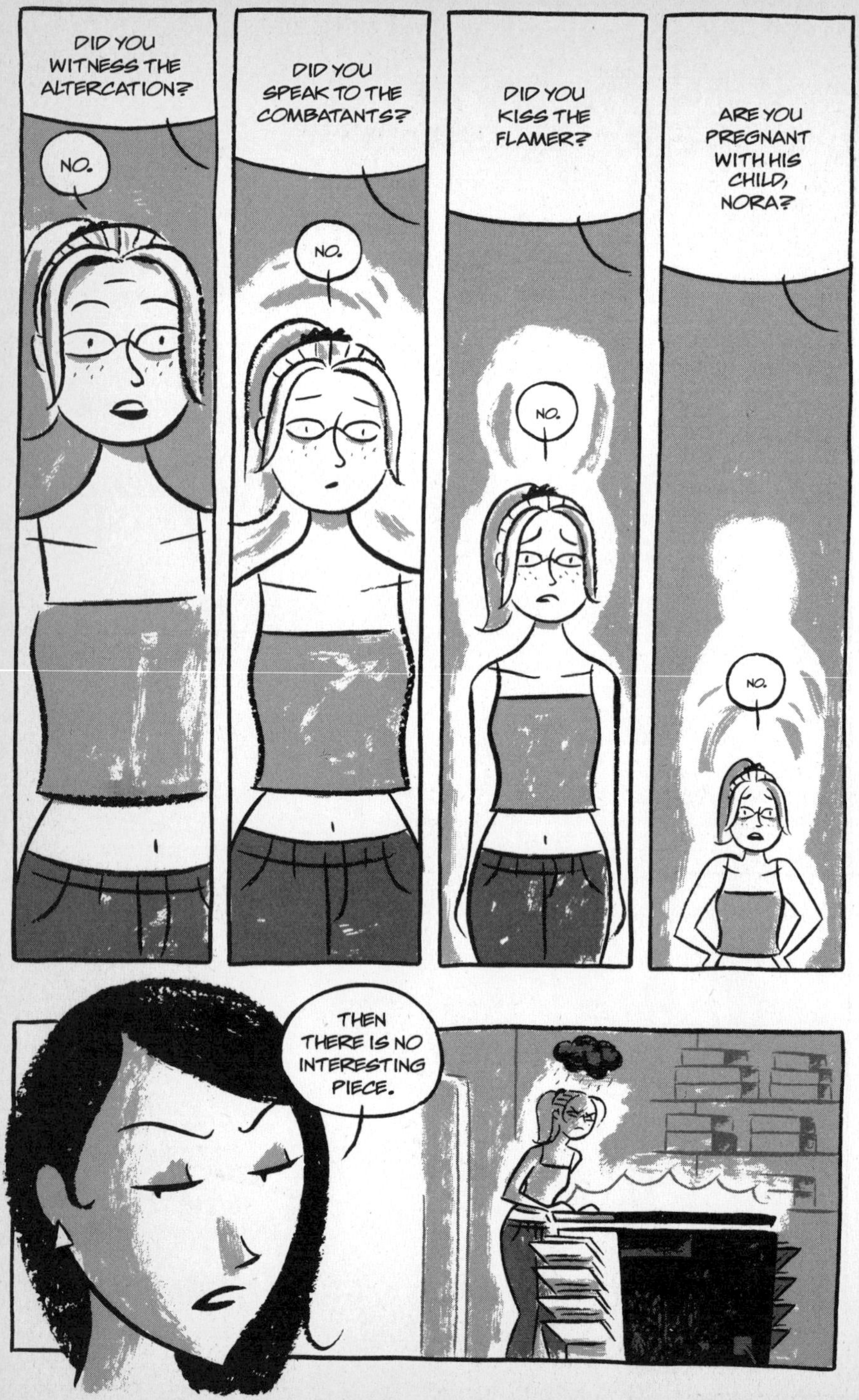
DID YOU WITNESS THE ALTERCATION?
NO.
DID YOU SPEAK TO THE COMBATANTS?
NO.
DID YOU KISS THE FLAMER?
NO.
ARE YOU PREGNANT WITH HIS CHILD, NORA?
NO.
THEN THERE IS NO INTERESTING PIECE.

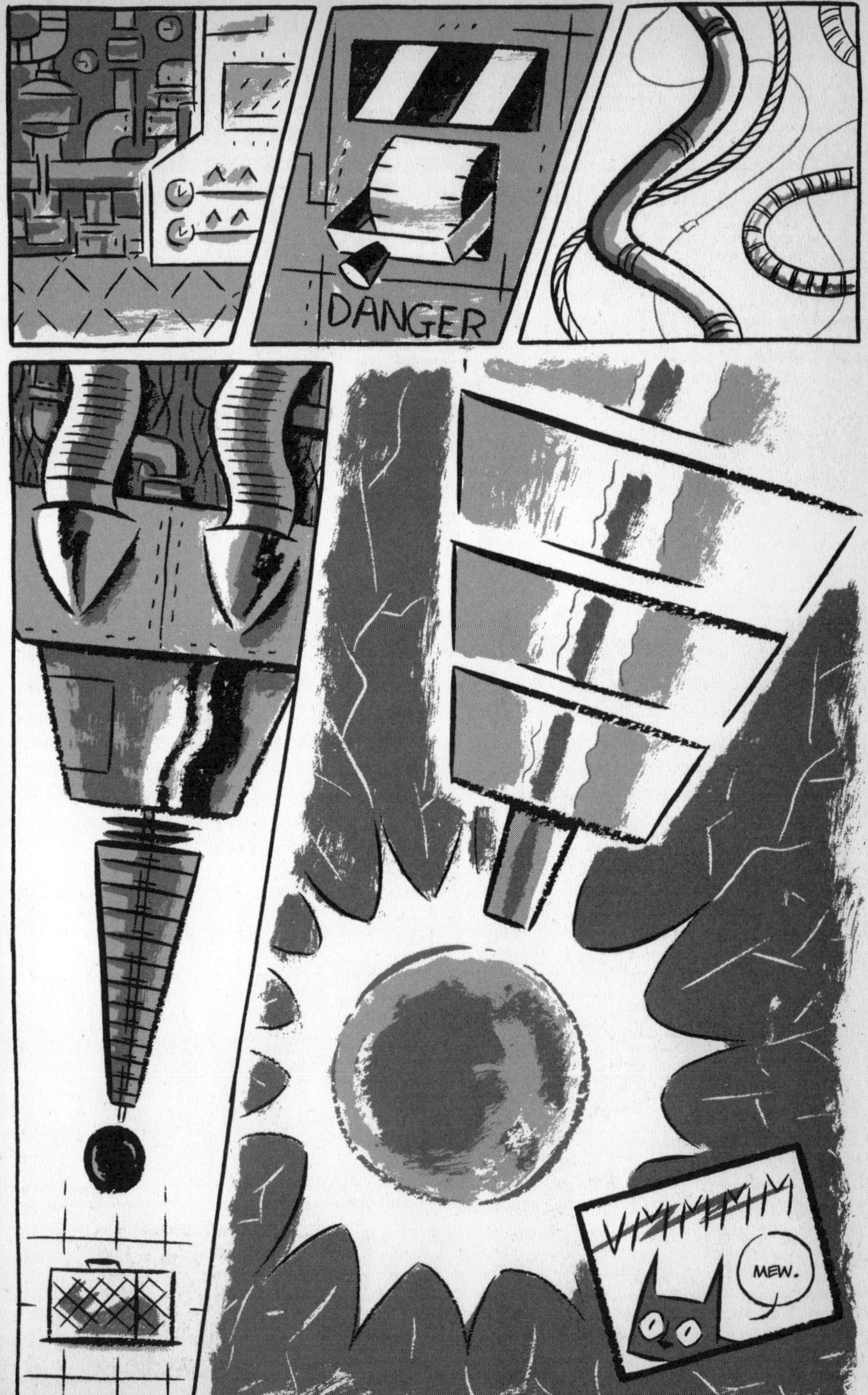
DANGER
MEW.

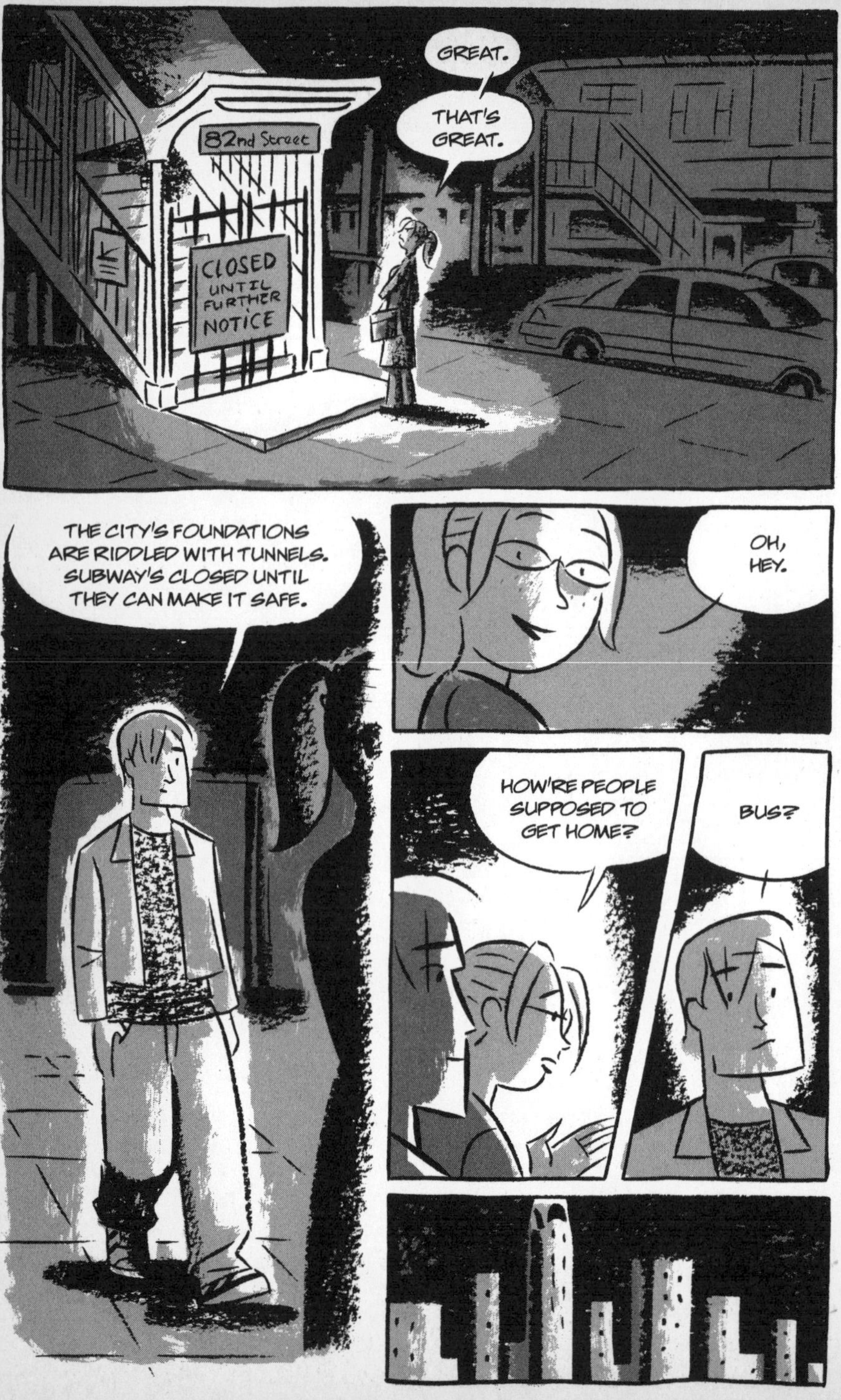
82nd Street
CLOSED UNTIL FURTHER NOTICE
GREAT.
THAT'S GREAT.
THE CITY'S FOUNDATIONS ARE RIDDLED WITH TUNNELS. SUBWAY'S CLOSED UNTIL THEY CAN MAKE IT SAFE.
OH, HEY.
HOW'RE PEOPLE SUPPOSED TO GET HOME?
BUS?

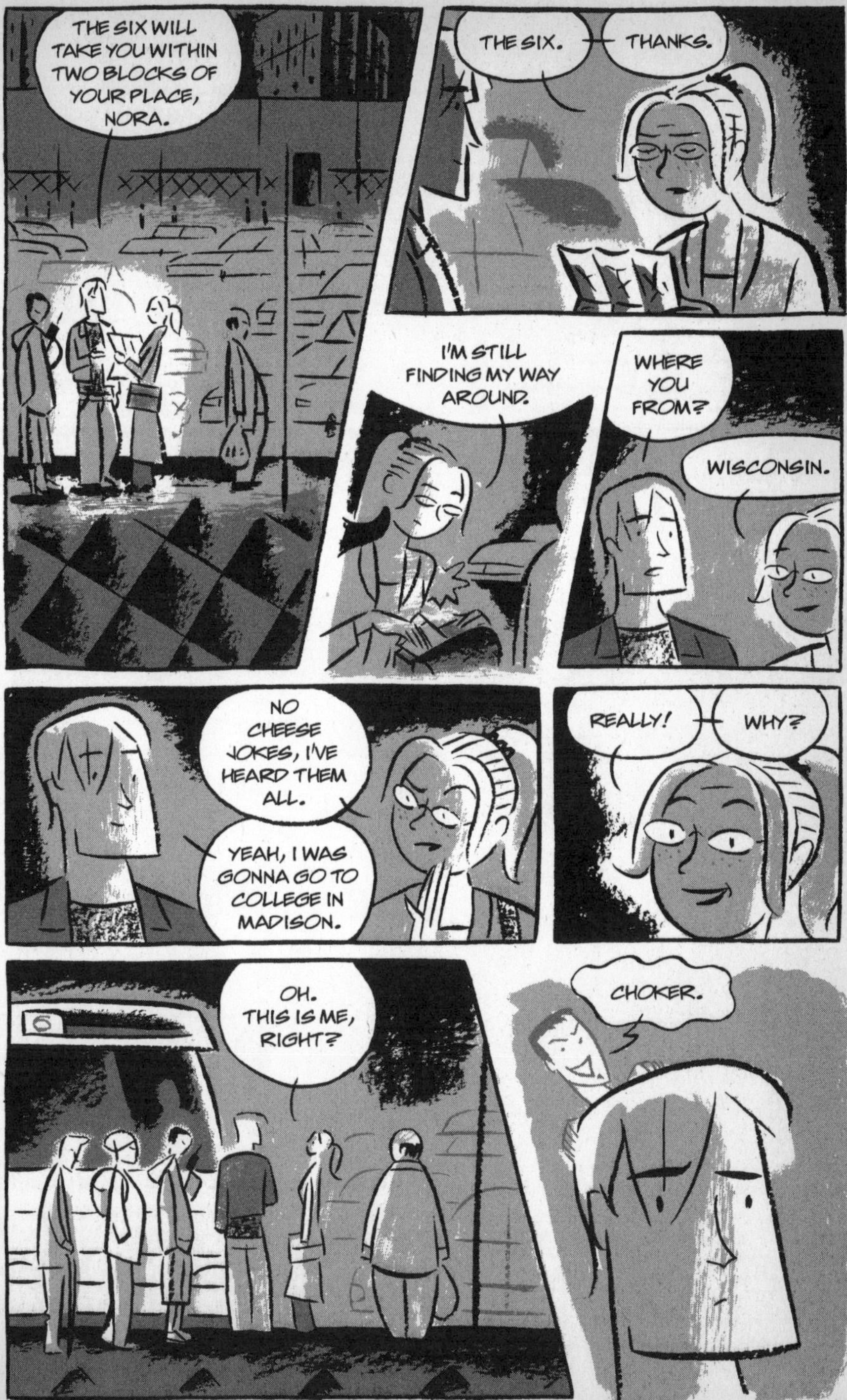
THE SIX WILL TAKE YOU WITHIN TWO BLOCKS OF YOUR PLACE, NORA.
THE SIX.
THANKS.
I'M STILL FINDING MY WAY AROUND.
WHERE YOU FROM?
WISCONSIN.
NO CHEESE JOKES, I'VE HEARD THEM ALL.
YEAH, I WAS GONNA GO TO COLLEGE IN MADISON.
REALLY!
WHY?
OH. THIS IS ME, RIGHT?
CHOKER.

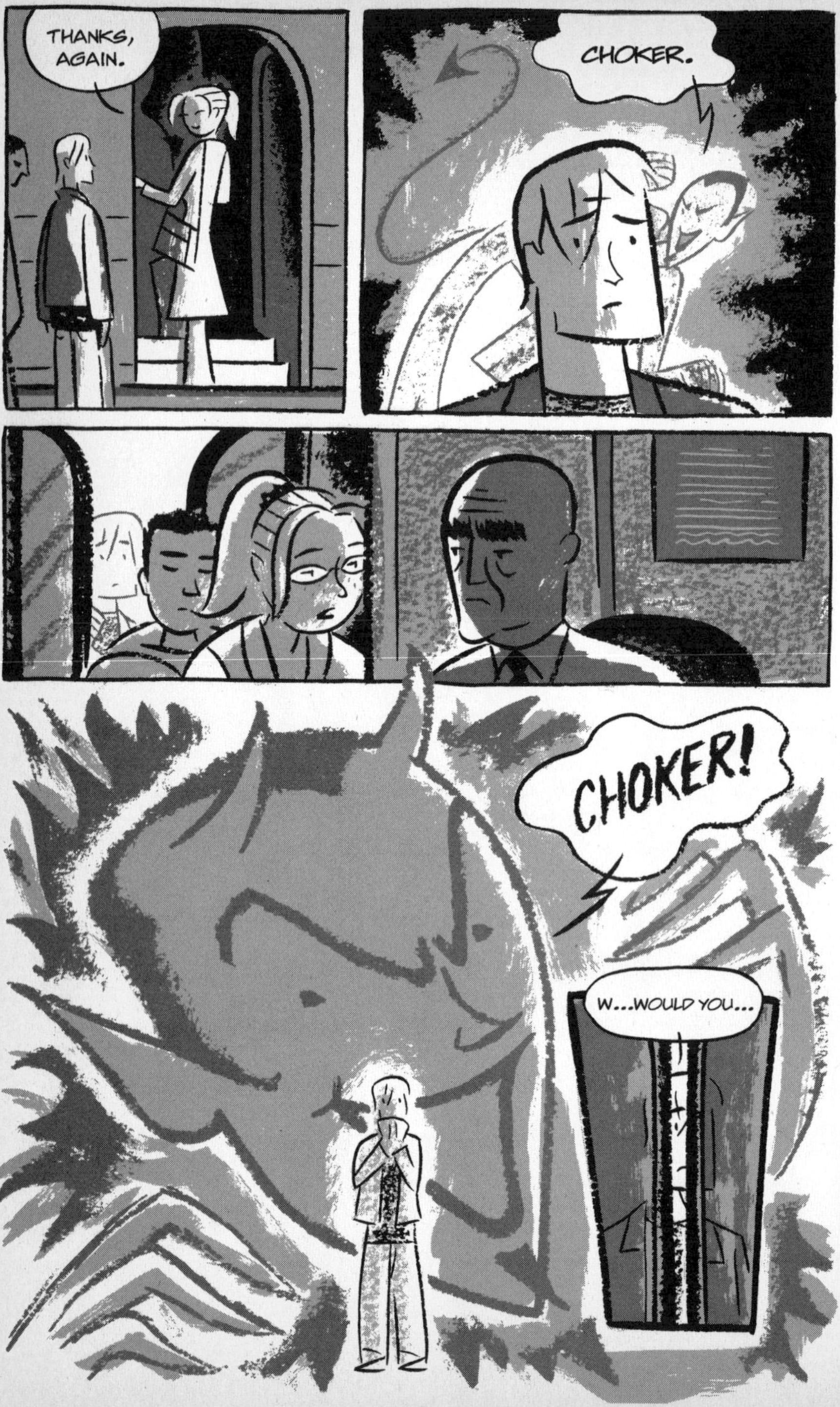
THANKS, AGAIN.
CHOKER.
CHOKER!
W...WOULD YOU...

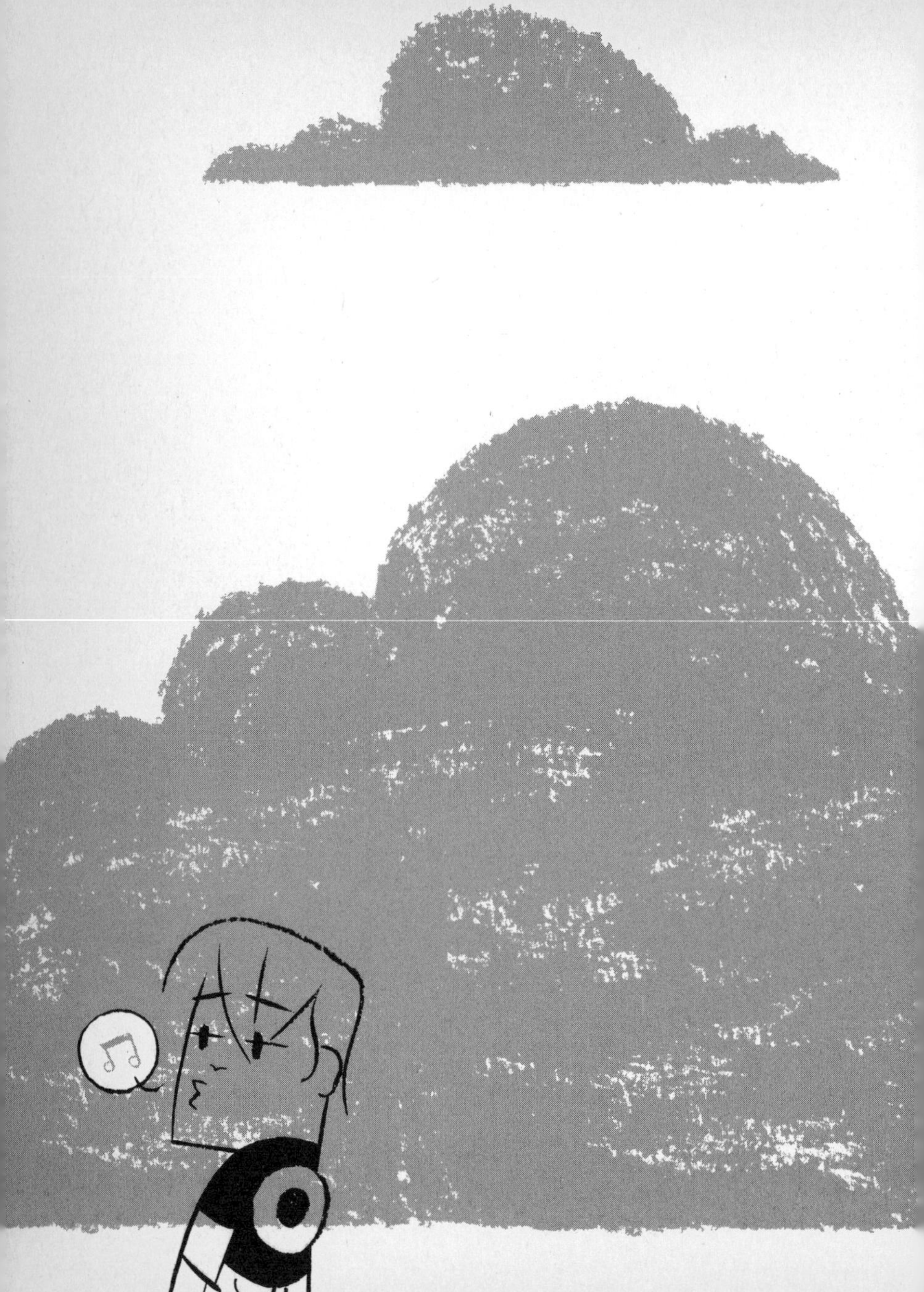

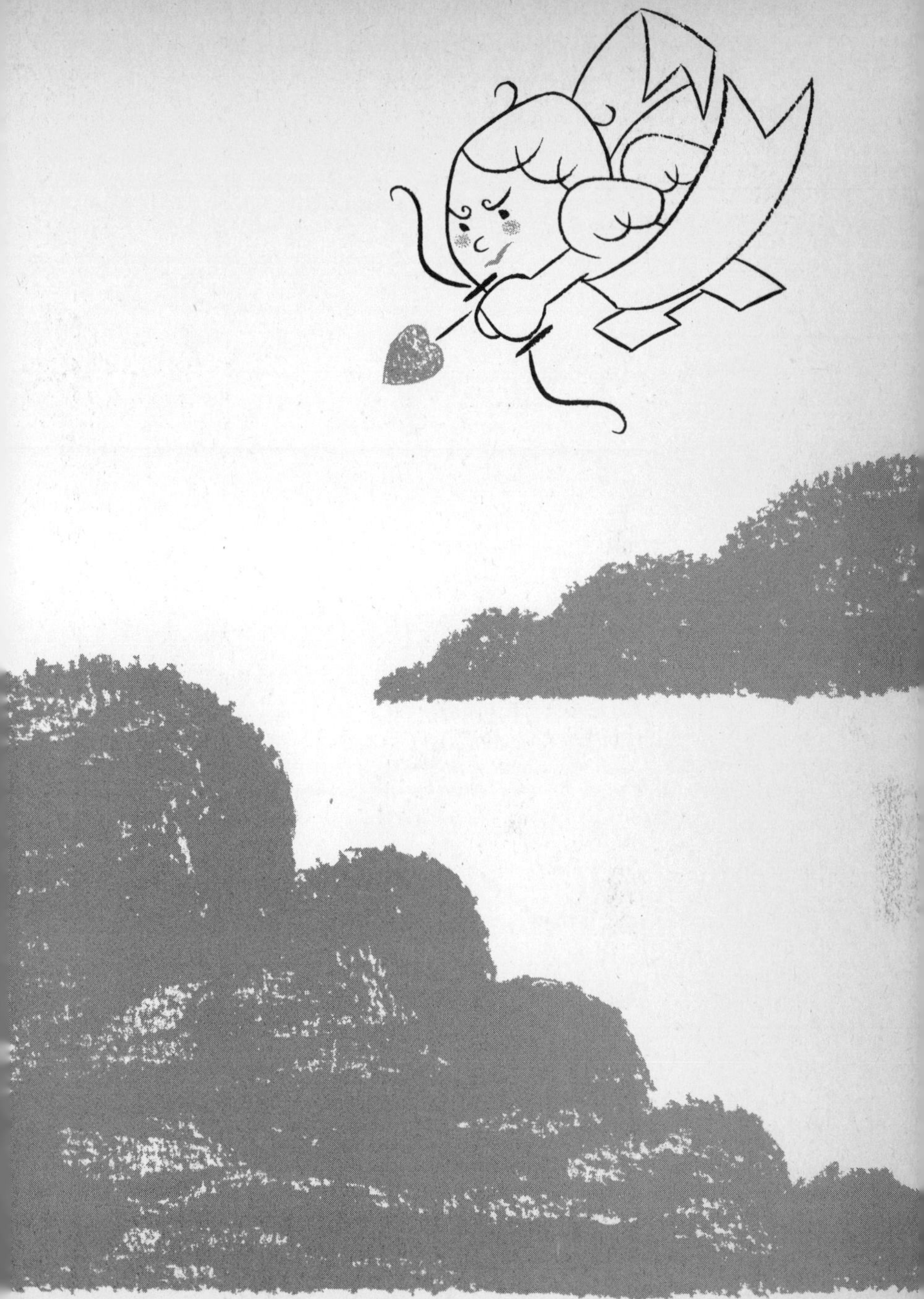

andi watson

ONI PRESS
$2.99 U.S., $4.60 CAN.

Love Fights™ #2

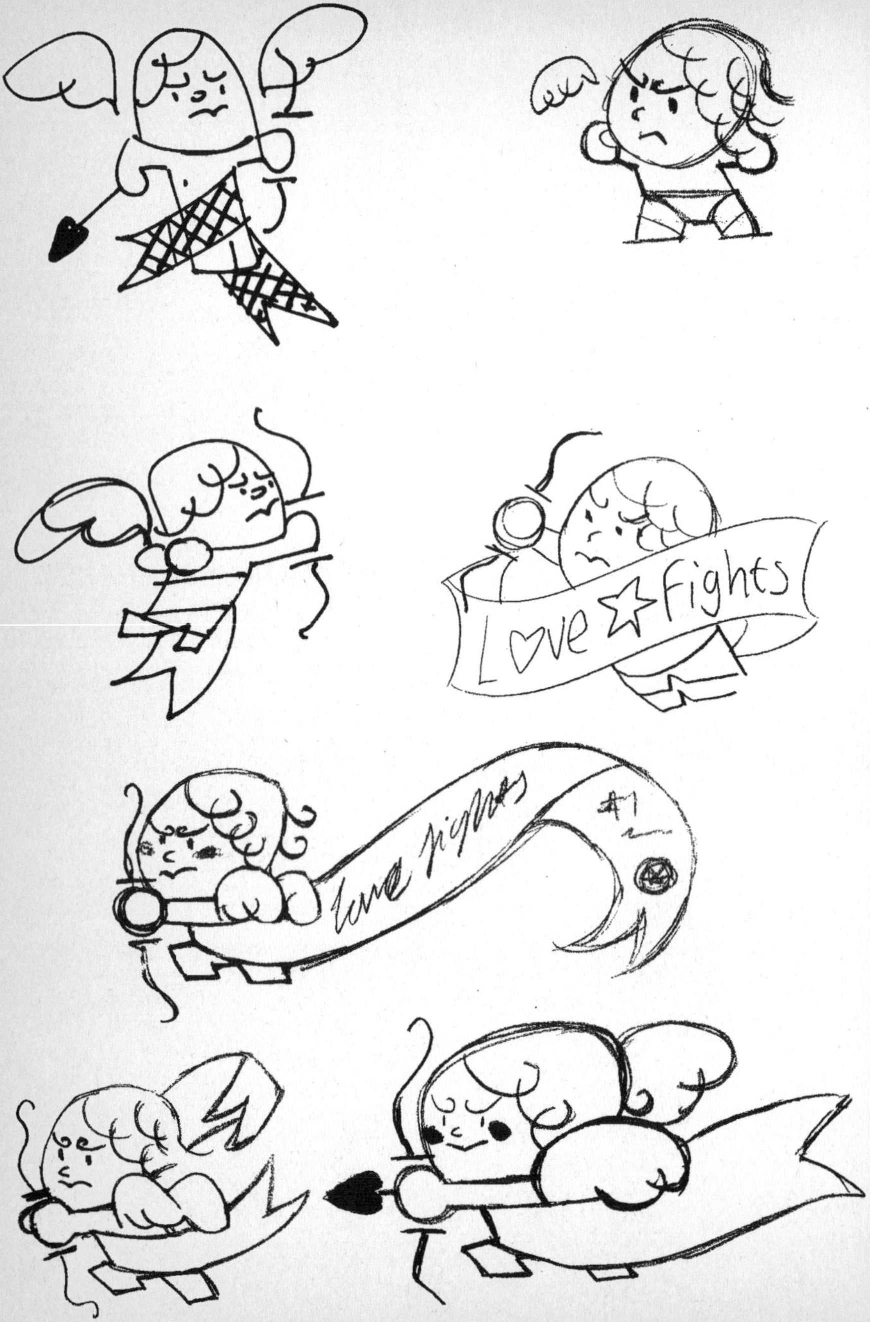
Love ☆ fights
#1

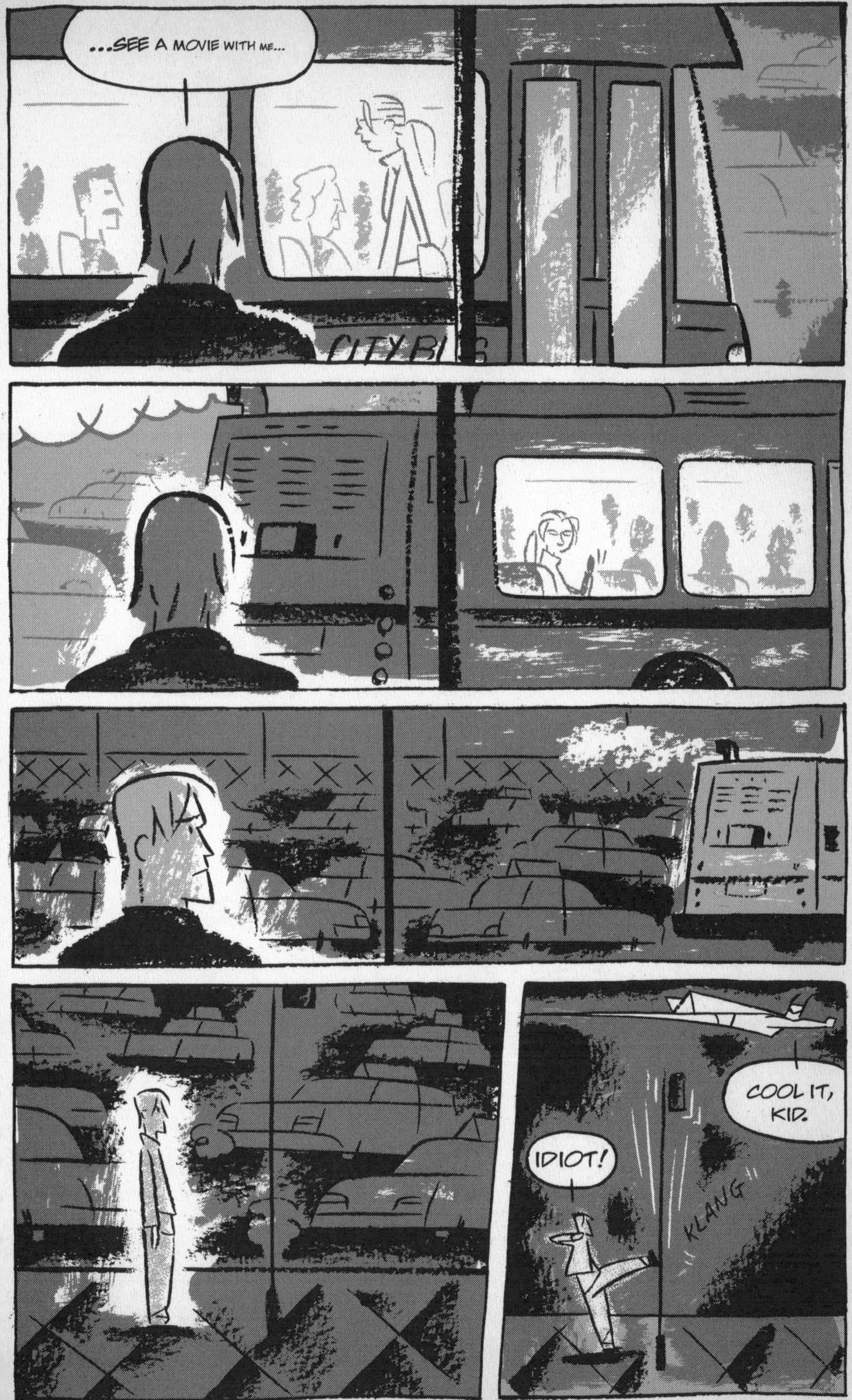
...SEE A MOVIE WITH ME...
CITY BUS
COOL IT, KID.
IDIOT!
KLANG

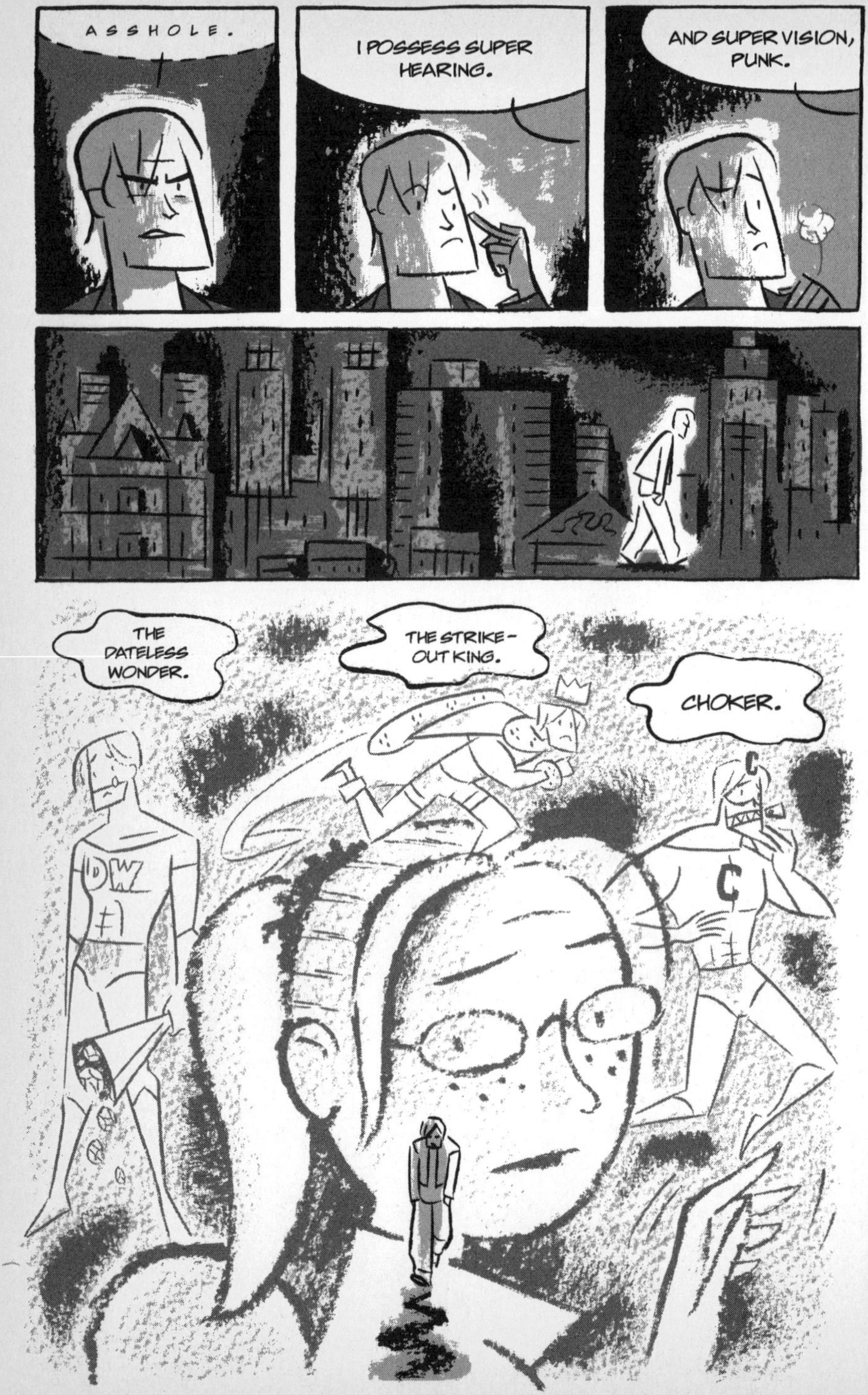
ASSHOLE.
I POSSESS SUPER HEARING.
AND SUPER VISION, PUNK.
THE DATELESS WONDER.
THE STRIKE-OUT KING.
CHOKER.

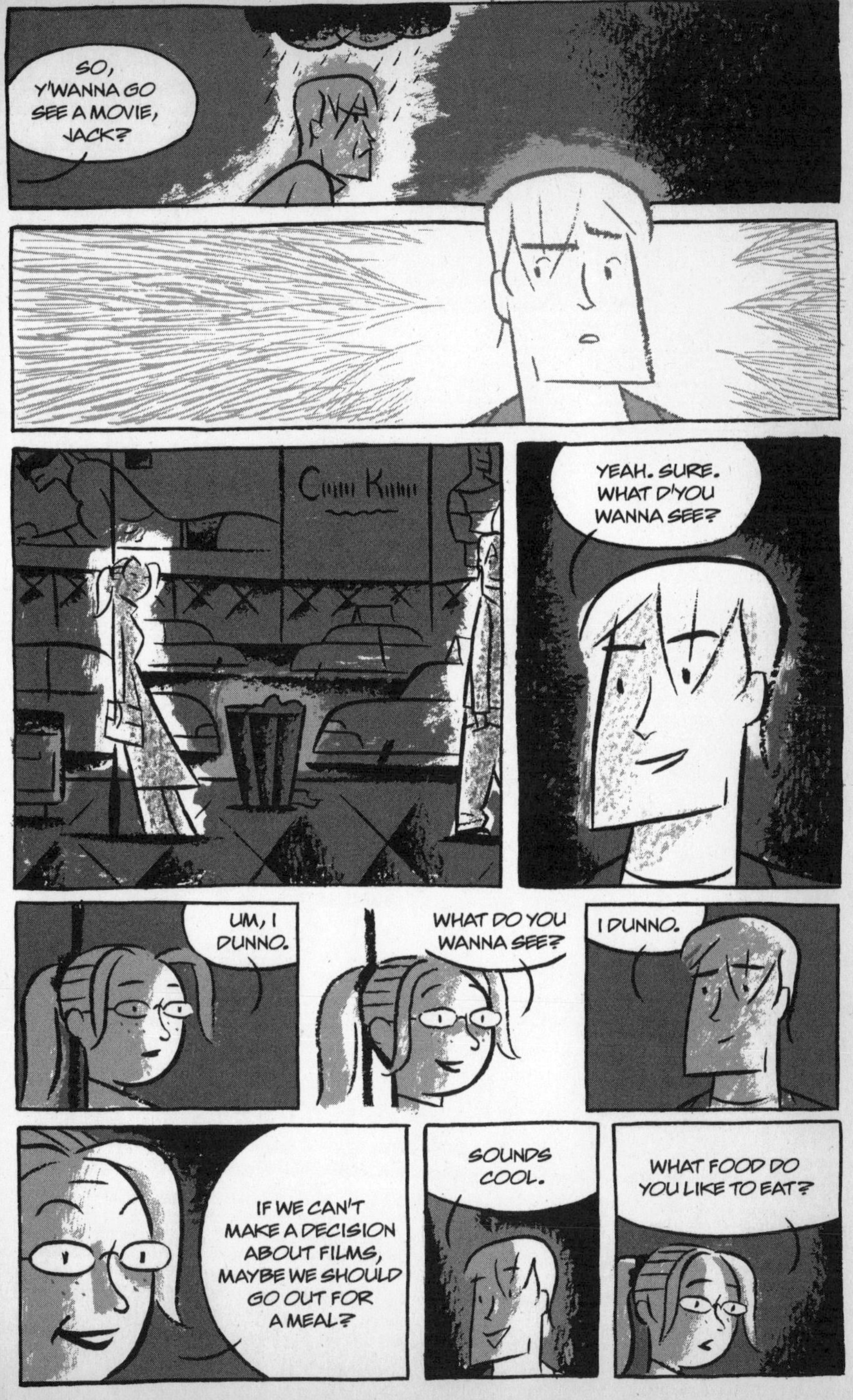
SO, Y'WANNA GO SEE A MOVIE, JACK?
Cinema Kinema
YEAH. SURE. WHAT D'YOU WANNA SEE?
UM, I DUNNO.
WHAT DO YOU WANNA SEE?
I DUNNO.
IF WE CAN'T MAKE A DECISION ABOUT FILMS, MAYBE WE SHOULD GO OUT FOR A MEAL?
SOUNDS COOL.
WHAT FOOD DO YOU LIKE TO EAT?

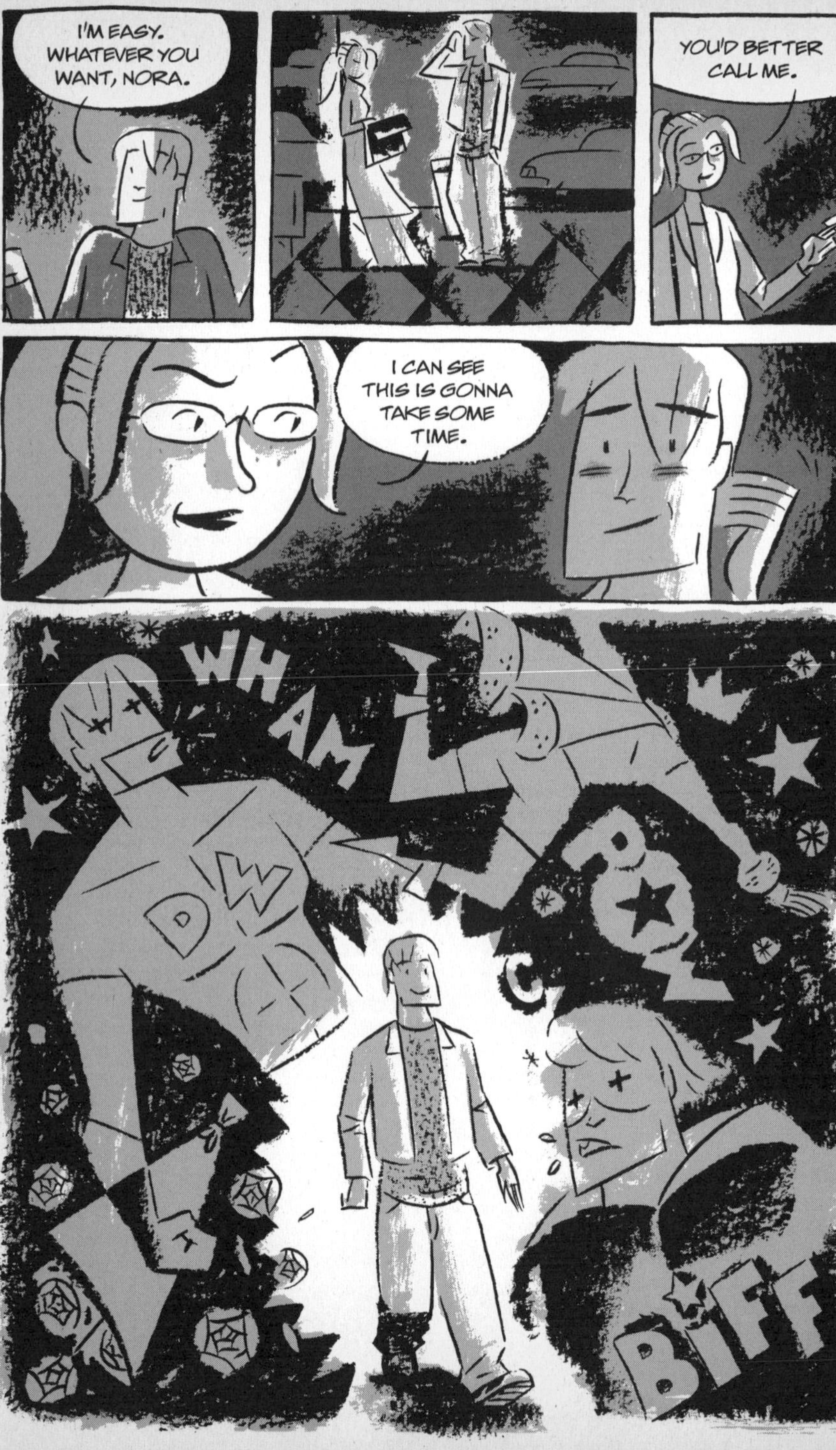
I'M EASY. WHATEVER YOU WANT, NORA.
YOU'D BETTER CALL ME.
I CAN SEE THIS IS GONNA TAKE SOME TIME.
WHAM
BIFF

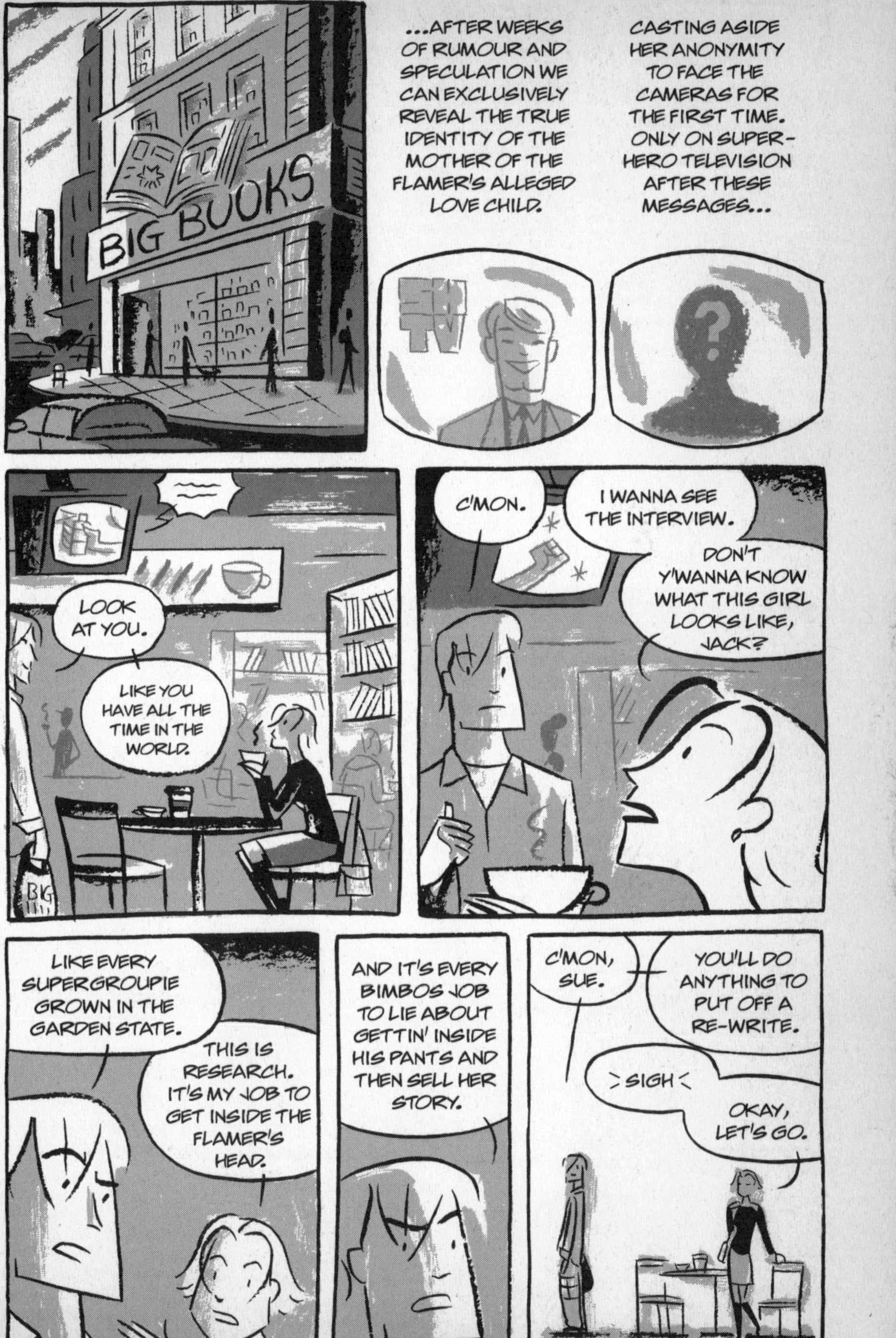
BIG BOOKS
...AFTER WEEKS OF RUMOUR AND SPECULATION WE CAN EXCLUSIVELY REVEAL THE TRUE IDENTITY OF THE MOTHER OF THE FLAMER'S ALLEGED LOVE CHILD.
CASTING ASIDE HER ANONYMITY TO FACE THE CAMERAS FOR THE FIRST TIME. ONLY ON SUPER-HERO TELEVISION AFTER THESE MESSAGES...
LOOK AT YOU.
LIKE YOU HAVE ALL THE TIME IN THE WORLD.
BIG
C'MON.
I WANNA SEE THE INTERVIEW.
DON'T Y'WANNA KNOW WHAT THIS GIRL LOOKS LIKE, JACK?
LIKE EVERY SUPERGROUPIE GROWN IN THE GARDEN STATE.
THIS IS RESEARCH. IT'S MY JOB TO GET INSIDE THE FLAMER'S HEAD.
AND IT'S EVERY BIMBOS JOB TO LIE ABOUT GETTIN' INSIDE HIS PANTS AND THEN SELL HER STORY.
C'MON, SUE.
YOU'LL DO ANYTHING TO PUT OFF A RE-WRITE.
>SIGH<
OKAY, LET'S GO.

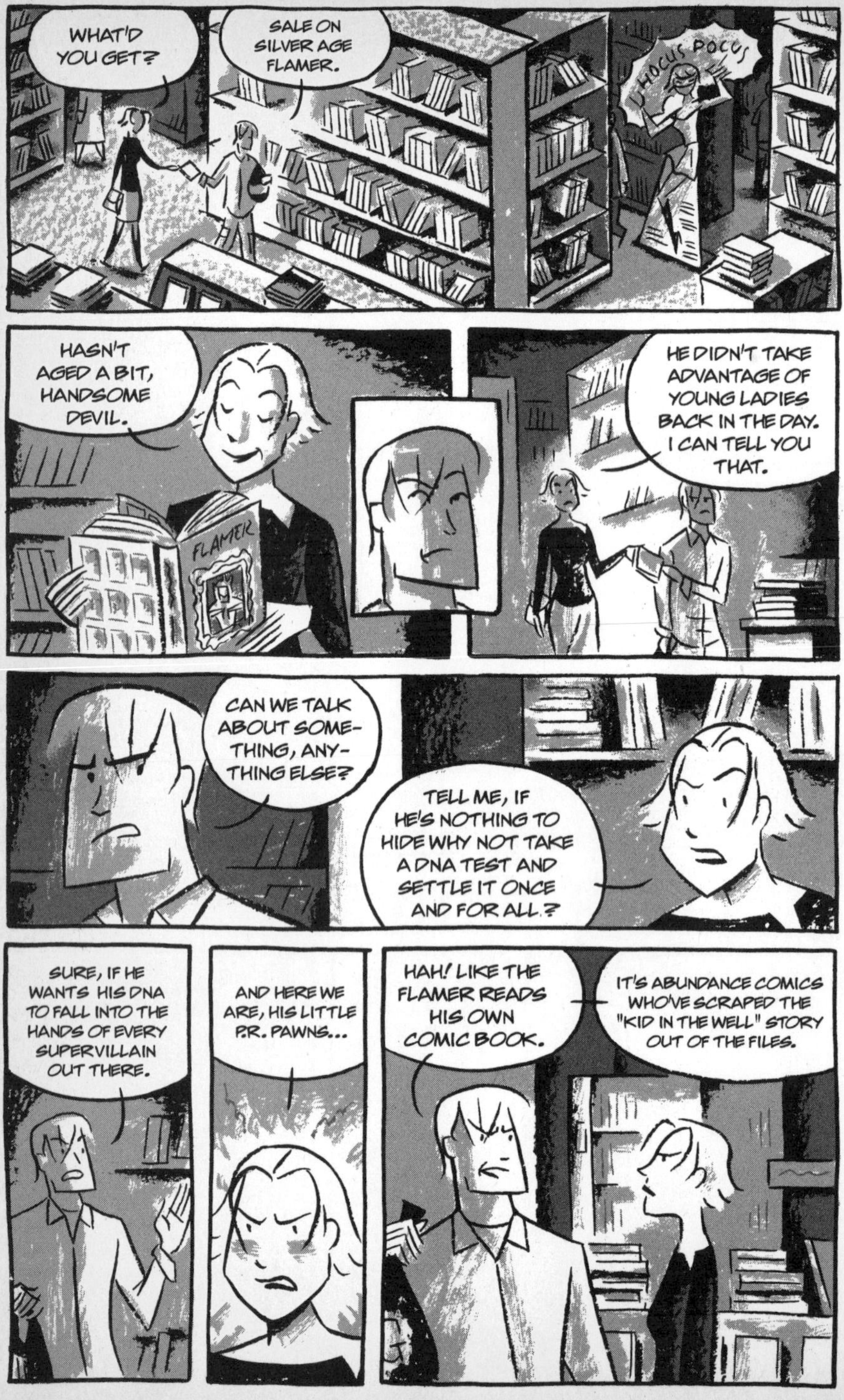
WHAT'D YOU GET?
SALE ON SILVER AGE FLAMER.
HOCUS POCUS
HASN'T AGED A BIT, HANDSOME DEVIL.
FLAMER
HE DIDN'T TAKE ADVANTAGE OF YOUNG LADIES BACK IN THE DAY. I CAN TELL YOU THAT.
CAN WE TALK ABOUT SOME-THING, ANY-THING ELSE?
TELL ME, IF HE'S NOTHING TO HIDE WHY NOT TAKE A DNA TEST AND SETTLE IT ONCE AND FOR ALL.?
SURE, IF HE WANTS HIS DNA TO FALL INTO THE HANDS OF EVERY SUPERVILLAIN OUT THERE.
AND HERE WE ARE, HIS LITTLE P.R. PAWNS...
HAH! LIKE THE FLAMER READS HIS OWN COMIC BOOK.
IT'S ABUNDANCE COMICS WHO'VE SCRAPED THE "KID IN THE WELL" STORY OUT OF THE FILES.

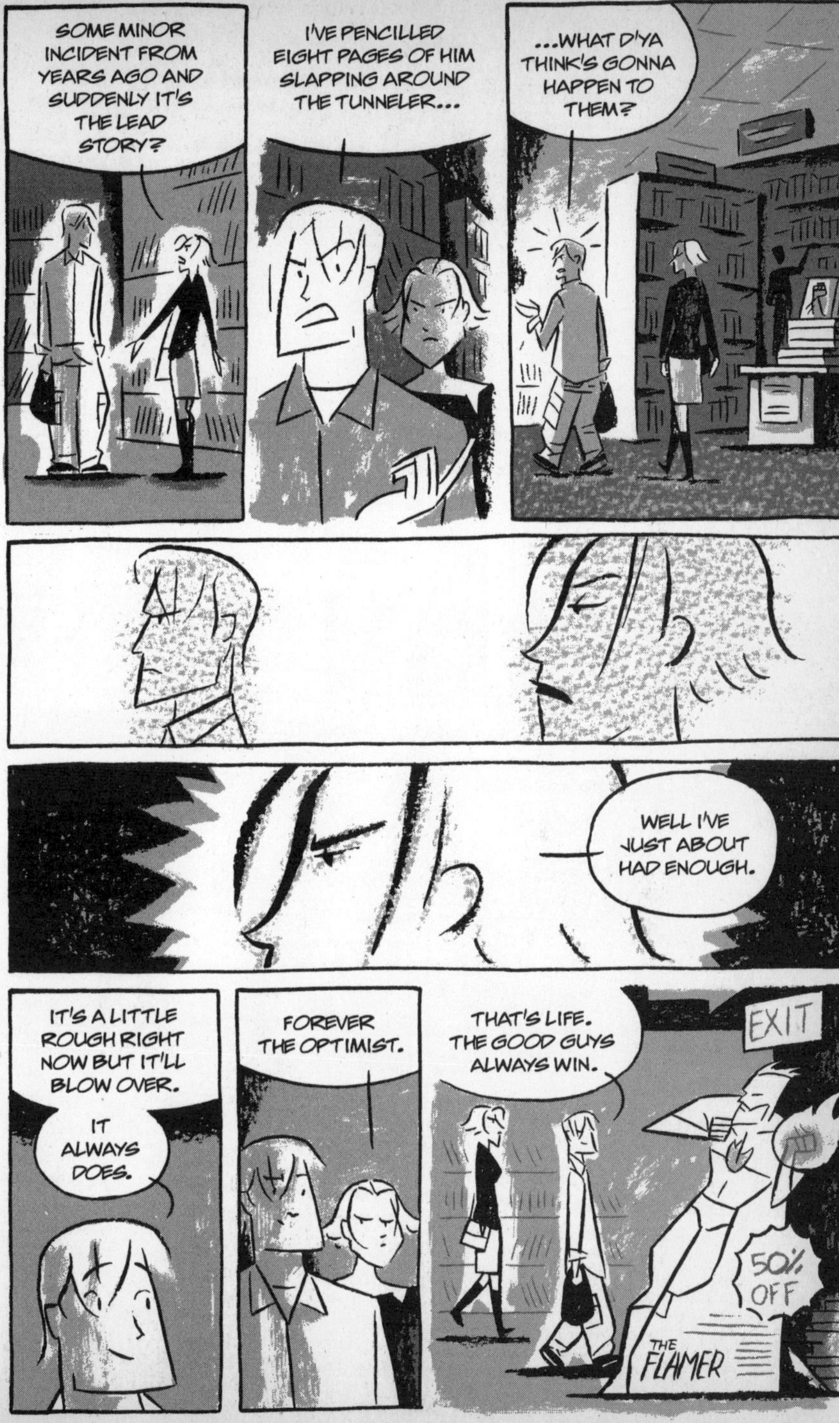
SOME MINOR INCIDENT FROM YEARS AGO AND SUDDENLY IT'S THE LEAD STORY?
I'VE PENCILLED EIGHT PAGES OF HIM SLAPPING AROUND THE TUNNELER...
...WHAT D'YA THINK'S GONNA HAPPEN TO THEM?
WELL I'VE JUST ABOUT HAD ENOUGH.
IT'S A LITTLE ROUGH RIGHT NOW BUT IT'LL BLOW OVER.
IT ALWAYS DOES.
FOREVER THE OPTIMIST.
THAT'S LIFE. THE GOOD GUYS ALWAYS WIN.
EXIT
50% OFF
THE FLAMER

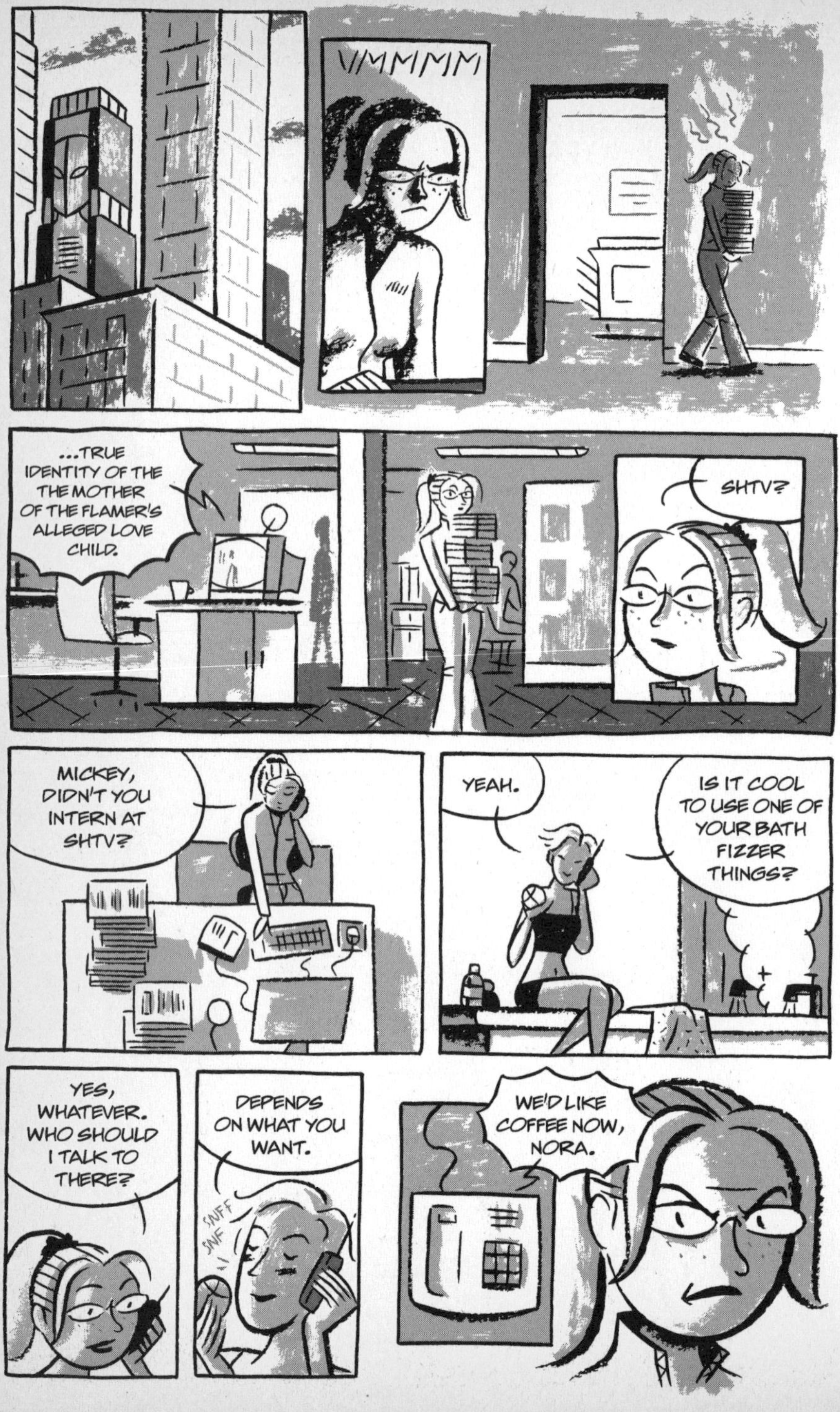
VMMMMM
...TRUE IDENTITY OF THE THE MOTHER OF THE FLAMER'S ALLEGED LOVE CHILD.
SHTV?
MICKEY, DIDN'T YOU INTERN AT SHTV?
YEAH.
IS IT COOL TO USE ONE OF YOUR BATH FIZZER THINGS?
YES, WHATEVER. WHO SHOULD I TALK TO THERE?
DEPENDS ON WHAT YOU WANT.
SNIFF SNIF
WE'D LIKE COFFEE NOW, NORA.

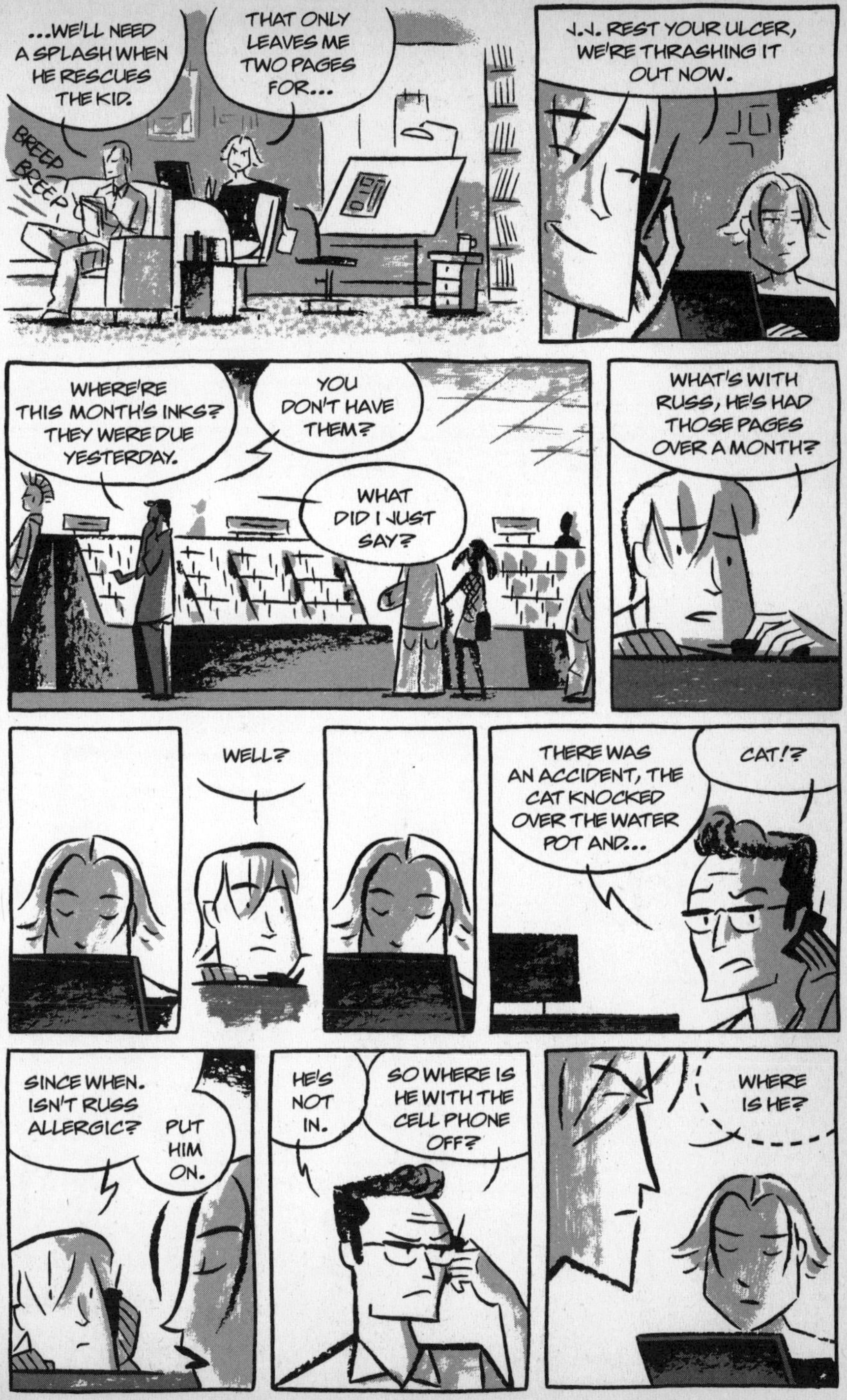
...WE'LL NEED A SPLASH WHEN HE RESCUES THE KID.
THAT ONLY LEAVES ME TWO PAGES FOR...
BREEP BREEP
J.J. REST YOUR ULCER, WE'RE THRASHING IT OUT NOW.
WHERE'RE THIS MONTH'S INKS? THEY WERE DUE YESTERDAY.
YOU DON'T HAVE THEM?
WHAT DID I JUST SAY?
WHAT'S WITH RUSS, HE'S HAD THOSE PAGES OVER A MONTH?
WELL?
THERE WAS AN ACCIDENT, THE CAT KNOCKED OVER THE WATER POT AND...
CAT!?
SINCE WHEN. ISN'T RUSS ALLERGIC?
PUT HIM ON.
HE'S NOT IN.
SO WHERE IS HE WITH THE CELL PHONE OFF?
WHERE IS HE?

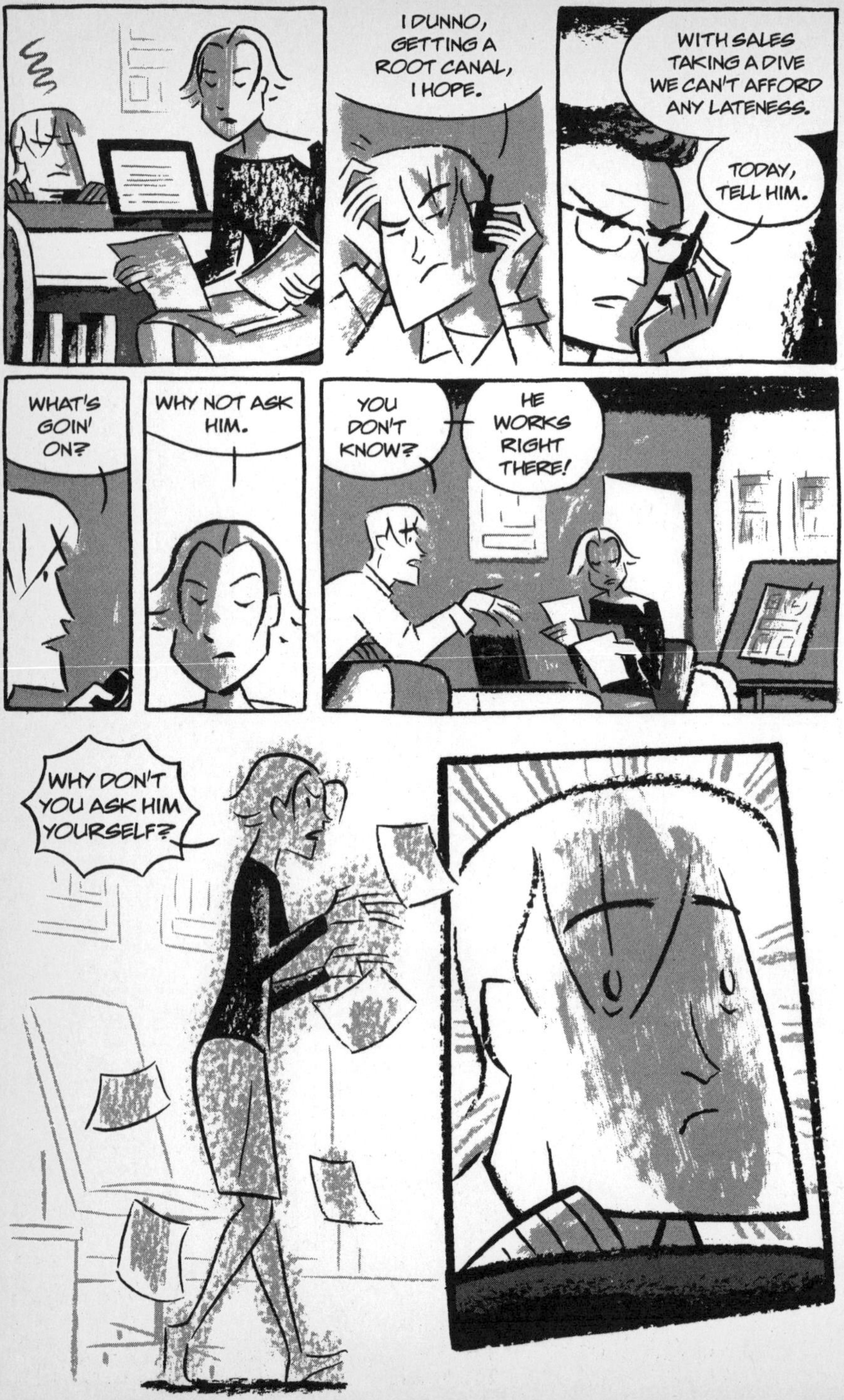
I DUNNO, GETTING A ROOT CANAL, I HOPE.
WITH SALES TAKING A DIVE WE CAN'T AFFORD ANY LATENESS.
TODAY, TELL HIM.
WHAT'S GOIN' ON?
WHY NOT ASK HIM.
YOU DON'T KNOW?
HE WORKS RIGHT THERE!
WHY DON'T YOU ASK HIM YOURSELF?

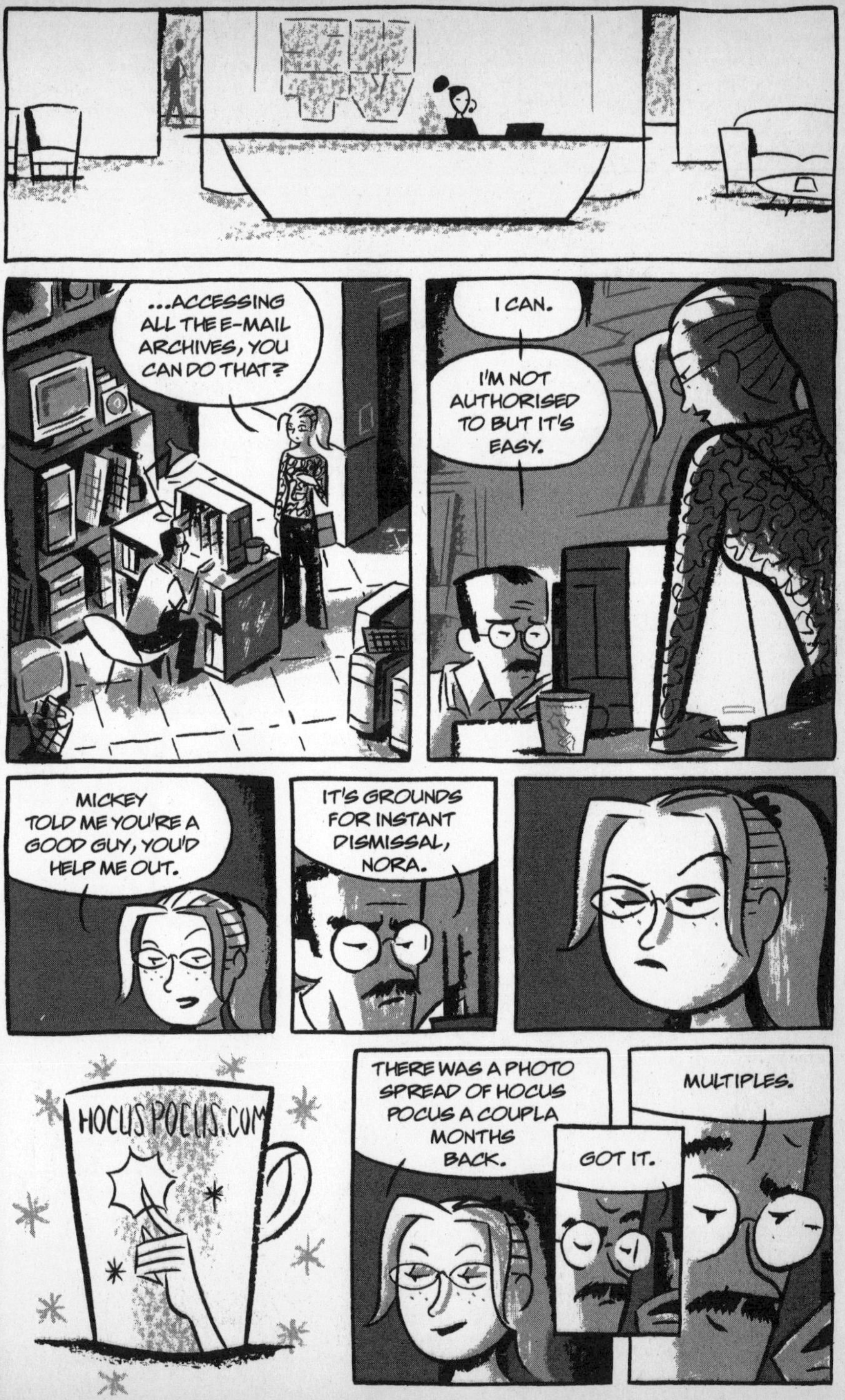

...ACCESSING ALL THE E-MAIL ARCHIVES, YOU CAN DO THAT?
I CAN.
I'M NOT AUTHORISED TO BUT IT'S EASY.
MICKEY TOLD ME YOU'RE A GOOD GUY, YOU'D HELP ME OUT.
IT'S GROUNDS FOR INSTANT DISMISSAL, NORA.
HOCUS POCUS.COM
THERE WAS A PHOTO SPREAD OF HOCUS POCUS A COUPLA MONTHS BACK.
GOT IT.
MULTIPLES.

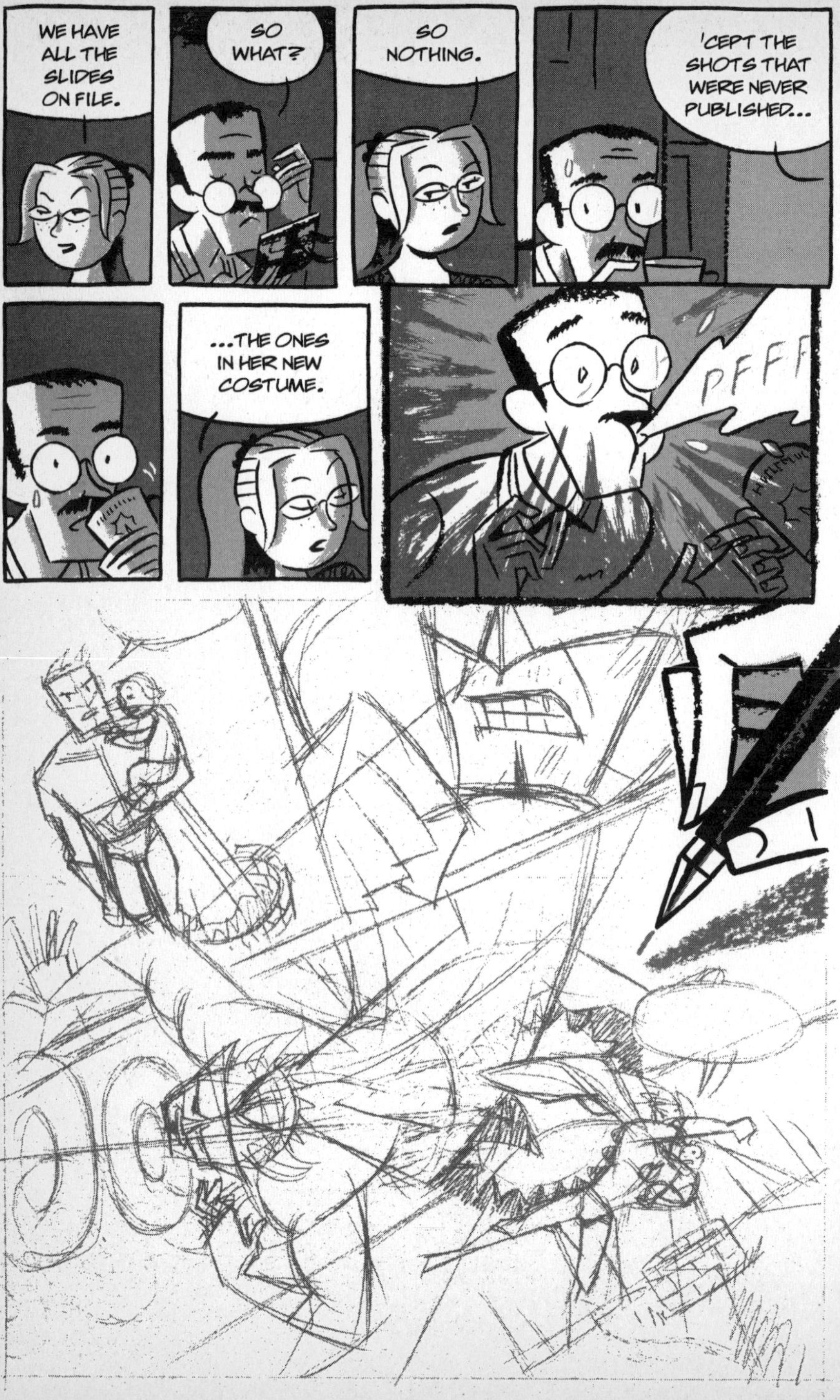
WE HAVE ALL THE SLIDES ON FILE.
SO WHAT?
SO NOTHING.
'CEPT THE SHOTS THAT WERE NEVER PUBLISHED...
...THE ONES IN HER NEW COSTUME.
PFFF

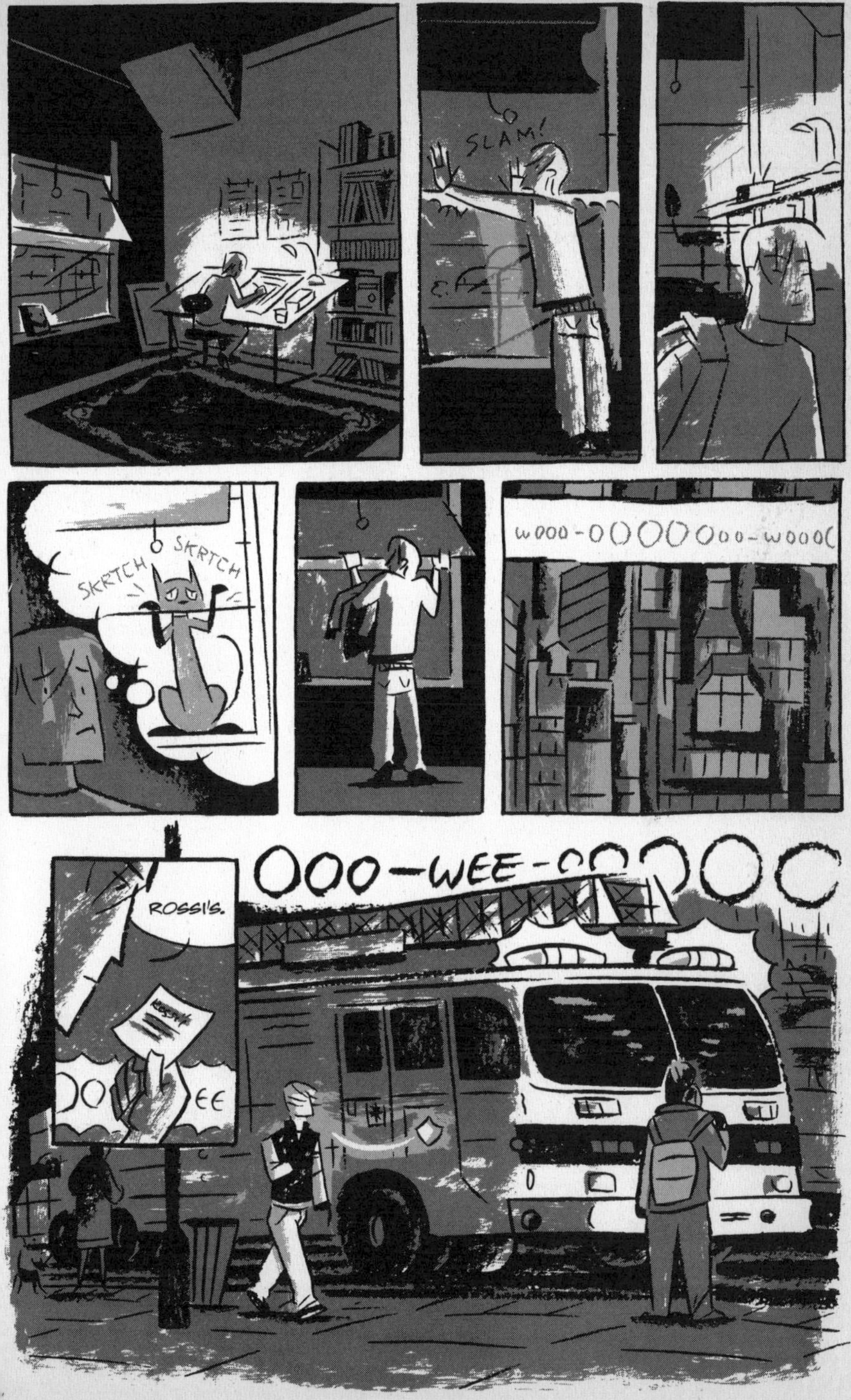
SLAM!
SKRTCH SKRTCH
wooo-OOOOOooo-woooO
ROSSI'S.
OOO-WEE-OOOOO

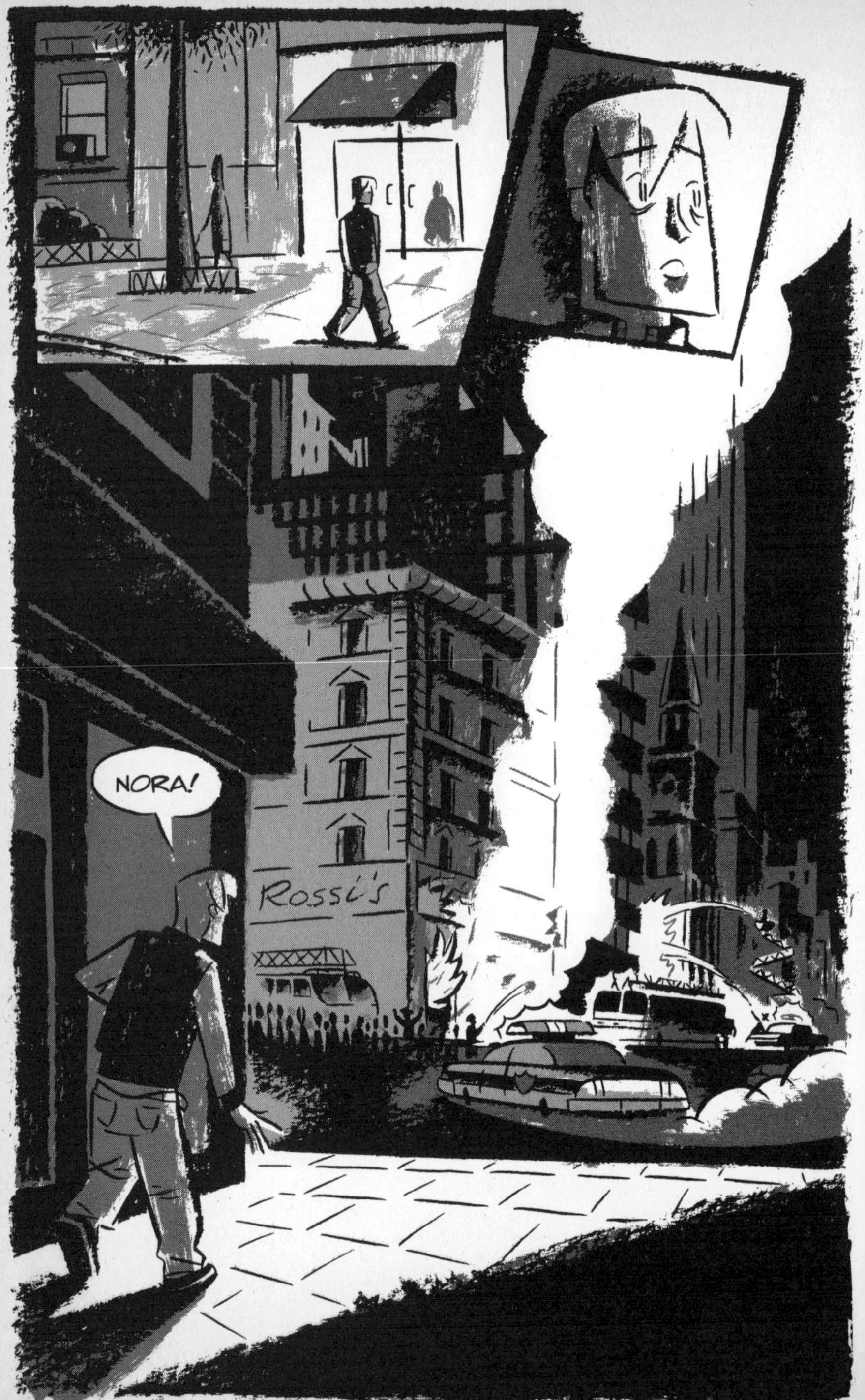
NORA!
Rossi's

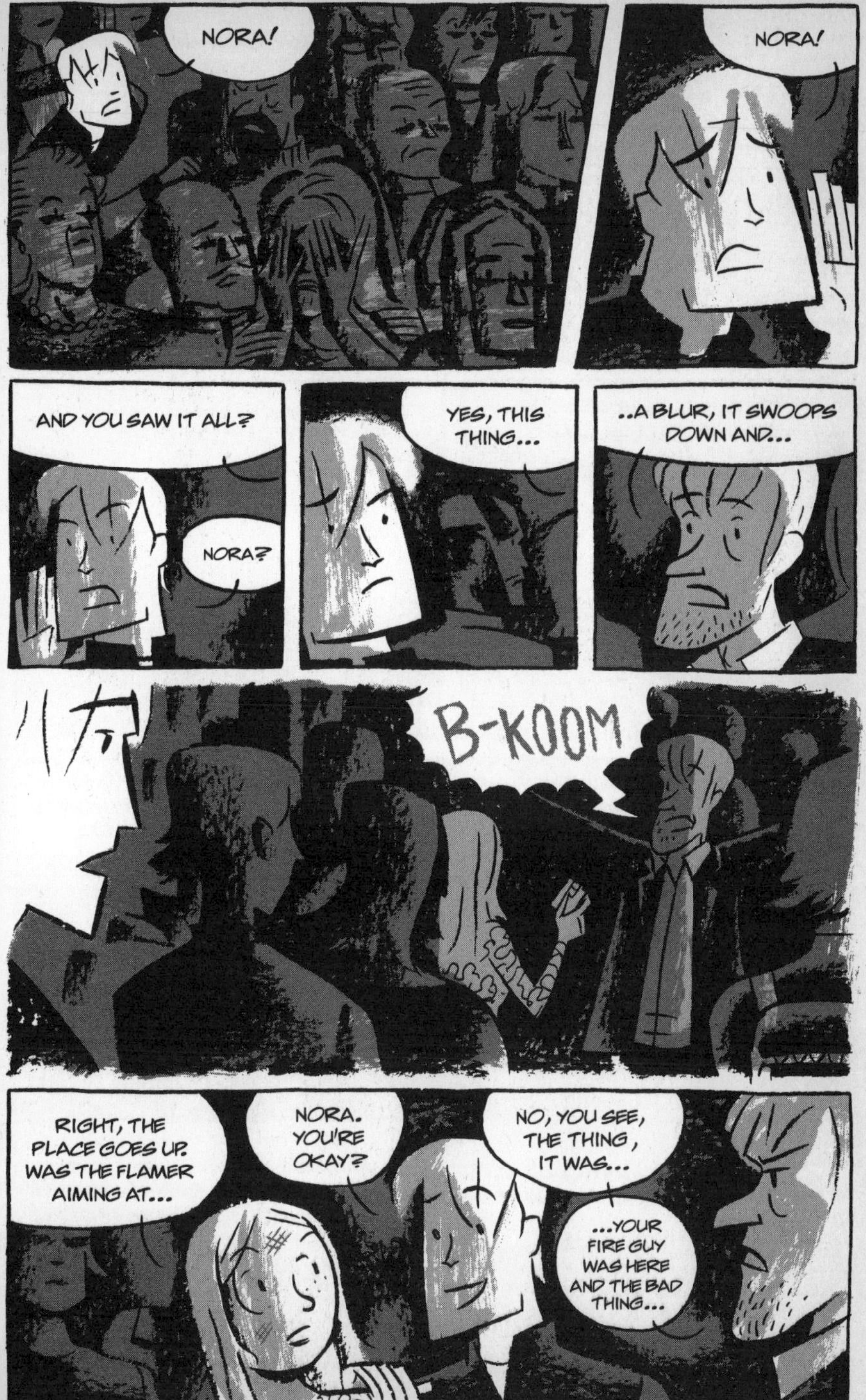
NORA!
NORA!
AND YOU SAW IT ALL?
NORA?
YES, THIS THING...
..A BLUR, IT SWOOPS DOWN AND...
B-KOOM
RIGHT, THE PLACE GOES UP. WAS THE FLAMER AIMING AT...
NORA. YOU'RE OKAY?
NO, YOU SEE, THE THING, IT WAS...
...YOUR FIRE GUY WAS HERE AND THE BAD THING...

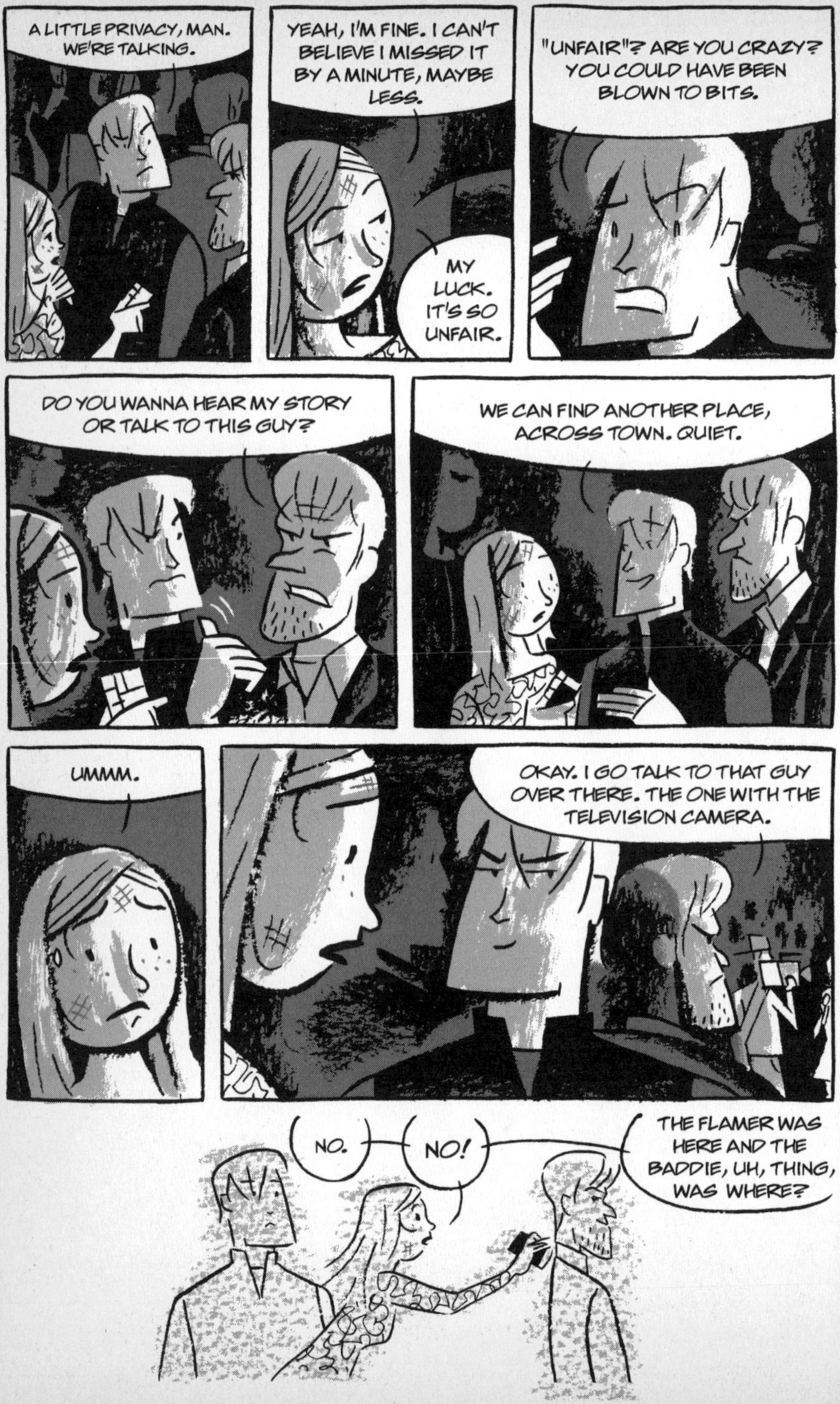
A LITTLE PRIVACY, MAN. WE'RE TALKING.
YEAH, I'M FINE. I CAN'T BELIEVE I MISSED IT BY A MINUTE, MAYBE LESS.
MY LUCK. IT'S SO UNFAIR.
"UNFAIR"? ARE YOU CRAZY? YOU COULD HAVE BEEN BLOWN TO BITS.
DO YOU WANNA HEAR MY STORY OR TALK TO THIS GUY?
WE CAN FIND ANOTHER PLACE, ACROSS TOWN. QUIET.
UMMM.
OKAY. I GO TALK TO THAT GUY OVER THERE. THE ONE WITH THE TELEVISION CAMERA.
NO.
NO!
THE FLAMER WAS HERE AND THE BADDIE, UH, THING, WAS WHERE?

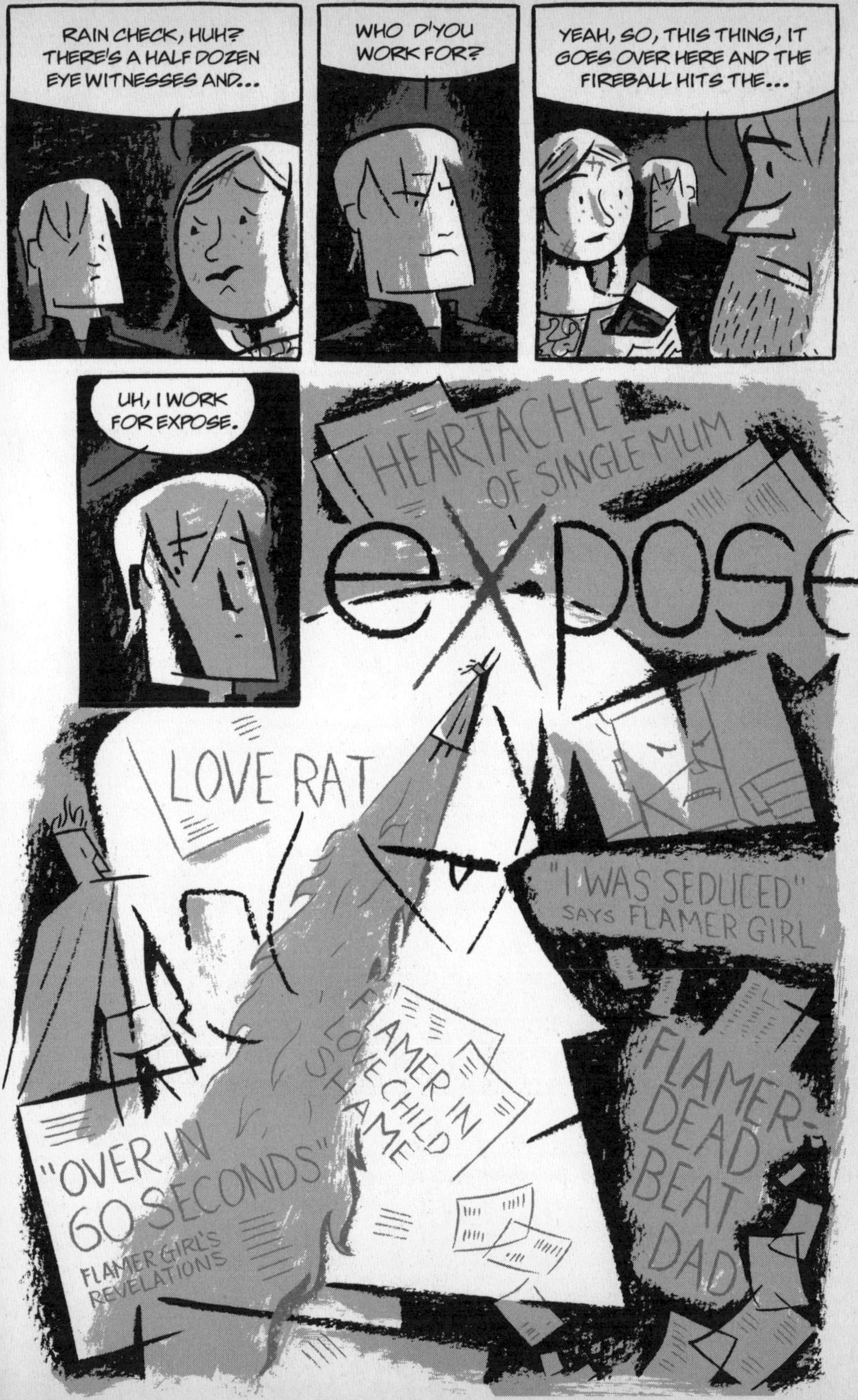
RAIN CHECK, HUH? THERE'S A HALF DOZEN EYE WITNESSES AND...
WHO D'YOU WORK FOR?
YEAH, SO, THIS THING, IT GOES OVER HERE AND THE FIREBALL HITS THE...
UH, I WORK FOR EXPOSE.
HEARTACHE OF SINGLE MUM
EXPOSE
LOVE RAT
"I WAS SEDUCED" SAYS FLAMER GIRL
FLAMER IN LOVE CHILD SHAME
FLAMER-DEAD BEAT DAD
"OVER IN 60 SECONDS"
FLAMER GIRL'S REVELATIONS

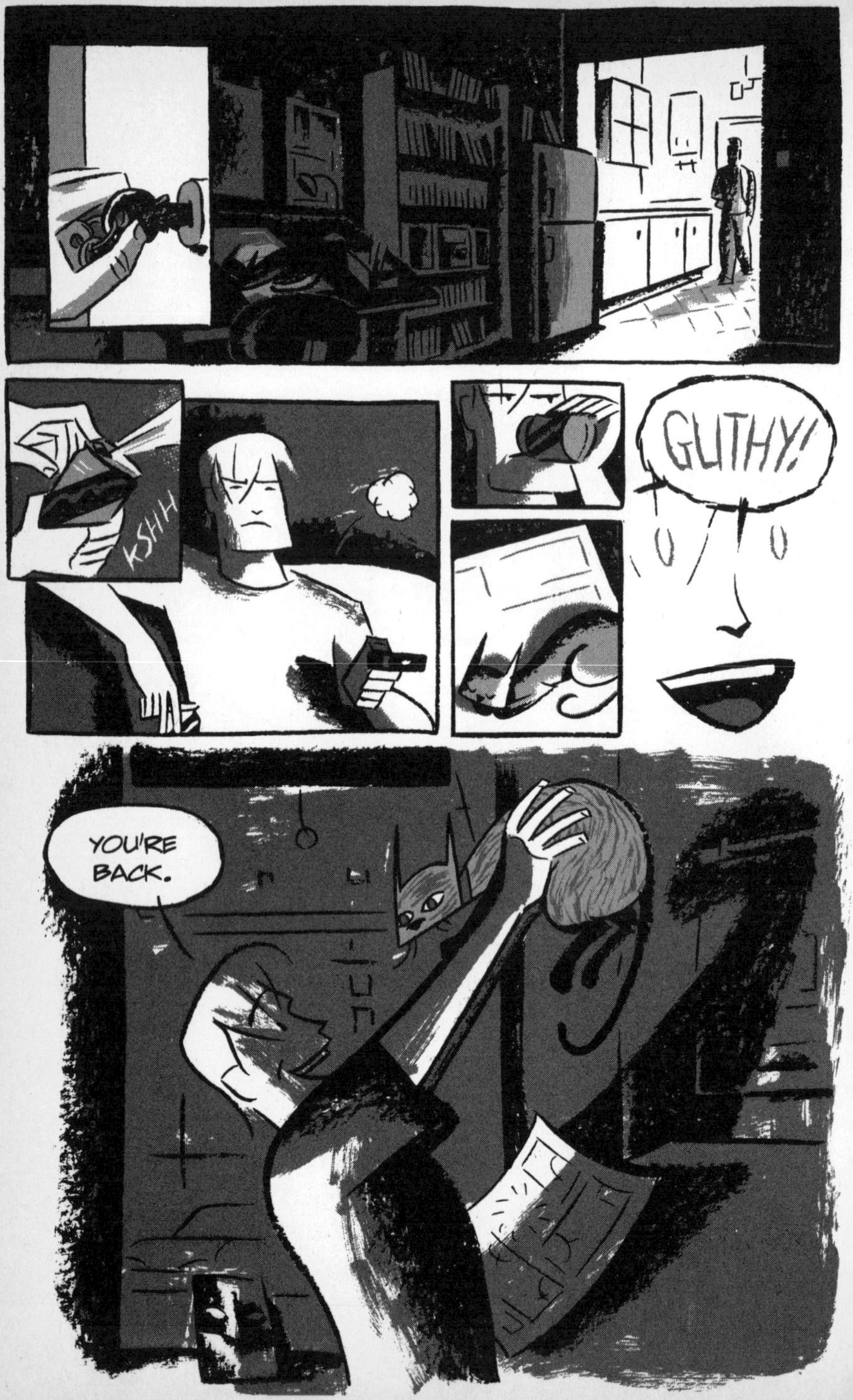
KSHH
GUTHY!
YOU'RE BACK.

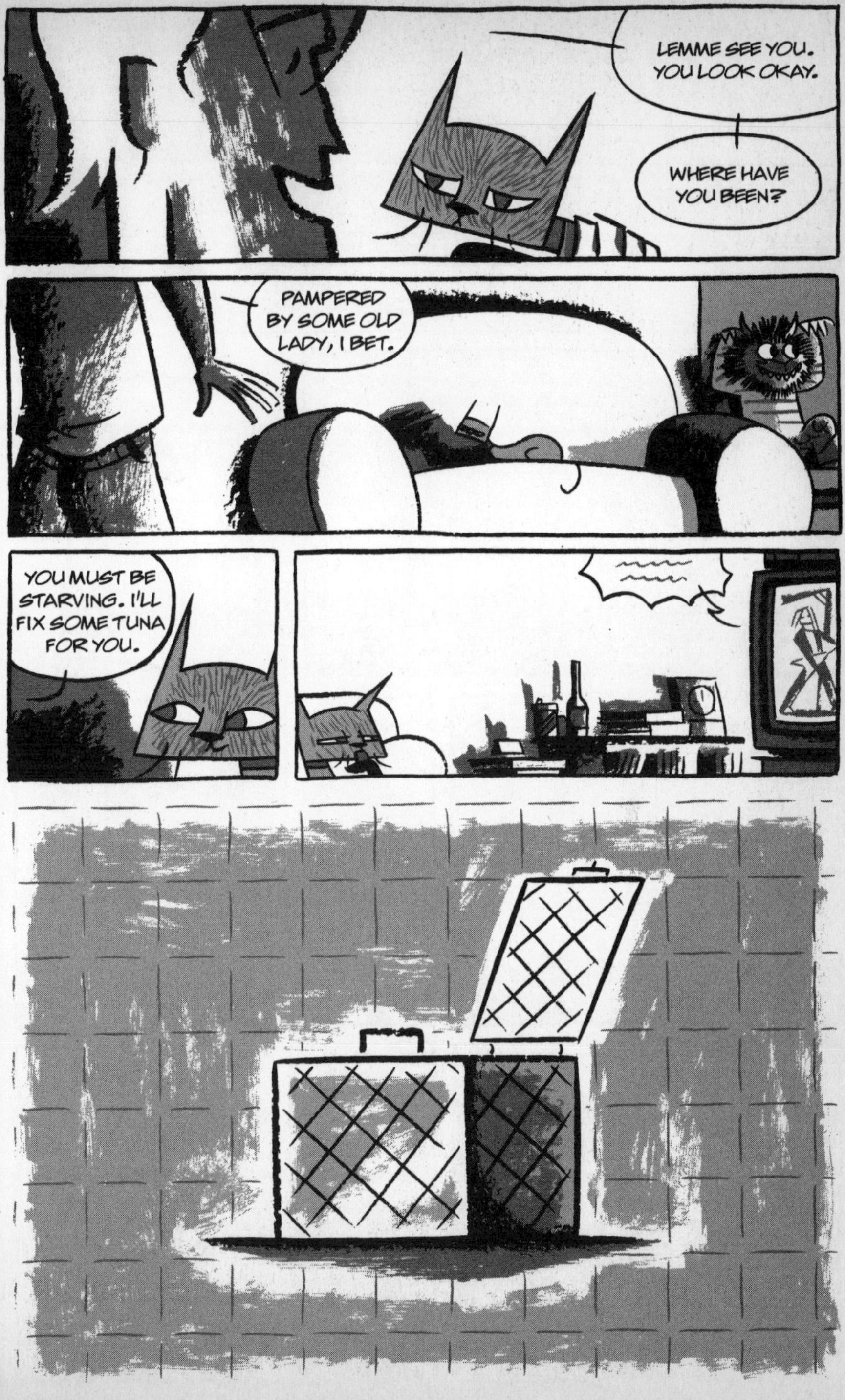
LEMME SEE YOU. YOU LOOK OKAY.
WHERE HAVE YOU BEEN?
PAMPERED BY SOME OLD LADY, I BET.
YOU MUST BE STARVING. I'LL FIX SOME TUNA FOR YOU.

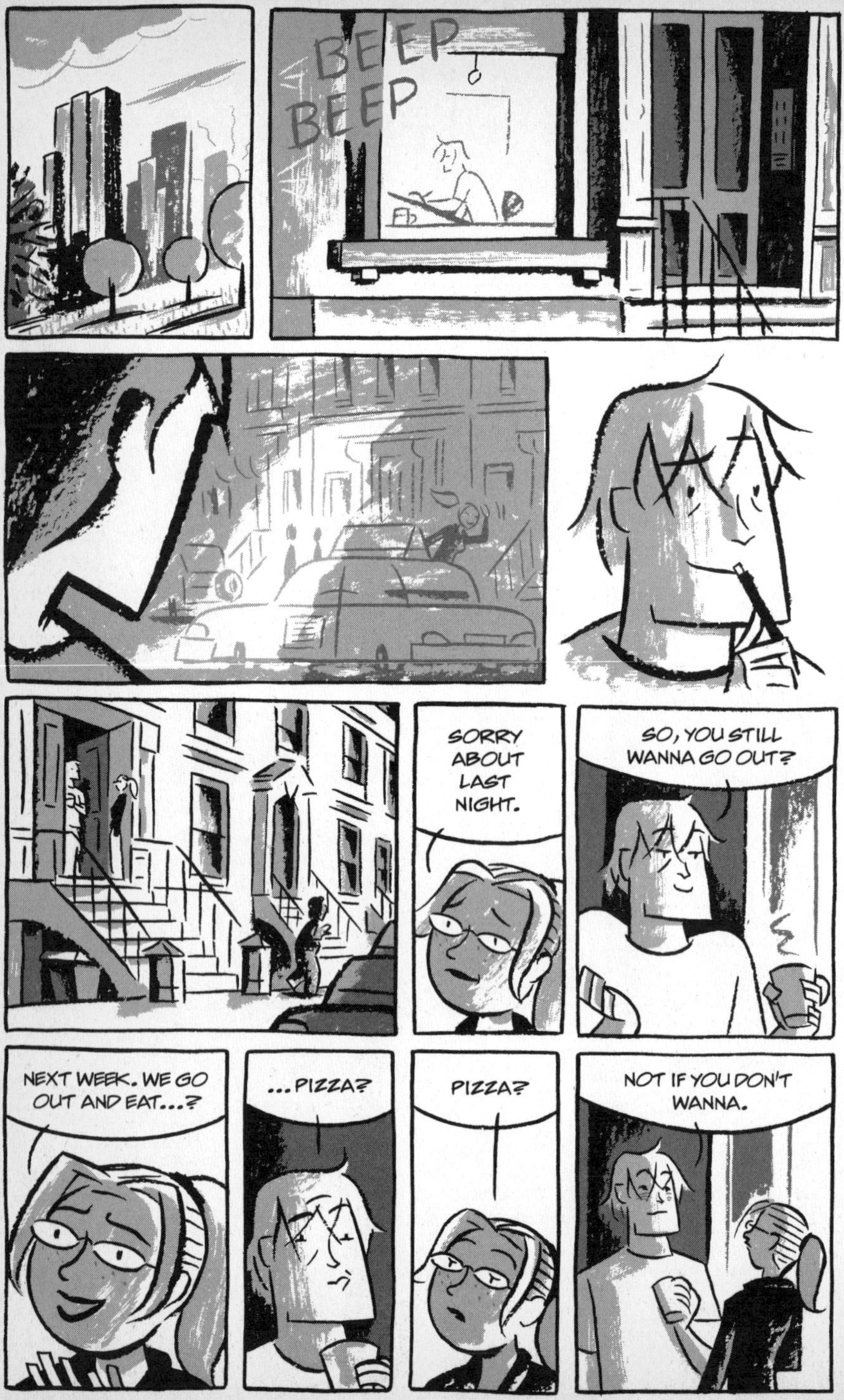
BEEP
BEEP
SORRY ABOUT LAST NIGHT.
SO, YOU STILL WANNA GO OUT?
NEXT WEEK. WE GO OUT AND EAT...?
...PIZZA?
PIZZA?
NOT IF YOU DON'T WANNA.

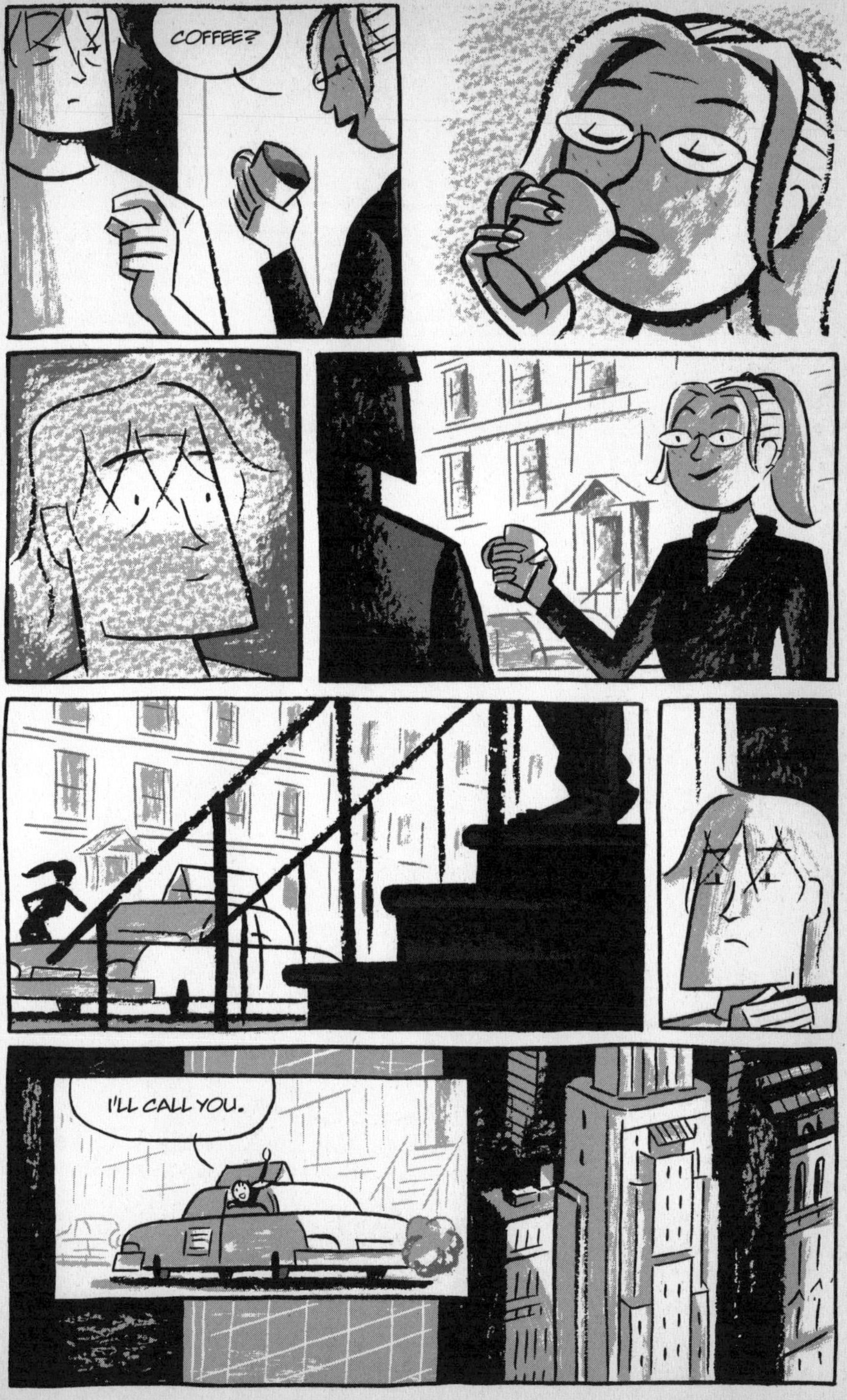
COFFEE?
I'LL CALL YOU.

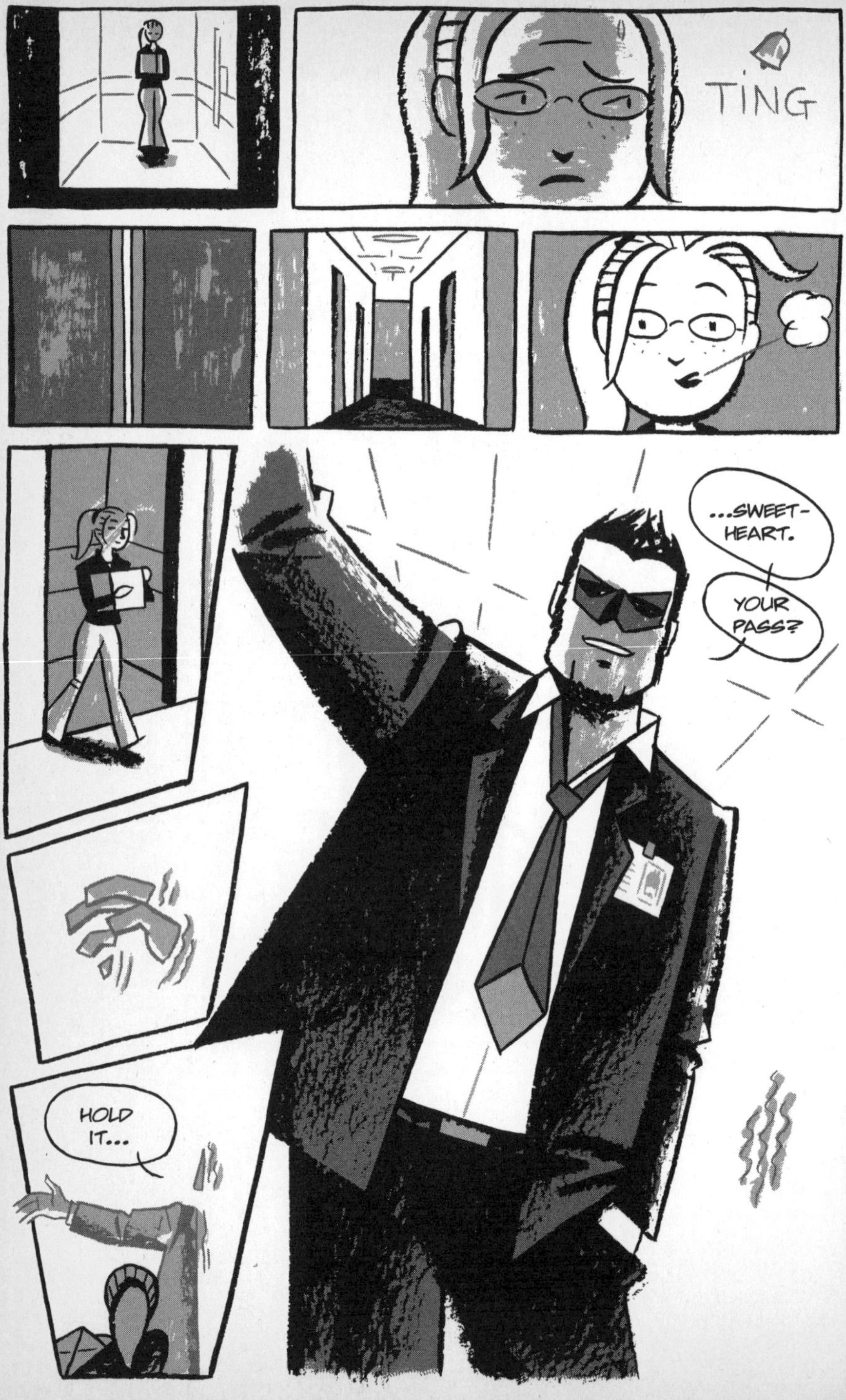
TING
...SWEET-HEART.
YOUR PASS?
HOLD IT...

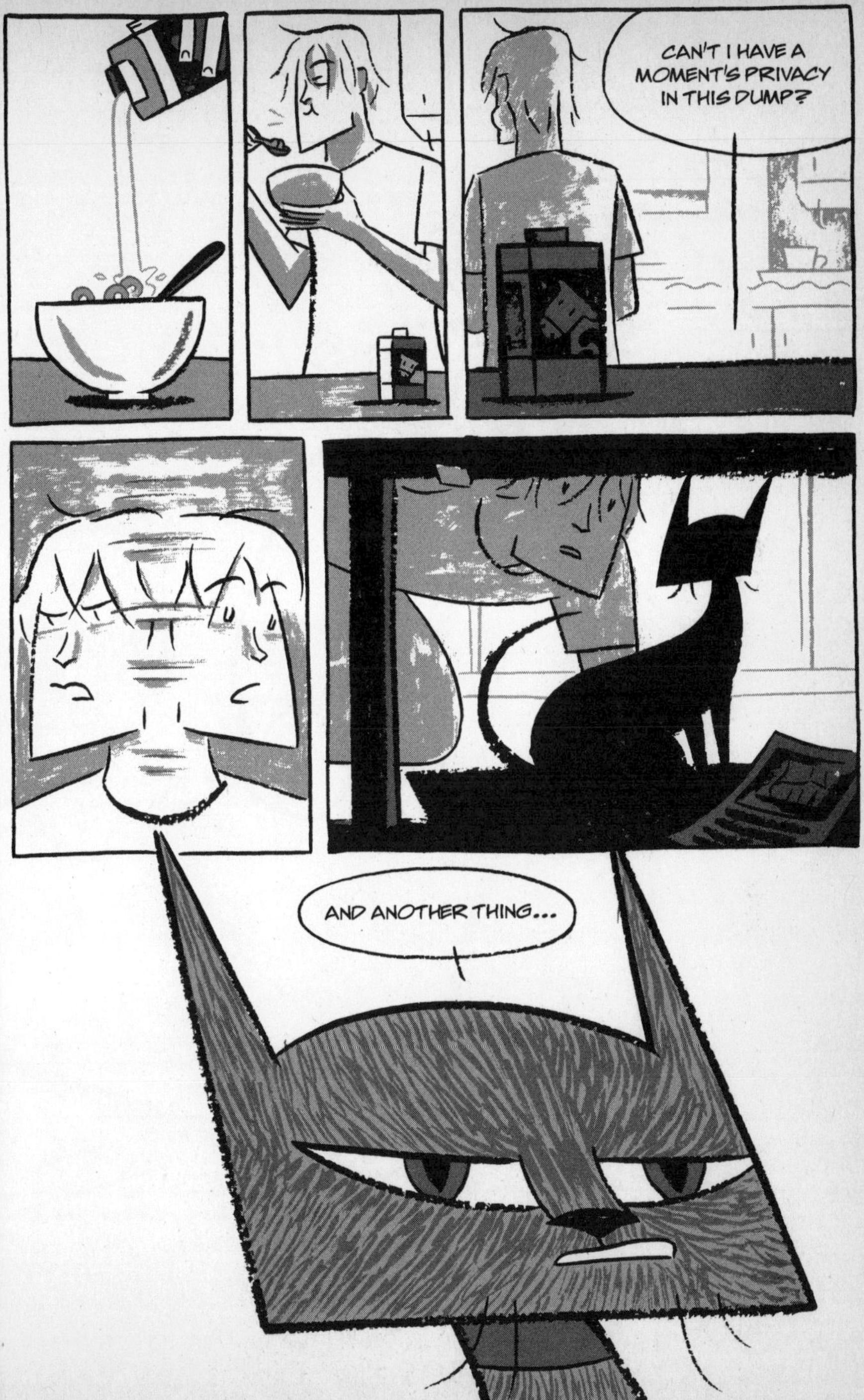
CAN'T I HAVE A MOMENT'S PRIVACY IN THIS DUMP?
AND ANOTHER THING...

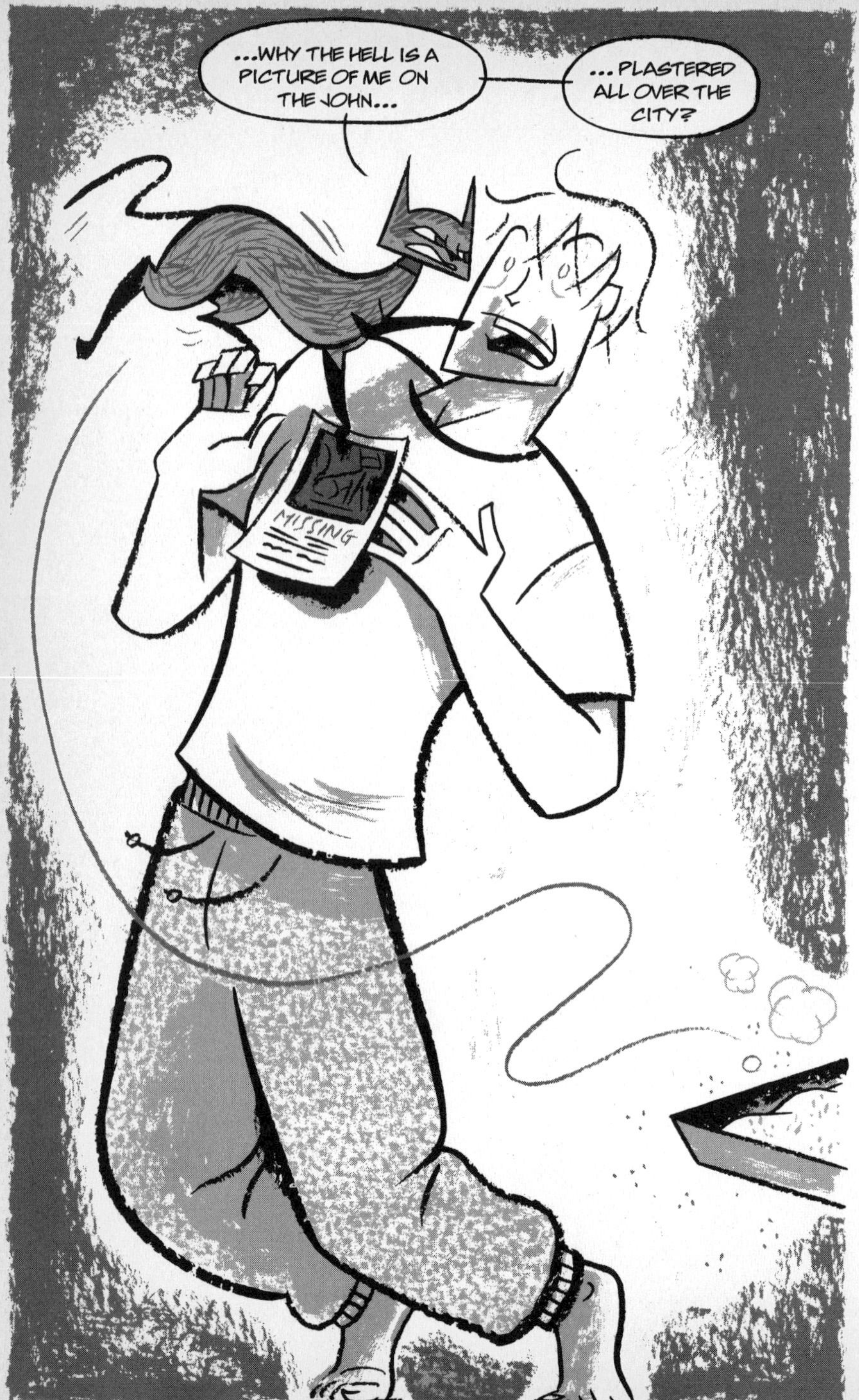
...WHY THE HELL IS A PICTURE OF ME ON THE JOHN...
... PLASTERED ALL OVER THE CITY?
MISSING

Love Fights™ #3

andi watson

ONI PRESS

$2.99 U.S., $4.60 CAN.

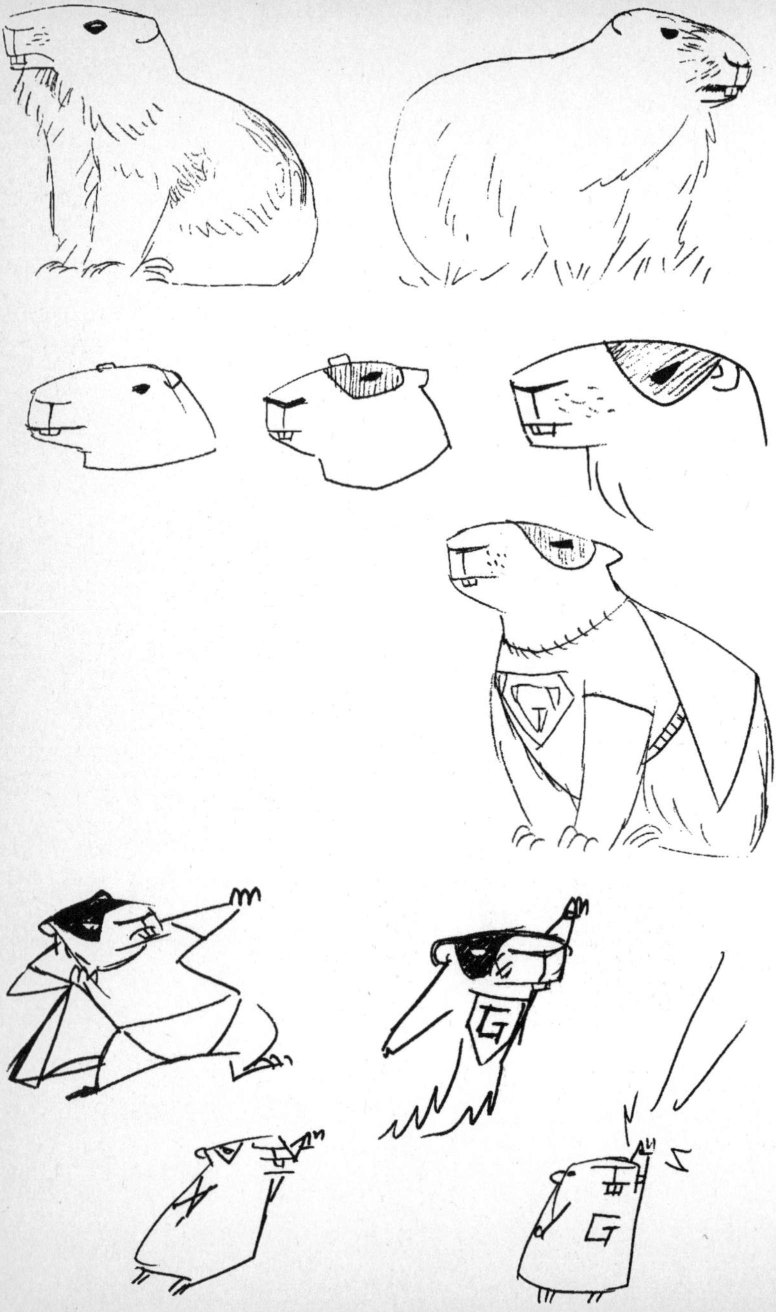

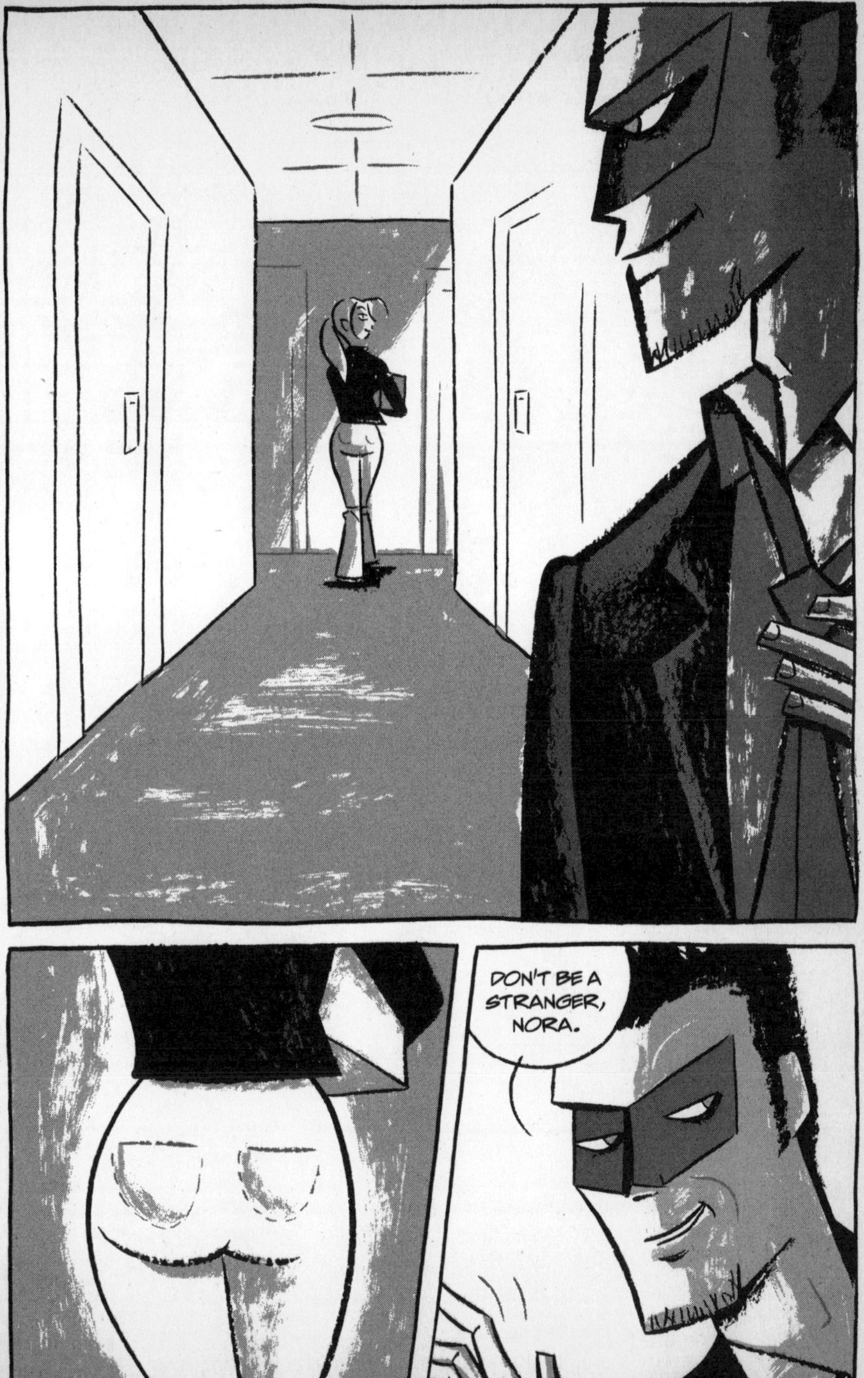
DON'T BE A STRANGER, NORA.

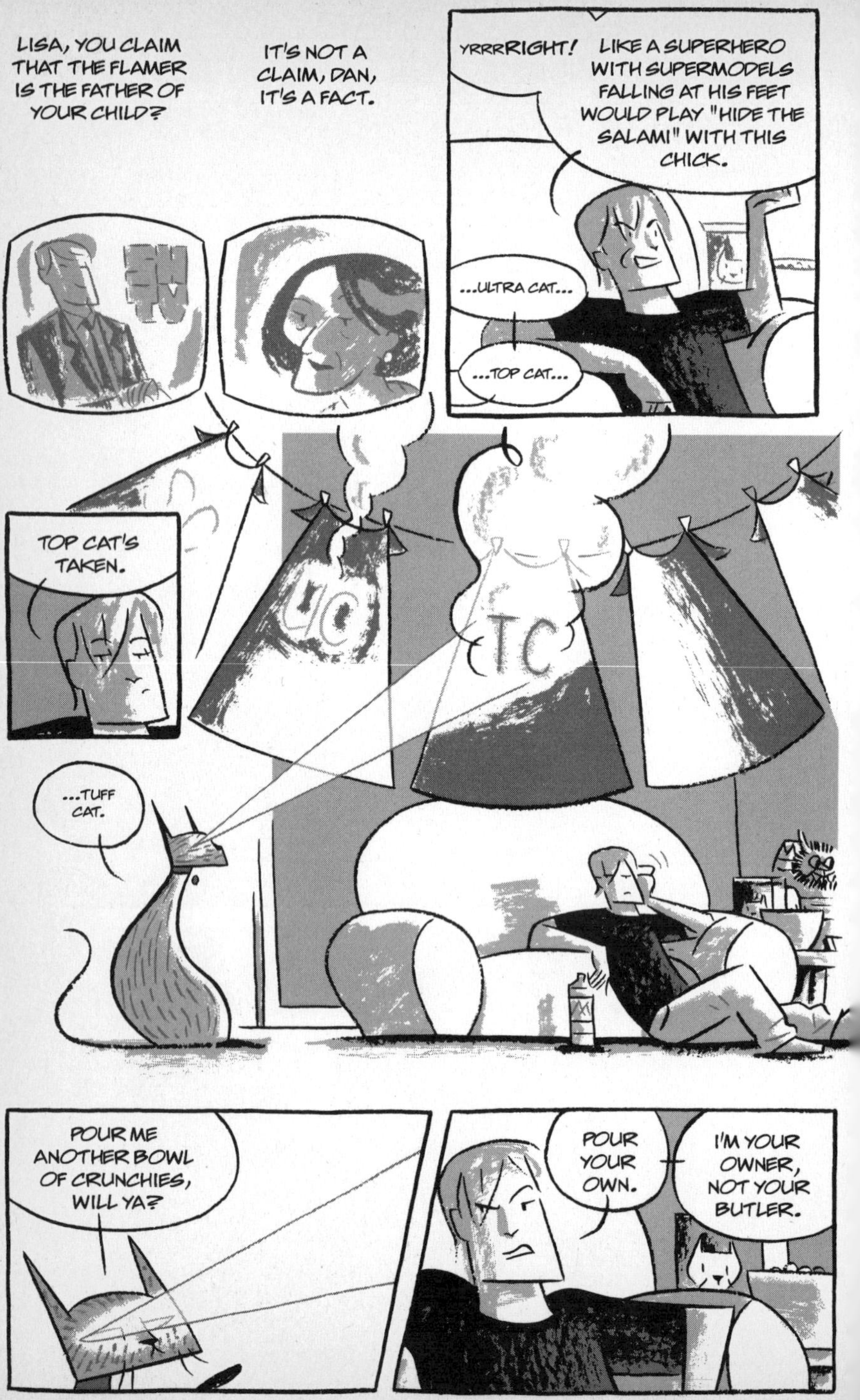
LISA, YOU CLAIM THAT THE FLAMER IS THE FATHER OF YOUR CHILD?
IT'S NOT A CLAIM, DAN, IT'S A FACT.
YRRRRIGHT!
LIKE A SUPERHERO WITH SUPERMODELS FALLING AT HIS FEET WOULD PLAY "HIDE THE SALAMI" WITH THIS CHICK.
...ULTRA CAT...
...TOP CAT...
TOP CAT'S TAKEN.
UC
TC
...TUFF CAT.
POUR ME ANOTHER BOWL OF CRUNCHIES, WILL YA?
POUR YOUR OWN.
I'M YOUR OWNER, NOT YOUR BUTLER.

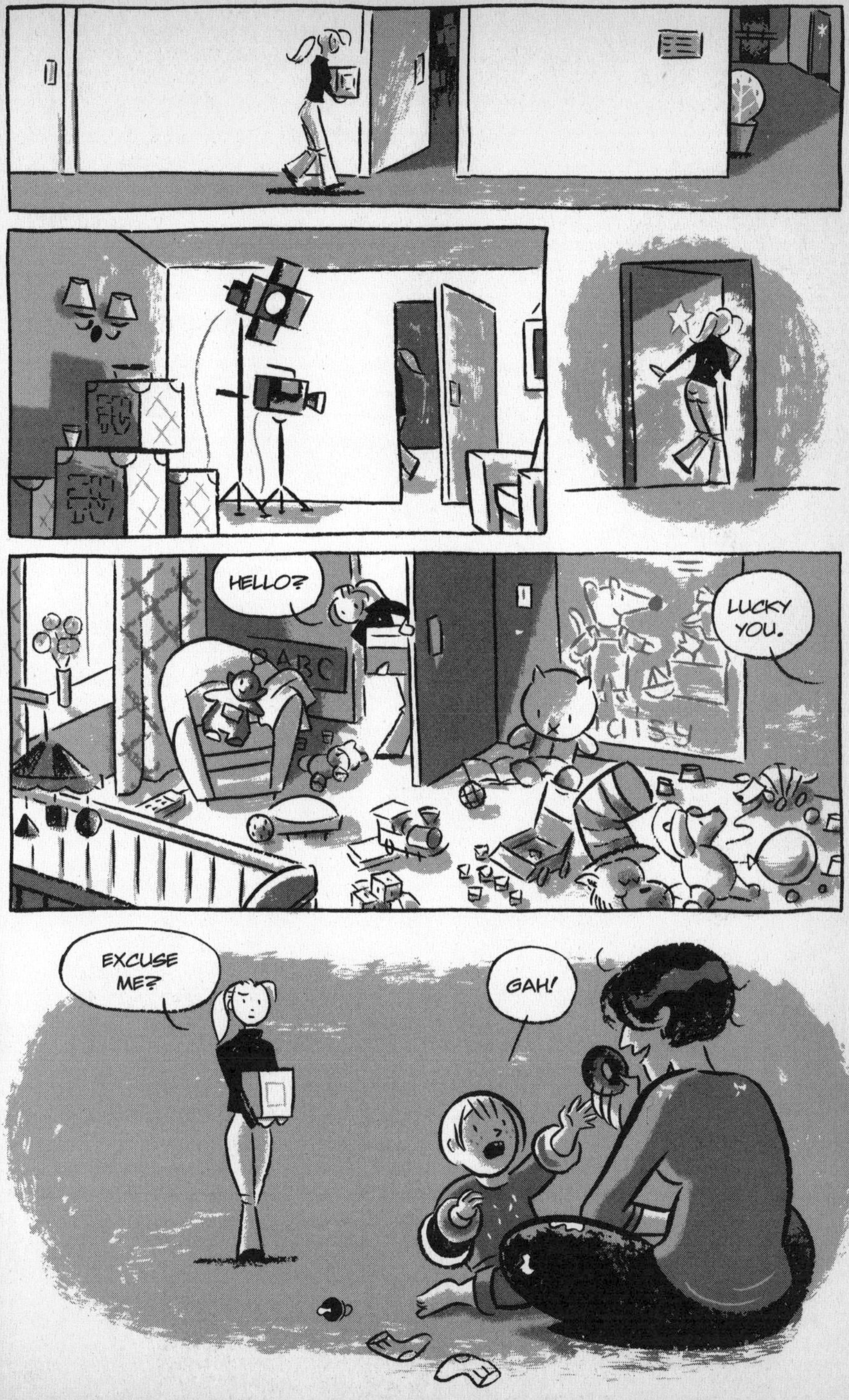
HELLO?
LUCKY YOU.
EXCUSE ME?
GAH!

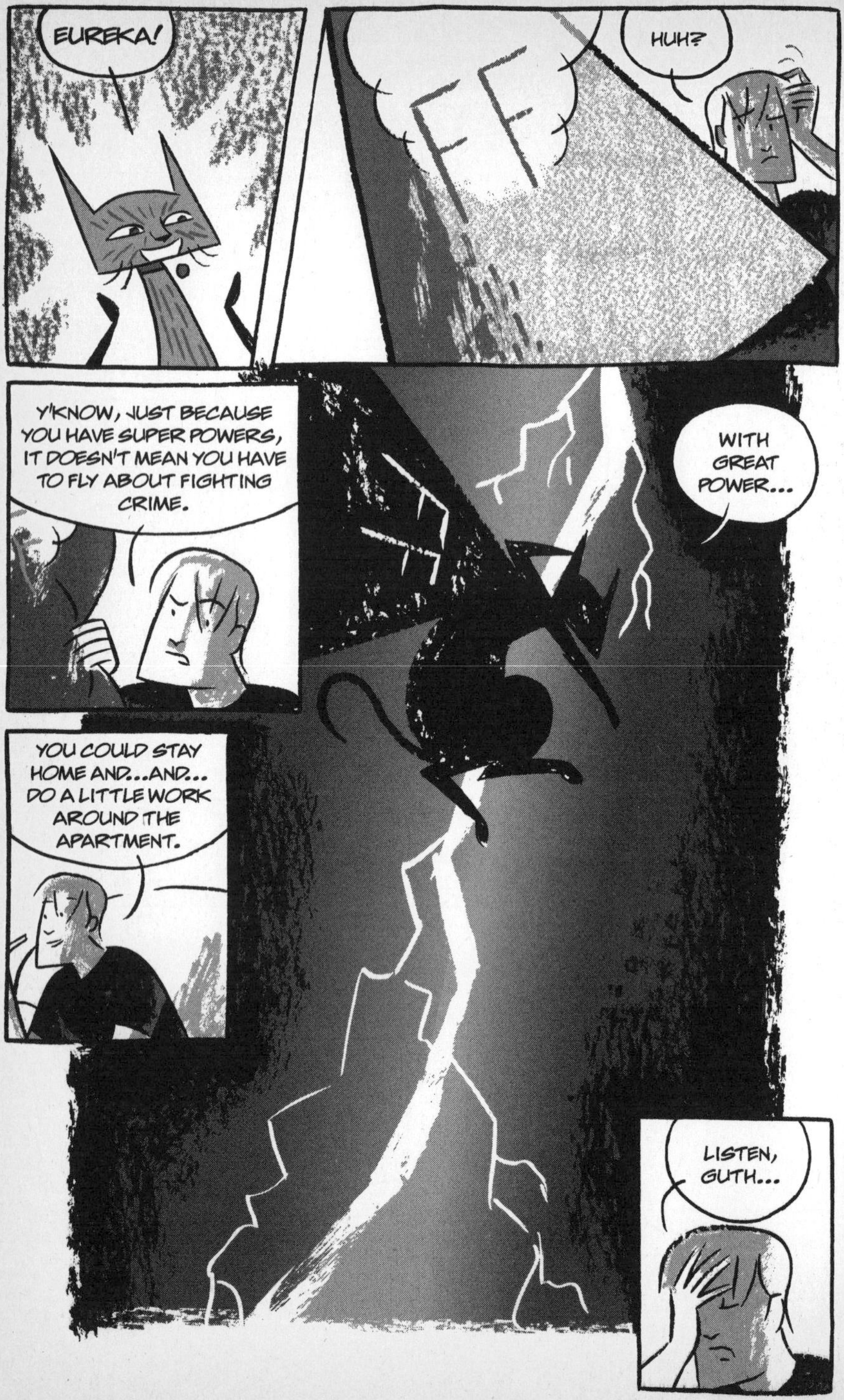
EUREKA!
HUH?
Y'KNOW, JUST BECAUSE YOU HAVE SUPER POWERS, IT DOESN'T MEAN YOU HAVE TO FLY ABOUT FIGHTING CRIME.
YOU COULD STAY HOME AND...AND... DO A LITTLE WORK AROUND THE APARTMENT.
WITH GREAT POWER...
LISTEN, GUTH...

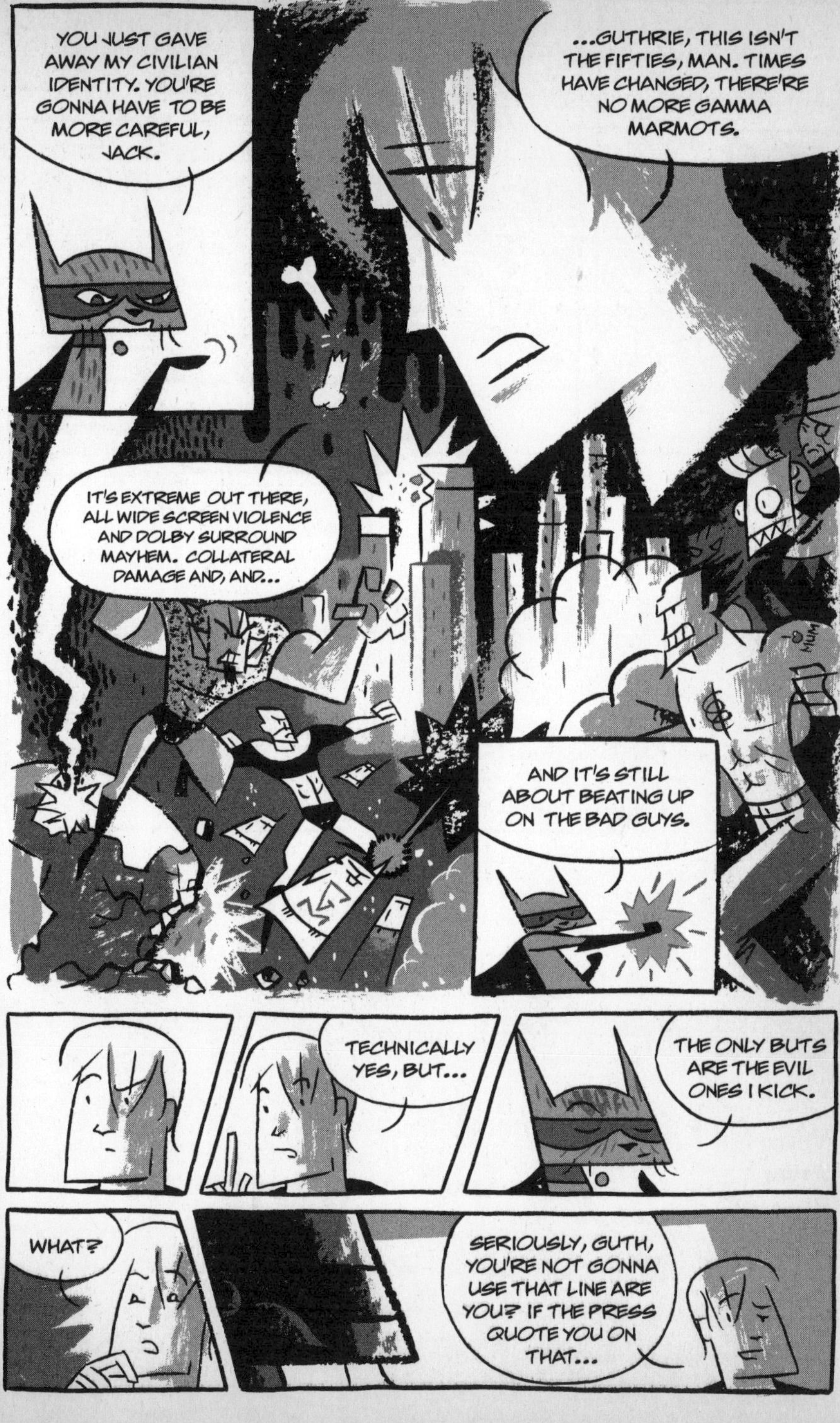
YOU JUST GAVE AWAY MY CIVILIAN IDENTITY. YOU'RE GONNA HAVE TO BE MORE CAREFUL, JACK.
...GUTHRIE, THIS ISN'T THE FIFTIES, MAN. TIMES HAVE CHANGED, THERE'RE NO MORE GAMMA MARMOTS.
IT'S EXTREME OUT THERE, ALL WIDE SCREEN VIOLENCE AND DOLBY SURROUND MAYHEM. COLLATERAL DAMAGE AND, AND...
MUM
AND IT'S STILL ABOUT BEATING UP ON THE BAD GUYS.
TECHNICALLY YES, BUT...
THE ONLY BUTS ARE THE EVIL ONES I KICK.
WHAT?
SERIOUSLY, GUTH, YOU'RE NOT GONNA USE THAT LINE ARE YOU? IF THE PRESS QUOTE YOU ON THAT...

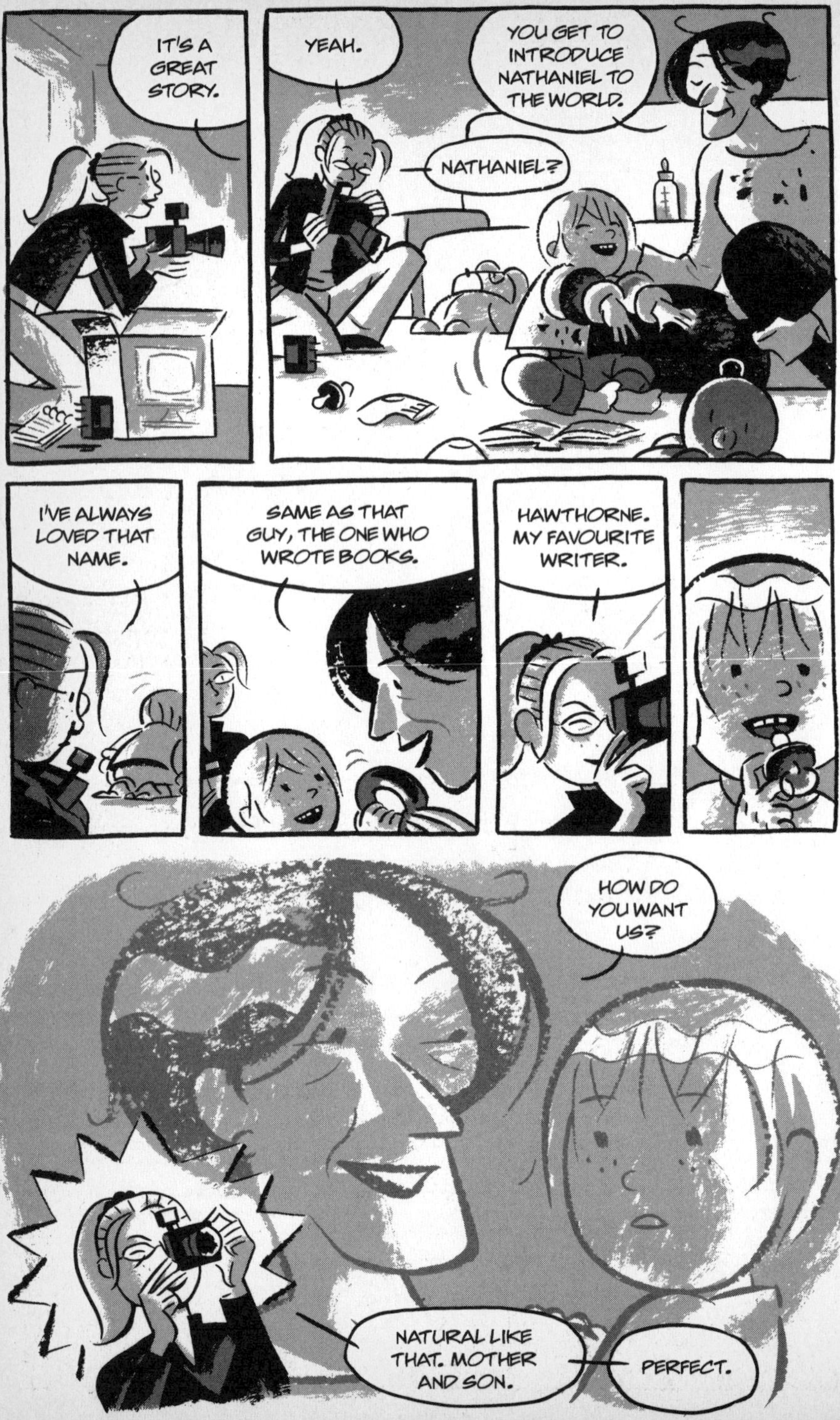
IT'S A GREAT STORY.
YEAH.
YOU GET TO INTRODUCE NATHANIEL TO THE WORLD.
NATHANIEL?
I'VE ALWAYS LOVED THAT NAME.
SAME AS THAT GUY, THE ONE WHO WROTE BOOKS.
HAWTHORNE. MY FAVOURITE WRITER.
HOW DO YOU WANT US?
NATURAL LIKE THAT. MOTHER AND SON.
PERFECT.

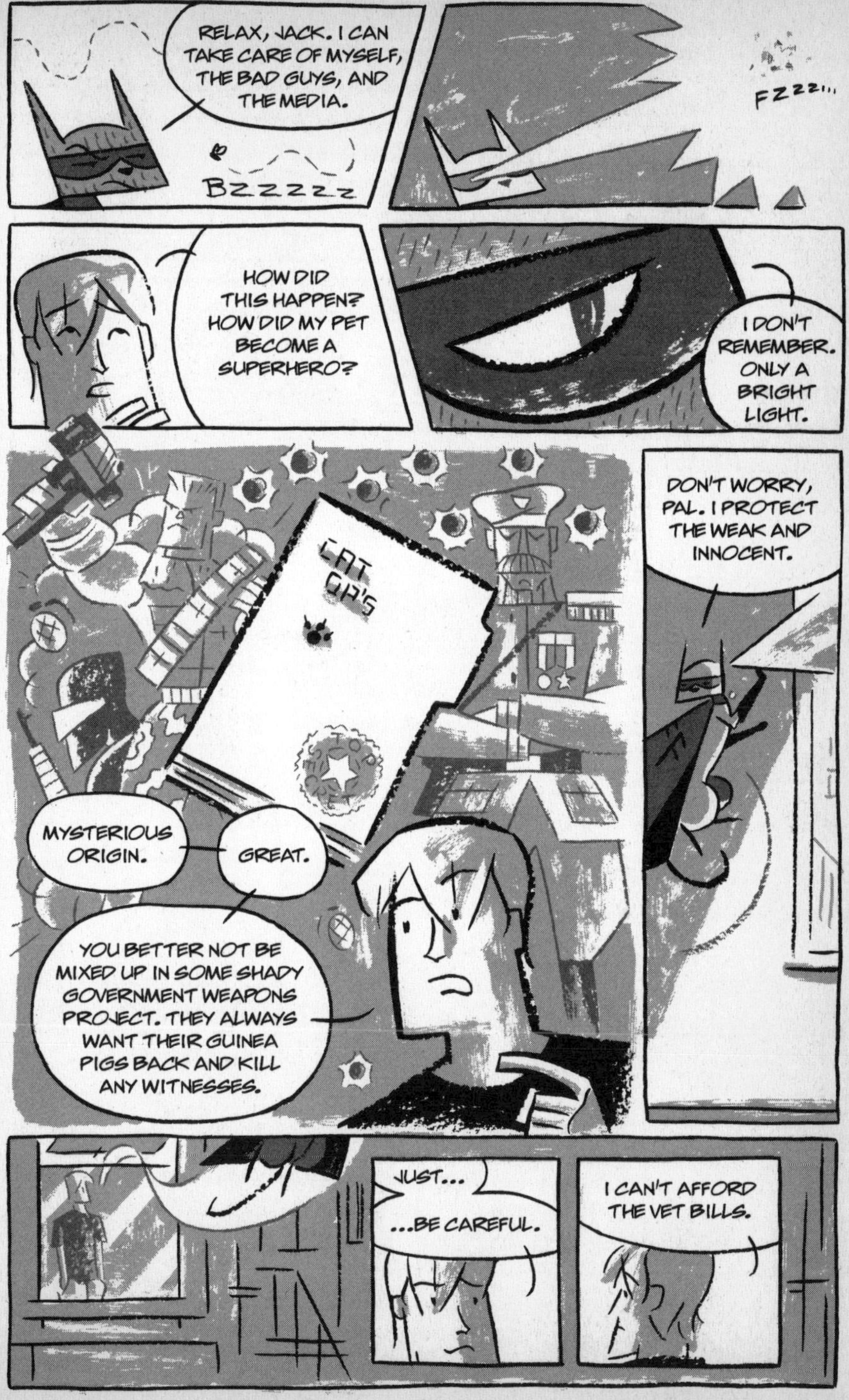
RELAX, JACK. I CAN TAKE CARE OF MYSELF, THE BAD GUYS, AND THE MEDIA.
BZZZZZ
FZZZ...
HOW DID THIS HAPPEN? HOW DID MY PET BECOME A SUPERHERO?
I DON'T REMEMBER. ONLY A BRIGHT LIGHT.
CAT OP'S
TOP SECRET
DON'T WORRY, PAL. I PROTECT THE WEAK AND INNOCENT.
MYSTERIOUS ORIGIN.
GREAT.
YOU BETTER NOT BE MIXED UP IN SOME SHADY GOVERNMENT WEAPONS PROJECT. THEY ALWAYS WANT THEIR GUINEA PIGS BACK AND KILL ANY WITNESSES.
JUST...
...BE CAREFUL.
I CAN'T AFFORD THE VET BILLS.

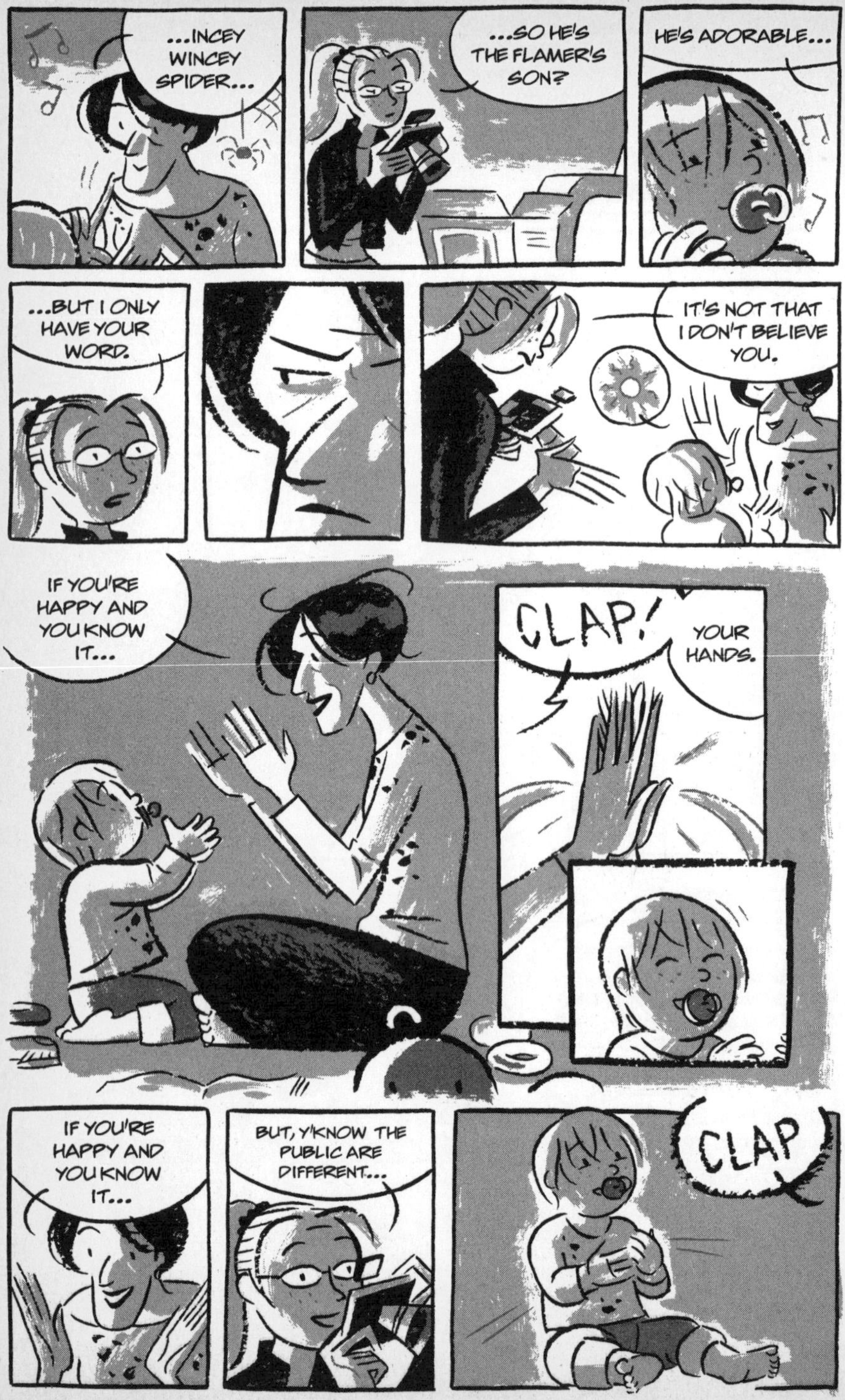
...INCEY WINCEY SPIDER...
...SO HE'S THE FLAMER'S SON?
HE'S ADORABLE...
...BUT I ONLY HAVE YOUR WORD.
IT'S NOT THAT I DON'T BELIEVE YOU.
IF YOU'RE HAPPY AND YOU KNOW IT...
CLAP!
YOUR HANDS.
IF YOU'RE HAPPY AND YOU KNOW IT...
BUT, Y'KNOW THE PUBLIC ARE DIFFERENT...
CLAP

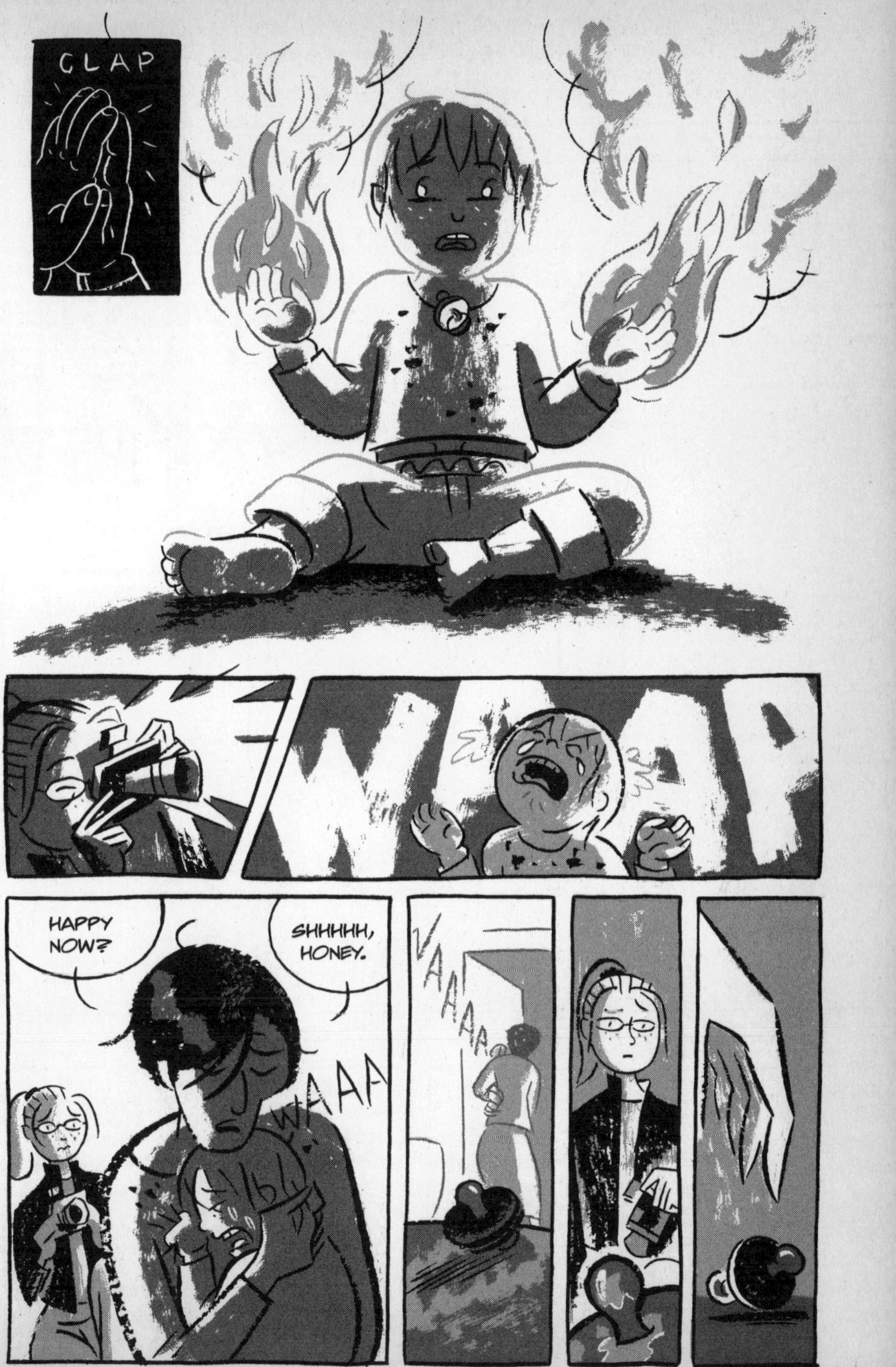
CLAP
WAAP
HAPPY NOW?
SHHHHH, HONEY.
WAAA
WAAAAA

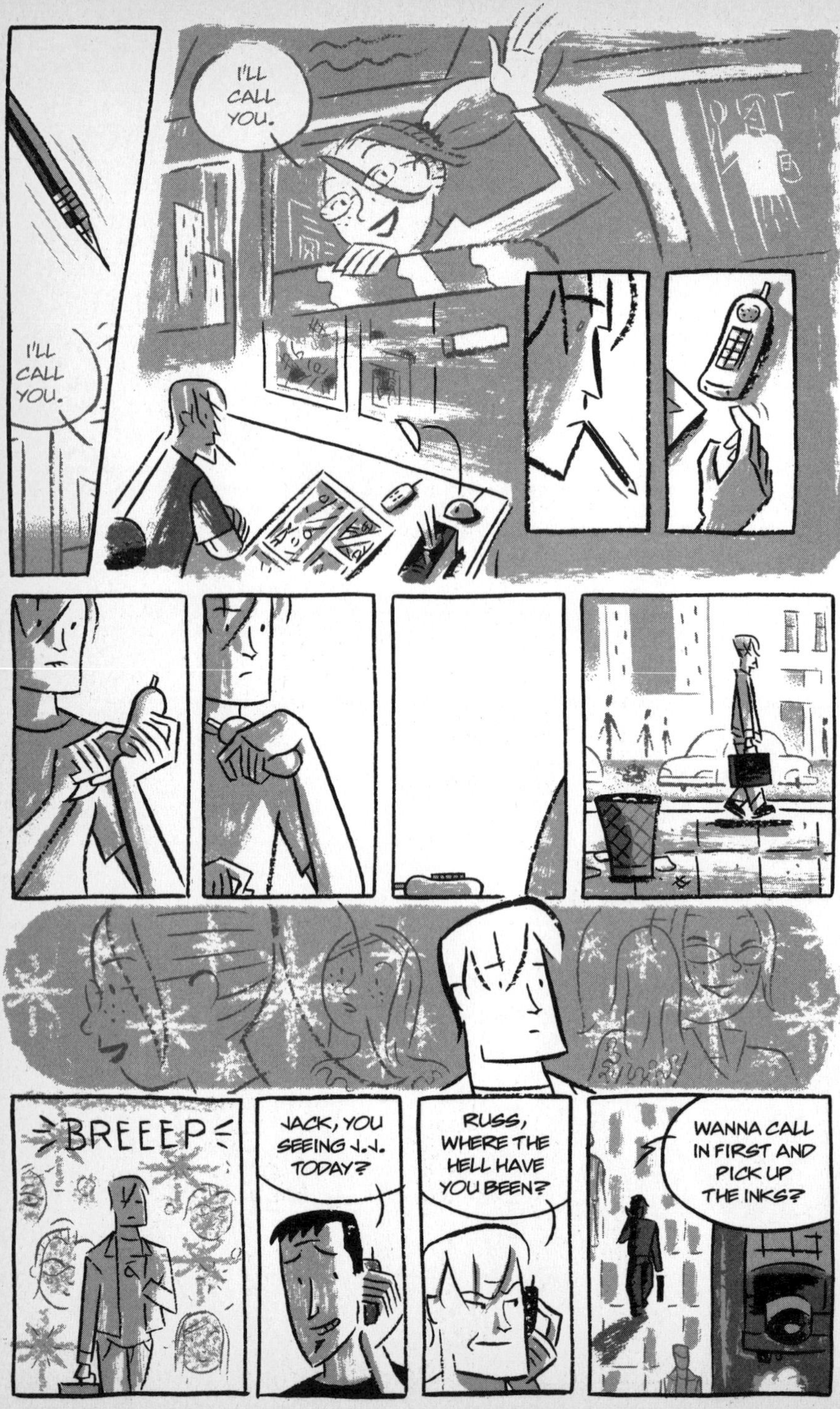

I'LL CALL YOU.
I'LL CALL YOU.
BREEEP
JACK, YOU SEEING J.J. TODAY?
RUSS, WHERE THE HELL HAVE YOU BEEN?
WANNA CALL IN FIRST AND PICK UP THE INKS?

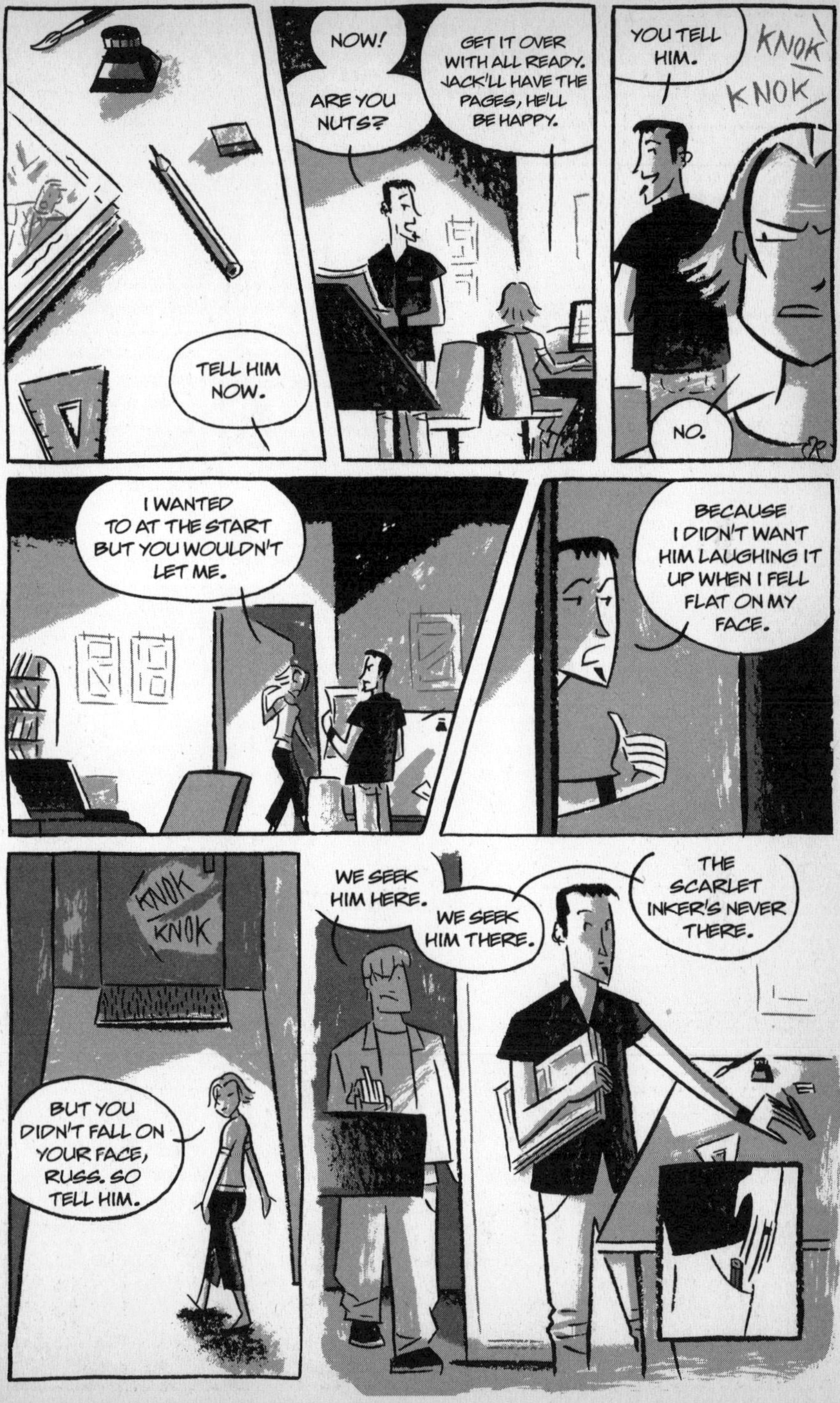
TELL HIM NOW.
NOW!
ARE YOU NUTS?
GET IT OVER WITH ALL READY. JACK'LL HAVE THE PAGES, HE'LL BE HAPPY.
YOU TELL HIM.
KNOK
KNOK
NO.
I WANTED TO AT THE START BUT YOU WOULDN'T LET ME.
BECAUSE I DIDN'T WANT HIM LAUGHING IT UP WHEN I FELL FLAT ON MY FACE.
KNOK
KNOK
BUT YOU DIDN'T FALL ON YOUR FACE, RUSS. SO TELL HIM.
WE SEEK HIM HERE.
WE SEEK HIM THERE.
THE SCARLET INKER'S NEVER THERE.

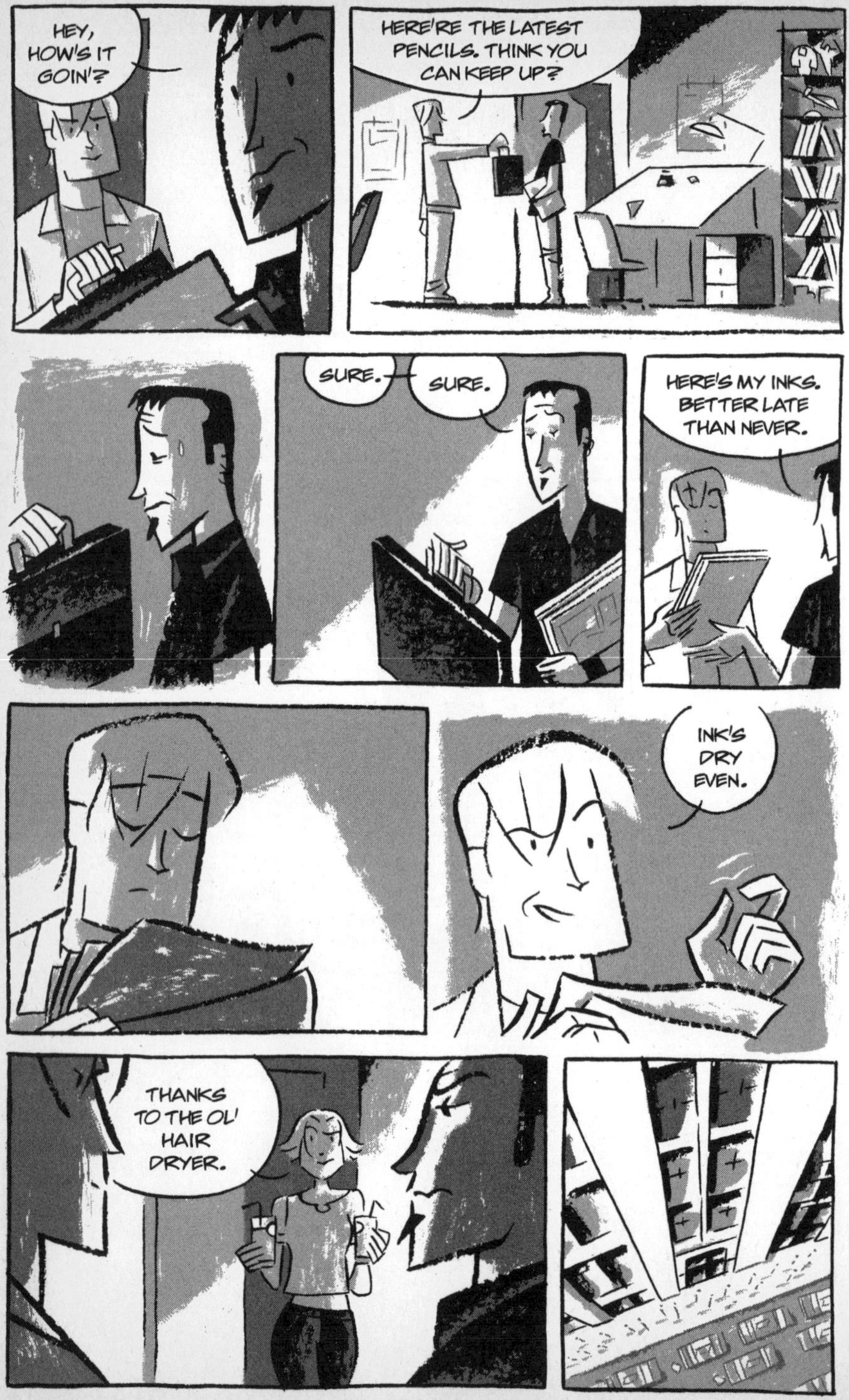
HEY, HOW'S IT GOIN'?
HERE'RE THE LATEST PENCILS. THINK YOU CAN KEEP UP?
SURE.
SURE.
HERE'S MY INKS. BETTER LATE THAN NEVER.
INK'S DRY EVEN.
THANKS TO THE OL' HAIR DRYER.

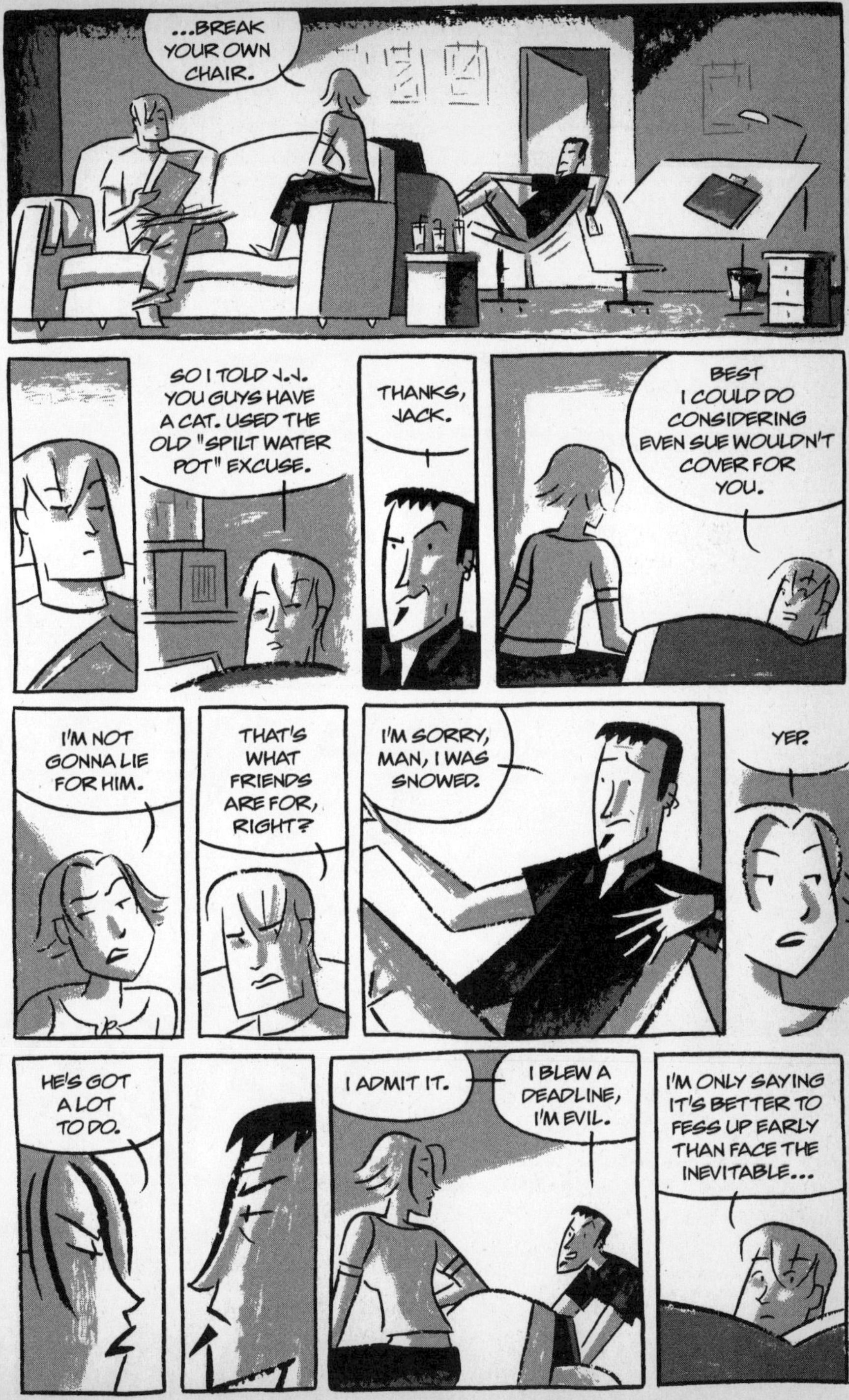
...BREAK YOUR OWN CHAIR.
SO I TOLD J.J. YOU GUYS HAVE A CAT. USED THE OLD "SPILT WATER POT" EXCUSE.
THANKS, JACK.
BEST I COULD DO CONSIDERING EVEN SUE WOULDN'T COVER FOR YOU.
I'M NOT GONNA LIE FOR HIM.
THAT'S WHAT FRIENDS ARE FOR, RIGHT?
I'M SORRY, MAN, I WAS SNOWED.
YEP.
HE'S GOT A LOT TO DO.
I ADMIT IT.
I BLEW A DEADLINE, I'M EVIL.
I'M ONLY SAYING IT'S BETTER TO FESS UP EARLY THAN FACE THE INEVITABLE...

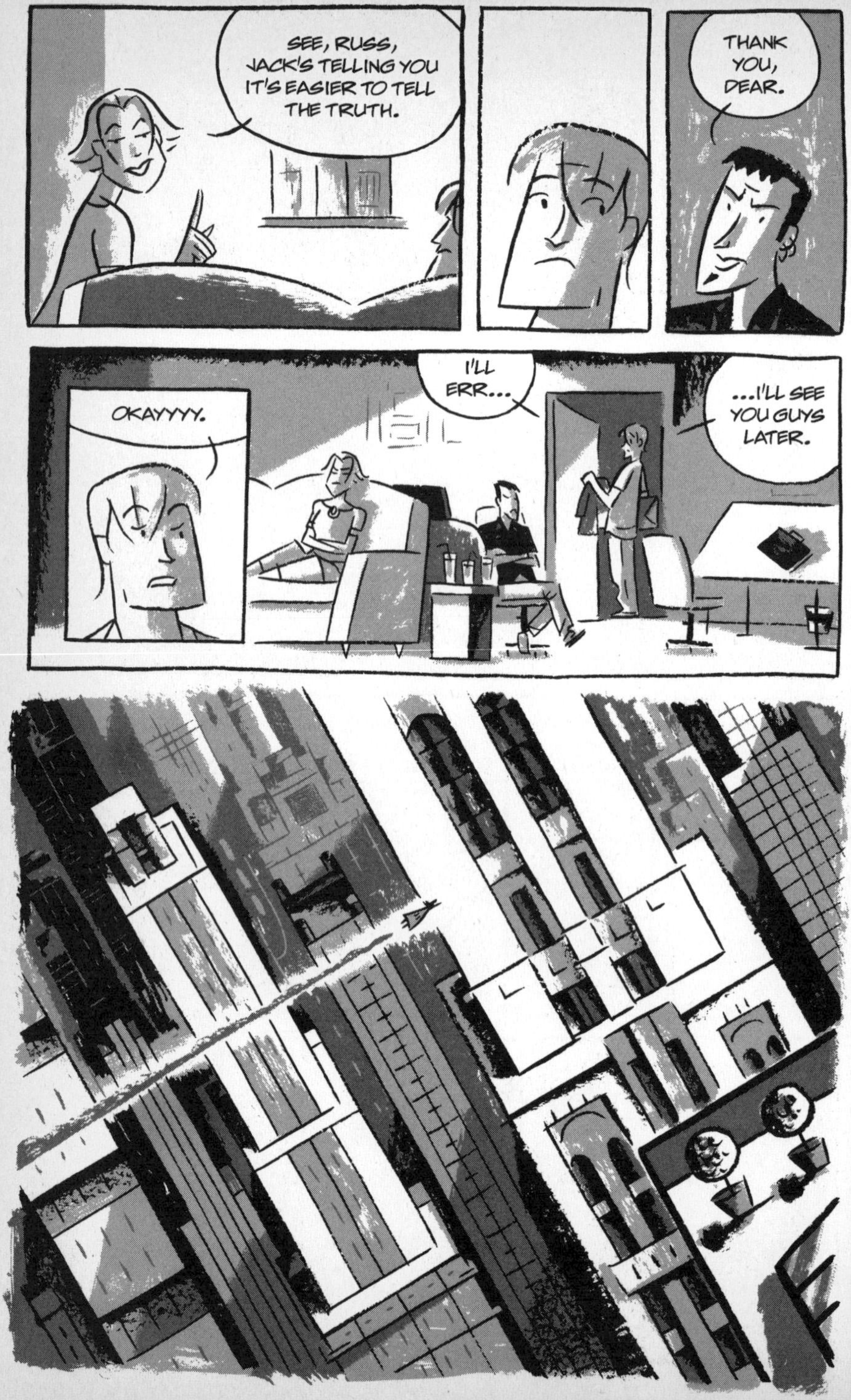
SEE, RUSS, JACK'S TELLING YOU IT'S EASIER TO TELL THE TRUTH.
THANK YOU, DEAR.
OKAYYYY.
I'LL ERR...
...I'LL SEE YOU GUYS LATER.

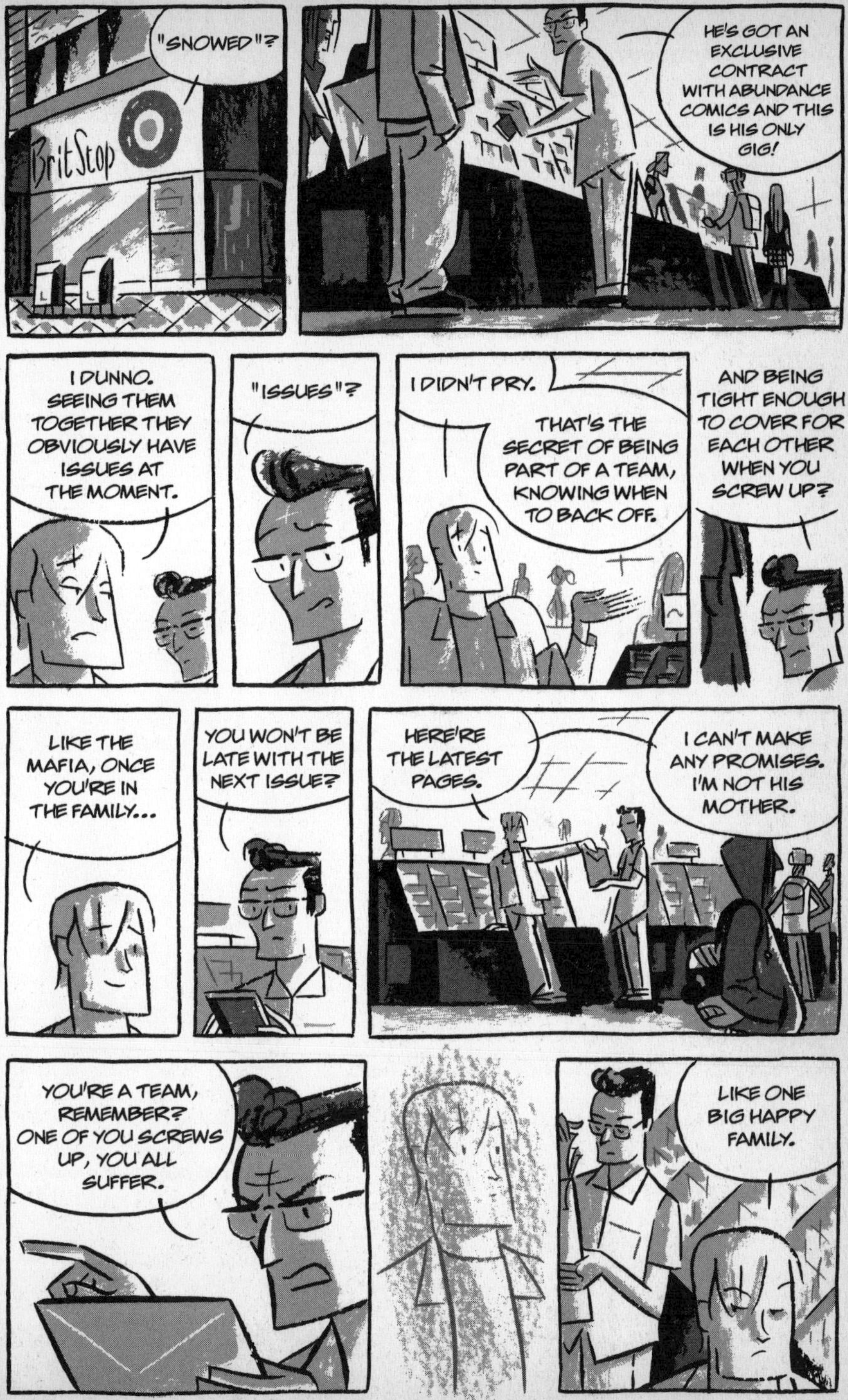

"SNOWED"?
BritStop
HE'S GOT AN EXCLUSIVE CONTRACT WITH ABUNDANCE COMICS AND THIS IS HIS ONLY GIG!
I DUNNO. SEEING THEM TOGETHER THEY OBVIOUSLY HAVE ISSUES AT THE MOMENT.
"ISSUES"?
I DIDN'T PRY.
THAT'S THE SECRET OF BEING PART OF A TEAM, KNOWING WHEN TO BACK OFF.
AND BEING TIGHT ENOUGH TO COVER FOR EACH OTHER WHEN YOU SCREW UP?
LIKE THE MAFIA, ONCE YOU'RE IN THE FAMILY...
YOU WON'T BE LATE WITH THE NEXT ISSUE?
HERE'RE THE LATEST PAGES.
I CAN'T MAKE ANY PROMISES. I'M NOT HIS MOTHER.
YOU'RE A TEAM, REMEMBER? ONE OF YOU SCREWS UP, YOU ALL SUFFER.
LIKE ONE BIG HAPPY FAMILY.

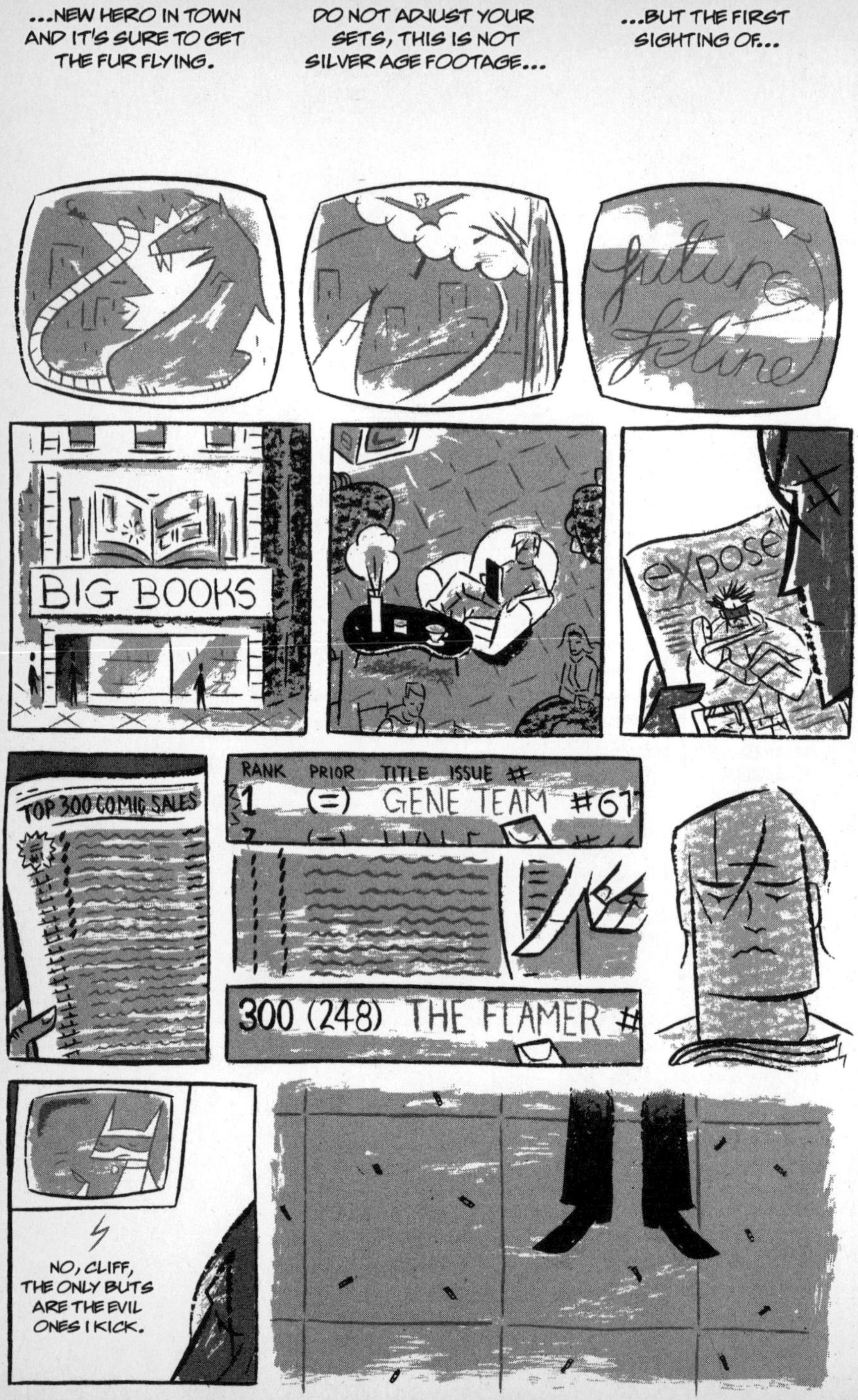
...NEW HERO IN TOWN AND IT'S SURE TO GET THE FUR FLYING.
DO NOT ADJUST YOUR SETS, THIS IS NOT SILVER AGE FOOTAGE...
...BUT THE FIRST SIGHTING OF...
BIG BOOKS
exposé
TOP 300 COMIC SALES
RANK PRIOR TITLE ISSUE #
1 (=) GENE TEAM #61
300 (248) THE FLAMER #
NO, CLIFF, THE ONLY BUTS ARE THE EVIL ONES I KICK.

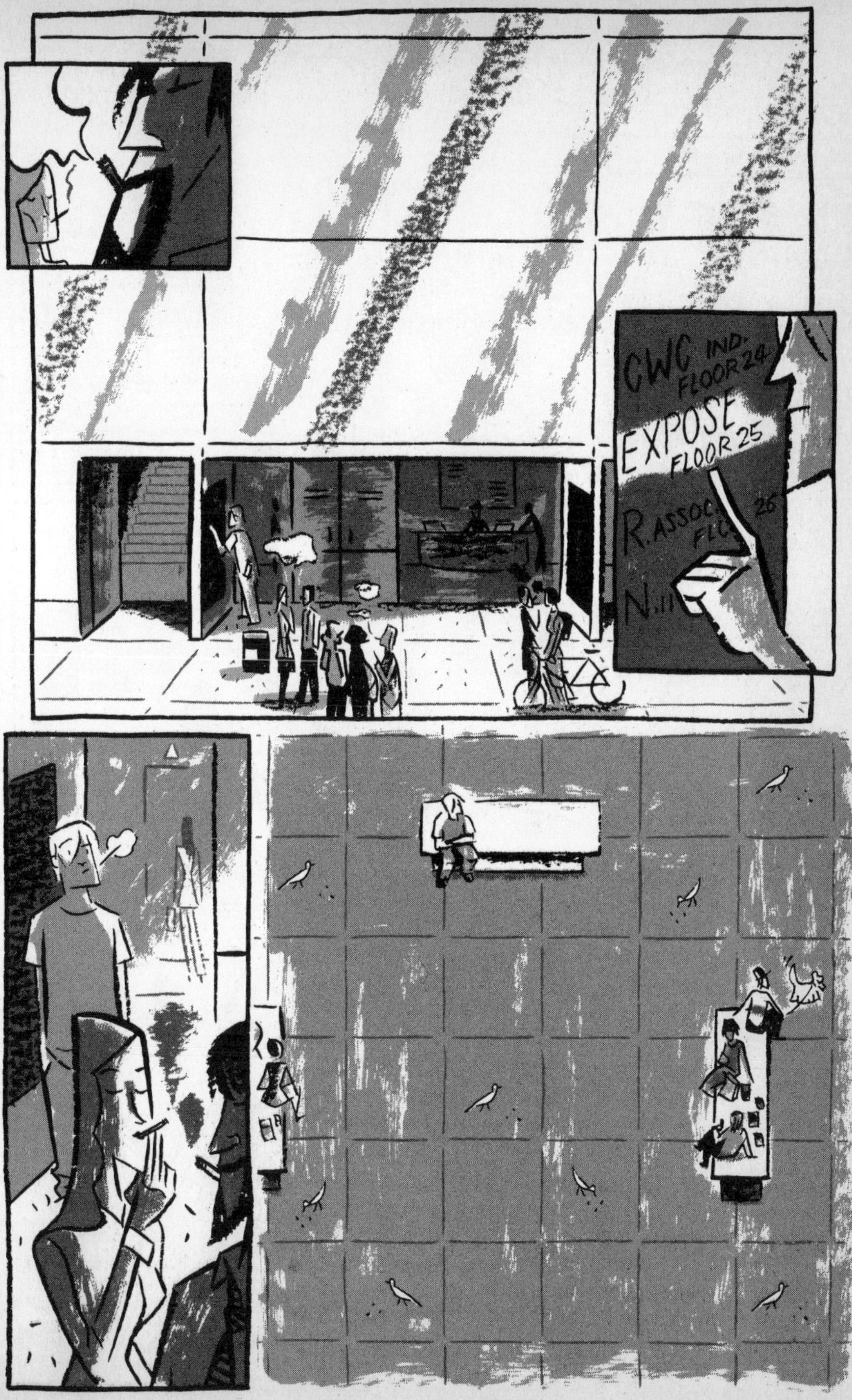
CWC IND.
FLOOR 24
EXPOSE
FLOOR 25

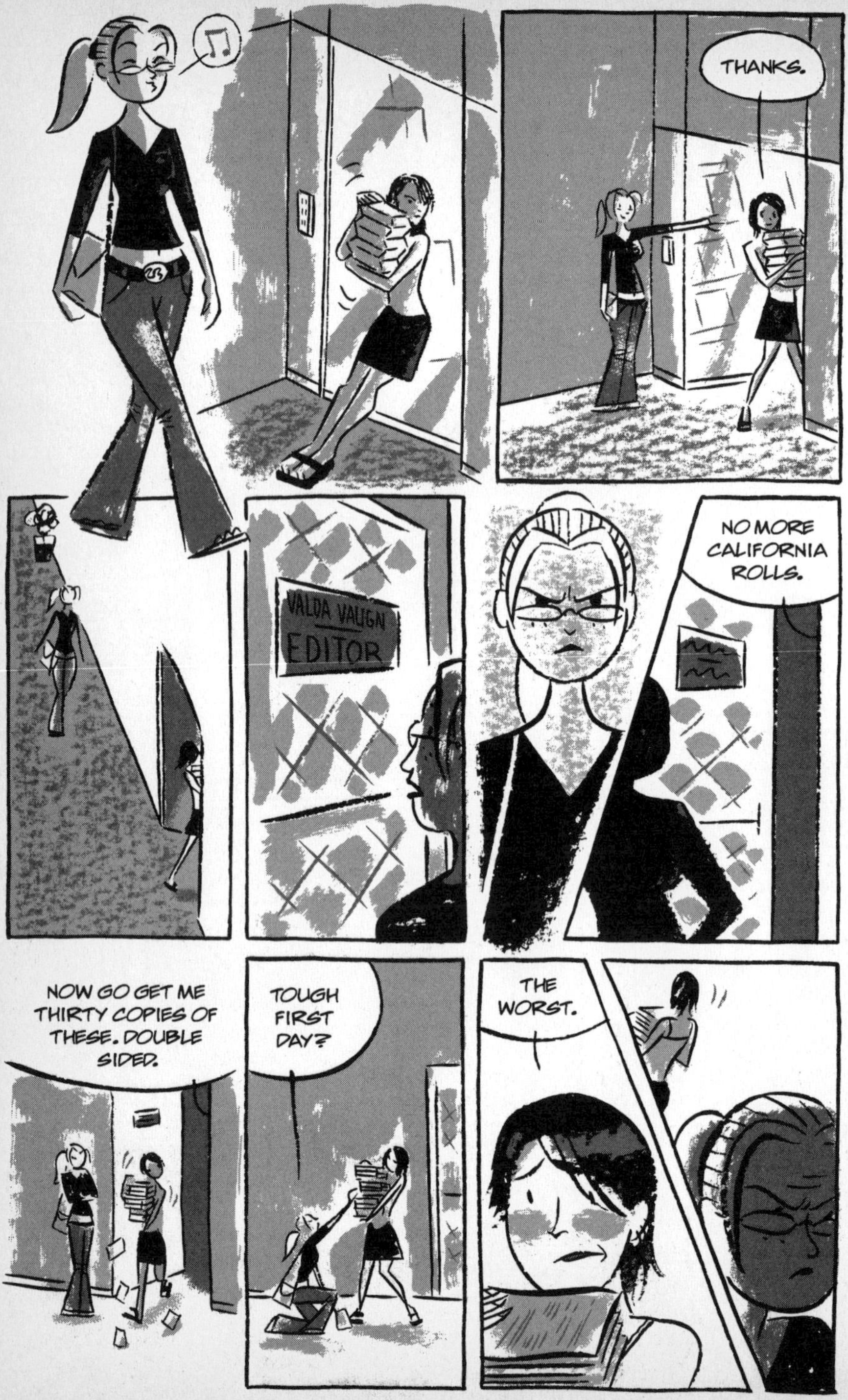
THANKS.
VALDA VAUGN
EDITOR
NO MORE CALIFORNIA ROLLS.
NOW GO GET ME THIRTY COPIES OF THESE. DOUBLE SIDED.
TOUGH FIRST DAY?
THE WORST.

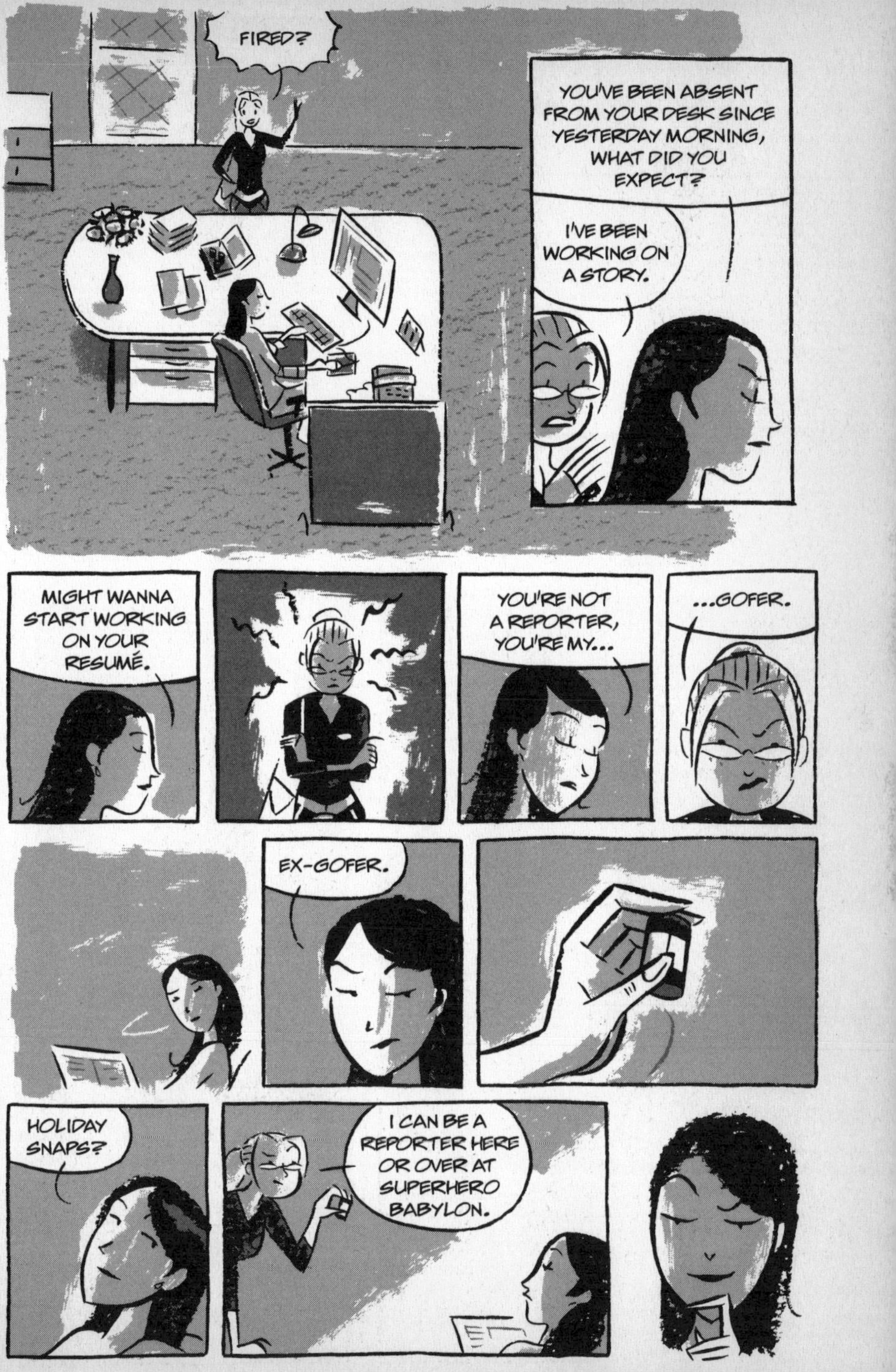
FIRED?
YOU'VE BEEN ABSENT FROM YOUR DESK SINCE YESTERDAY MORNING, WHAT DID YOU EXPECT?
I'VE BEEN WORKING ON A STORY.
MIGHT WANNA START WORKING ON YOUR RESUMÉ.
YOU'RE NOT A REPORTER, YOU'RE MY...
...GOFER.
EX-GOFER.
HOLIDAY SNAPS?
I CAN BE A REPORTER HERE OR OVER AT SUPERHERO BABYLON.

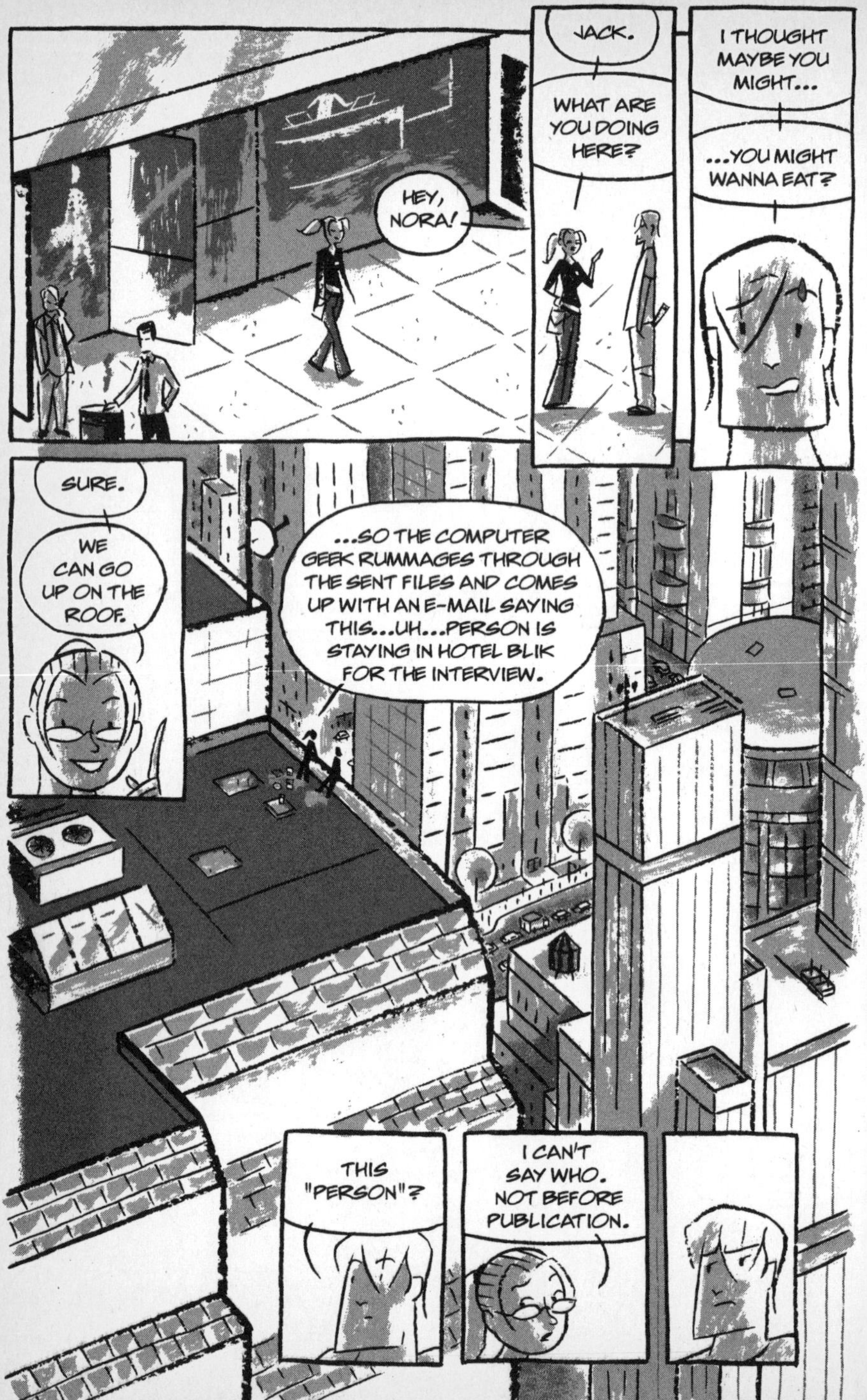
HEY, NORA!
JACK.
WHAT ARE YOU DOING HERE?
I THOUGHT MAYBE YOU MIGHT...
...YOU MIGHT WANNA EAT?
SURE.
WE CAN GO UP ON THE ROOF.
...SO THE COMPUTER GEEK RUMMAGES THROUGH THE SENT FILES AND COMES UP WITH AN E-MAIL SAYING THIS...UH...PERSON IS STAYING IN HOTEL BLIK FOR THE INTERVIEW.
THIS "PERSON"?
I CAN'T SAY WHO. NOT BEFORE PUBLICATION.

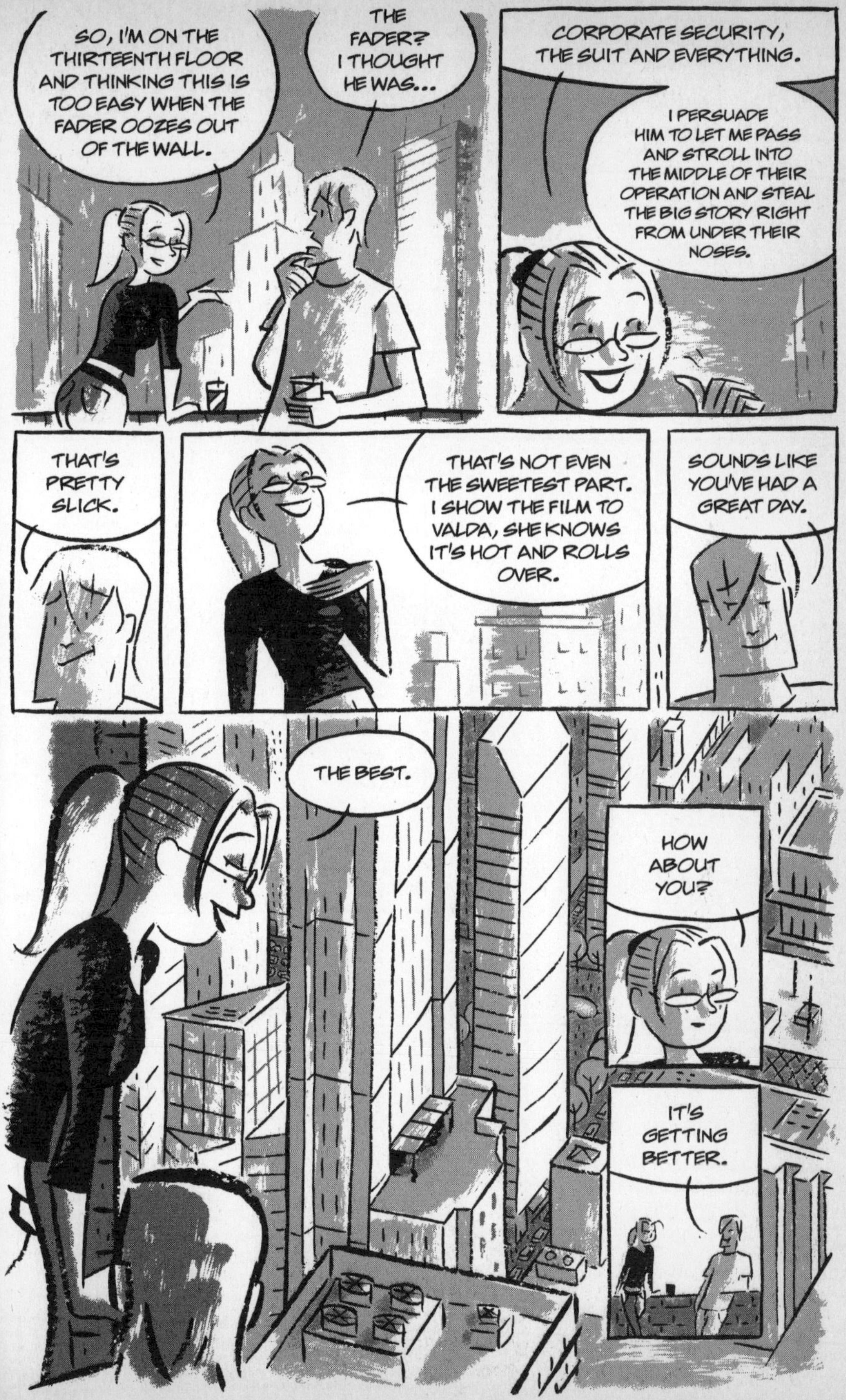
SO, I'M ON THE THIRTEENTH FLOOR AND THINKING THIS IS TOO EASY WHEN THE FADER OOZES OUT OF THE WALL.
THE FADER? I THOUGHT HE WAS...
CORPORATE SECURITY, THE SUIT AND EVERYTHING.
I PERSUADE HIM TO LET ME PASS AND STROLL INTO THE MIDDLE OF THEIR OPERATION AND STEAL THE BIG STORY RIGHT FROM UNDER THEIR NOSES.
THAT'S PRETTY SLICK.
THAT'S NOT EVEN THE SWEETEST PART. I SHOW THE FILM TO VALDA, SHE KNOWS IT'S HOT AND ROLLS OVER.
SOUNDS LIKE YOU'VE HAD A GREAT DAY.
THE BEST.
HOW ABOUT YOU?
IT'S GETTING BETTER.

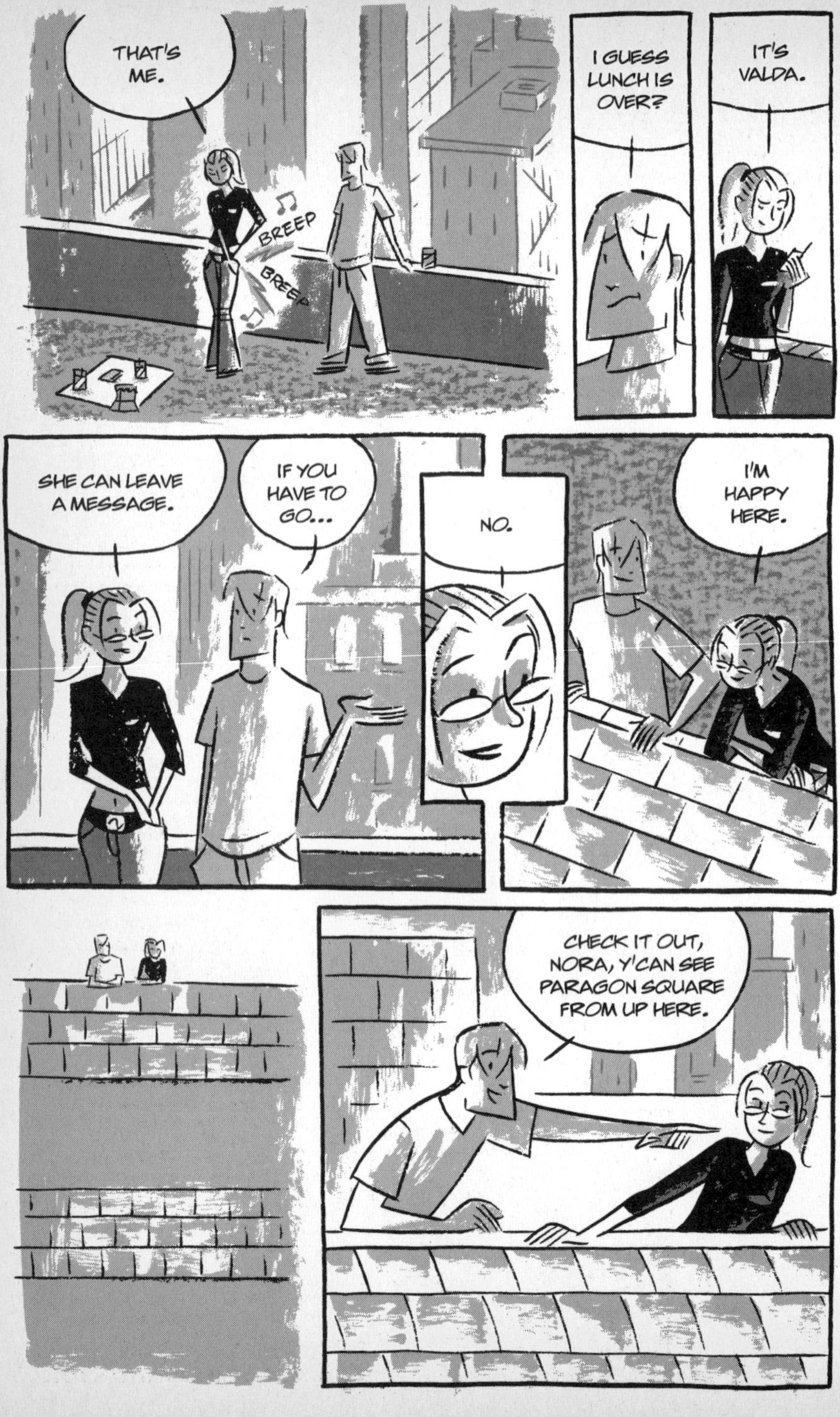
THAT'S ME.
BREEP
BREEP
I GUESS LUNCH IS OVER?
IT'S VALDA.
SHE CAN LEAVE A MESSAGE.
IF YOU HAVE TO GO...
NO.
I'M HAPPY HERE.
CHECK IT OUT, NORA, Y'CAN SEE PARAGON SQUARE FROM UP HERE.

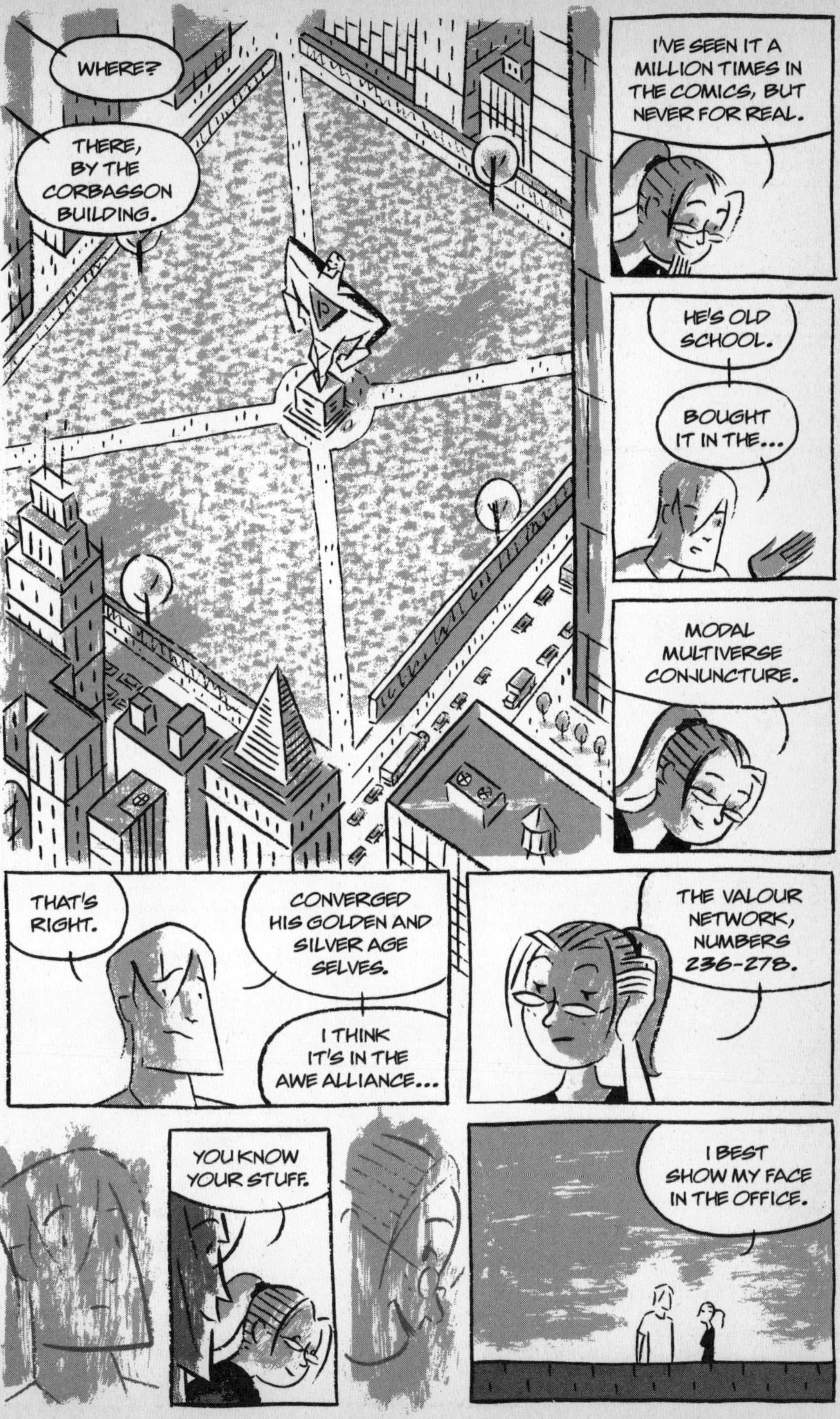
WHERE?
THERE, BY THE CORBASSON BUILDING.
I'VE SEEN IT A MILLION TIMES IN THE COMICS, BUT NEVER FOR REAL.
HE'S OLD SCHOOL.
BOUGHT IT IN THE...
MODAL MULTIVERSE CONJUNCTURE.
THAT'S RIGHT.
CONVERGED HIS GOLDEN AND SILVER AGE SELVES.
I THINK IT'S IN THE AWE ALLIANCE...
THE VALOUR NETWORK, NUMBERS 236-278.
YOU KNOW YOUR STUFF.
I BEST SHOW MY FACE IN THE OFFICE.

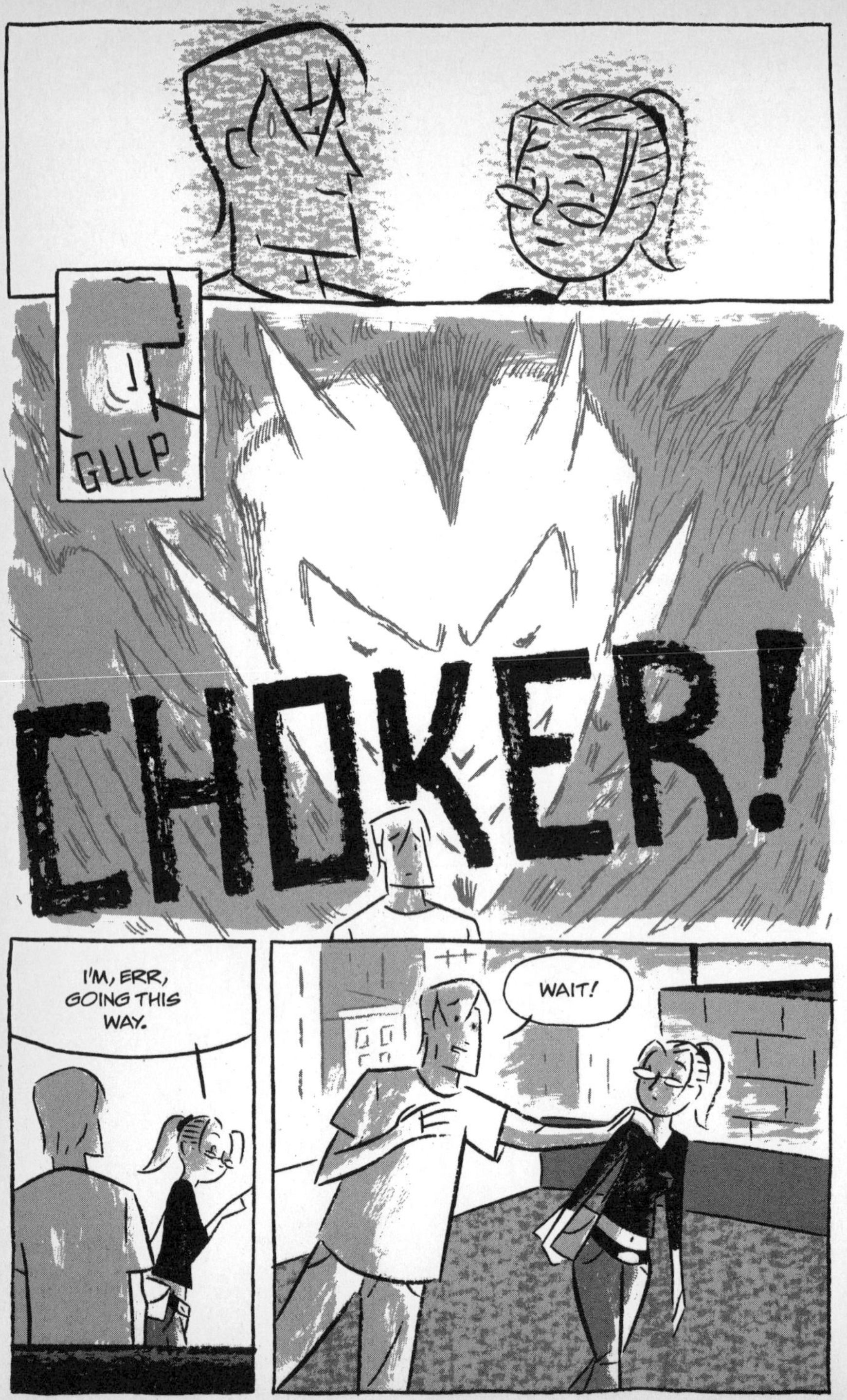
GULP
CHOKER!
I'M, ERR, GOING THIS WAY.
WAIT!

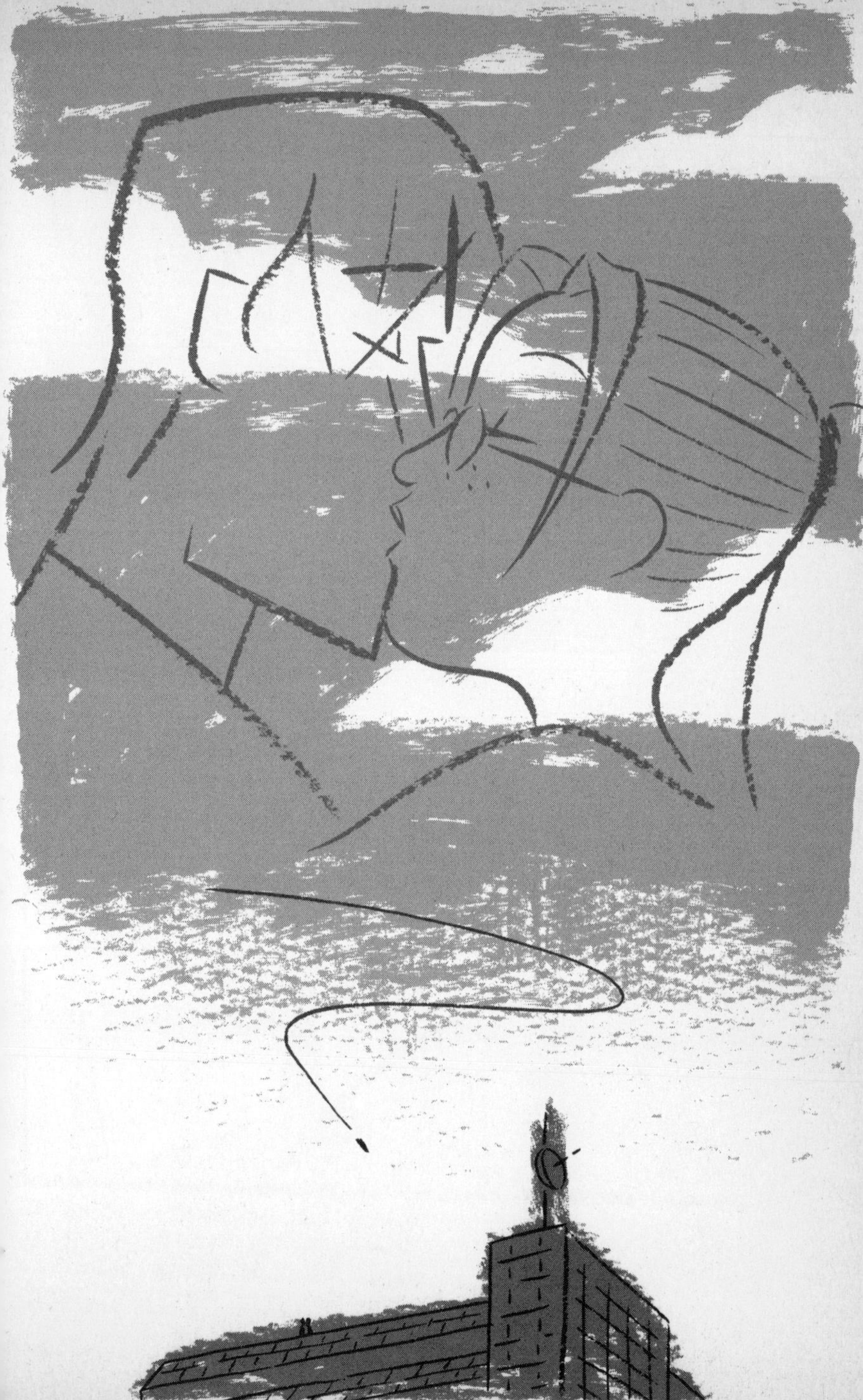

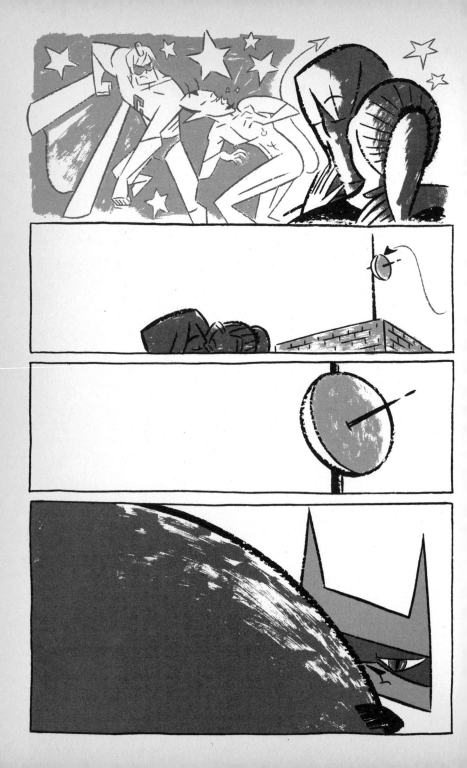

Love Fights™ #4

andi watson

oni PRESS

$2.99 U.S., $4.60 CAN.

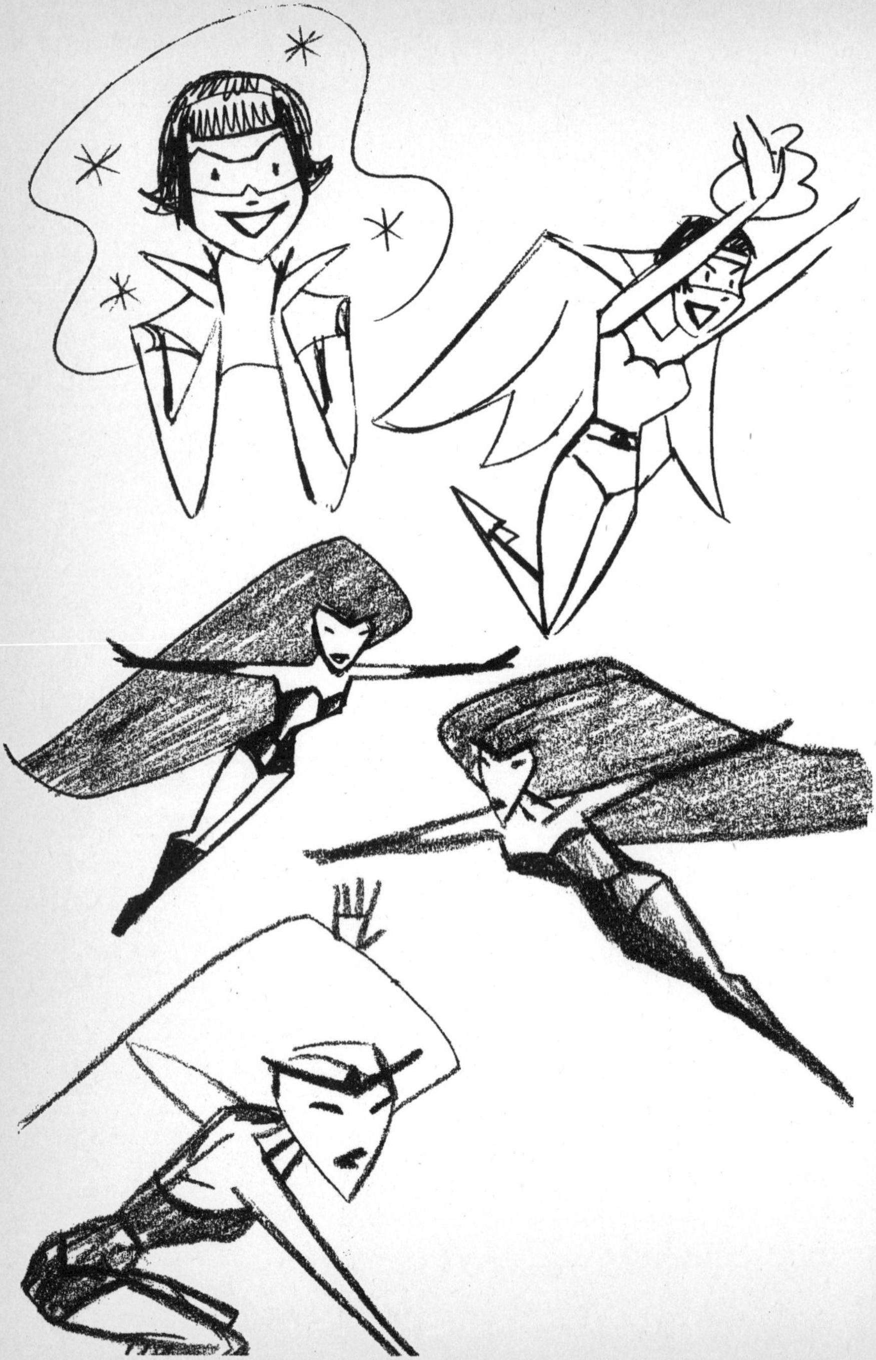

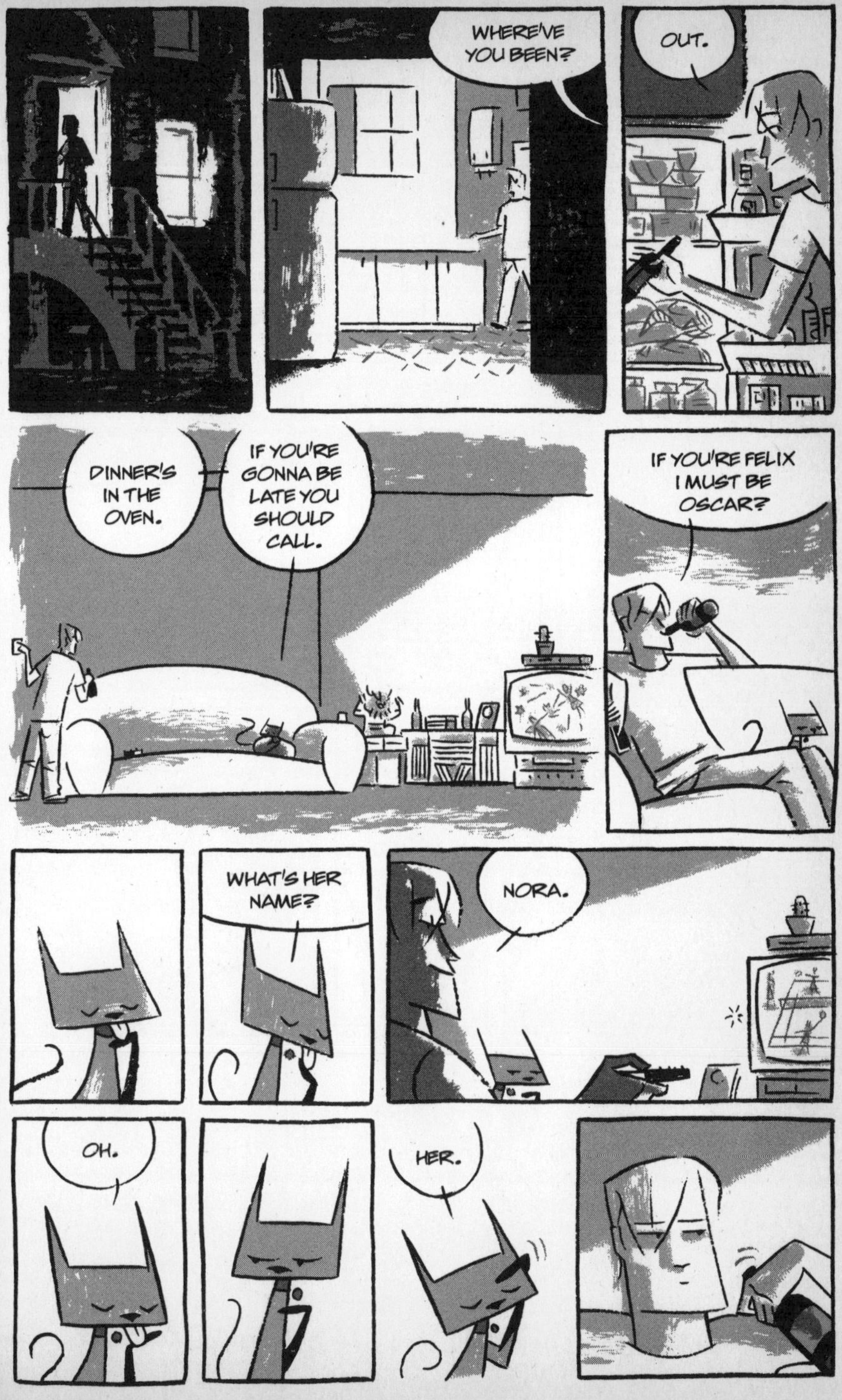
WHERE'VE YOU BEEN?
OUT.
DINNER'S IN THE OVEN.
IF YOU'RE GONNA BE LATE YOU SHOULD CALL.
IF YOU'RE FELIX I MUST BE OSCAR?
WHAT'S HER NAME?
NORA.
OH.
HER.

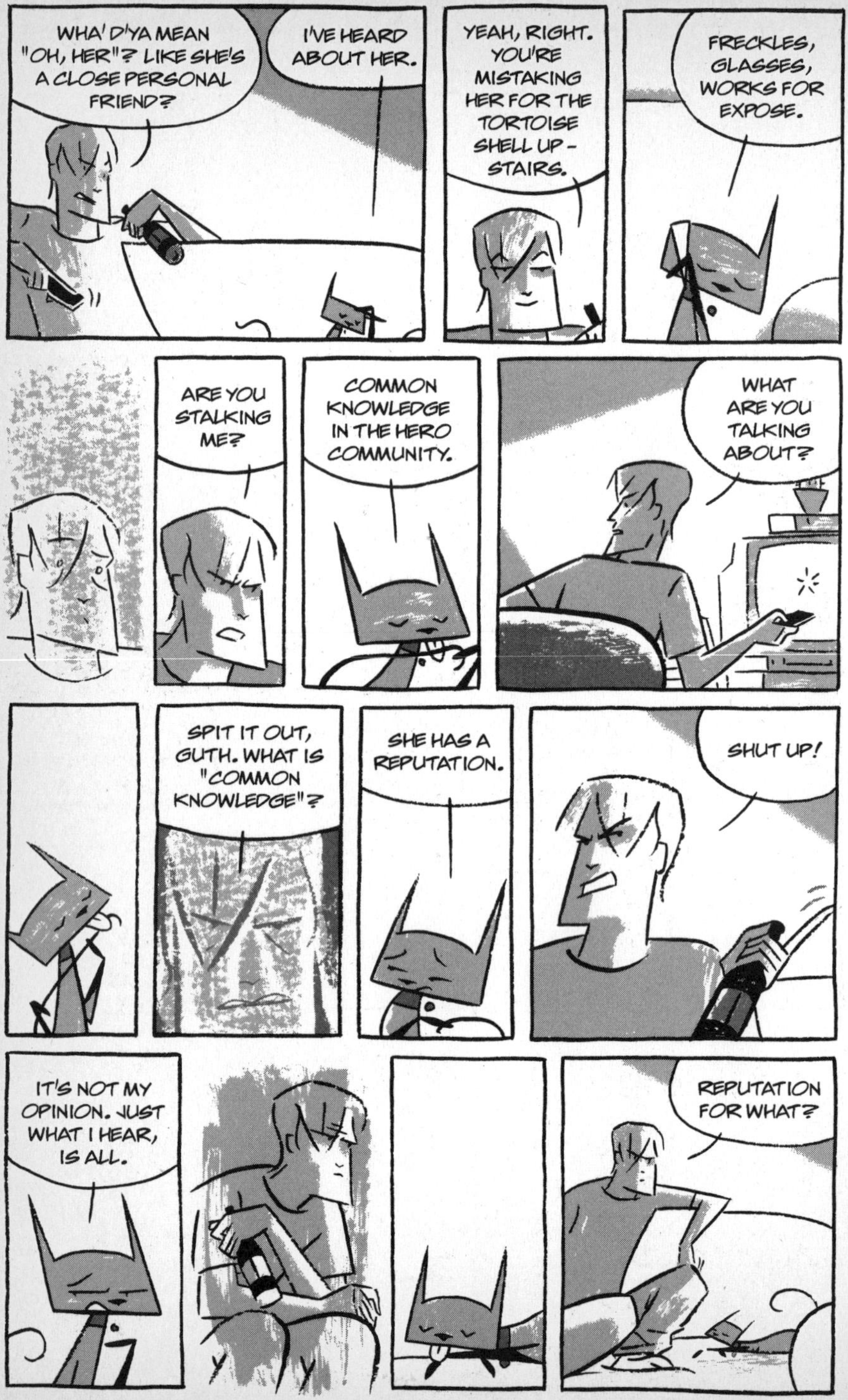

WHA' D'YA MEAN "OH, HER"? LIKE SHE'S A CLOSE PERSONAL FRIEND?
I'VE HEARD ABOUT HER.
YEAH, RIGHT. YOU'RE MISTAKING HER FOR THE TORTOISE SHELL UP-STAIRS.
FRECKLES, GLASSES, WORKS FOR EXPOSE.
ARE YOU STALKING ME?
COMMON KNOWLEDGE IN THE HERO COMMUNITY.
WHAT ARE YOU TALKING ABOUT?
SPIT IT OUT, GUTH. WHAT IS "COMMON KNOWLEDGE"?
SHE HAS A REPUTATION.
SHUT UP!
IT'S NOT MY OPINION. JUST WHAT I HEAR, IS ALL.
REPUTATION FOR WHAT?

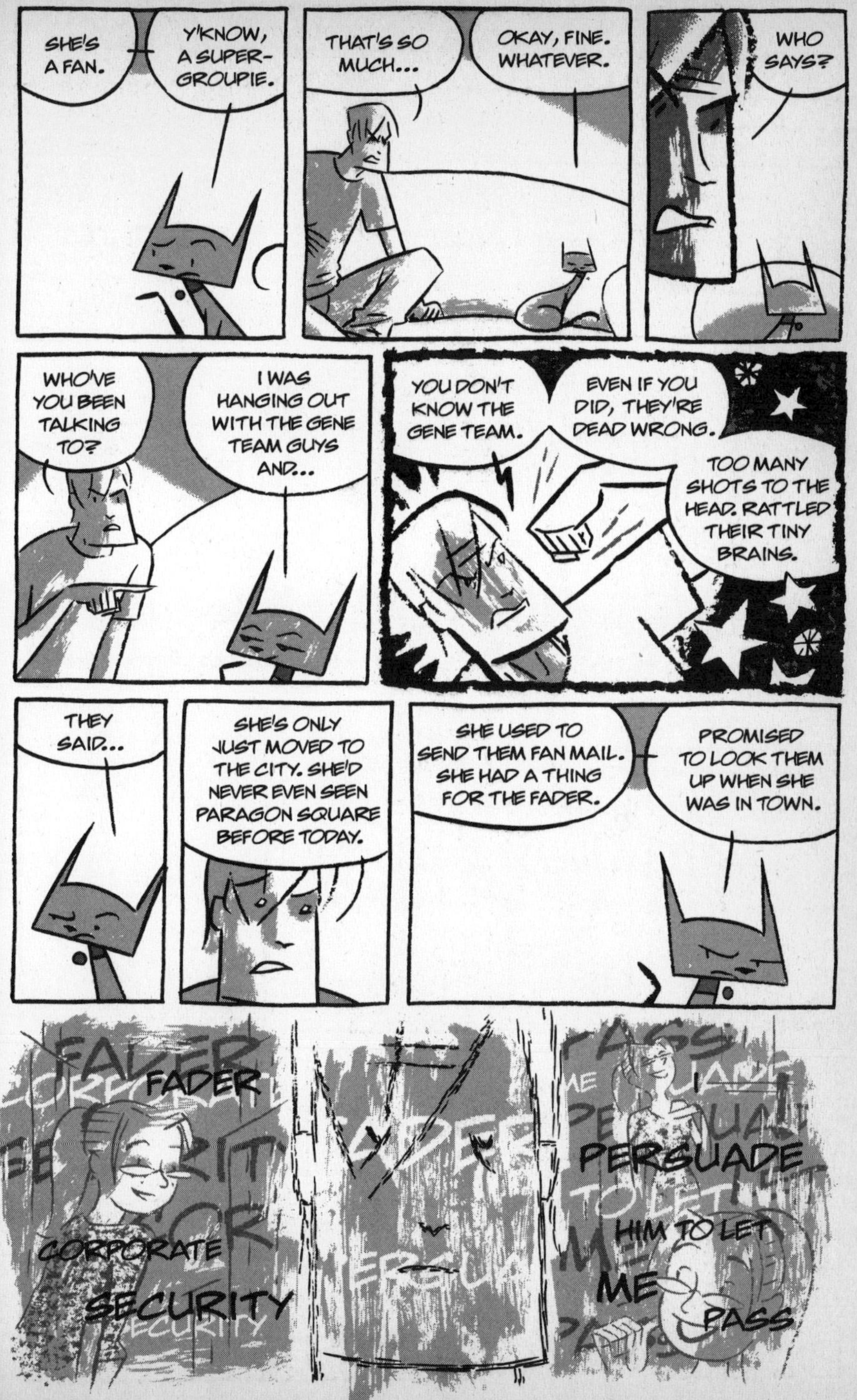
SHE'S A FAN.
Y'KNOW, A SUPER-GROUPIE.
THAT'S SO MUCH...
OKAY, FINE. WHATEVER.
WHO SAYS?
WHO'VE YOU BEEN TALKING TO?
I WAS HANGING OUT WITH THE GENE TEAM GUYS AND...
YOU DON'T KNOW THE GENE TEAM.
EVEN IF YOU DID, THEY'RE DEAD WRONG.
TOO MANY SHOTS TO THE HEAD. RATTLED THEIR TINY BRAINS.
THEY SAID...
SHE'S ONLY JUST MOVED TO THE CITY. SHE'D NEVER EVEN SEEN PARAGON SQUARE BEFORE TODAY.
SHE USED TO SEND THEM FAN MAIL. SHE HAD A THING FOR THE FADER.
PROMISED TO LOOK THEM UP WHEN SHE WAS IN TOWN.
FADER
CORPORATE
SECURITY
I
PERSUADE
HIM TO LET
ME
PASS

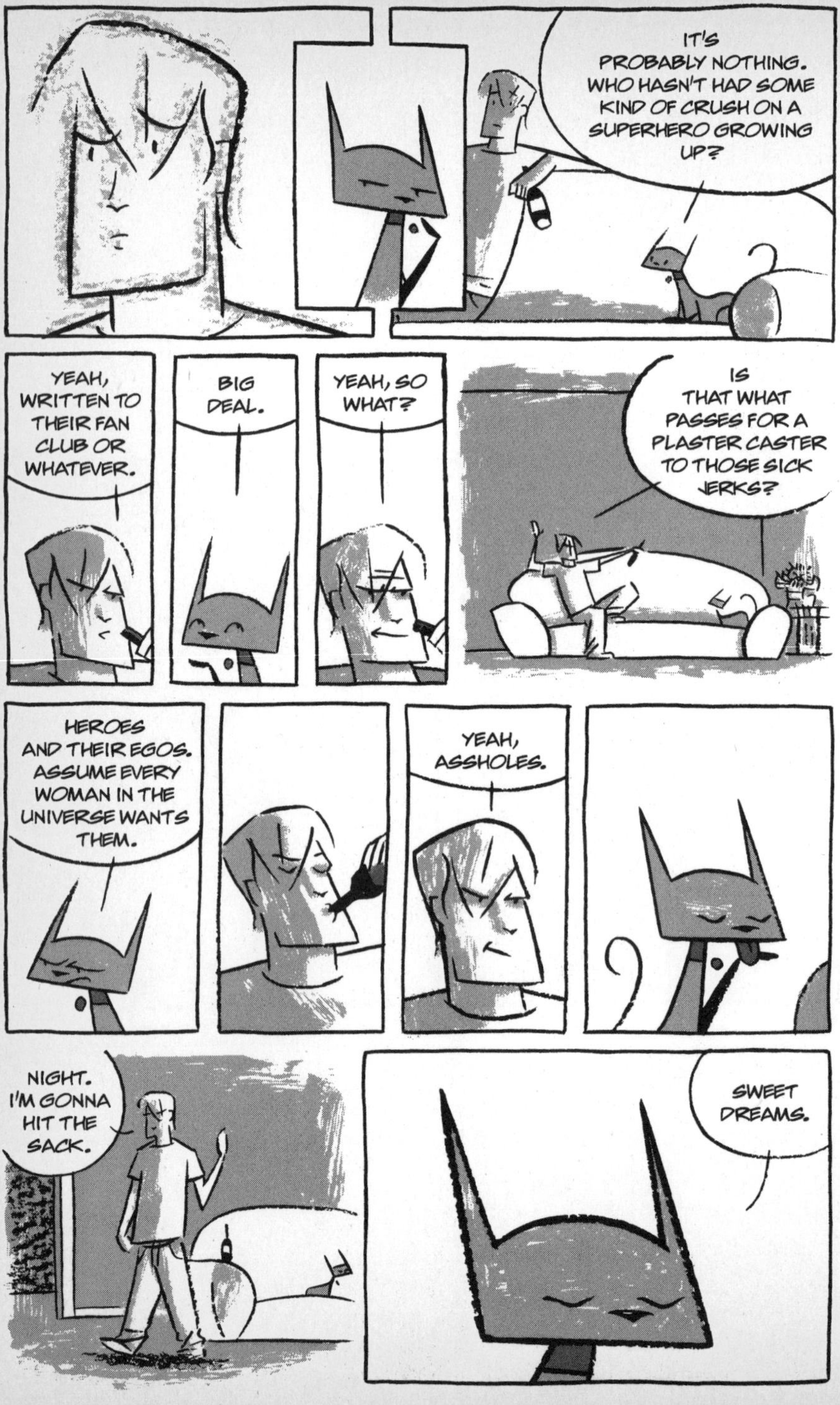
IT'S PROBABLY NOTHING. WHO HASN'T HAD SOME KIND OF CRUSH ON A SUPERHERO GROWING UP?
YEAH, WRITTEN TO THEIR FAN CLUB OR WHATEVER.
BIG DEAL.
YEAH, SO WHAT?
IS THAT WHAT PASSES FOR A PLASTER CASTER TO THOSE SICK JERKS?
HEROES AND THEIR EGOS. ASSUME EVERY WOMAN IN THE UNIVERSE WANTS THEM.
YEAH, ASSHOLES.
NIGHT. I'M GONNA HIT THE SACK.
SWEET DREAMS.

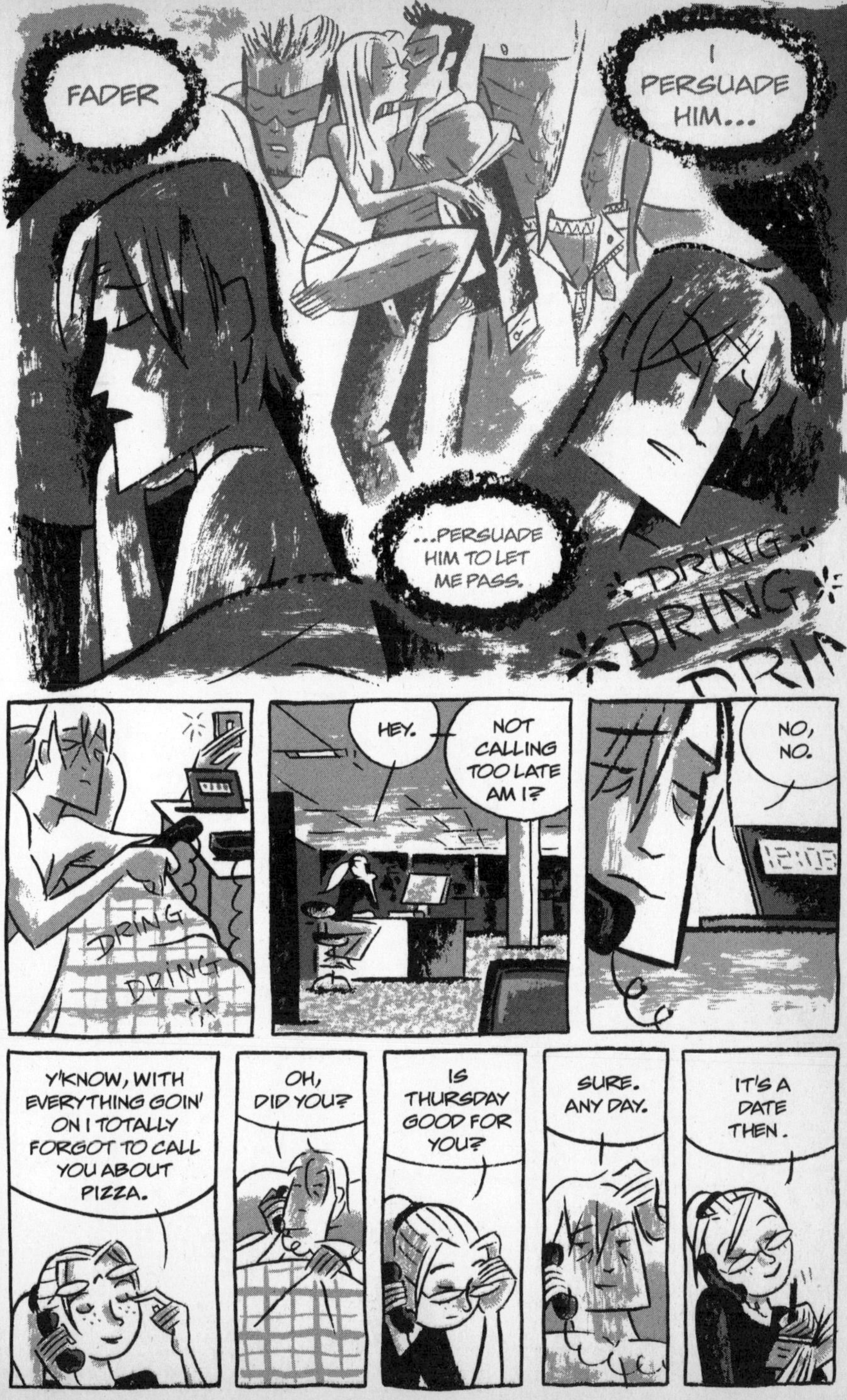
FADER
I PERSUADE HIM...
...PERSUADE HIM TO LET ME PASS.
DRING DRING DRIN
DRING DRING
HEY.
NOT CALLING TOO LATE AM I?
NO, NO.
Y'KNOW, WITH EVERYTHING GOIN' ON I TOTALLY FORGOT TO CALL YOU ABOUT PIZZA.
OH, DID YOU?
IS THURSDAY GOOD FOR YOU?
SURE. ANY DAY.
IT'S A DATE THEN.

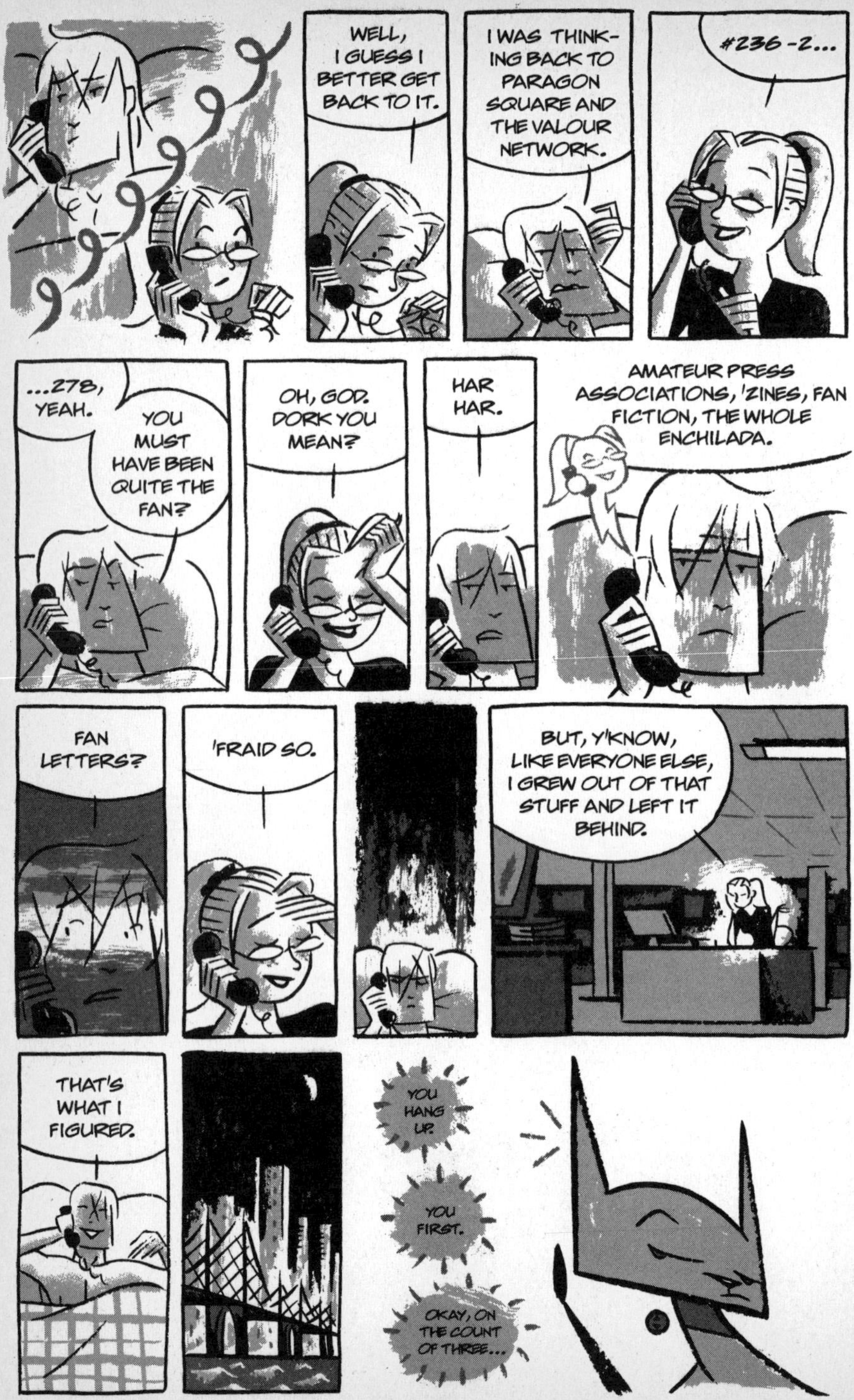
WELL, I GUESS I BETTER GET BACK TO IT.
I WAS THINKING BACK TO PARAGON SQUARE AND THE VALOUR NETWORK.
#236-2...
...278, YEAH.
YOU MUST HAVE BEEN QUITE THE FAN?
OH, GOD. DORK YOU MEAN?
HAR HAR.
AMATEUR PRESS ASSOCIATIONS, 'ZINES, FAN FICTION, THE WHOLE ENCHILADA.
FAN LETTERS?
'FRAID SO.
BUT, Y'KNOW, LIKE EVERYONE ELSE, I GREW OUT OF THAT STUFF AND LEFT IT BEHIND.
THAT'S WHAT I FIGURED.
YOU HANG UP.
YOU FIRST.
OKAY, ON THE COUNT OF THREE...

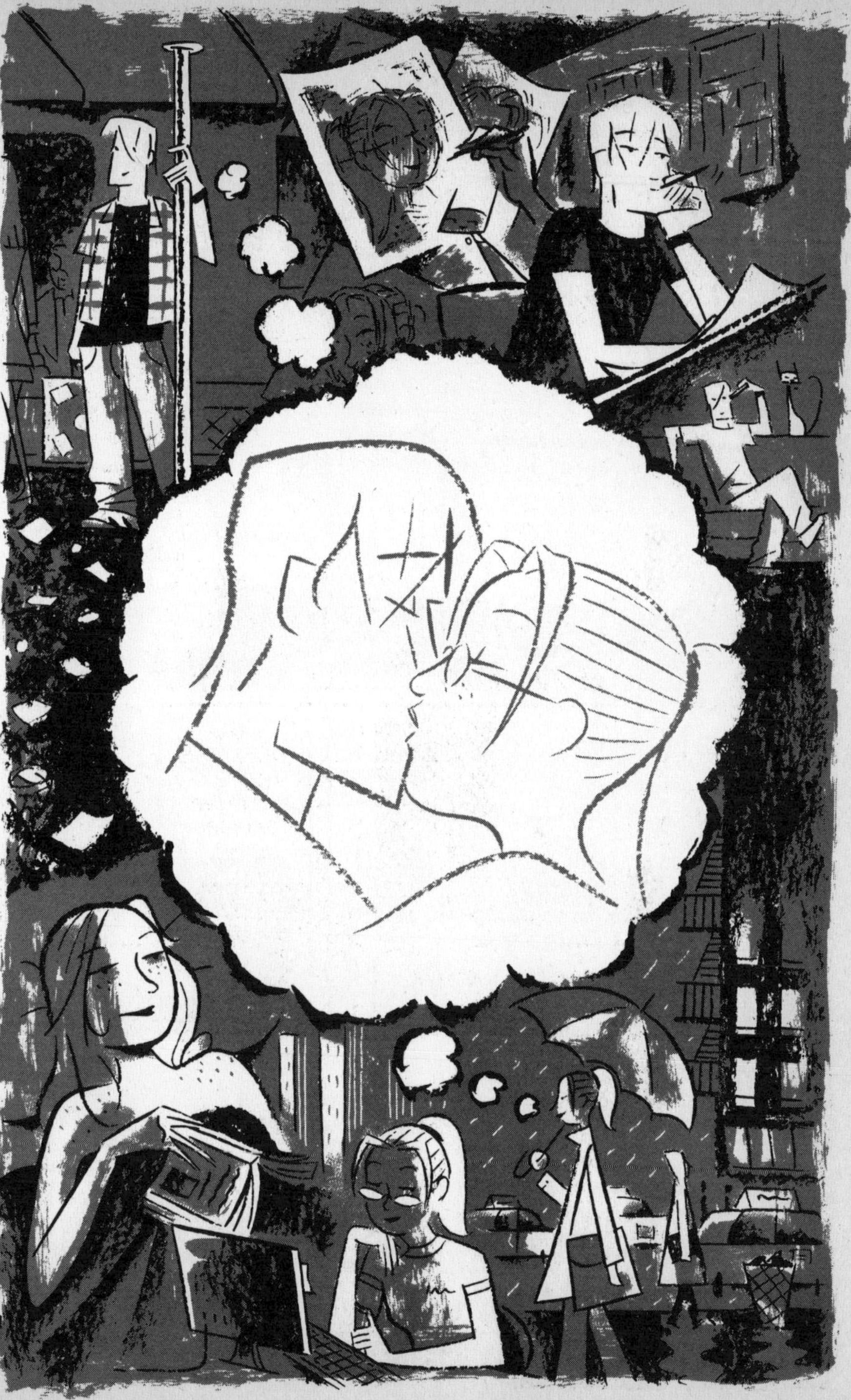

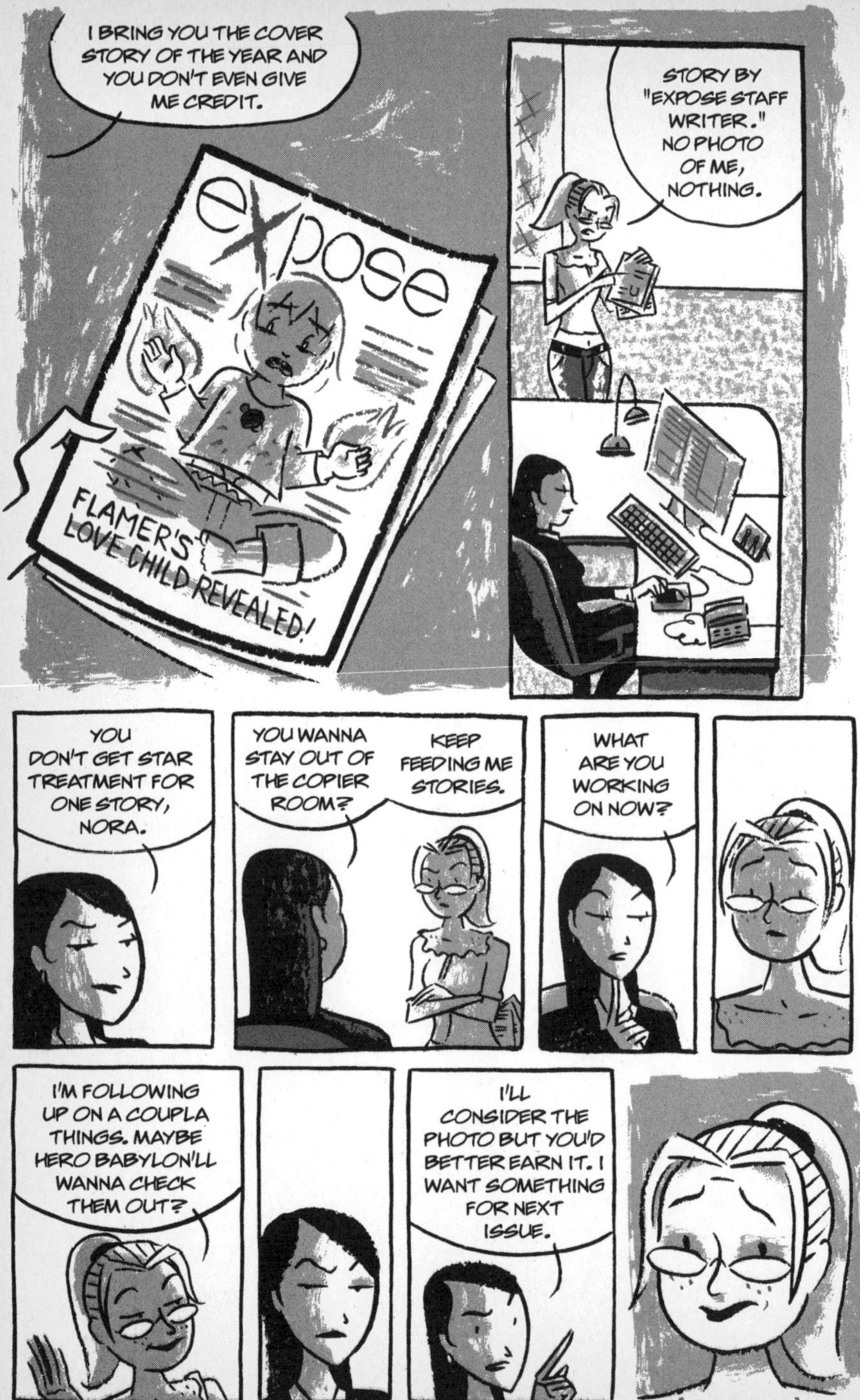
I BRING YOU THE COVER STORY OF THE YEAR AND YOU DON'T EVEN GIVE ME CREDIT.
expose
FLAMER'S LOVE CHILD REVEALED!
STORY BY "EXPOSE STAFF WRITER." NO PHOTO OF ME, NOTHING.
YOU DON'T GET STAR TREATMENT FOR ONE STORY, NORA.
YOU WANNA STAY OUT OF THE COPIER ROOM?
KEEP FEEDING ME STORIES.
WHAT ARE YOU WORKING ON NOW?
I'M FOLLOWING UP ON A COUPLA THINGS. MAYBE HERO BABYLON'LL WANNA CHECK THEM OUT?
I'LL CONSIDER THE PHOTO BUT YOU'D BETTER EARN IT. I WANT SOMETHING FOR NEXT ISSUE.

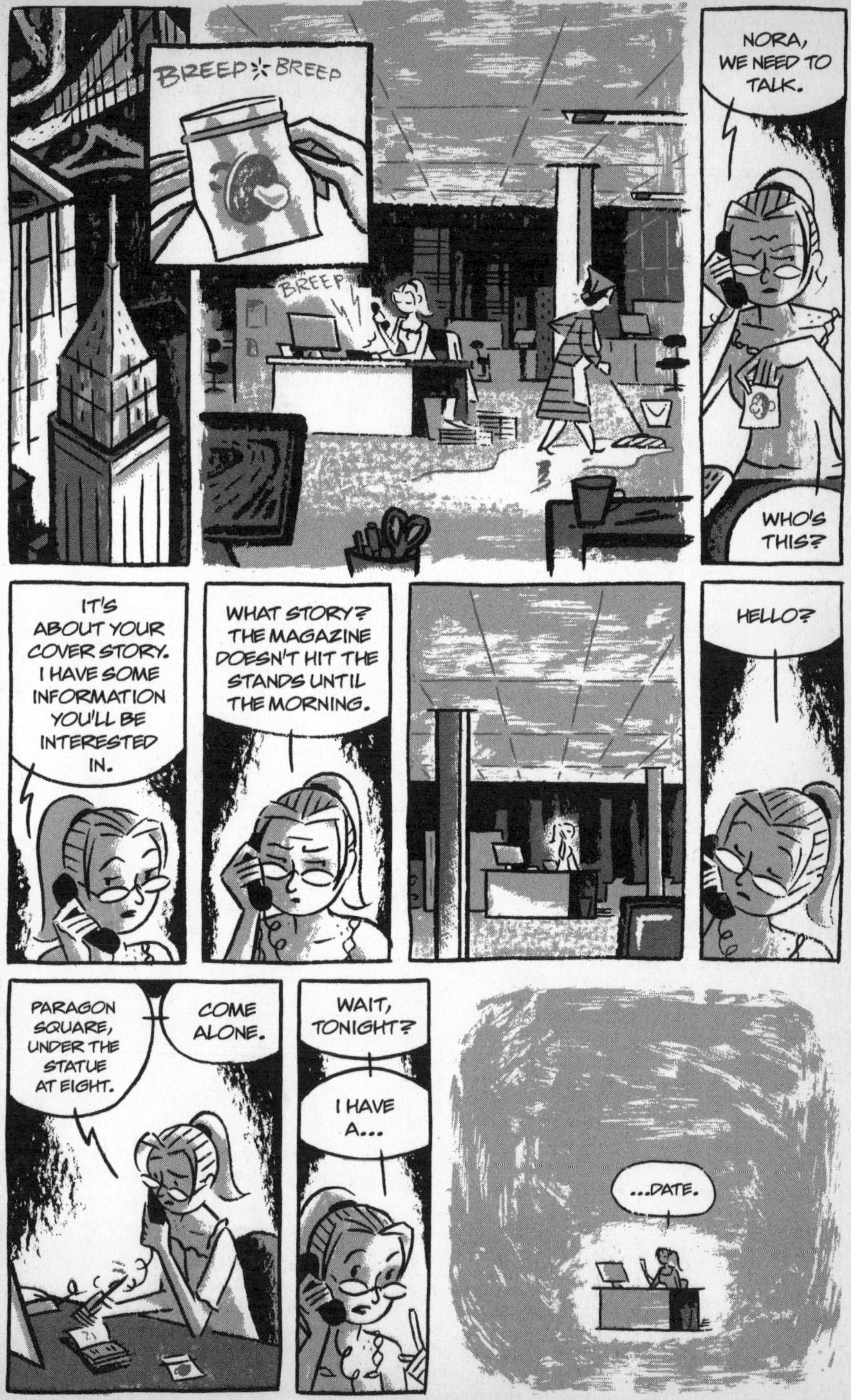
BREEP BREEP
BREEP
NORA, WE NEED TO TALK.
WHO'S THIS?
IT'S ABOUT YOUR COVER STORY. I HAVE SOME INFORMATION YOU'LL BE INTERESTED IN.
WHAT STORY? THE MAGAZINE DOESN'T HIT THE STANDS UNTIL THE MORNING.
HELLO?
PARAGON SQUARE, UNDER THE STATUE AT EIGHT.
COME ALONE.
WAIT, TONIGHT?
I HAVE A...
...DATE.

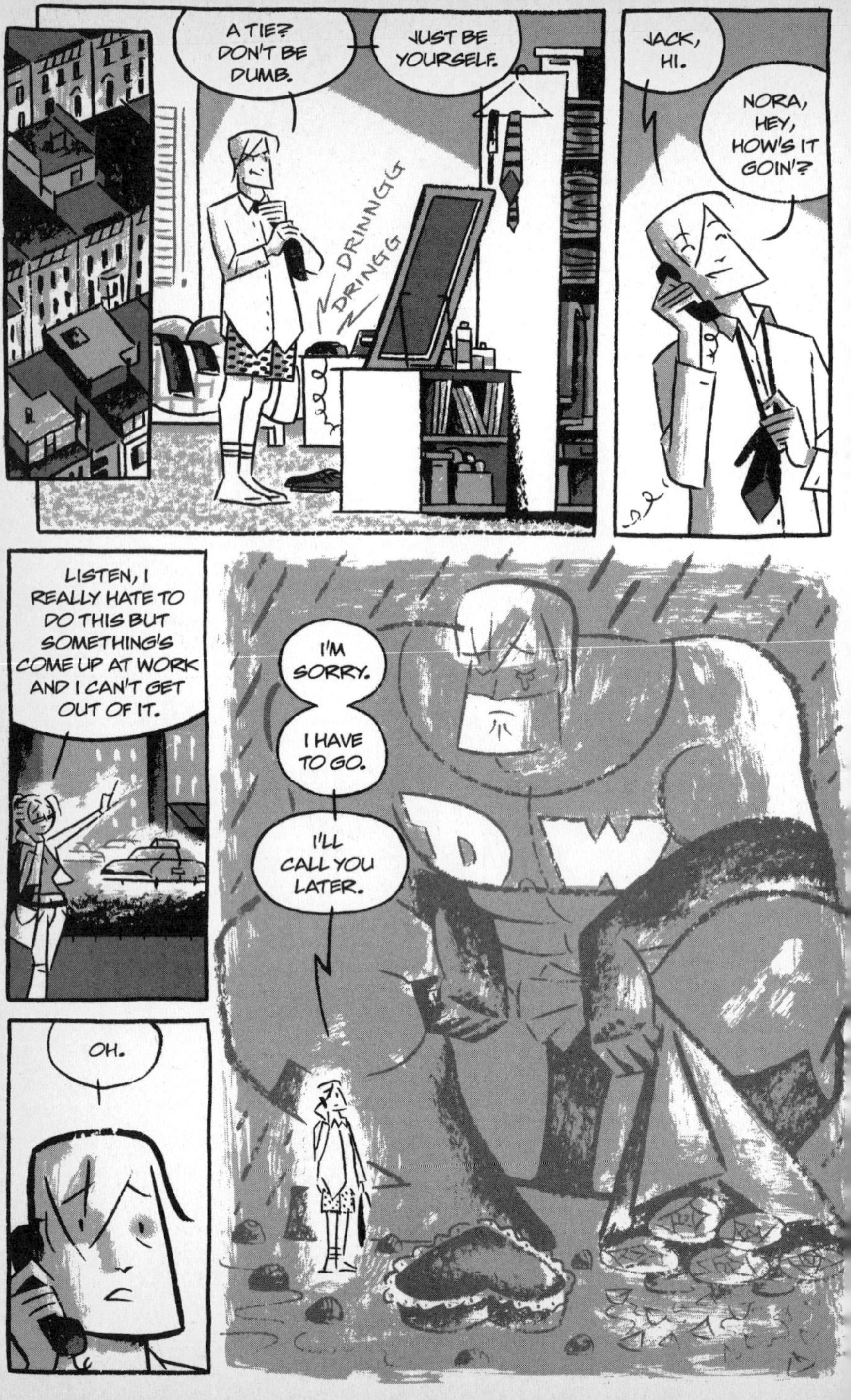
A TIE? DON'T BE DUMB.
JUST BE YOURSELF.
DRINNNGG
DRINGG
JACK, HI.
NORA, HEY, HOW'S IT GOIN'?
LISTEN, I REALLY HATE TO DO THIS BUT SOMETHING'S COME UP AT WORK AND I CAN'T GET OUT OF IT.
I'M SORRY.
I HAVE TO GO.
I'LL CALL YOU LATER.
OH.

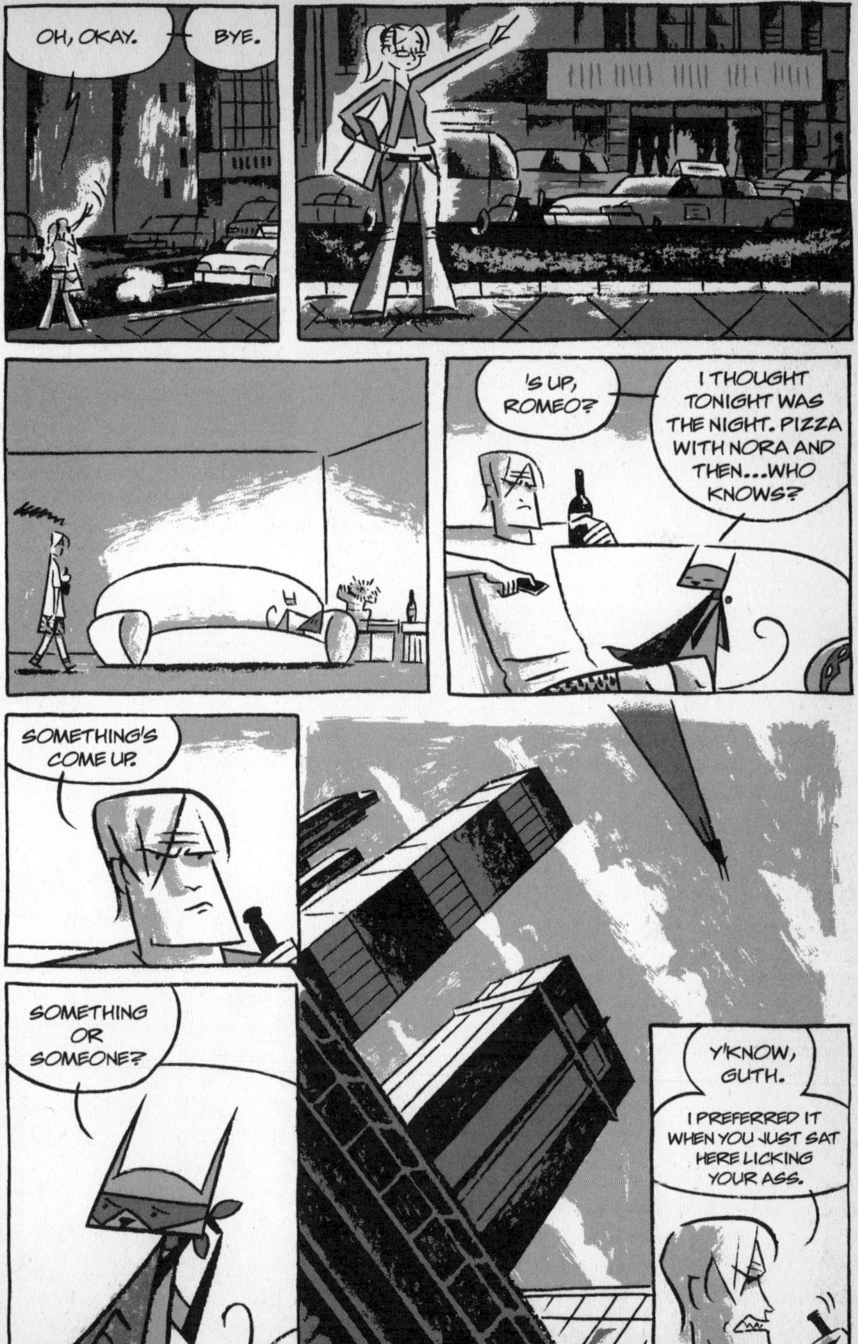
OH, OKAY.
BYE.
'S UP, ROMEO?
I THOUGHT TONIGHT WAS THE NIGHT. PIZZA WITH NORA AND THEN...WHO KNOWS?
SOMETHING'S COME UP.
SOMETHING OR SOMEONE?
Y'KNOW, GUTH.
I PREFERRED IT WHEN YOU JUST SAT HERE LICKING YOUR ASS.

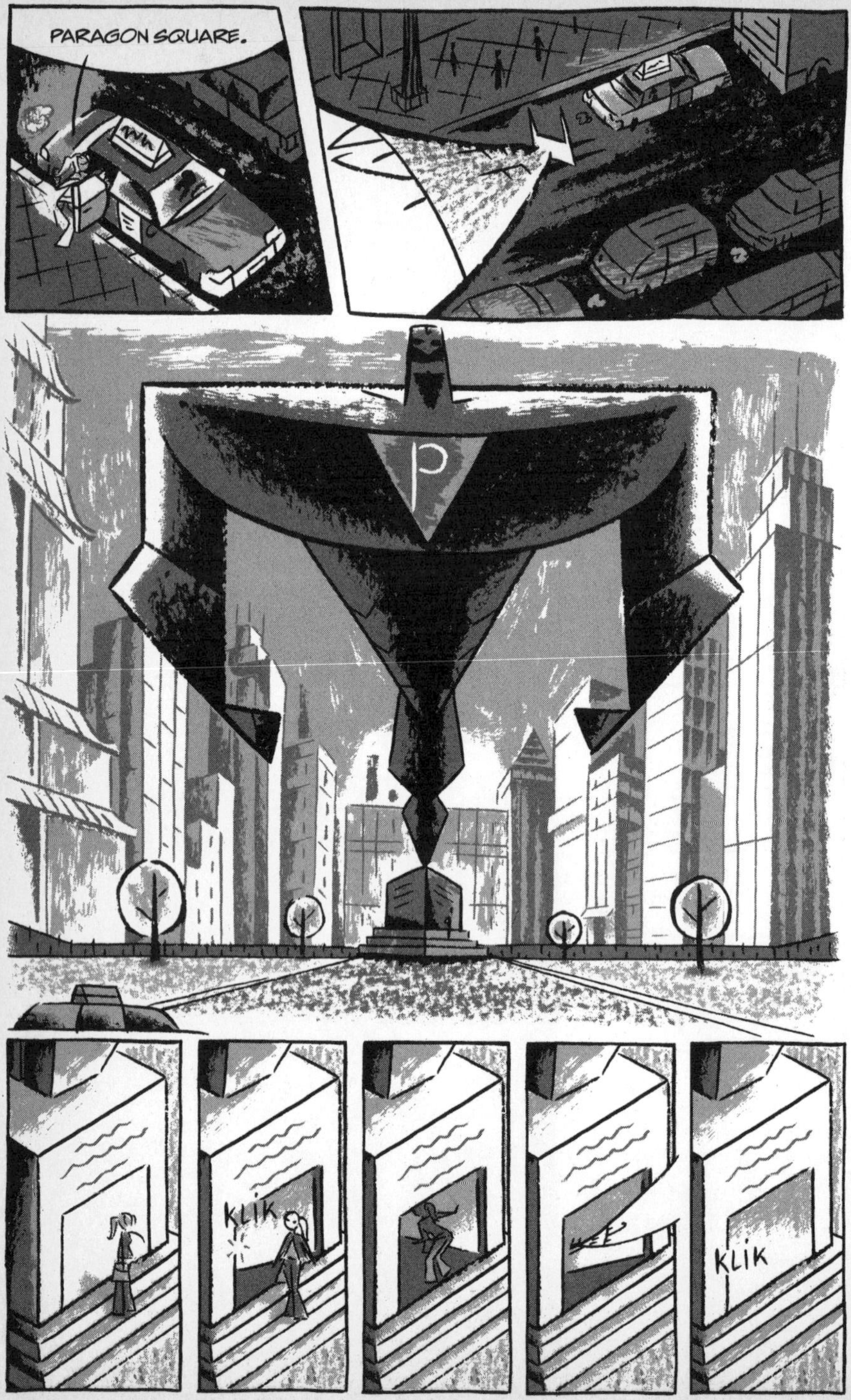
PARAGON SQUARE.
KLIK
KLIK

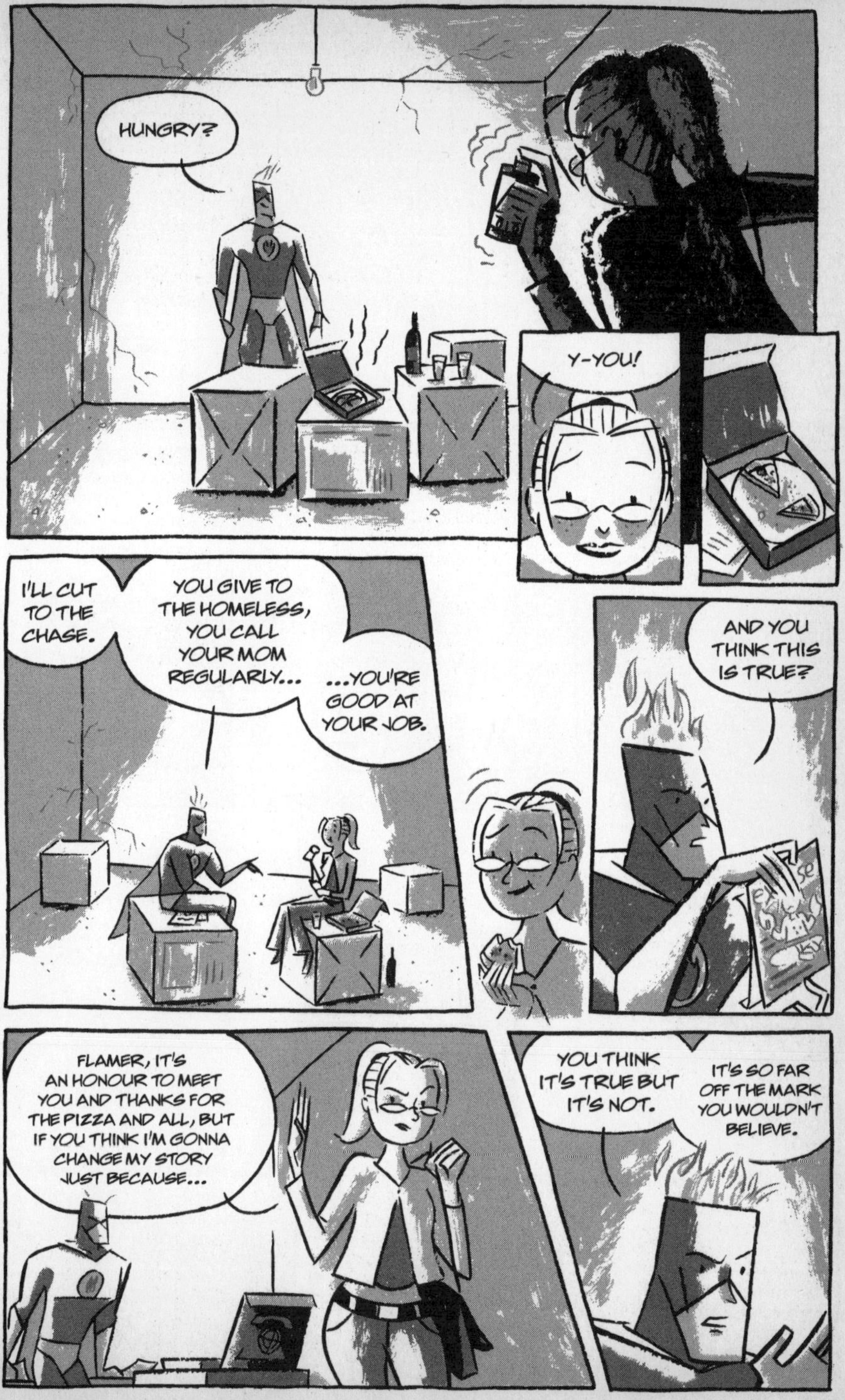
HUNGRY?
Y-YOU!
I'LL CUT TO THE CHASE.
YOU GIVE TO THE HOMELESS, YOU CALL YOUR MOM REGULARLY...
...YOU'RE GOOD AT YOUR JOB.
AND YOU THINK THIS IS TRUE?
FLAMER, IT'S AN HONOUR TO MEET YOU AND THANKS FOR THE PIZZA AND ALL, BUT IF YOU THINK I'M GONNA CHANGE MY STORY JUST BECAUSE...
YOU THINK IT'S TRUE BUT IT'S NOT.
IT'S SO FAR OFF THE MARK YOU WOULDN'T BELIEVE.

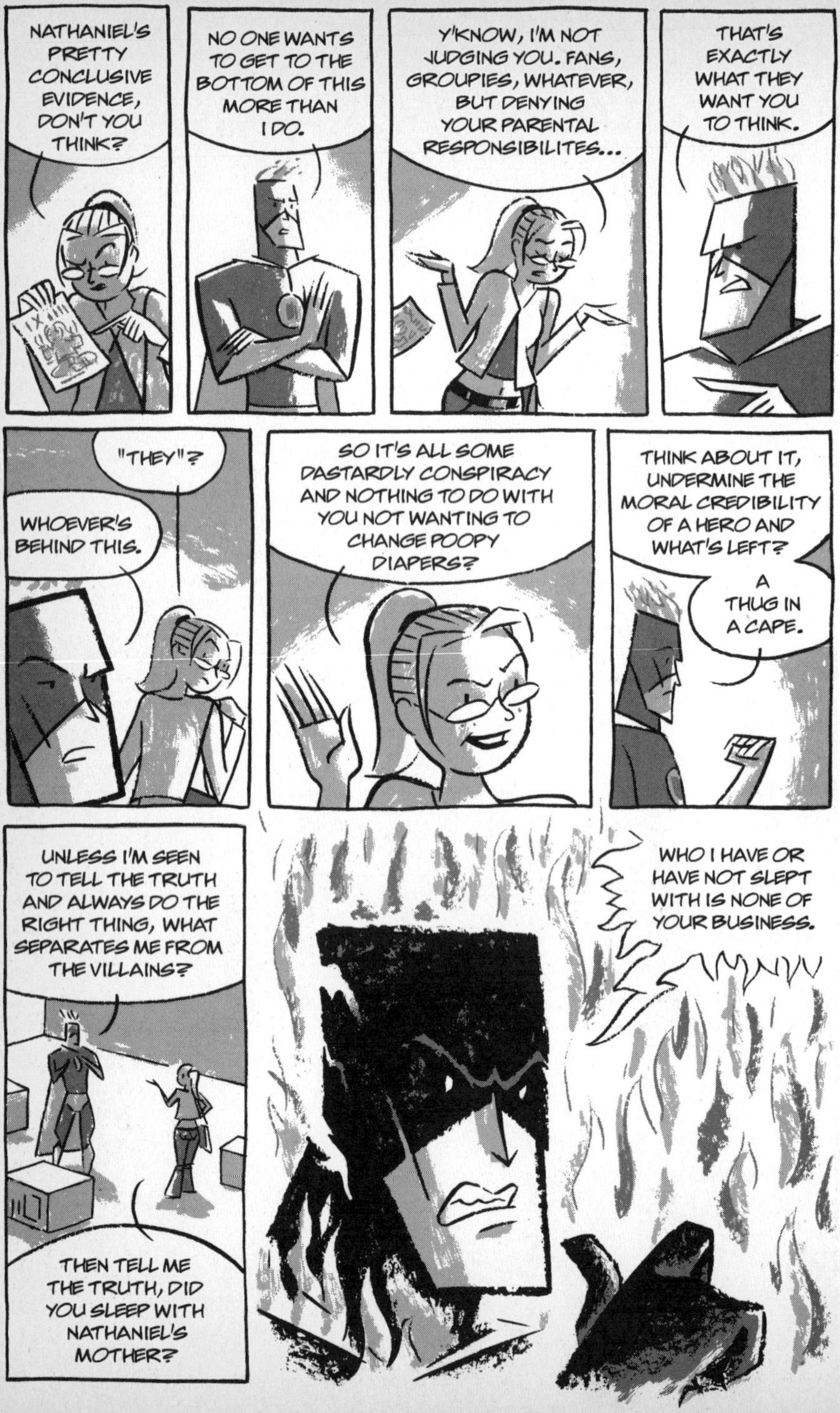
NATHANIEL'S PRETTY CONCLUSIVE EVIDENCE, DON'T YOU THINK?
NO ONE WANTS TO GET TO THE BOTTOM OF THIS MORE THAN I DO.
Y'KNOW, I'M NOT JUDGING YOU. FANS, GROUPIES, WHATEVER, BUT DENYING YOUR PARENTAL RESPONSIBILITES...
THAT'S EXACTLY WHAT THEY WANT YOU TO THINK.
"THEY"?
WHOEVER'S BEHIND THIS.
SO IT'S ALL SOME DASTARDLY CONSPIRACY AND NOTHING TO DO WITH YOU NOT WANTING TO CHANGE POOPY DIAPERS?
THINK ABOUT IT, UNDERMINE THE MORAL CREDIBILITY OF A HERO AND WHAT'S LEFT?
A THUG IN A CAPE.
UNLESS I'M SEEN TO TELL THE TRUTH AND ALWAYS DO THE RIGHT THING, WHAT SEPARATES ME FROM THE VILLAINS?
THEN TELL ME THE TRUTH, DID YOU SLEEP WITH NATHANIEL'S MOTHER?
WHO I HAVE OR HAVE NOT SLEPT WITH IS NONE OF YOUR BUSINESS.

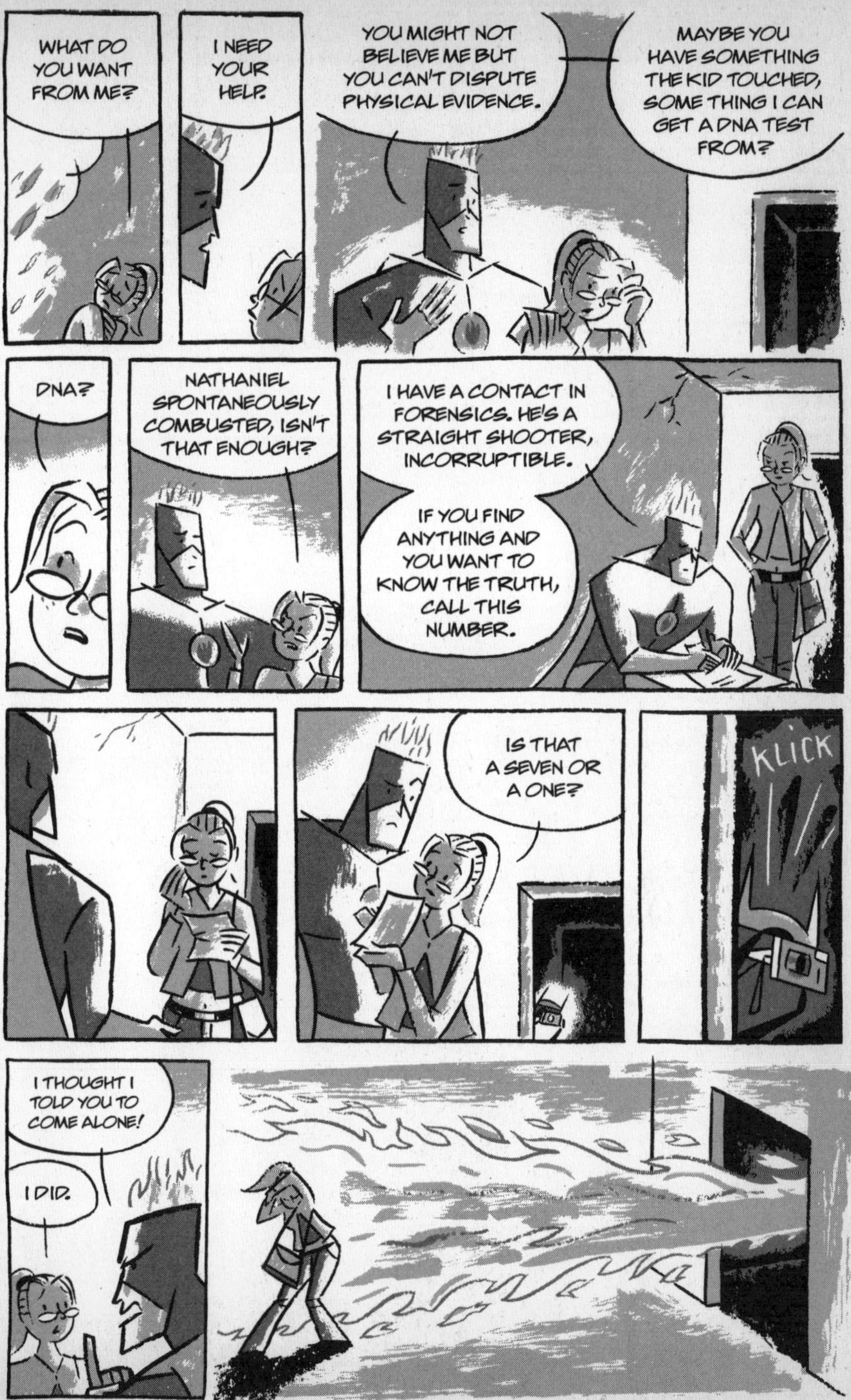
WHAT DO YOU WANT FROM ME?
I NEED YOUR HELP.
YOU MIGHT NOT BELIEVE ME BUT YOU CAN'T DISPUTE PHYSICAL EVIDENCE.
MAYBE YOU HAVE SOMETHING THE KID TOUCHED, SOME THING I CAN GET A DNA TEST FROM?
DNA?
NATHANIEL SPONTANEOUSLY COMBUSTED, ISN'T THAT ENOUGH?
I HAVE A CONTACT IN FORENSICS. HE'S A STRAIGHT SHOOTER, INCORRUPTIBLE.
IF YOU FIND ANYTHING AND YOU WANT TO KNOW THE TRUTH, CALL THIS NUMBER.
IS THAT A SEVEN OR A ONE?
KLICK
I THOUGHT I TOLD YOU TO COME ALONE!
I DID.

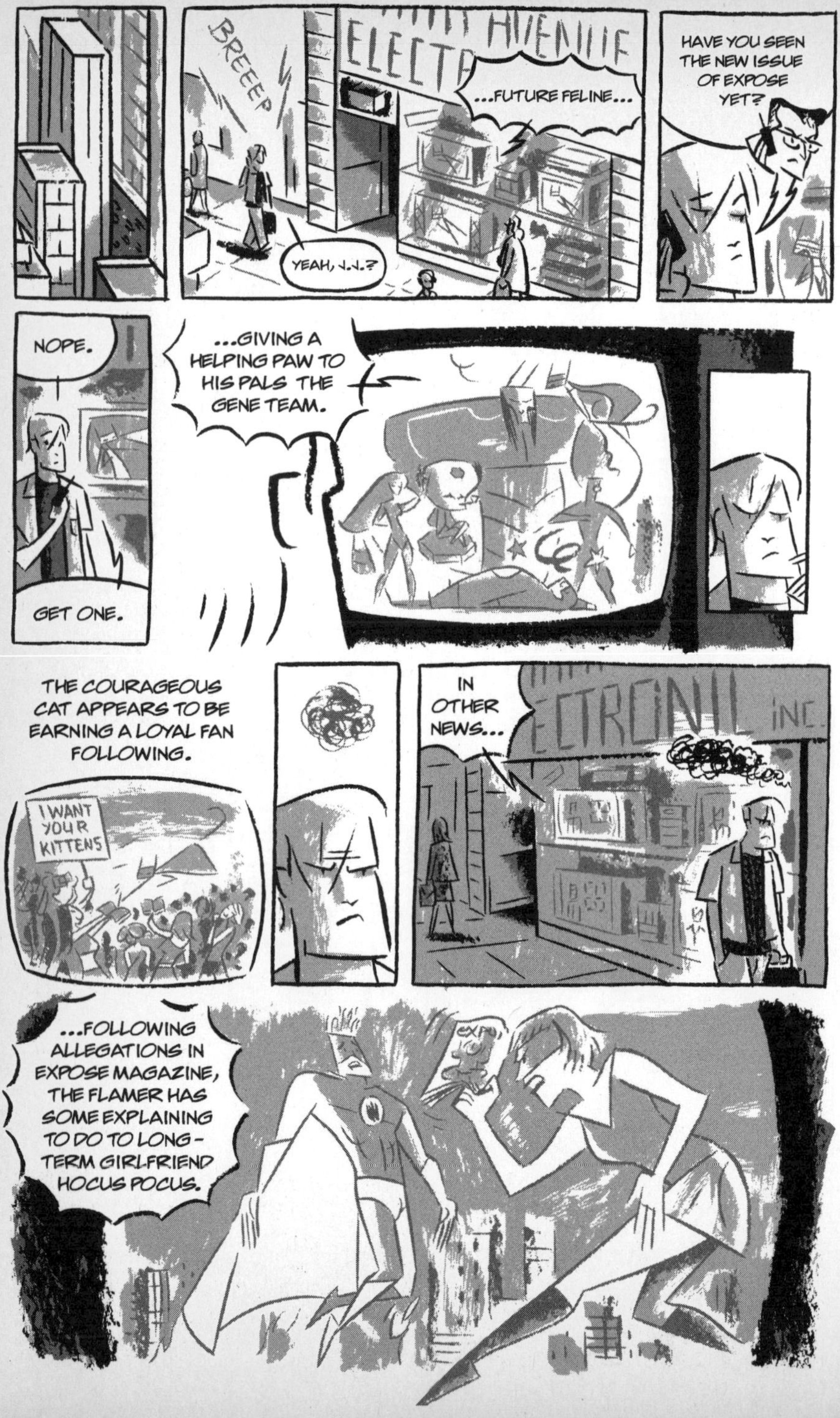
AVENUE
ELECTR
BREEEP
...FUTURE FELINE...
YEAH, J.J.?
HAVE YOU SEEN THE NEW ISSUE OF EXPOSE YET?
NOPE.
GET ONE.
...GIVING A HELPING PAW TO HIS PALS THE GENE TEAM.
THE COURAGEOUS CAT APPEARS TO BE EARNING A LOYAL FAN FOLLOWING.
I WANT YOUR KITTENS
IN OTHER NEWS...
ECTRONI INC.
...FOLLOWING ALLEGATIONS IN EXPOSE MAGAZINE, THE FLAMER HAS SOME EXPLAINING TO DO TO LONG-TERM GIRLFRIEND HOCUS POCUS.

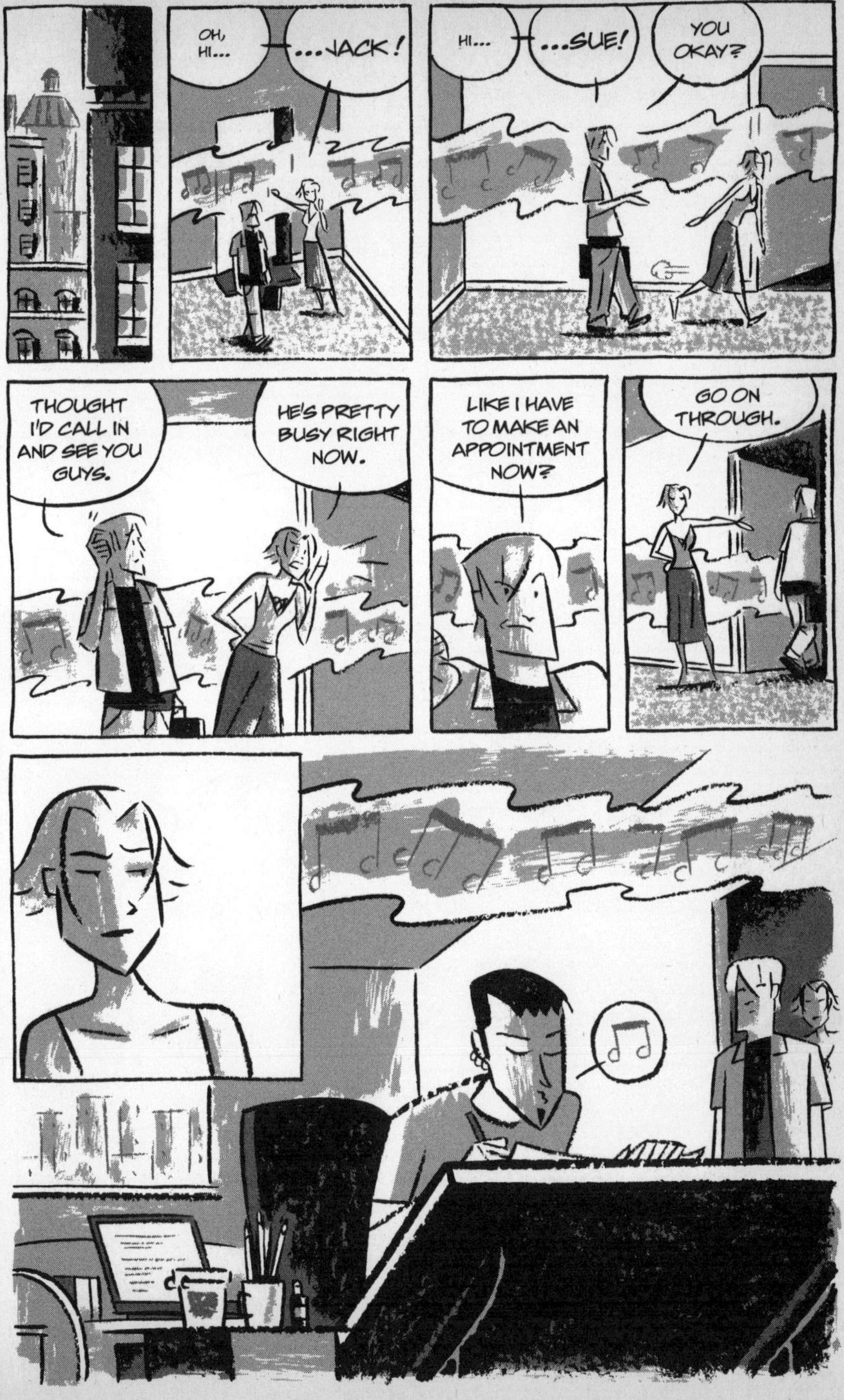
OH, HI...
...JACK!
HI...
...SUE!
YOU OKAY?
THOUGHT I'D CALL IN AND SEE YOU GUYS.
HE'S PRETTY BUSY RIGHT NOW.
LIKE I HAVE TO MAKE AN APPOINTMENT NOW?
GO ON THROUGH.

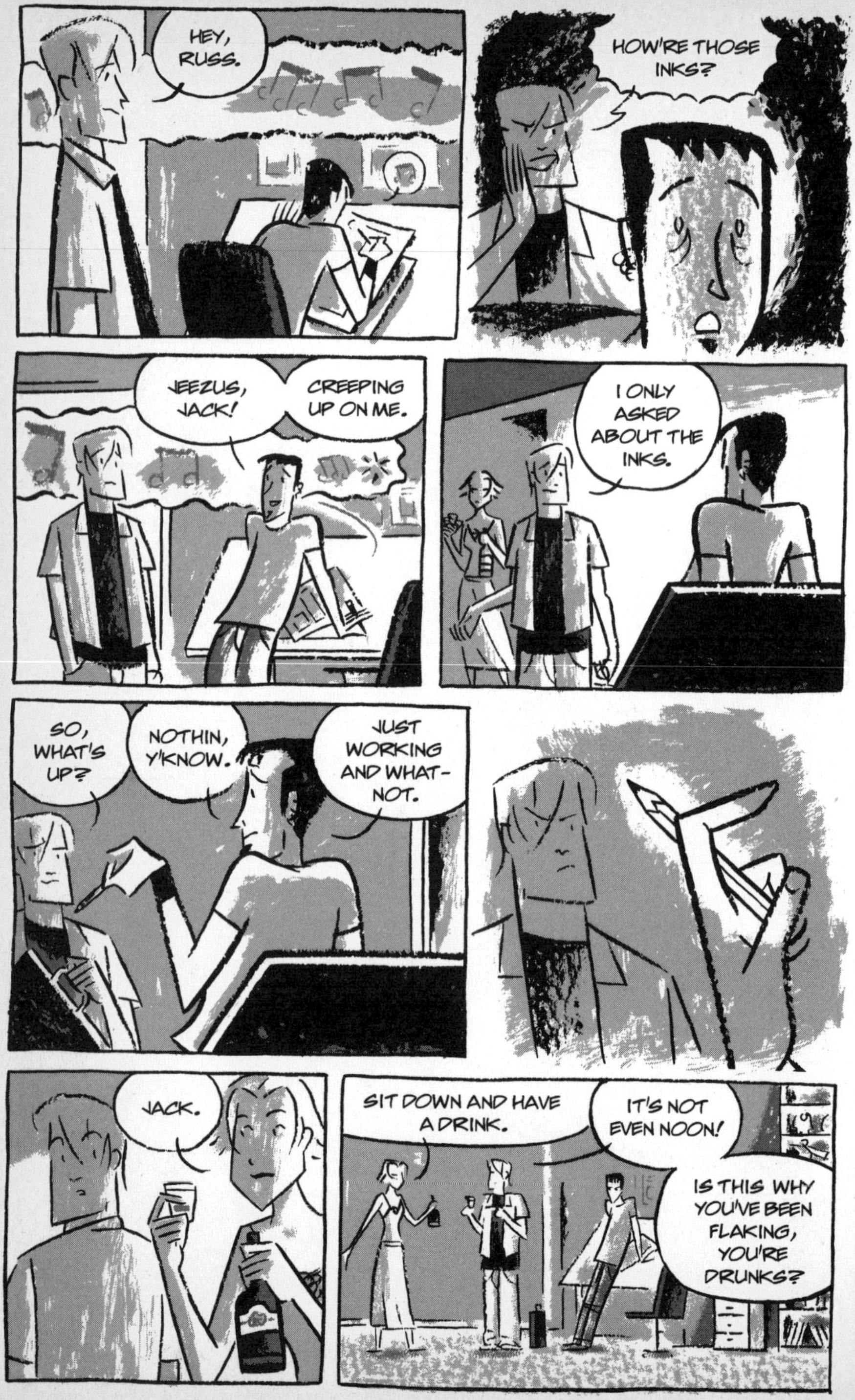
HEY, RUSS.
HOW'RE THOSE INKS?
JEEZUS, JACK!
CREEPING UP ON ME.
I ONLY ASKED ABOUT THE INKS.
SO, WHAT'S UP?
NOTHIN, Y'KNOW.
JUST WORKING AND WHAT-NOT.
JACK.
SIT DOWN AND HAVE A DRINK.
IT'S NOT EVEN NOON!
IS THIS WHY YOU'VE BEEN FLAKING, YOU'RE DRUNK?

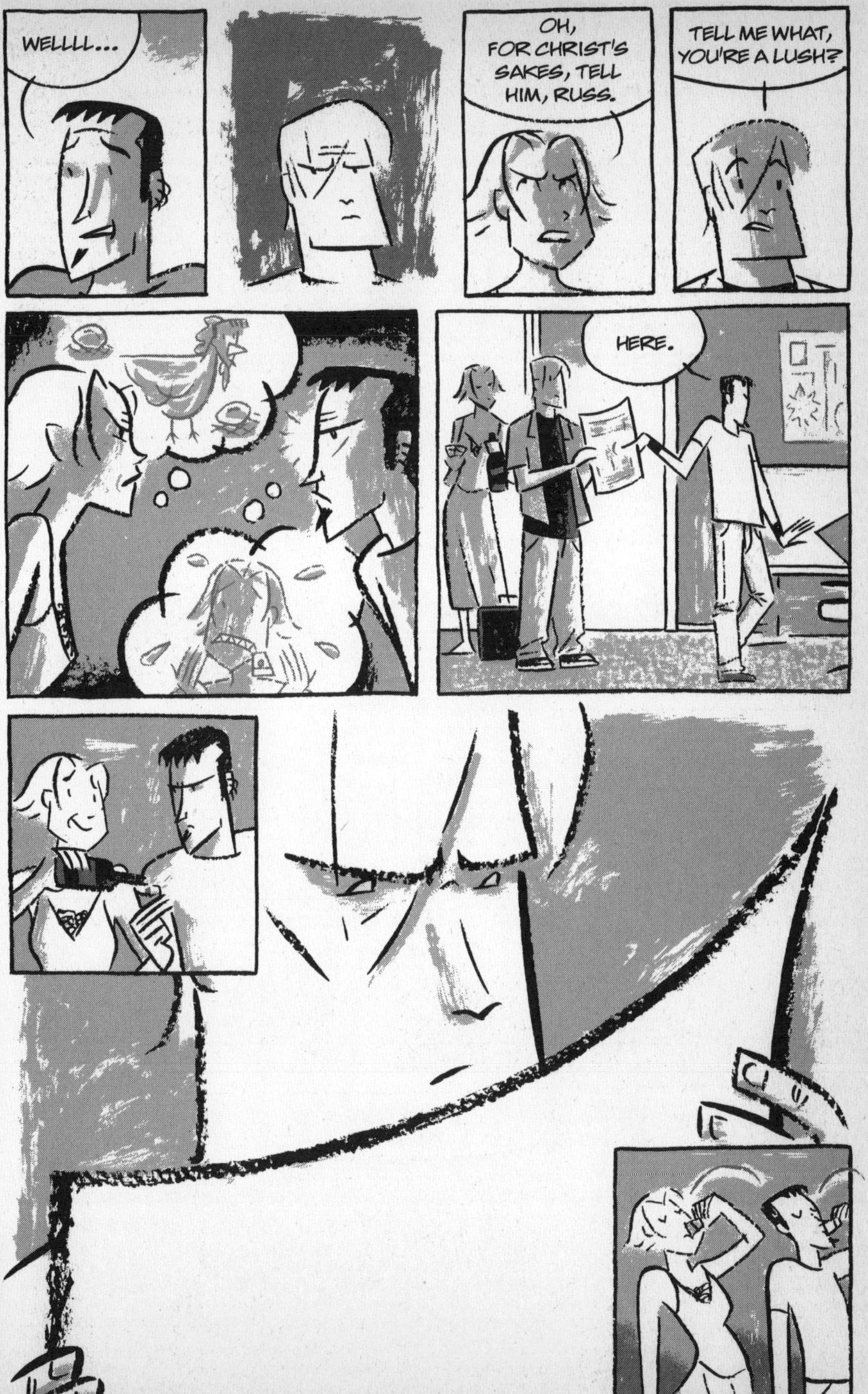
WELLLL...
OH, FOR CHRIST'S SAKES, TELL HIM, RUSS.
TELL ME WHAT, YOU'RE A LUSH?
HERE.

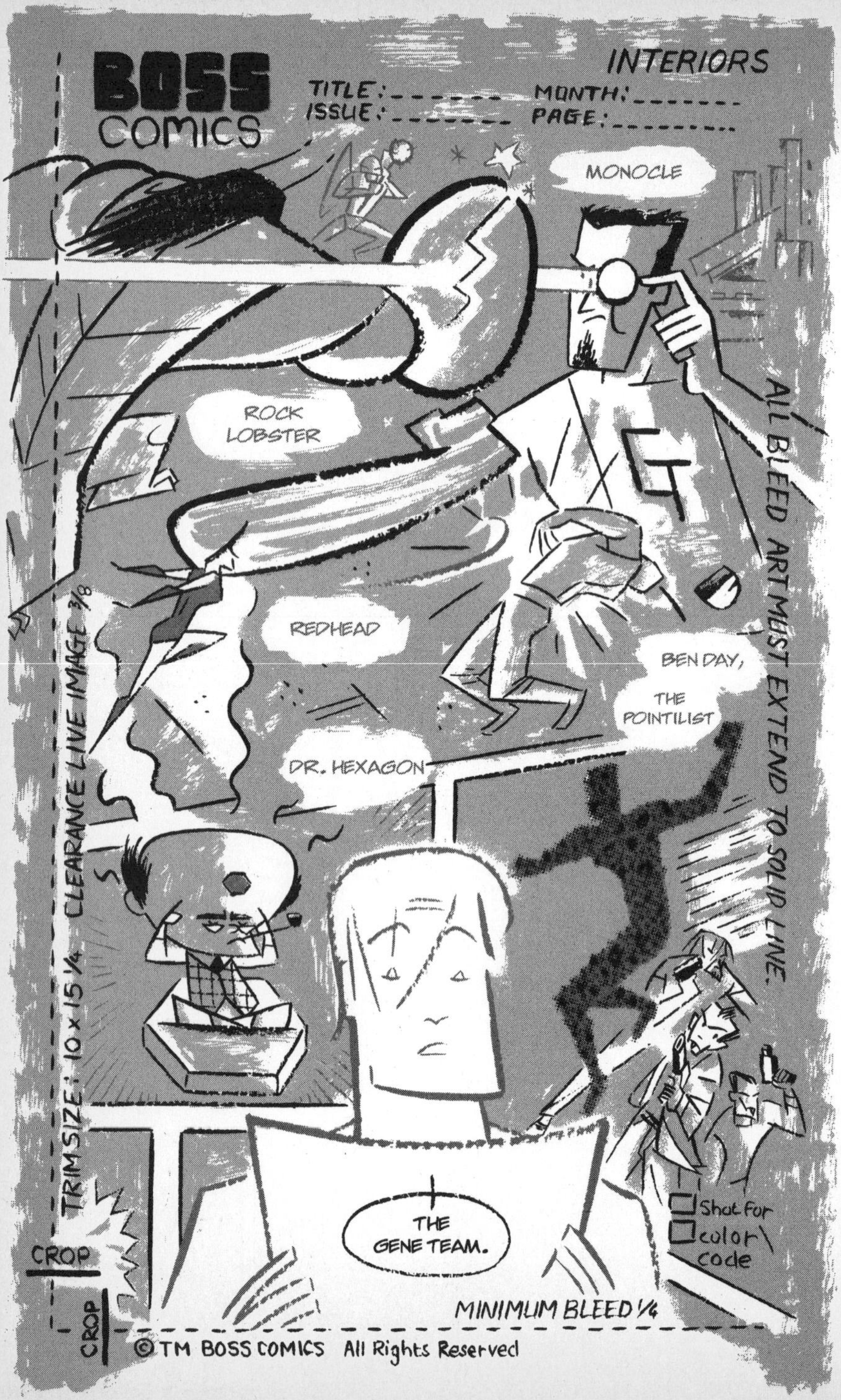
BOSS
COMICS
INTERIORS
TITLE:
ISSUE:
MONTH:
PAGE:
MONOCLE
ROCK LOBSTER
REDHEAD
BEN DAY, THE POINTILIST
DR. HEXAGON
THE GENE TEAM.
ALL BLEED ART MUST EXTEND TO SOLID LINE.
TRIM SIZE: 10 x 15 1/4 CLEARANCE LIVE IMAGE 3/8
Shot for color code
CROP
CROP
MINIMUM BLEED 1/4
©TM BOSS COMICS All Rights Reserved

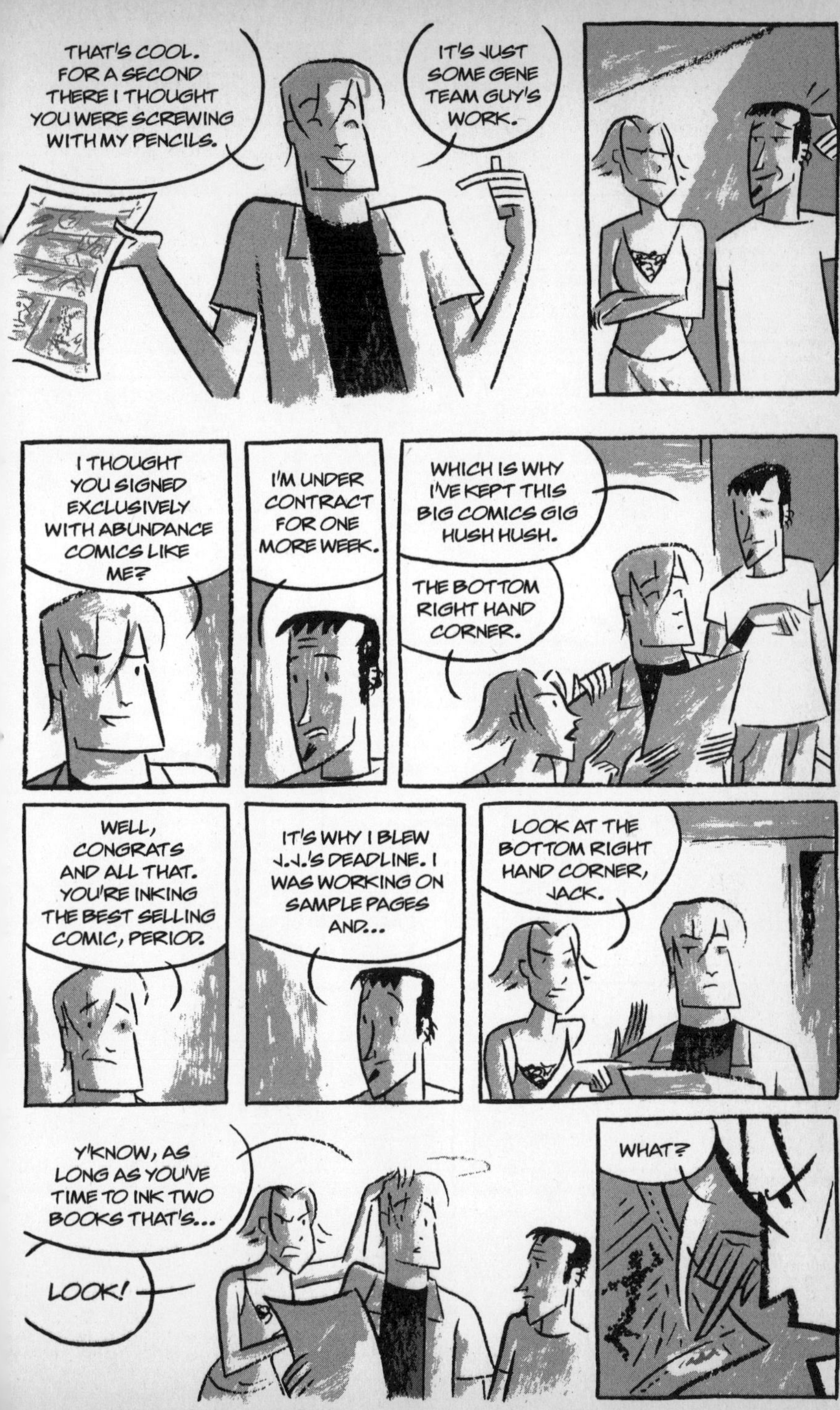
THAT'S COOL. FOR A SECOND THERE I THOUGHT YOU WERE SCREWING WITH MY PENCILS.
IT'S JUST SOME GENE TEAM GUY'S WORK.
I THOUGHT YOU SIGNED EXCLUSIVELY WITH ABUNDANCE COMICS LIKE ME?
I'M UNDER CONTRACT FOR ONE MORE WEEK.
WHICH IS WHY I'VE KEPT THIS BIG COMICS GIG HUSH HUSH.
THE BOTTOM RIGHT HAND CORNER.
WELL, CONGRATS AND ALL THAT. YOU'RE INKING THE BEST SELLING COMIC, PERIOD.
IT'S WHY I BLEW J.J.'S DEADLINE. I WAS WORKING ON SAMPLE PAGES AND...
LOOK AT THE BOTTOM RIGHT HAND CORNER, JACK.
Y'KNOW, AS LONG AS YOU'VE TIME TO INK TWO BOOKS THAT'S...
LOOK!
WHAT?

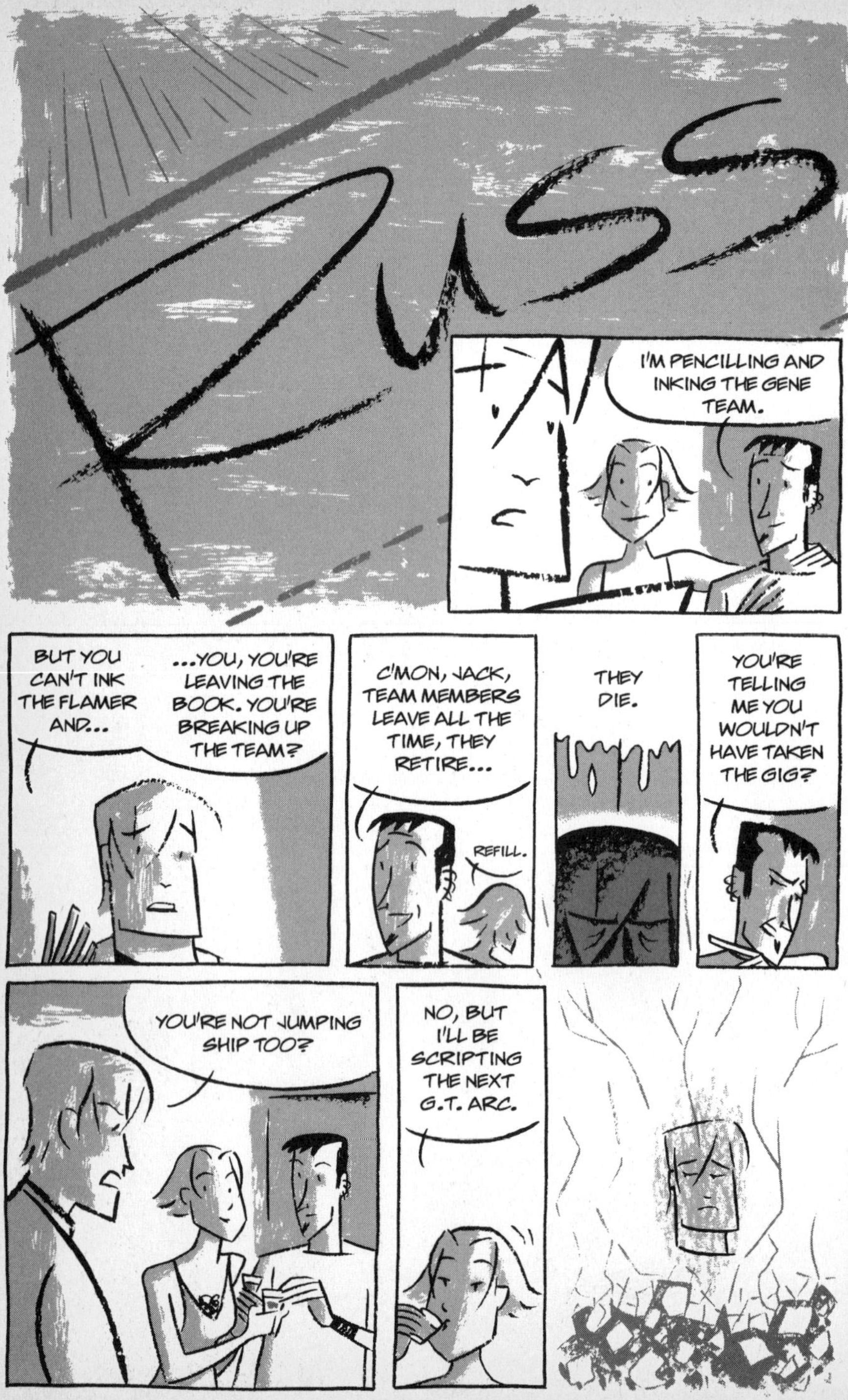
RUSS
I'M PENCILLING AND INKING THE GENE TEAM.
BUT YOU CAN'T INK THE FLAMER AND...
...YOU, YOU'RE LEAVING THE BOOK. YOU'RE BREAKING UP THE TEAM?
C'MON, JACK, TEAM MEMBERS LEAVE ALL THE TIME, THEY RETIRE...
REFILL.
THEY DIE.
YOU'RE TELLING ME YOU WOULDN'T HAVE TAKEN THE GIG?
YOU'RE NOT JUMPING SHIP TOO?
NO, BUT I'LL BE SCRIPTING THE NEXT G.T. ARC.

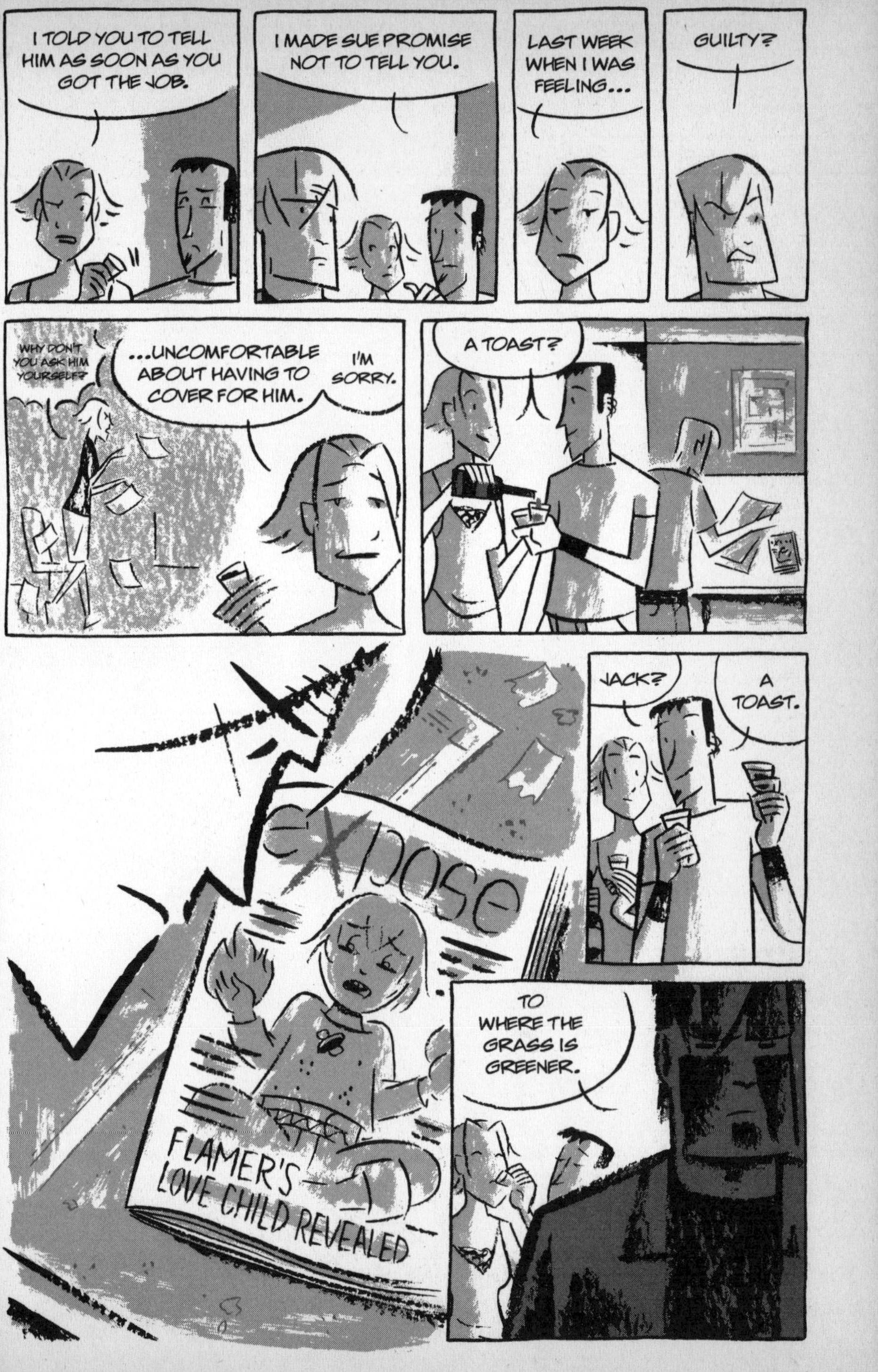

I TOLD YOU TO TELL HIM AS SOON AS YOU GOT THE JOB.
I MADE SUE PROMISE NOT TO TELL YOU.
LAST WEEK WHEN I WAS FEELING...
GUILTY?
WHY DON'T YOU ASK HIM YOURSELF?
...UNCOMFORTABLE ABOUT HAVING TO COVER FOR HIM.
I'M SORRY.
A TOAST?
EXPOSE
FLAMER'S LOVE CHILD REVEALED
JACK?
A TOAST.
TO WHERE THE GRASS IS GREENER.

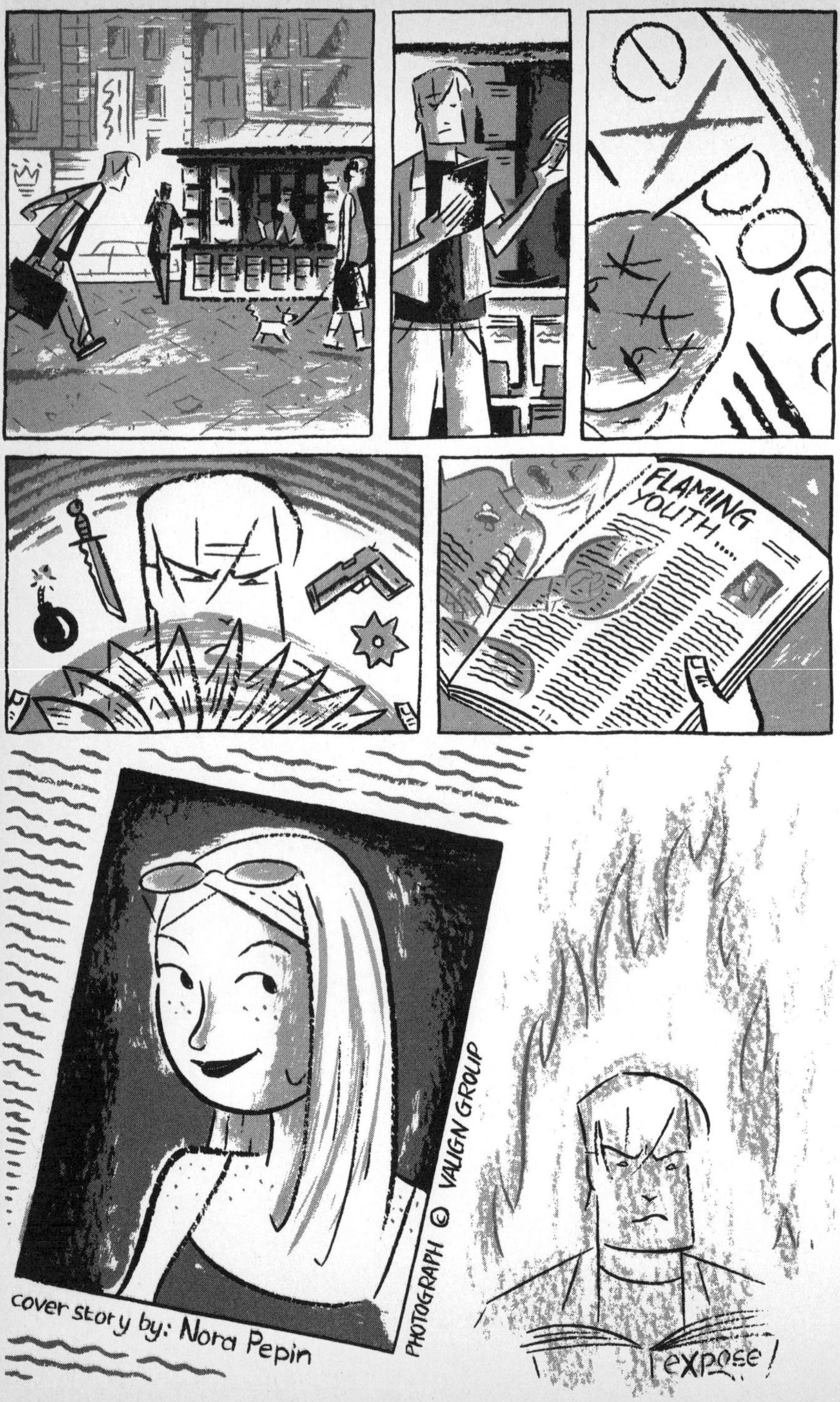

expose
FLAMING YOUTH....
cover story by: Nora Pepin
PHOTOGRAPH © VAUGN GROUP
expose!

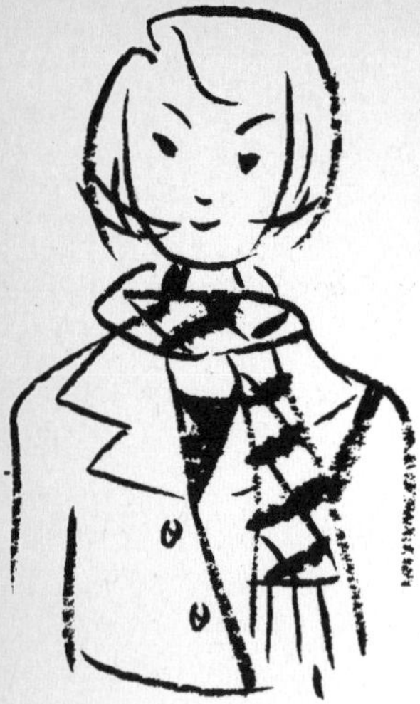
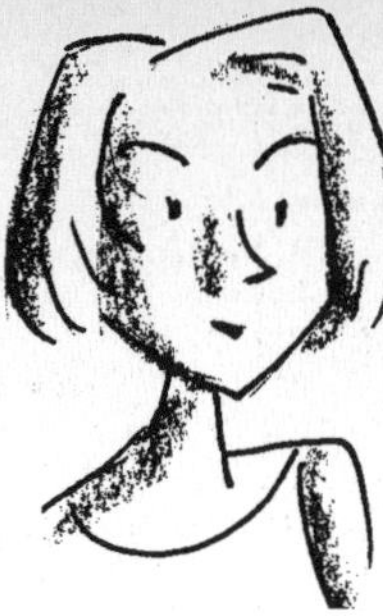
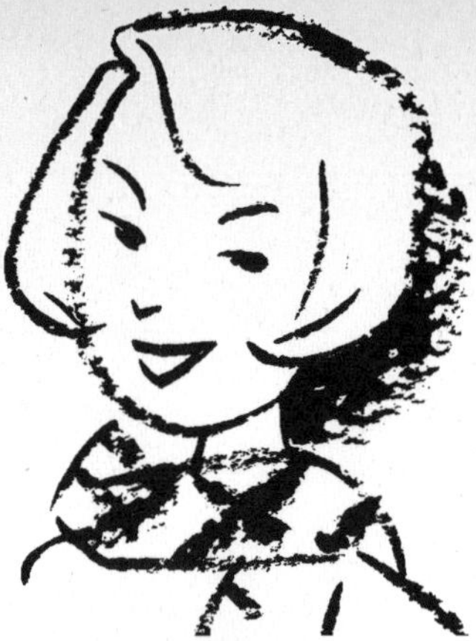
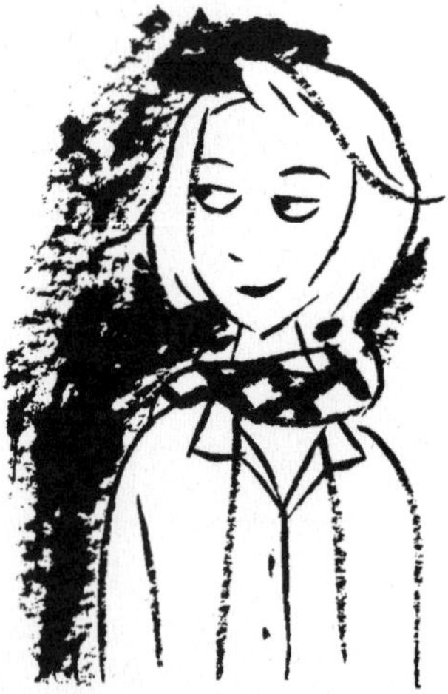
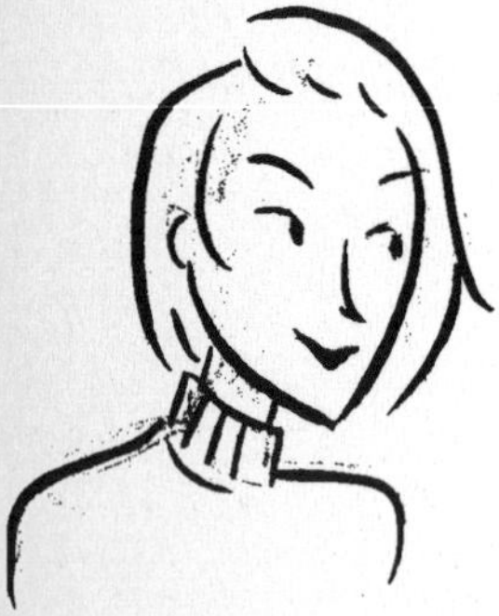
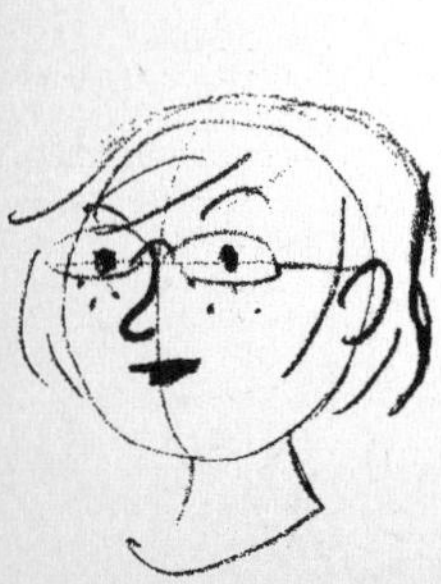
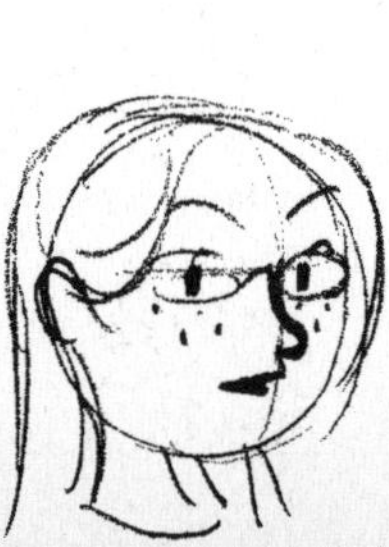
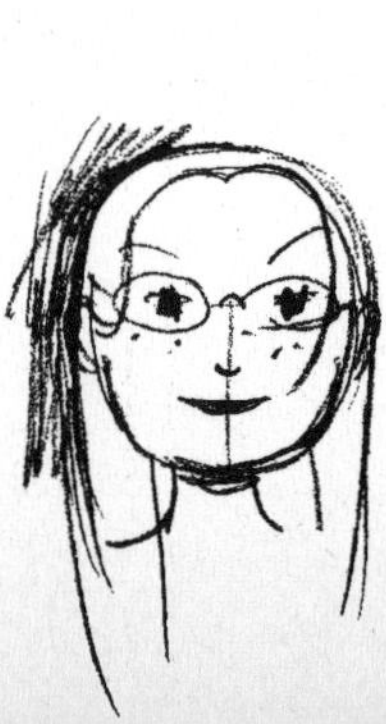

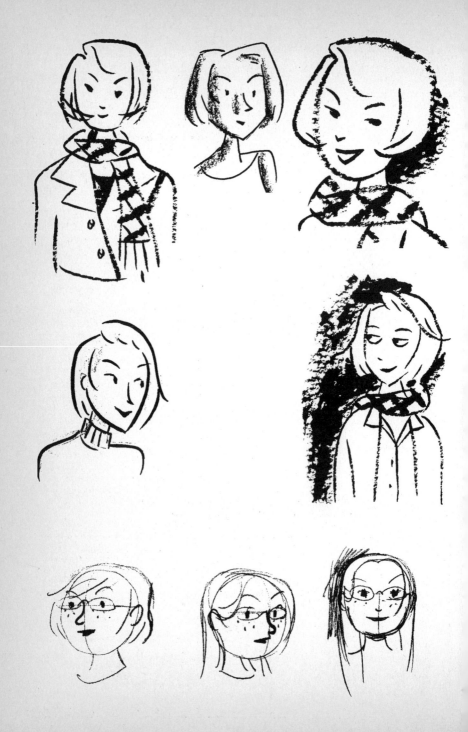

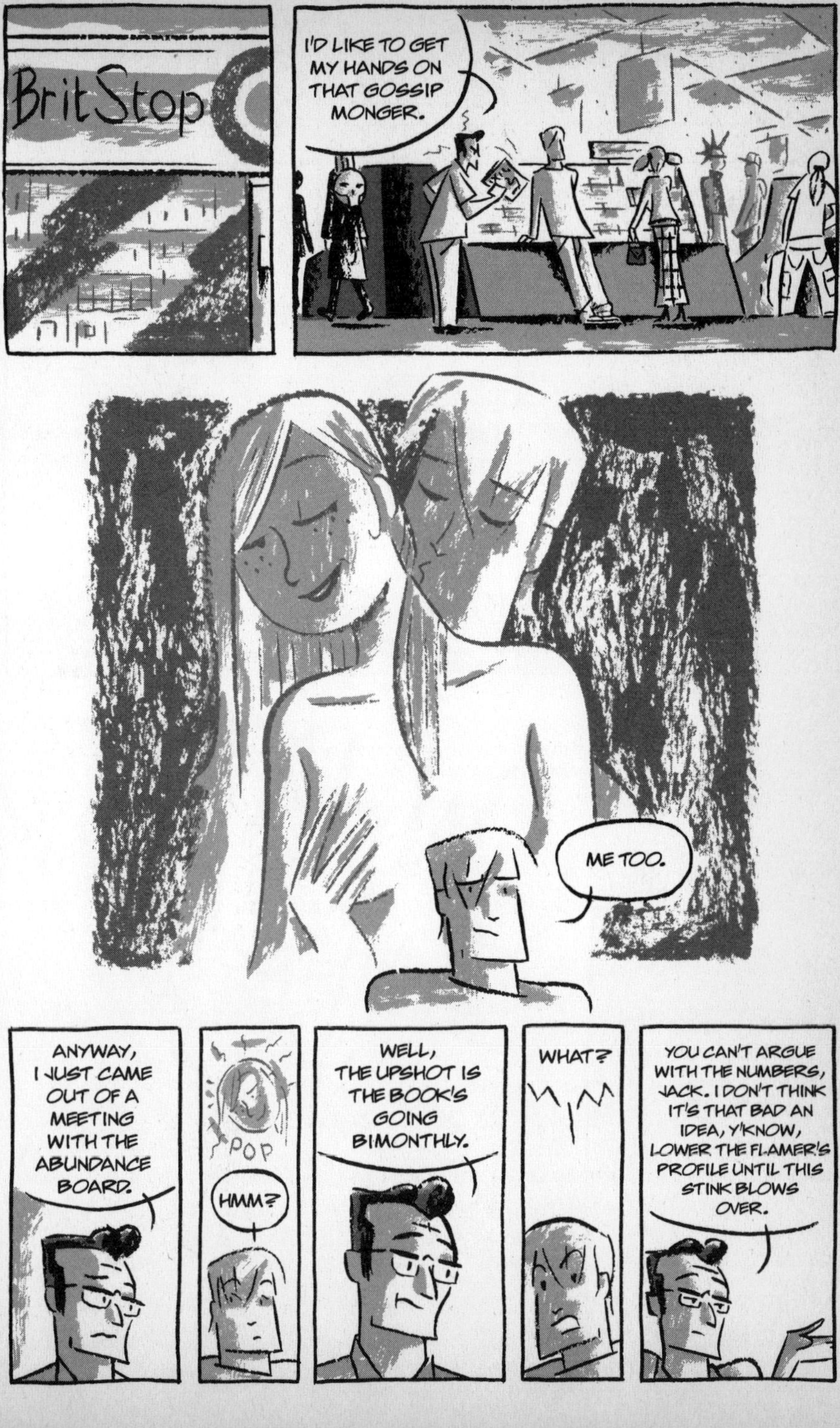
BritStop
I'D LIKE TO GET MY HANDS ON THAT GOSSIP MONGER.
ME TOO.
ANYWAY, I JUST CAME OUT OF A MEETING WITH THE ABUNDANCE BOARD.
POP
HMM?
WELL, THE UPSHOT IS THE BOOK'S GOING BIMONTHLY.
WHAT?
YOU CAN'T ARGUE WITH THE NUMBERS, JACK. I DON'T THINK IT'S THAT BAD AN IDEA, Y'KNOW, LOWER THE FLAMER'S PROFILE UNTIL THIS STINK BLOWS OVER.

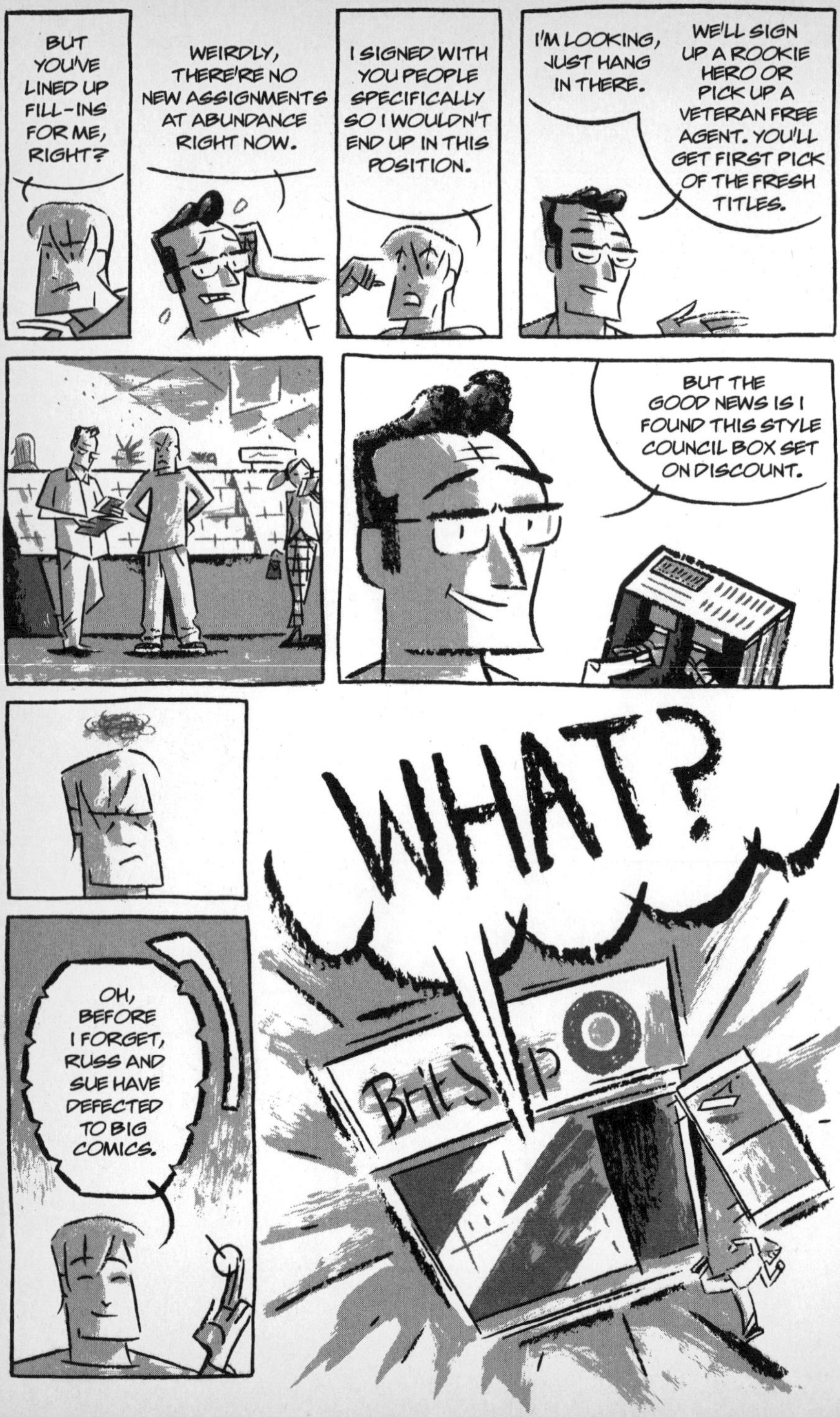
BUT YOU'VE LINED UP FILL-INS FOR ME, RIGHT?
WEIRDLY, THERE'RE NO NEW ASSIGNMENTS AT ABUNDANCE RIGHT NOW.
I SIGNED WITH YOU PEOPLE SPECIFICALLY SO I WOULDN'T END UP IN THIS POSITION.
I'M LOOKING, JUST HANG IN THERE.
WE'LL SIGN UP A ROOKIE HERO OR PICK UP A VETERAN FREE AGENT. YOU'LL GET FIRST PICK OF THE FRESH TITLES.
BUT THE GOOD NEWS IS I FOUND THIS STYLE COUNCIL BOX SET ON DISCOUNT.
OH, BEFORE I FORGET, RUSS AND SUE HAVE DEFECTED TO BIG COMICS.
WHAT?

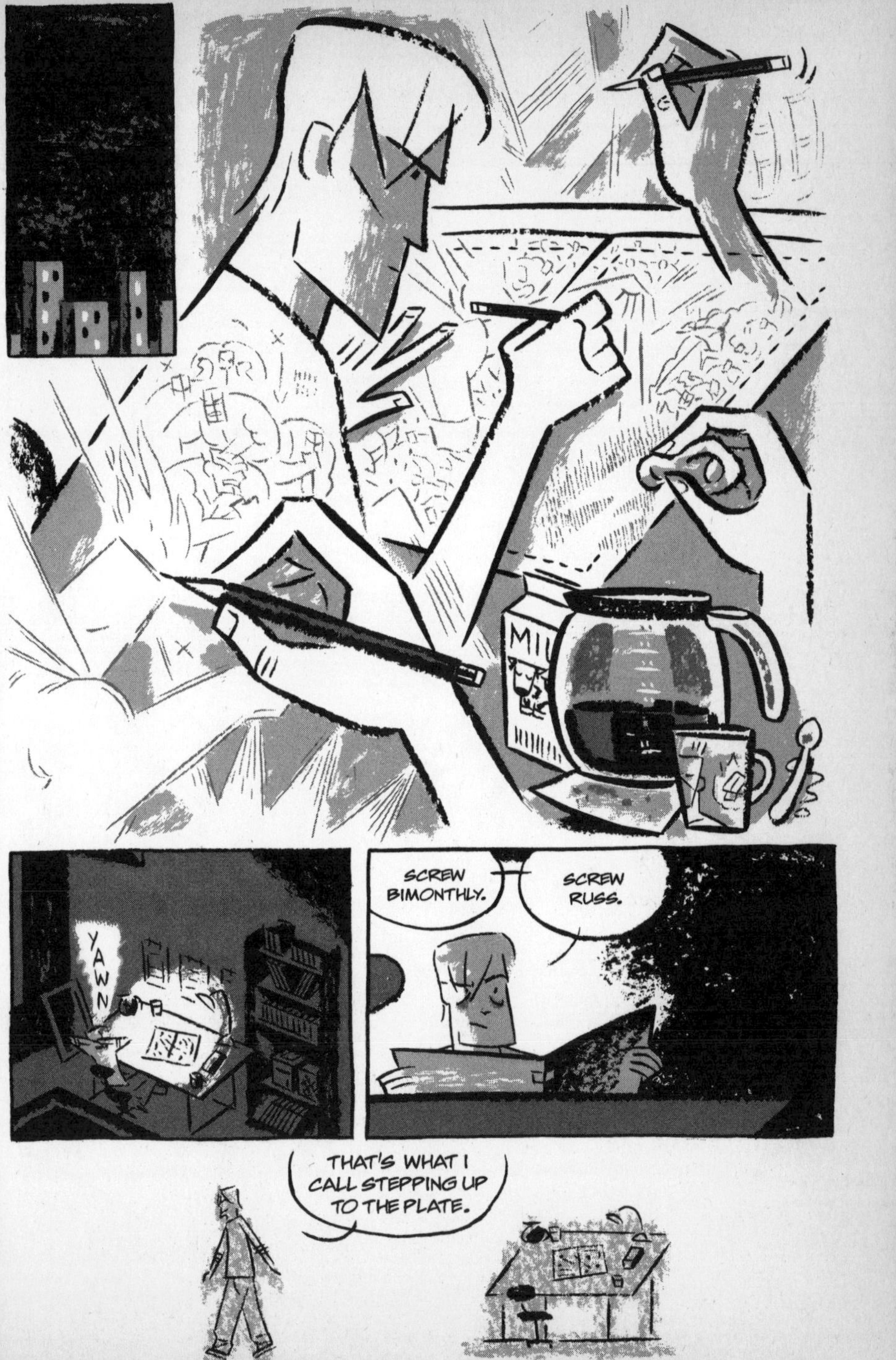
YAWN
SCREW BIMONTHLY.
SCREW RUSS.
THAT'S WHAT I CALL STEPPING UP TO THE PLATE.

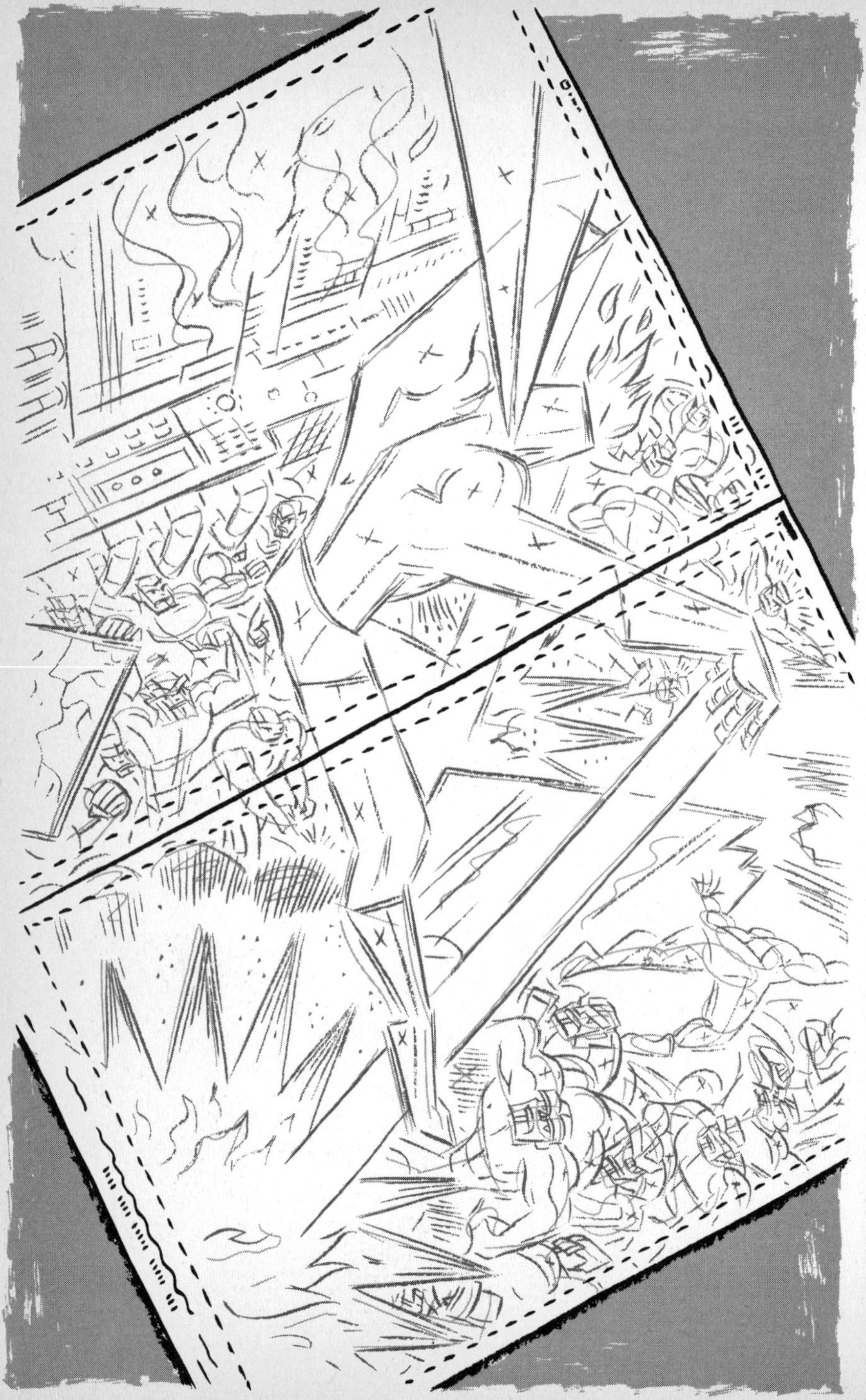

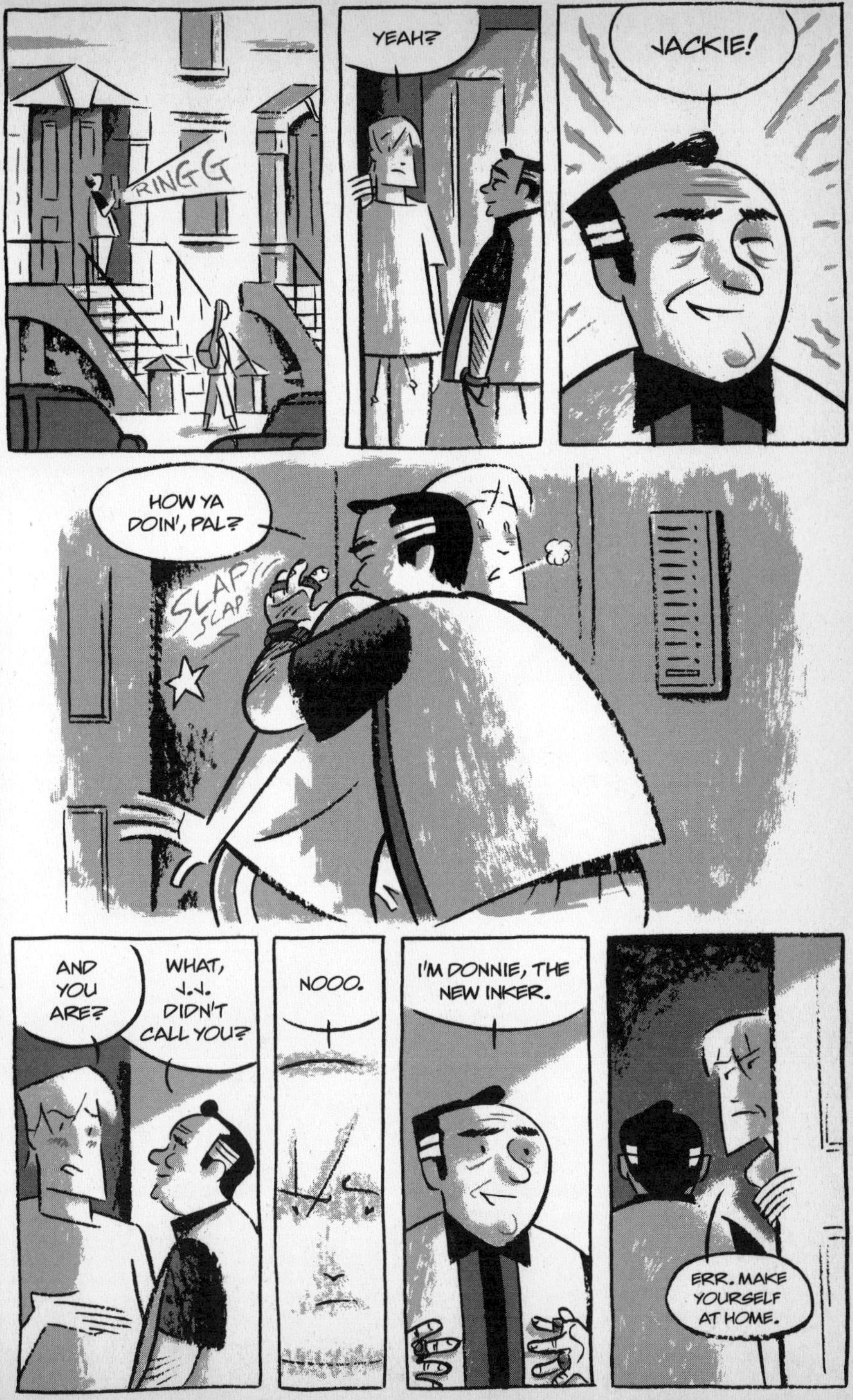
RINGG
YEAH?
JACKIE!
HOW YA DOIN', PAL?
SLAP SLAP
AND YOU ARE?
WHAT, J.J. DIDN'T CALL YOU?
NOOO.
I'M DONNIE, THE NEW INKER.
ERR. MAKE YOURSELF AT HOME.

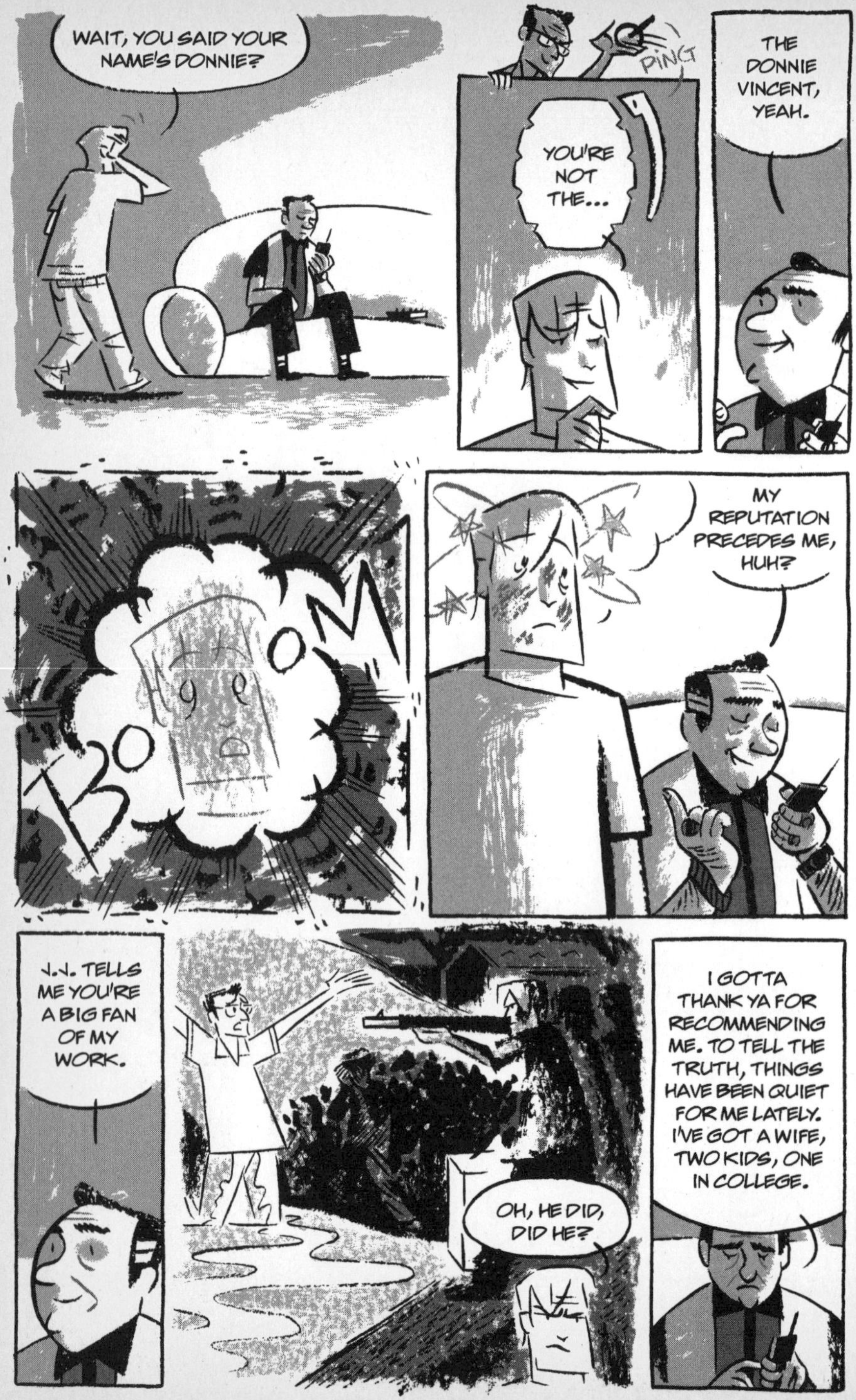
WAIT, YOU SAID YOUR NAME'S DONNIE?
PING
YOU'RE NOT THE...
THE DONNIE VINCENT, YEAH.
BOOM
MY REPUTATION PRECEDES ME, HUH?
J.J. TELLS ME YOU'RE A BIG FAN OF MY WORK.
OH, HE DID, DID HE?
I GOTTA THANK YA FOR RECOMMENDING ME. TO TELL THE TRUTH, THINGS HAVE BEEN QUIET FOR ME LATELY. I'VE GOT A WIFE, TWO KIDS, ONE IN COLLEGE.

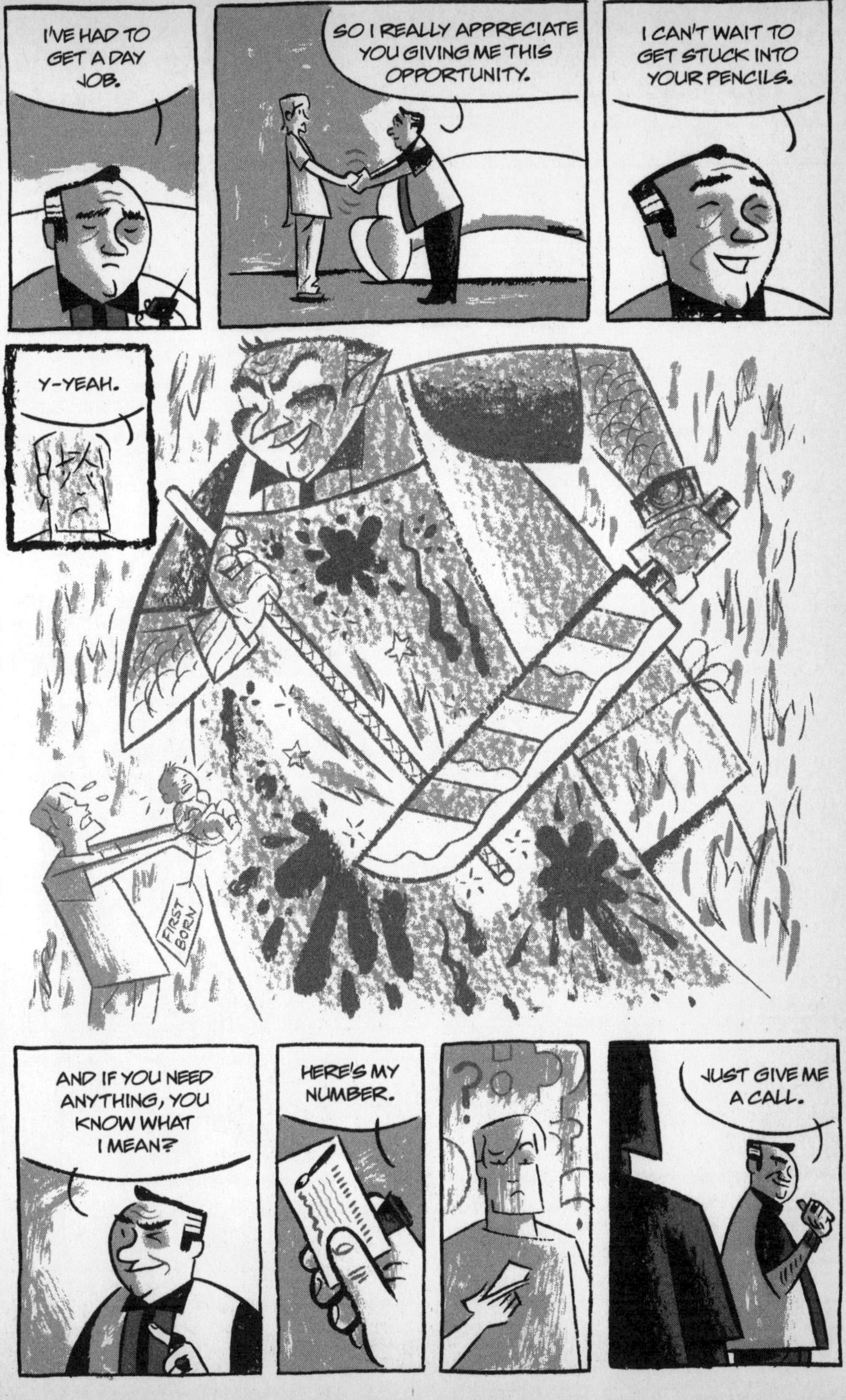
I'VE HAD TO GET A DAY JOB.
SO I REALLY APPRECIATE YOU GIVING ME THIS OPPORTUNITY.
I CAN'T WAIT TO GET STUCK INTO YOUR PENCILS.
Y-YEAH.
FIRST BORN
AND IF YOU NEED ANYTHING, YOU KNOW WHAT I MEAN?
HERE'S MY NUMBER.
JUST GIVE ME A CALL.

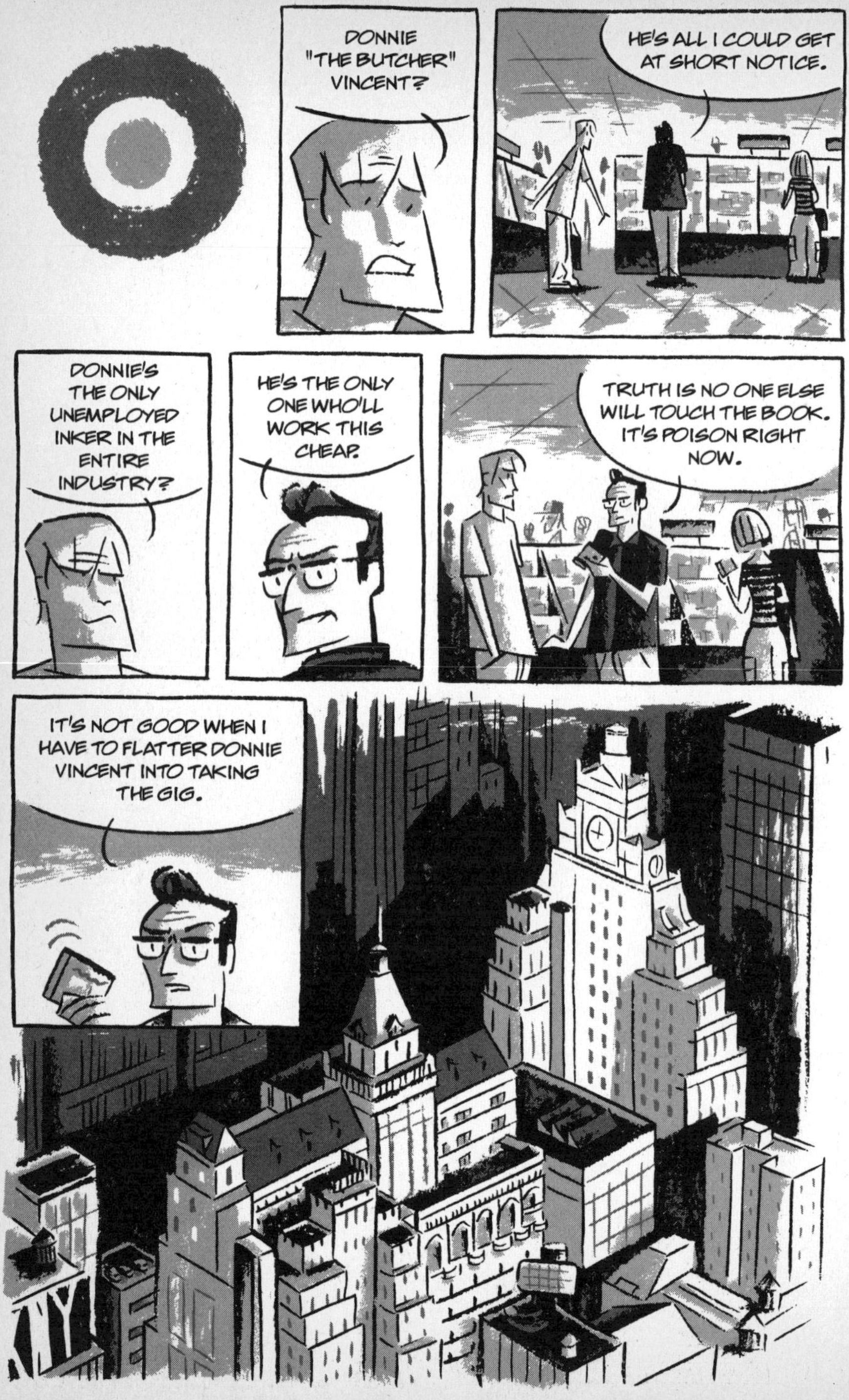
DONNIE "THE BUTCHER" VINCENT?
HE'S ALL I COULD GET AT SHORT NOTICE.
DONNIE'S THE ONLY UNEMPLOYED INKER IN THE ENTIRE INDUSTRY?
HE'S THE ONLY ONE WHO'LL WORK THIS CHEAP.
TRUTH IS NO ONE ELSE WILL TOUCH THE BOOK. IT'S POISON RIGHT NOW.
IT'S NOT GOOD WHEN I HAVE TO FLATTER DONNIE VINCENT INTO TAKING THE GIG.

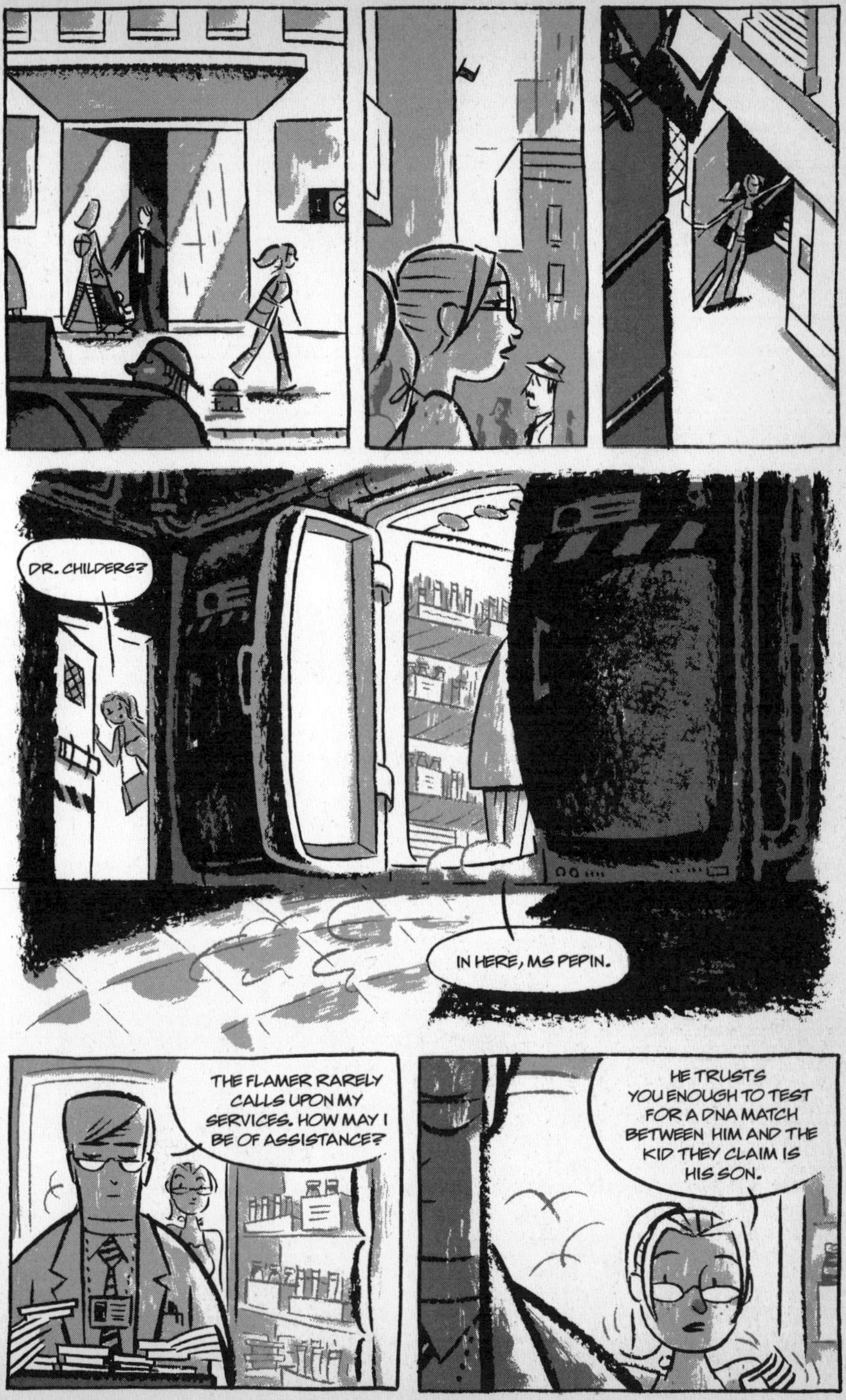
DR. CHILDERS?
IN HERE, MS PEPIN.
THE FLAMER RARELY CALLS UPON MY SERVICES. HOW MAY I BE OF ASSISTANCE?
HE TRUSTS YOU ENOUGH TO TEST FOR A DNA MATCH BETWEEN HIM AND THE KID THEY CLAIM IS HIS SON.

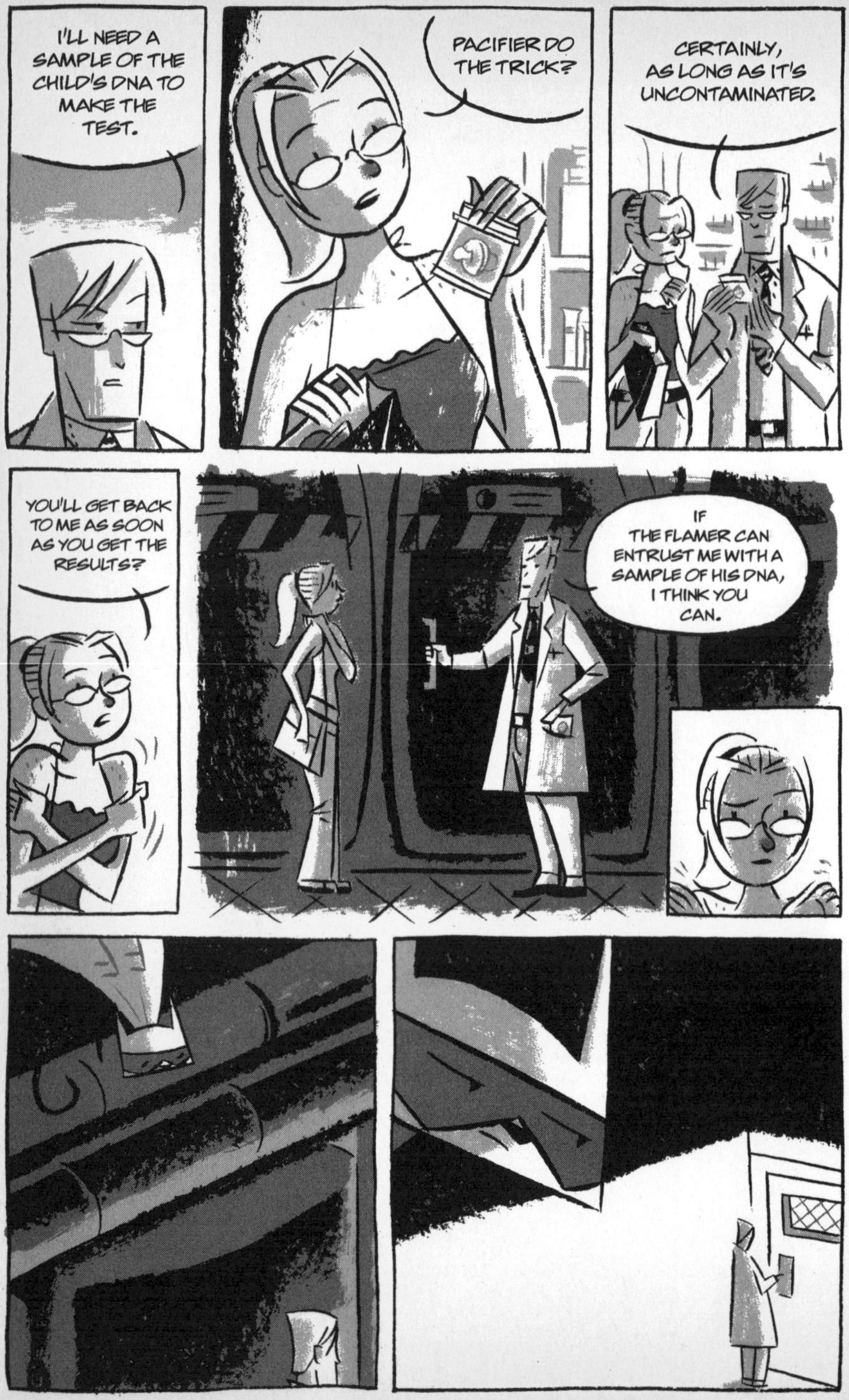
I'LL NEED A SAMPLE OF THE CHILD'S DNA TO MAKE THE TEST.
PACIFIER DO THE TRICK?
CERTAINLY, AS LONG AS IT'S UNCONTAMINATED.
YOU'LL GET BACK TO ME AS SOON AS YOU GET THE RESULTS?
IF THE FLAMER CAN ENTRUST ME WITH A SAMPLE OF HIS DNA, I THINK YOU CAN.

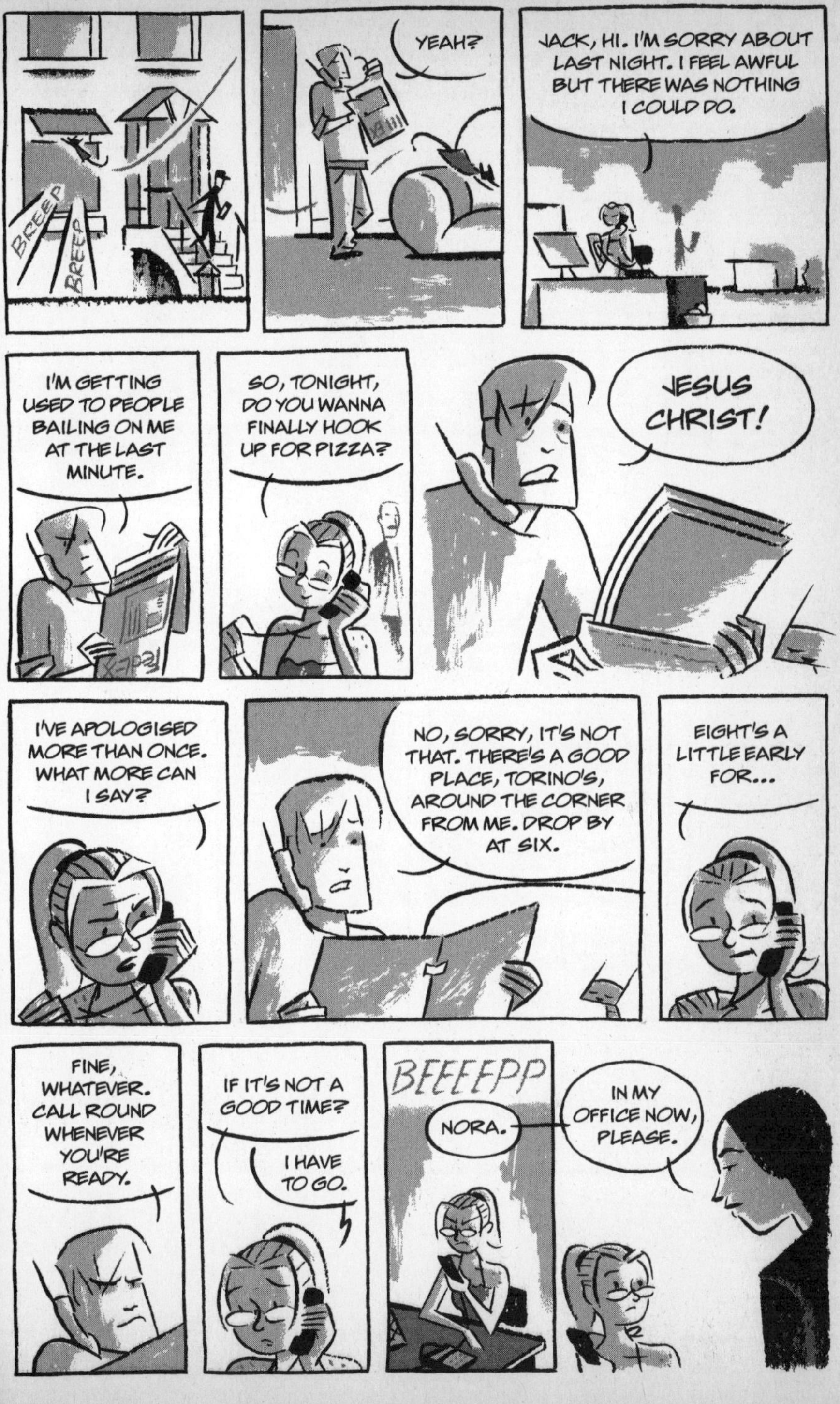
BREEP
BREEP
YEAH?
JACK, HI. I'M SORRY ABOUT LAST NIGHT. I FEEL AWFUL BUT THERE WAS NOTHING I COULD DO.
I'M GETTING USED TO PEOPLE BAILING ON ME AT THE LAST MINUTE.
SO, TONIGHT, DO YOU WANNA FINALLY HOOK UP FOR PIZZA?
JESUS CHRIST!
I'VE APOLOGISED MORE THAN ONCE. WHAT MORE CAN I SAY?
NO, SORRY, IT'S NOT THAT. THERE'S A GOOD PLACE, TORINO'S, AROUND THE CORNER FROM ME. DROP BY AT SIX.
EIGHT'S A LITTLE EARLY FOR...
FINE, WHATEVER. CALL ROUND WHENEVER YOU'RE READY.
IF IT'S NOT A GOOD TIME?
I HAVE TO GO.
BEEEEPP
NORA.
IN MY OFFICE NOW, PLEASE.

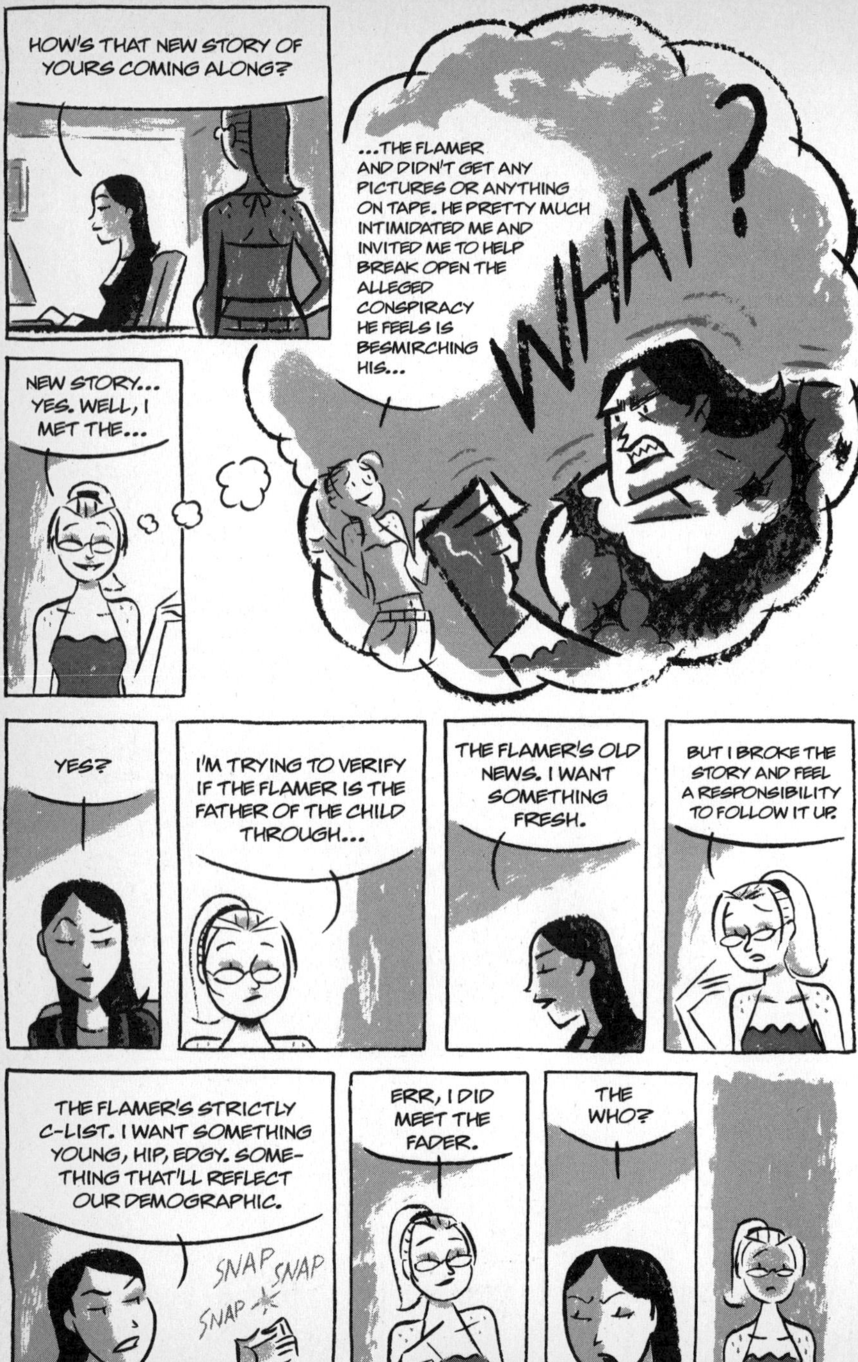
HOW'S THAT NEW STORY OF YOURS COMING ALONG?
NEW STORY... YES. WELL, I MET THE...
...THE FLAMER AND DIDN'T GET ANY PICTURES OR ANYTHING ON TAPE. HE PRETTY MUCH INTIMIDATED ME AND INVITED ME TO HELP BREAK OPEN THE ALLEGED CONSPIRACY HE FEELS IS BESMIRCHING HIS...
WHAT?
YES?
I'M TRYING TO VERIFY IF THE FLAMER IS THE FATHER OF THE CHILD THROUGH...
THE FLAMER'S OLD NEWS. I WANT SOMETHING FRESH.
BUT I BROKE THE STORY AND FEEL A RESPONSIBILITY TO FOLLOW IT UP.
THE FLAMER'S STRICTLY C-LIST. I WANT SOMETHING YOUNG, HIP, EDGY. SOMETHING THAT'LL REFLECT OUR DEMOGRAPHIC.
SNAP SNAP
SNAP
ERR, I DID MEET THE FADER.
THE WHO?

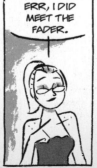

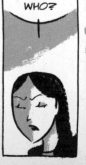

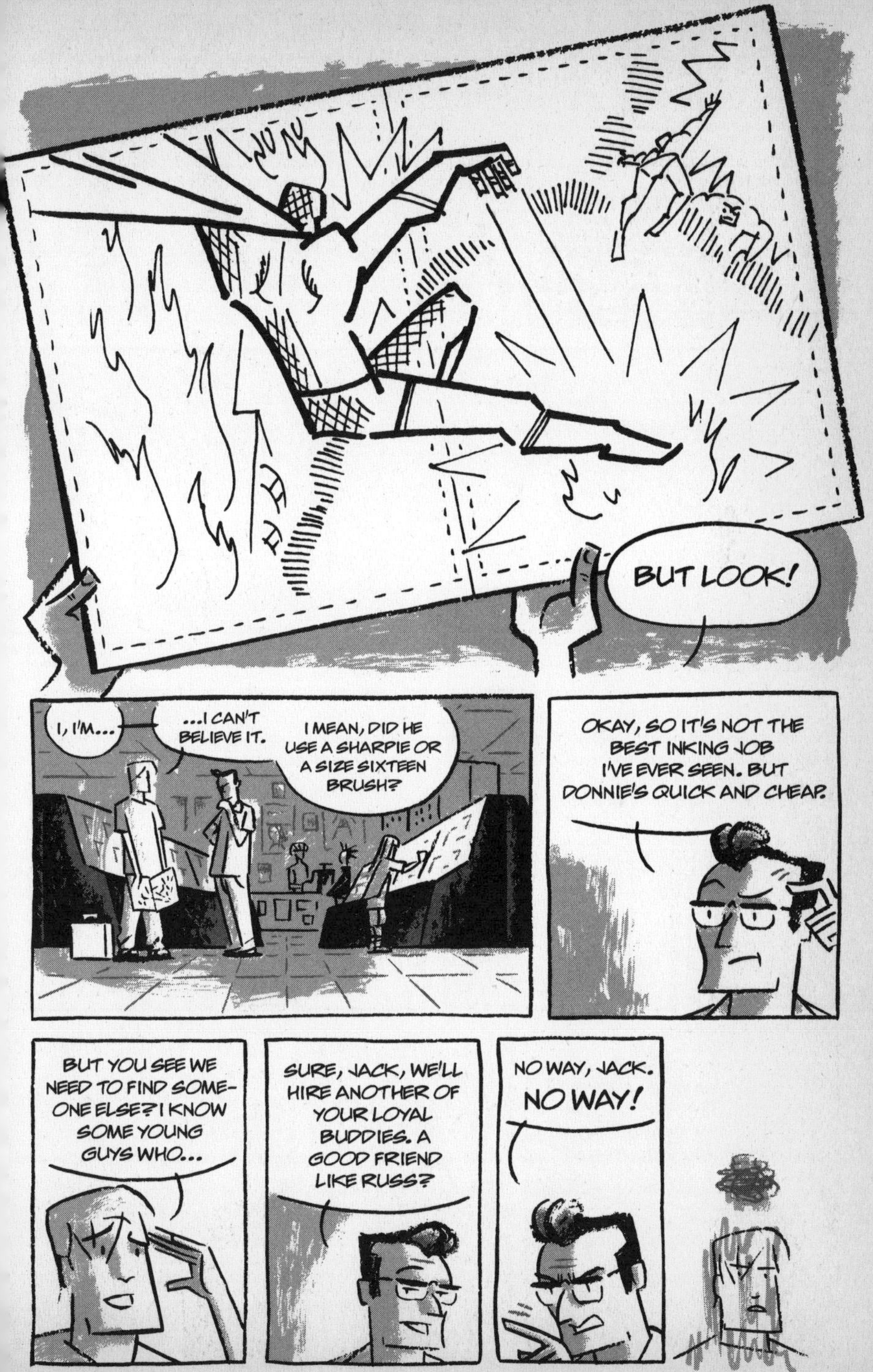
BUT LOOK!
I, I'M...
...I CAN'T BELIEVE IT.
I MEAN, DID HE USE A SHARPIE OR A SIZE SIXTEEN BRUSH?
OKAY, SO IT'S NOT THE BEST INKING JOB I'VE EVER SEEN. BUT DONNIE'S QUICK AND CHEAP.
BUT YOU SEE WE NEED TO FIND SOME-ONE ELSE? I KNOW SOME YOUNG GUYS WHO...
SURE, JACK, WE'LL HIRE ANOTHER OF YOUR LOYAL BUDDIES. A GOOD FRIEND LIKE RUSS?
NO WAY, JACK.
NO WAY!

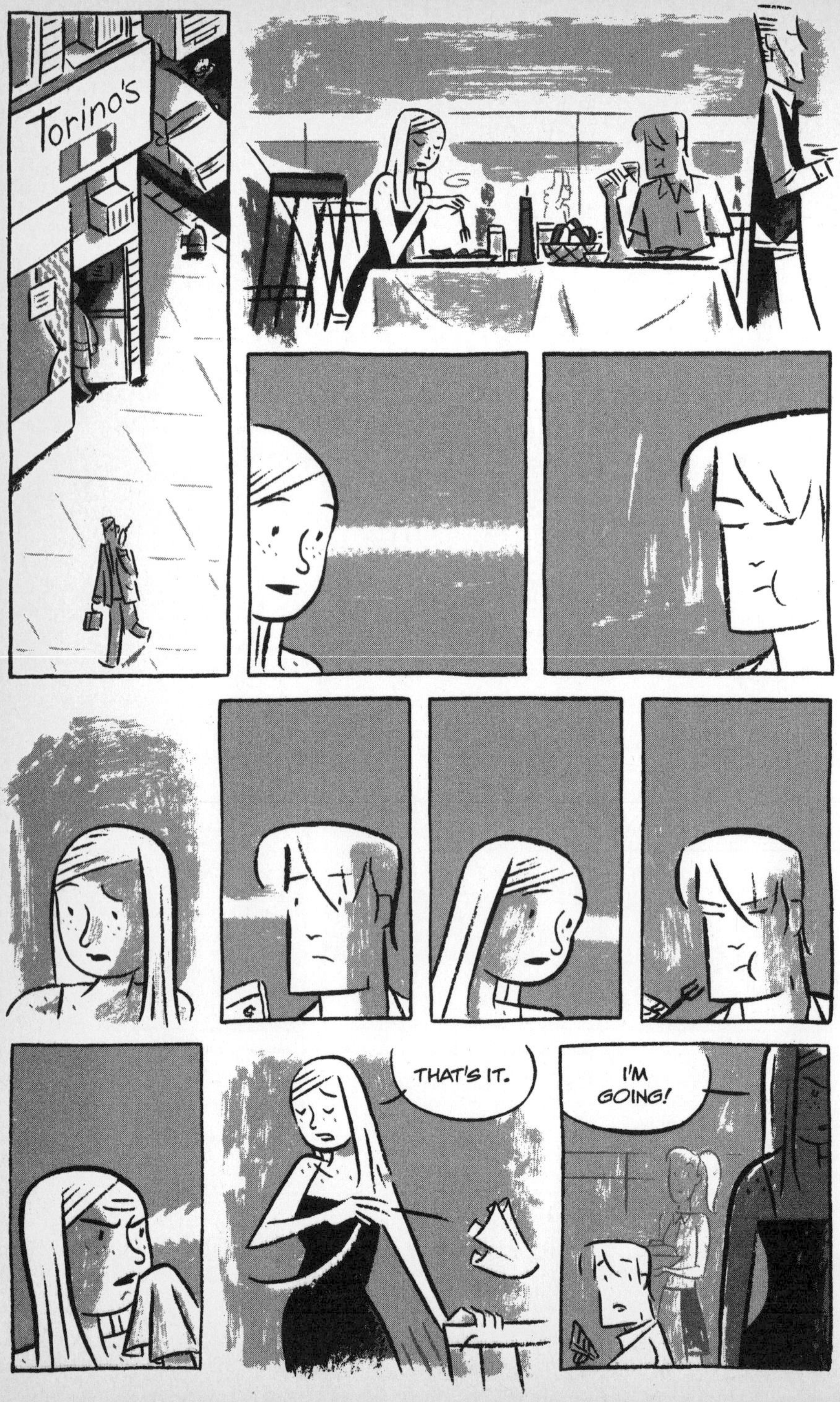
Torino's
THAT'S IT.
I'M GOING!

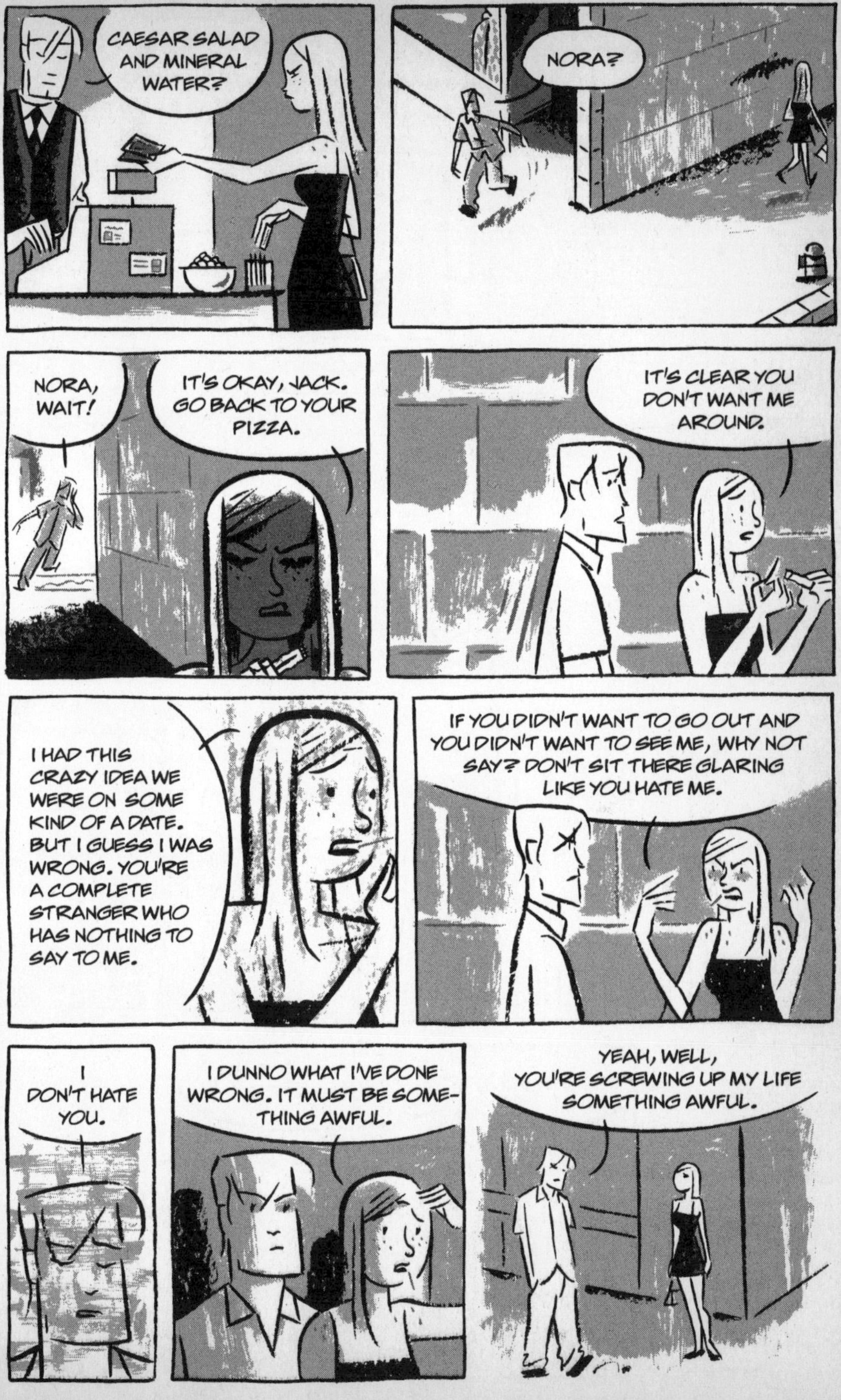
CAESAR SALAD AND MINERAL WATER?
NORA?
NORA, WAIT!
IT'S OKAY, JACK. GO BACK TO YOUR PIZZA.
IT'S CLEAR YOU DON'T WANT ME AROUND.
I HAD THIS CRAZY IDEA WE WERE ON SOME KIND OF A DATE. BUT I GUESS I WAS WRONG. YOU'RE A COMPLETE STRANGER WHO HAS NOTHING TO SAY TO ME.
IF YOU DIDN'T WANT TO GO OUT AND YOU DIDN'T WANT TO SEE ME, WHY NOT SAY? DON'T SIT THERE GLARING LIKE YOU HATE ME.
I DON'T HATE YOU.
I DUNNO WHAT I'VE DONE WRONG. IT MUST BE SOMETHING AWFUL.
YEAH, WELL, YOU'RE SCREWING UP MY LIFE SOMETHING AWFUL.

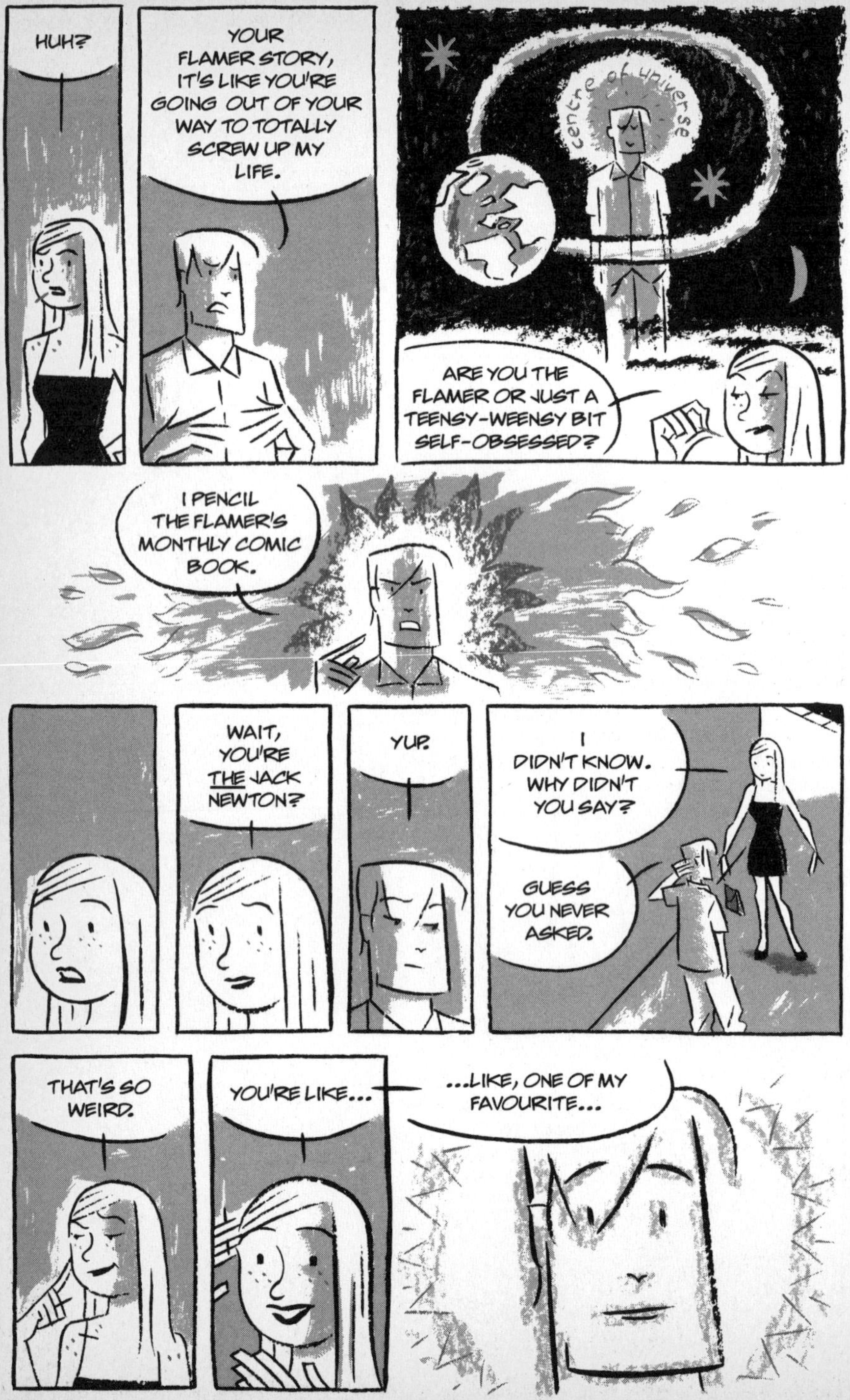
HUH?
YOUR FLAMER STORY, IT'S LIKE YOU'RE GOING OUT OF YOUR WAY TO TOTALLY SCREW UP MY LIFE.
centre of universe
ARE YOU THE FLAMER OR JUST A TEENSY-WEENSY BIT SELF-OBSESSED?
I PENCIL THE FLAMER'S MONTHLY COMIC BOOK.
WAIT, YOU'RE THE JACK NEWTON?
YUP.
I DIDN'T KNOW. WHY DIDN'T YOU SAY?
GUESS YOU NEVER ASKED.
THAT'S SO WEIRD.
YOU'RE LIKE...
...LIKE, ONE OF MY FAVOURITE...

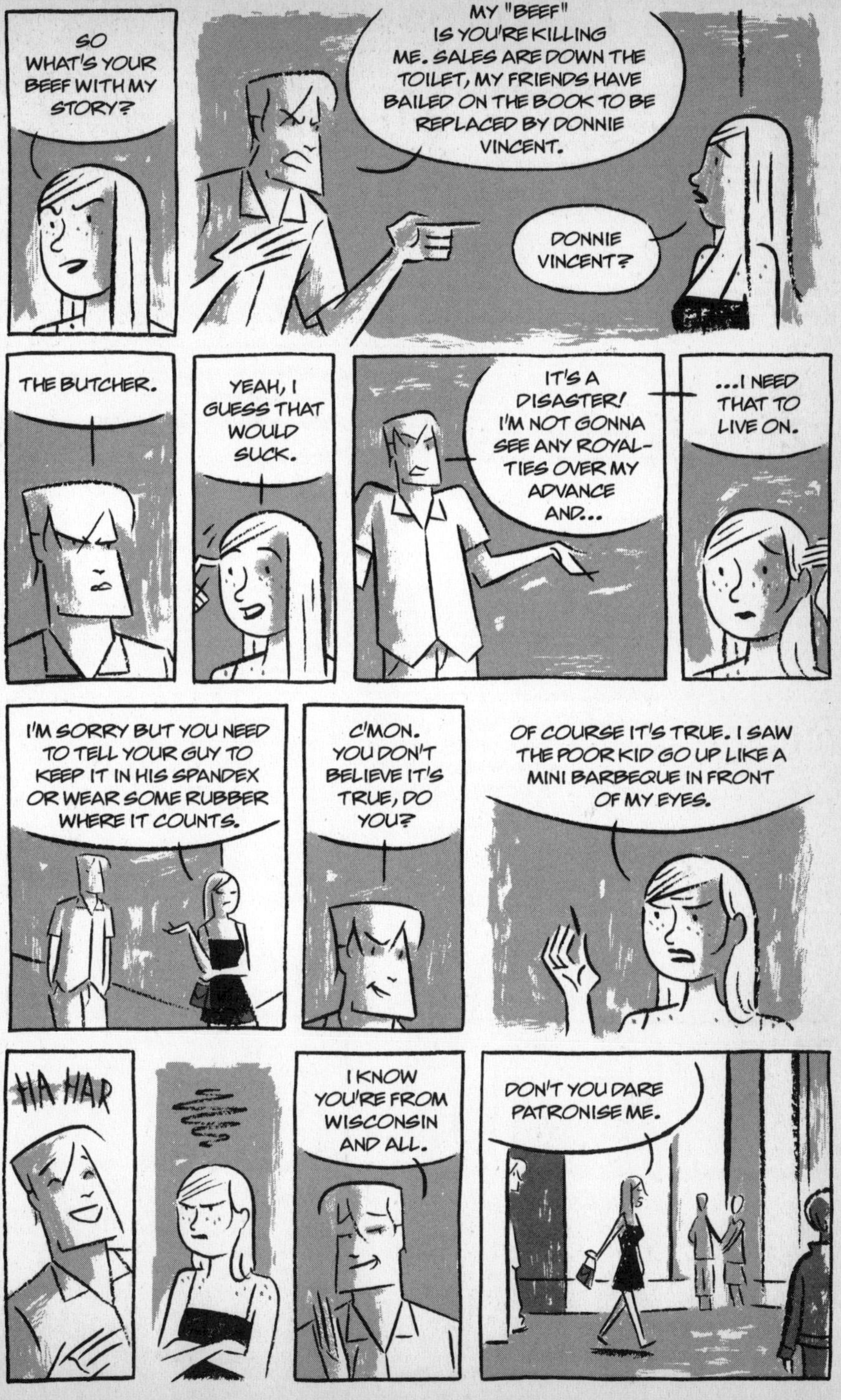
SO WHAT'S YOUR BEEF WITH MY STORY?
MY "BEEF" IS YOU'RE KILLING ME. SALES ARE DOWN THE TOILET, MY FRIENDS HAVE BAILED ON THE BOOK TO BE REPLACED BY DONNIE VINCENT.
DONNIE VINCENT?
THE BUTCHER.
YEAH, I GUESS THAT WOULD SUCK.
IT'S A DISASTER! I'M NOT GONNA SEE ANY ROYAL-TIES OVER MY ADVANCE AND...
...I NEED THAT TO LIVE ON.
I'M SORRY BUT YOU NEED TO TELL YOUR GUY TO KEEP IT IN HIS SPANDEX OR WEAR SOME RUBBER WHERE IT COUNTS.
C'MON. YOU DON'T BELIEVE IT'S TRUE, DO YOU?
OF COURSE IT'S TRUE. I SAW THE POOR KID GO UP LIKE A MINI BARBEQUE IN FRONT OF MY EYES.
HA HAR
I KNOW YOU'RE FROM WISCONSIN AND ALL.
DON'T YOU DARE PATRONISE ME.

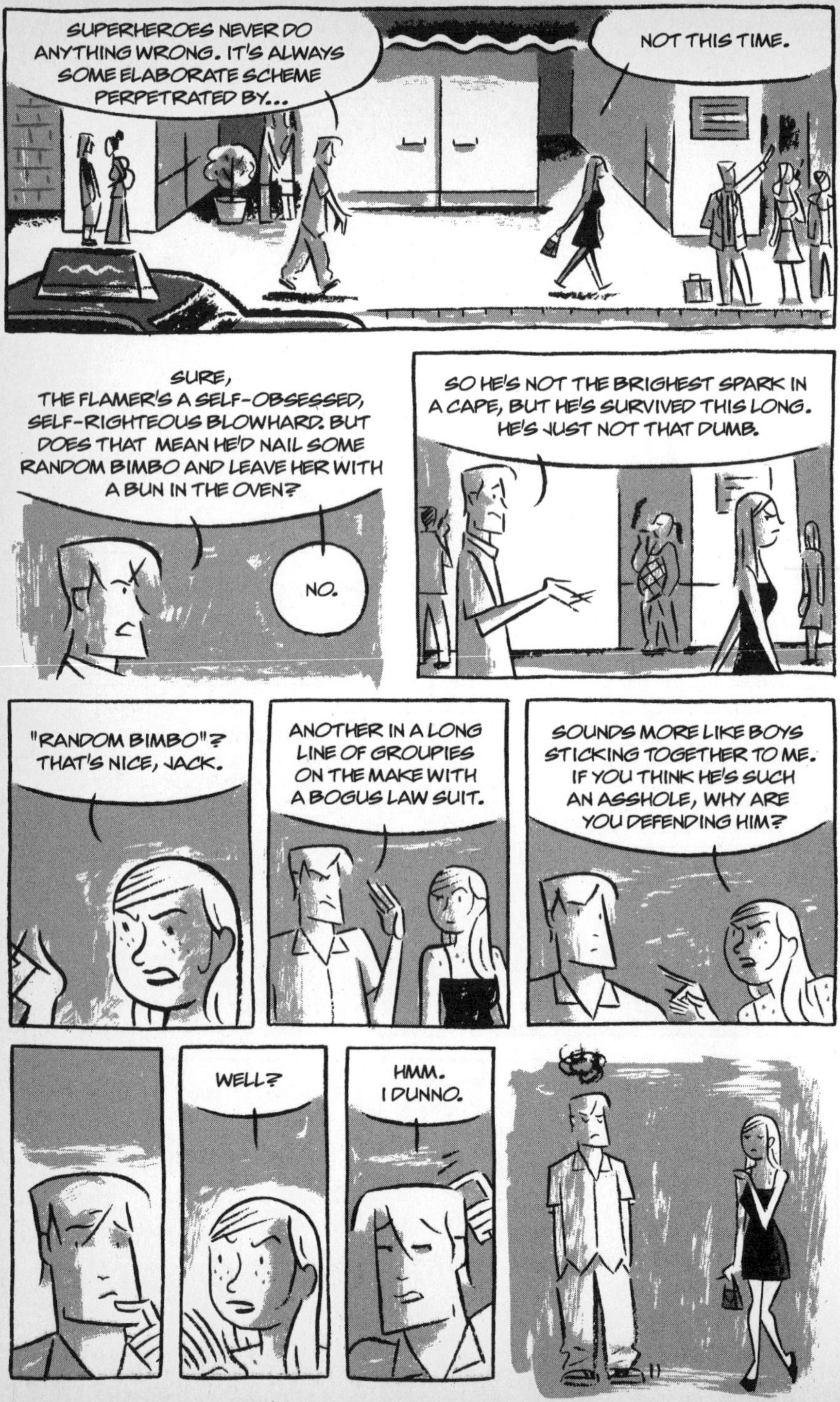
SUPERHEROES NEVER DO ANYTHING WRONG. IT'S ALWAYS SOME ELABORATE SCHEME PERPETRATED BY...
NOT THIS TIME.
SURE, THE FLAMER'S A SELF-OBSESSED, SELF-RIGHTEOUS BLOWHARD. BUT DOES THAT MEAN HE'D NAIL SOME RANDOM BIMBO AND LEAVE HER WITH A BUN IN THE OVEN?
NO.
SO HE'S NOT THE BRIGHEST SPARK IN A CAPE, BUT HE'S SURVIVED THIS LONG. HE'S JUST NOT THAT DUMB.
"RANDOM BIMBO"? THAT'S NICE, JACK.
ANOTHER IN A LONG LINE OF GROUPIES ON THE MAKE WITH A BOGUS LAW SUIT.
SOUNDS MORE LIKE BOYS STICKING TOGETHER TO ME. IF YOU THINK HE'S SUCH AN ASSHOLE, WHY ARE YOU DEFENDING HIM?
WELL?
HMM. I DUNNO.

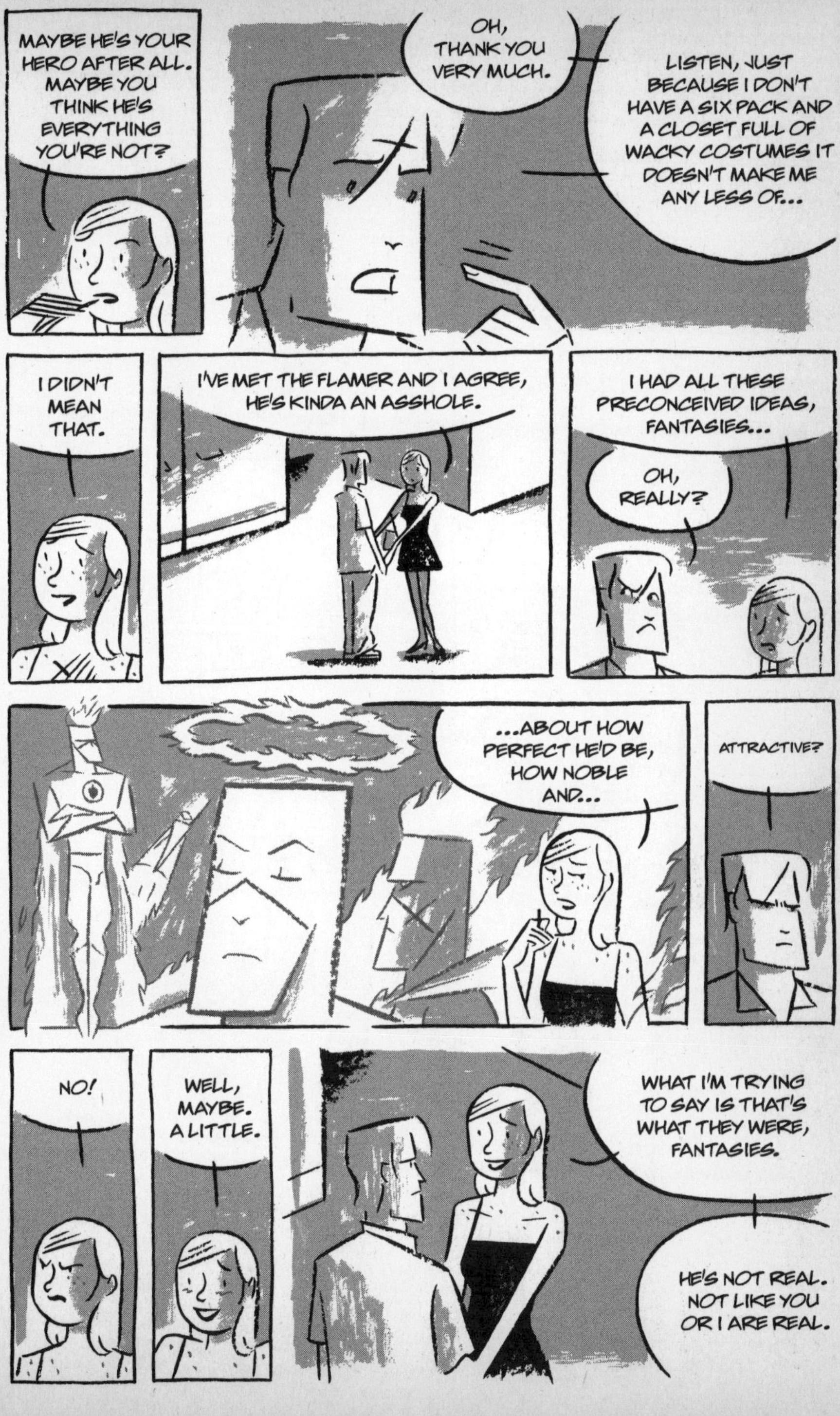
MAYBE HE'S YOUR HERO AFTER ALL. MAYBE YOU THINK HE'S EVERYTHING YOU'RE NOT?
OH, THANK YOU VERY MUCH.
LISTEN, JUST BECAUSE I DON'T HAVE A SIX PACK AND A CLOSET FULL OF WACKY COSTUMES IT DOESN'T MAKE ME ANY LESS OF...
I DIDN'T MEAN THAT.
I'VE MET THE FLAMER AND I AGREE, HE'S KINDA AN ASSHOLE.
I HAD ALL THESE PRECONCEIVED IDEAS, FANTASIES...
OH, REALLY?
...ABOUT HOW PERFECT HE'D BE, HOW NOBLE AND...
ATTRACTIVE?
NO!
WELL, MAYBE. A LITTLE.
WHAT I'M TRYING TO SAY IS THAT'S WHAT THEY WERE, FANTASIES.
HE'S NOT REAL. NOT LIKE YOU OR I ARE REAL.

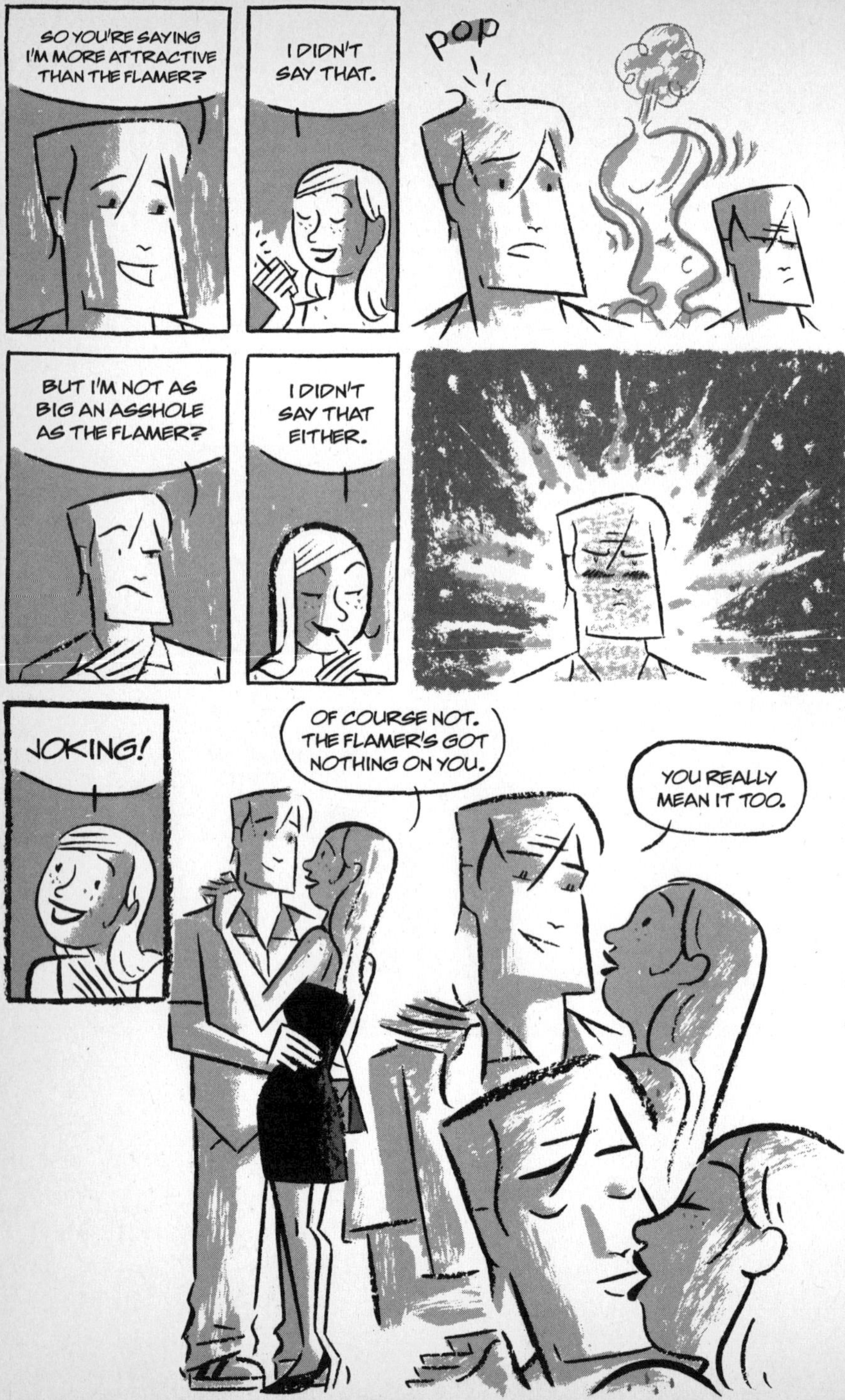
SO YOU'RE SAYING I'M MORE ATTRACTIVE THAN THE FLAMER?
I DIDN'T SAY THAT.
POP
BUT I'M NOT AS BIG AN ASSHOLE AS THE FLAMER?
I DIDN'T SAY THAT EITHER.
JOKING!
OF COURSE NOT. THE FLAMER'S GOT NOTHING ON YOU.
YOU REALLY MEAN IT TOO.

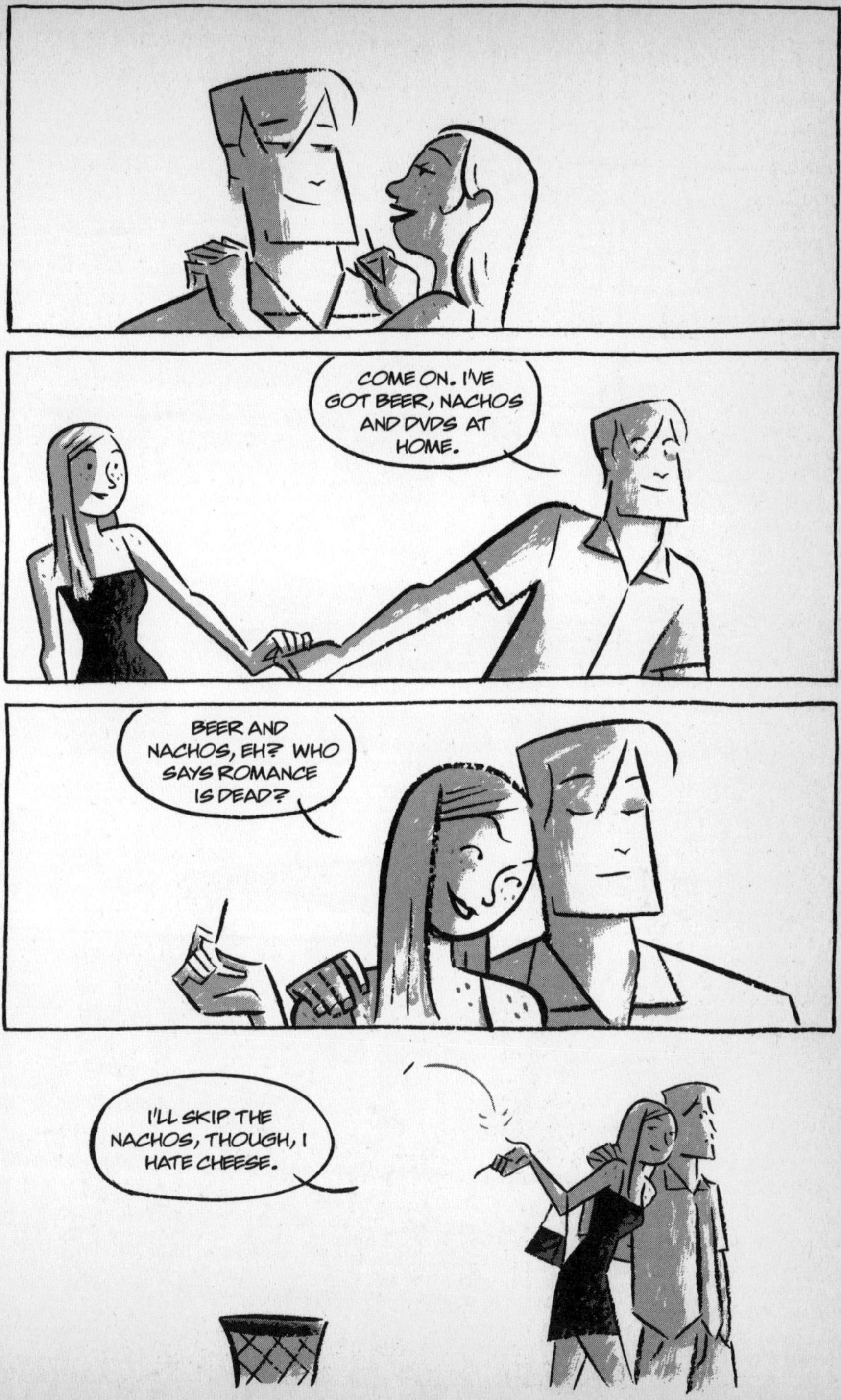
COME ON. I'VE GOT BEER, NACHOS AND DVDS AT HOME.
BEER AND NACHOS, EH? WHO SAYS ROMANCE IS DEAD?
I'LL SKIP THE NACHOS, THOUGH, I HATE CHEESE.

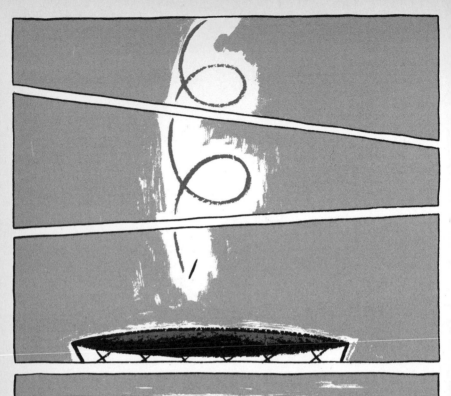

Love Fights™ #6

ONI PRESS

$2.99 U.S., $4.60 CAN.

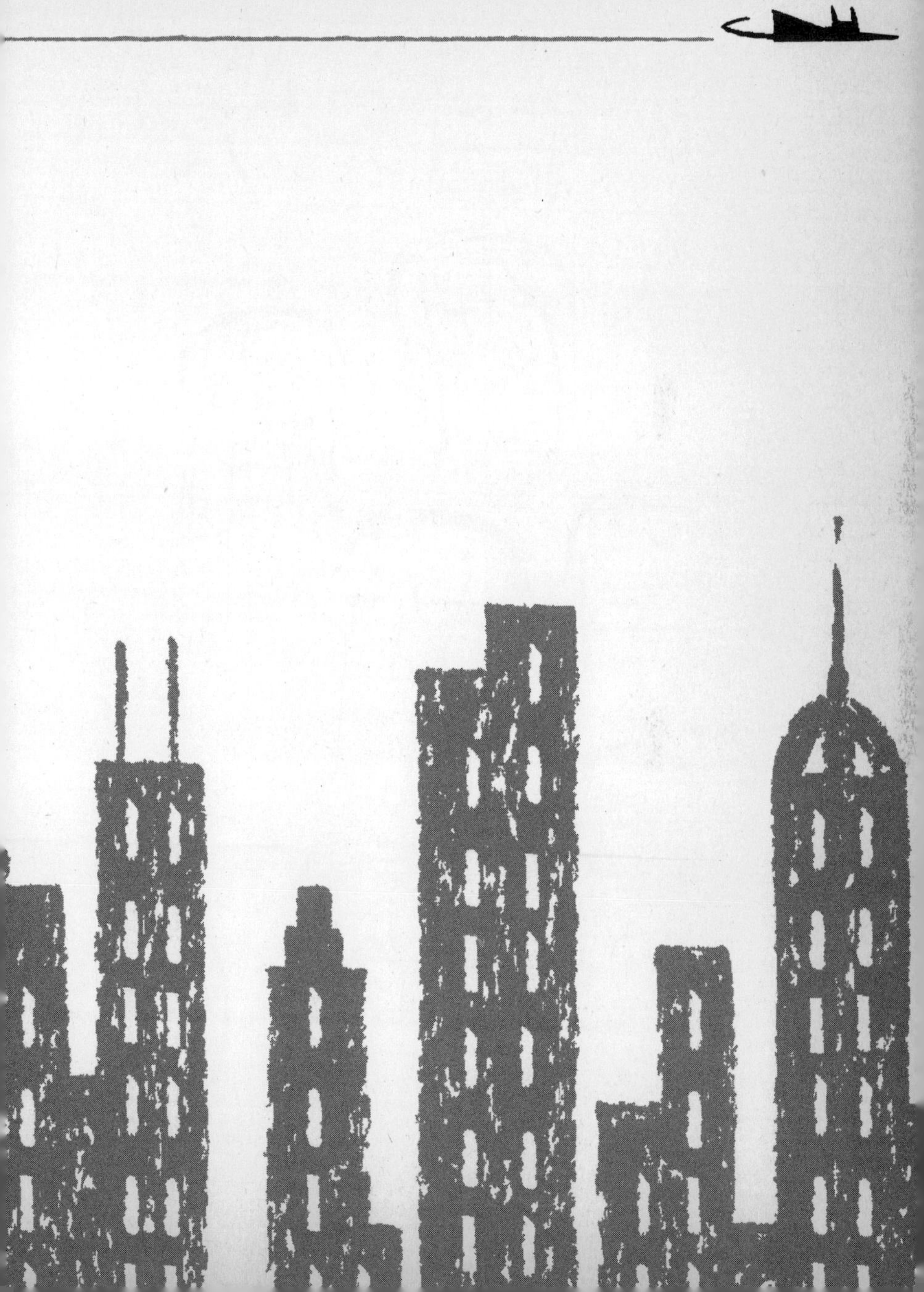

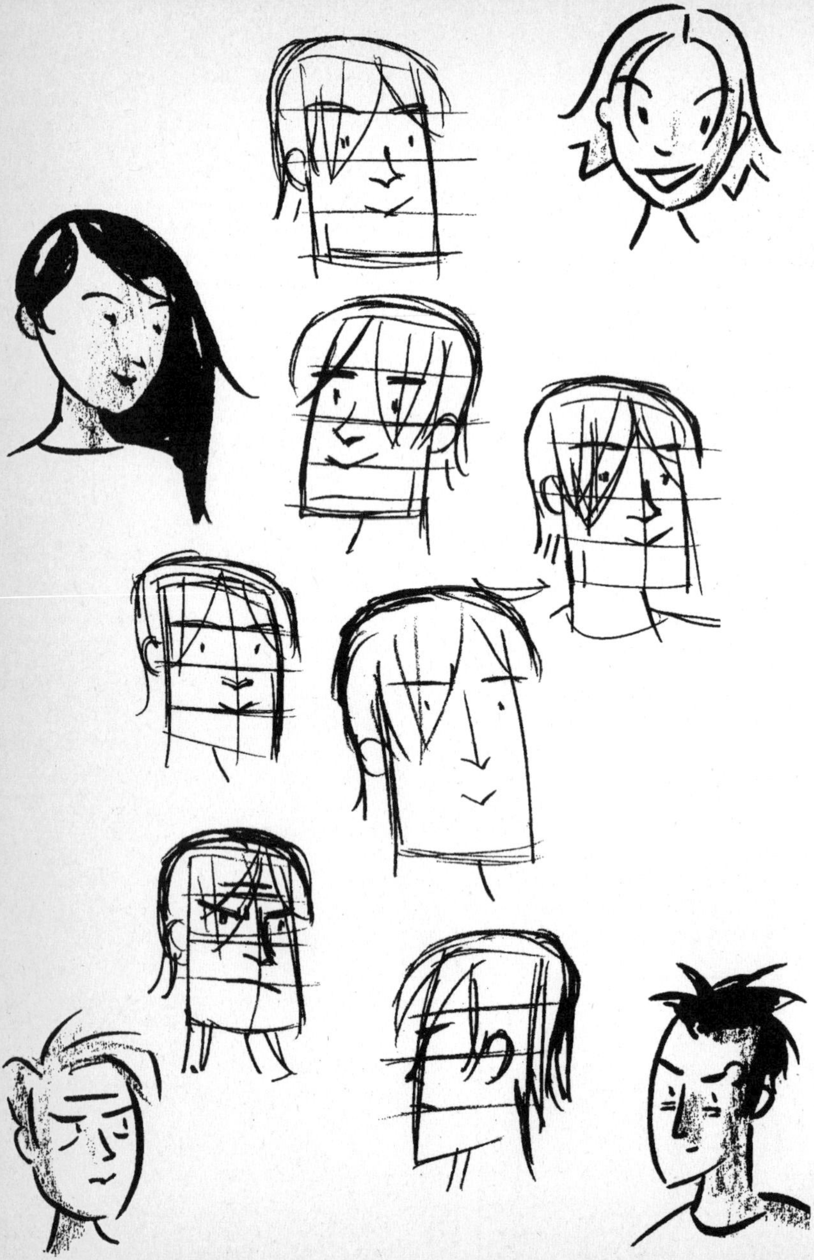

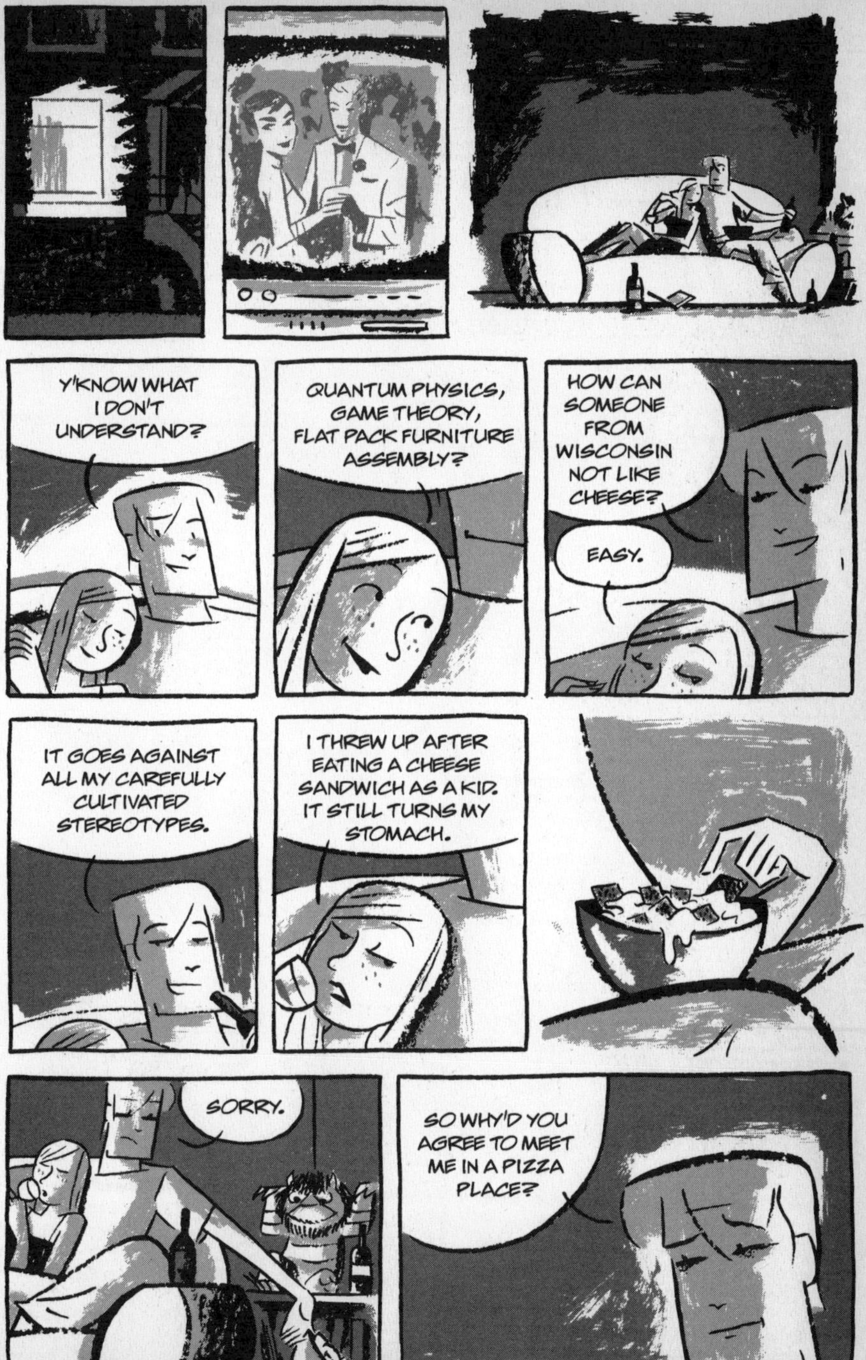

Y'KNOW WHAT I DON'T UNDERSTAND?
QUANTUM PHYSICS, GAME THEORY, FLAT PACK FURNITURE ASSEMBLY?
HOW CAN SOMEONE FROM WISCONSIN NOT LIKE CHEESE?
EASY.
IT GOES AGAINST ALL MY CAREFULLY CULTIVATED STEREOTYPES.
I THREW UP AFTER EATING A CHEESE SANDWICH AS A KID. IT STILL TURNS MY STOMACH.
SORRY.
SO WHY'D YOU AGREE TO MEET ME IN A PIZZA PLACE?

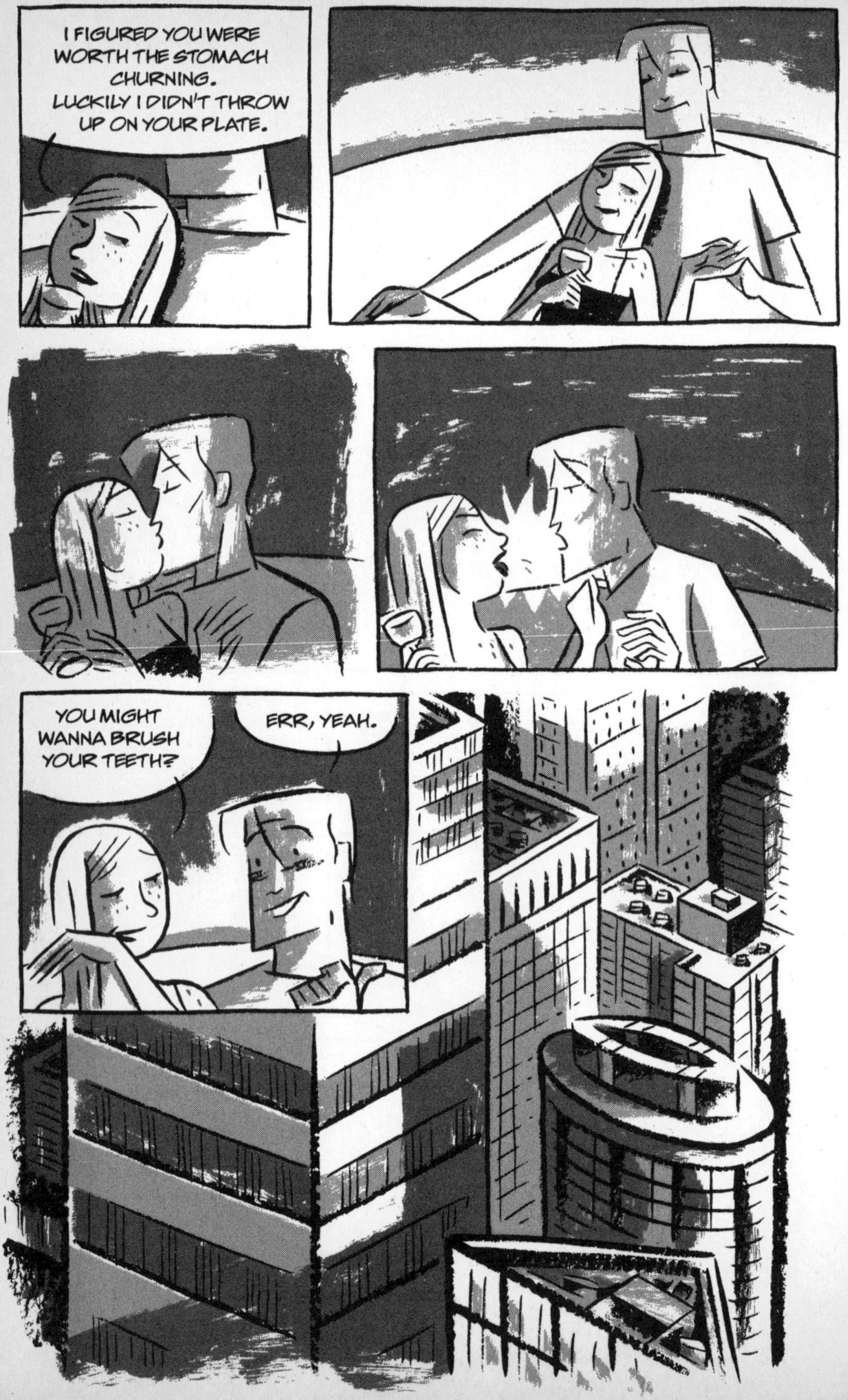
I FIGURED YOU WERE WORTH THE STOMACH CHURNING. LUCKILY I DIDN'T THROW UP ON YOUR PLATE.
YOU MIGHT WANNA BRUSH YOUR TEETH?
ERR, YEAH.

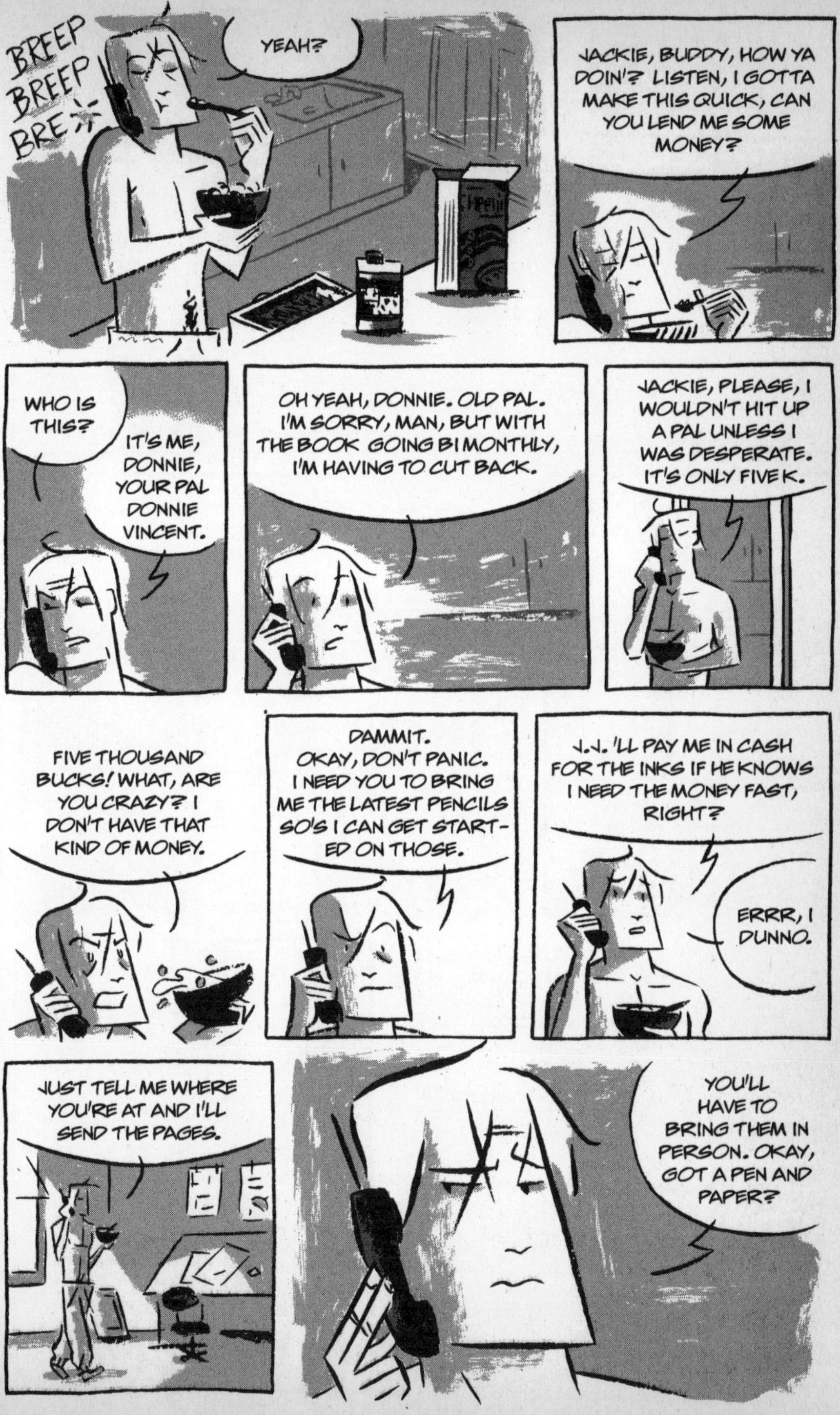
BREEP BREEP BRE
YEAH?
JACKIE, BUDDY, HOW YA DOIN'? LISTEN, I GOTTA MAKE THIS QUICK, CAN YOU LEND ME SOME MONEY?
WHO IS THIS?
IT'S ME, DONNIE, YOUR PAL DONNIE VINCENT.
OH YEAH, DONNIE. OLD PAL. I'M SORRY, MAN, BUT WITH THE BOOK GOING BI MONTHLY, I'M HAVING TO CUT BACK.
JACKIE, PLEASE, I WOULDN'T HIT UP A PAL UNLESS I WAS DESPERATE. IT'S ONLY FIVE K.
FIVE THOUSAND BUCKS! WHAT, ARE YOU CRAZY? I DON'T HAVE THAT KIND OF MONEY.
DAMMIT. OKAY, DON'T PANIC. I NEED YOU TO BRING ME THE LATEST PENCILS SO'S I CAN GET START-ED ON THOSE.
J.J. 'LL PAY ME IN CASH FOR THE INKS IF HE KNOWS I NEED THE MONEY FAST, RIGHT?
ERRR, I DUNNO.
JUST TELL ME WHERE YOU'RE AT AND I'LL SEND THE PAGES.
YOU'LL HAVE TO BRING THEM IN PERSON. OKAY, GOT A PEN AND PAPER?

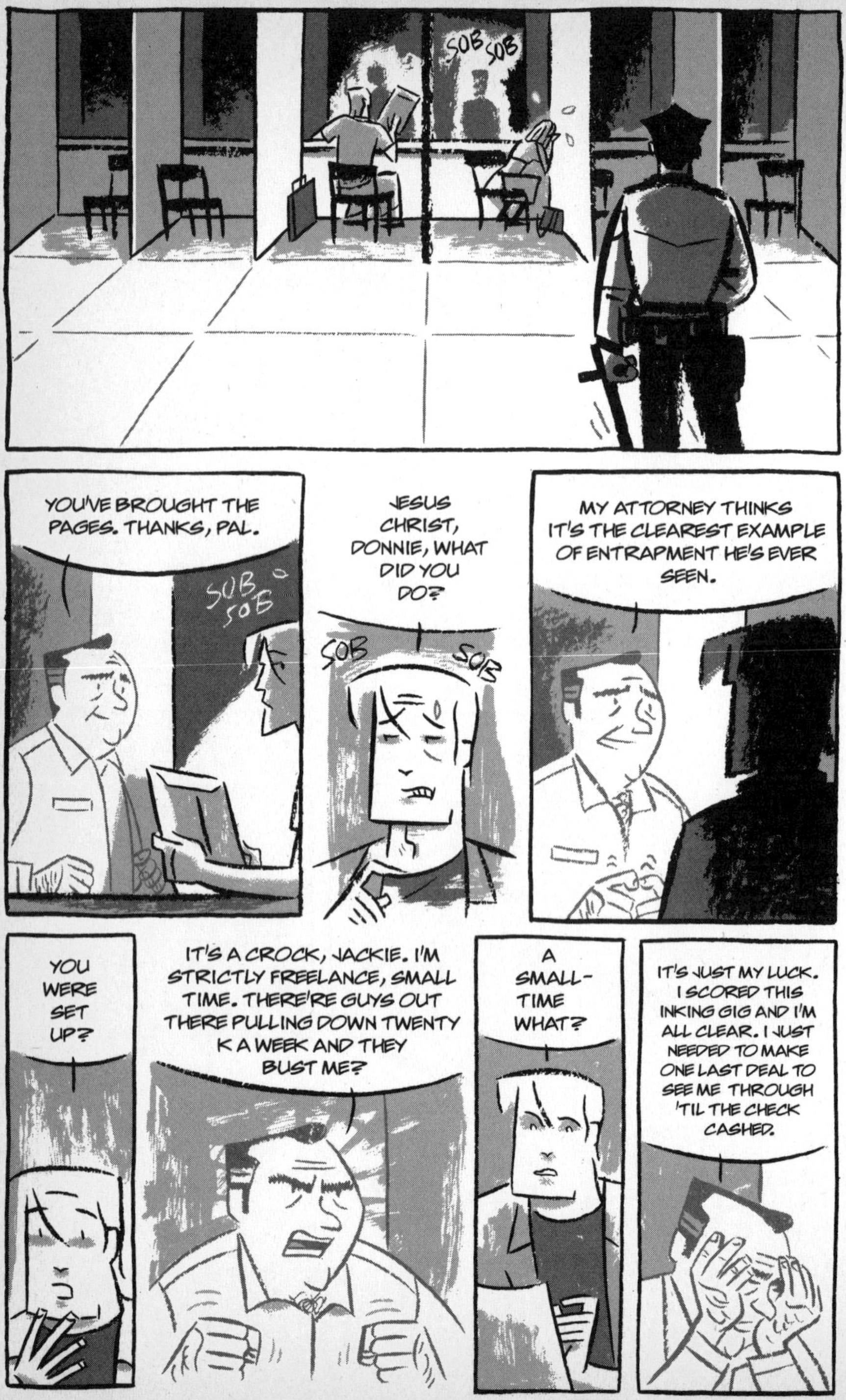
SOB SOB
YOU'VE BROUGHT THE PAGES. THANKS, PAL.
SOB SOB
JESUS CHRIST, DONNIE, WHAT DID YOU DO?
SOB SOB
MY ATTORNEY THINKS IT'S THE CLEAREST EXAMPLE OF ENTRAPMENT HE'S EVER SEEN.
YOU WERE SET UP?
IT'S A CROCK, JACKIE. I'M STRICTLY FREELANCE, SMALL TIME. THERE'RE GUYS OUT THERE PULLING DOWN TWENTY K A WEEK AND THEY BUST ME?
A SMALL-TIME WHAT?
IT'S JUST MY LUCK. I SCORED THIS INKING GIG AND I'M ALL CLEAR. I JUST NEEDED TO MAKE ONE LAST DEAL TO SEE ME THROUGH 'TIL THE CHECK CASHED.

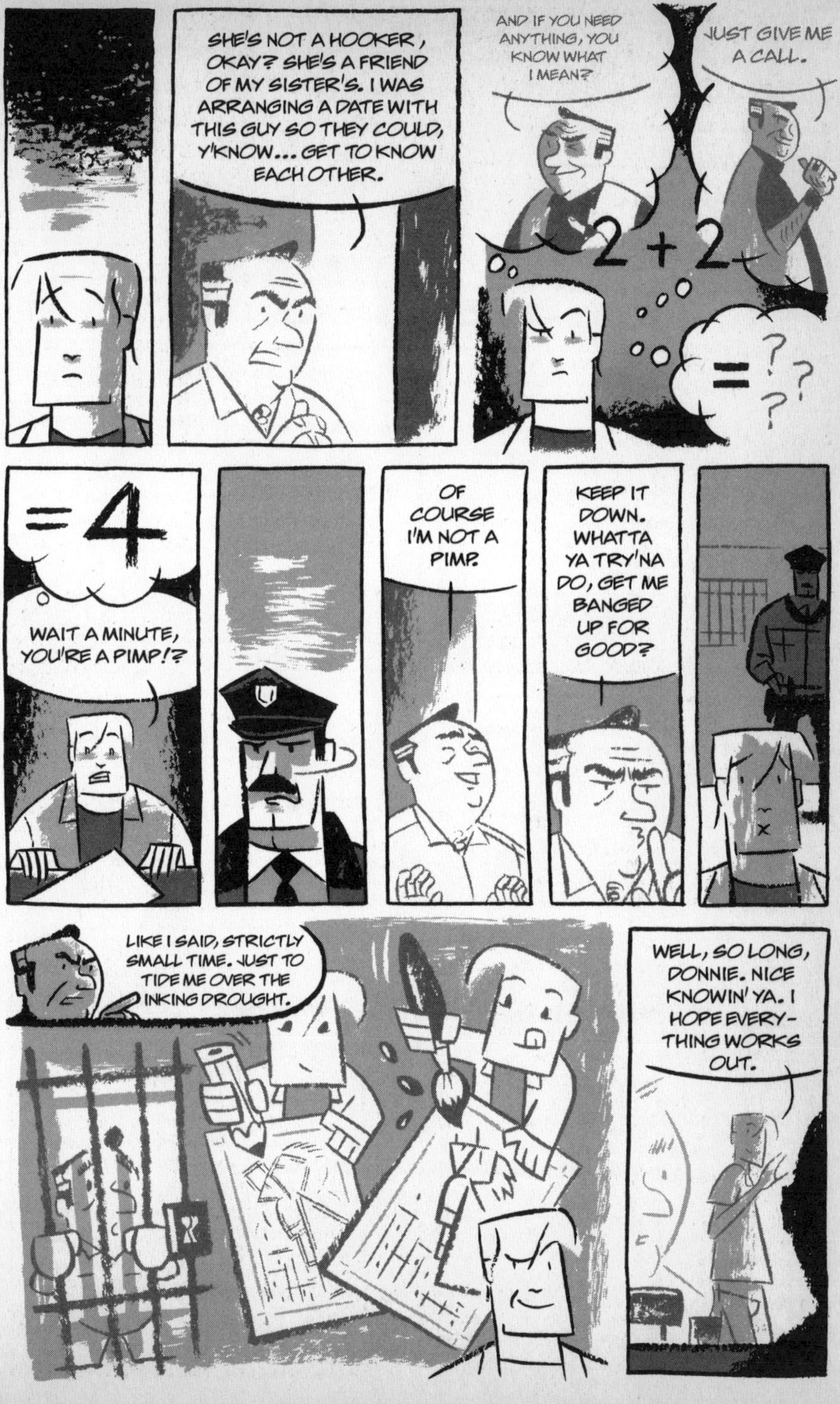
SHE'S NOT A HOOKER, OKAY? SHE'S A FRIEND OF MY SISTER'S. I WAS ARRANGING A DATE WITH THIS GUY SO THEY COULD, Y'KNOW... GET TO KNOW EACH OTHER.
AND IF YOU NEED ANYTHING, YOU KNOW WHAT I MEAN?
JUST GIVE ME A CALL.
2 + 2
= ? ? ?
= 4
WAIT A MINUTE, YOU'RE A PIMP!?
OF COURSE I'M NOT A PIMP.
KEEP IT DOWN. WHATTA YA TRY'NA DO, GET ME BANGED UP FOR GOOD?
LIKE I SAID, STRICTLY SMALL TIME. JUST TO TIDE ME OVER THE INKING DROUGHT.
WELL, SO LONG, DONNIE. NICE KNOWIN' YA. I HOPE EVERY-THING WORKS OUT.

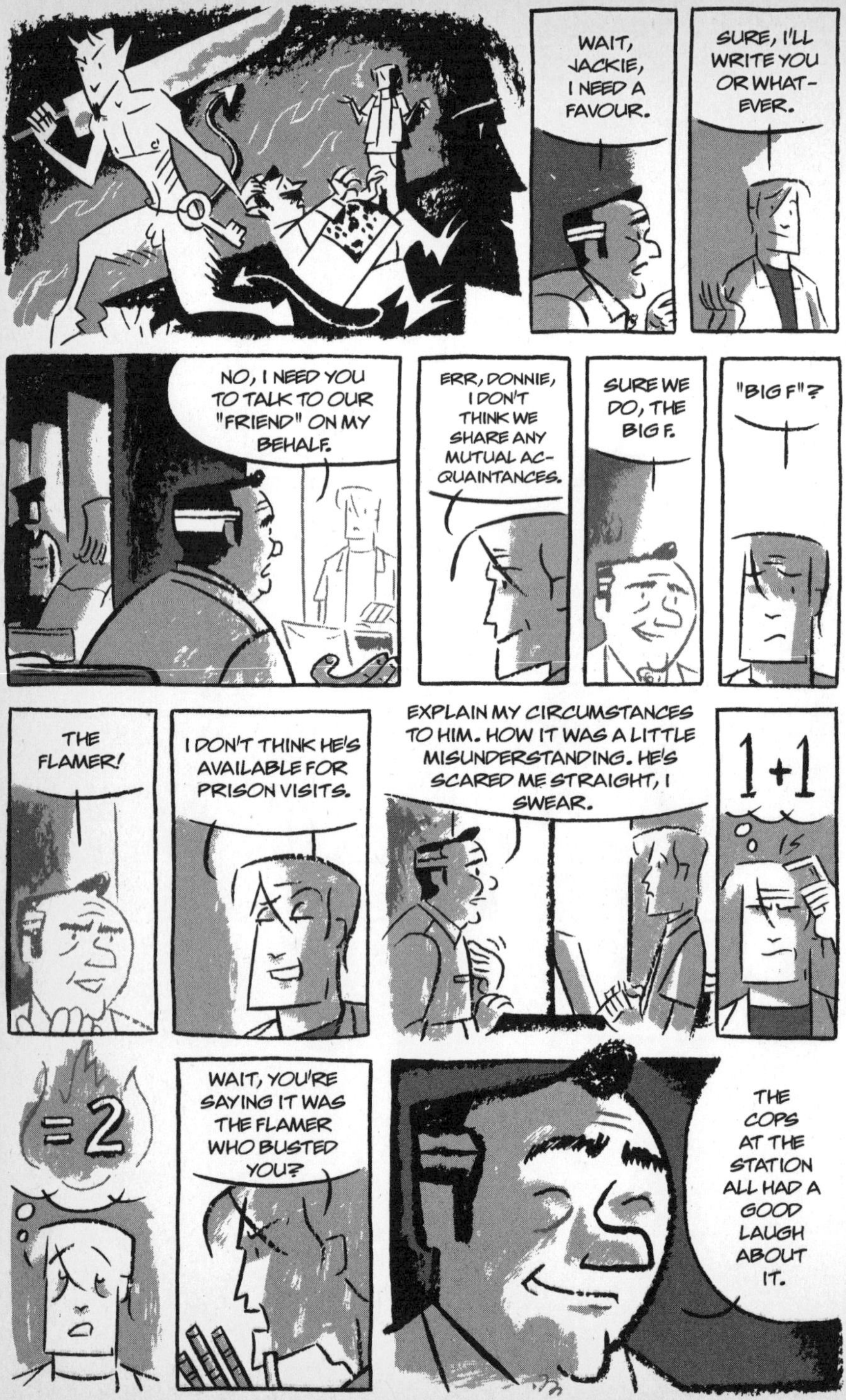
WAIT, JACKIE, I NEED A FAVOUR.
SURE, I'LL WRITE YOU OR WHAT-EVER.
NO, I NEED YOU TO TALK TO OUR "FRIEND" ON MY BEHALF.
ERR, DONNIE, I DON'T THINK WE SHARE ANY MUTUAL AC-QUAINTANCES.
SURE WE DO, THE BIG F.
"BIG F"?
THE FLAMER!
I DON'T THINK HE'S AVAILABLE FOR PRISON VISITS.
EXPLAIN MY CIRCUMSTANCES TO HIM. HOW IT WAS A LITTLE MISUNDERSTANDING. HE'S SCARED ME STRAIGHT, I SWEAR.
1+1
=2
WAIT, YOU'RE SAYING IT WAS THE FLAMER WHO BUSTED YOU?
THE COPS AT THE STATION ALL HAD A GOOD LAUGH ABOUT IT.

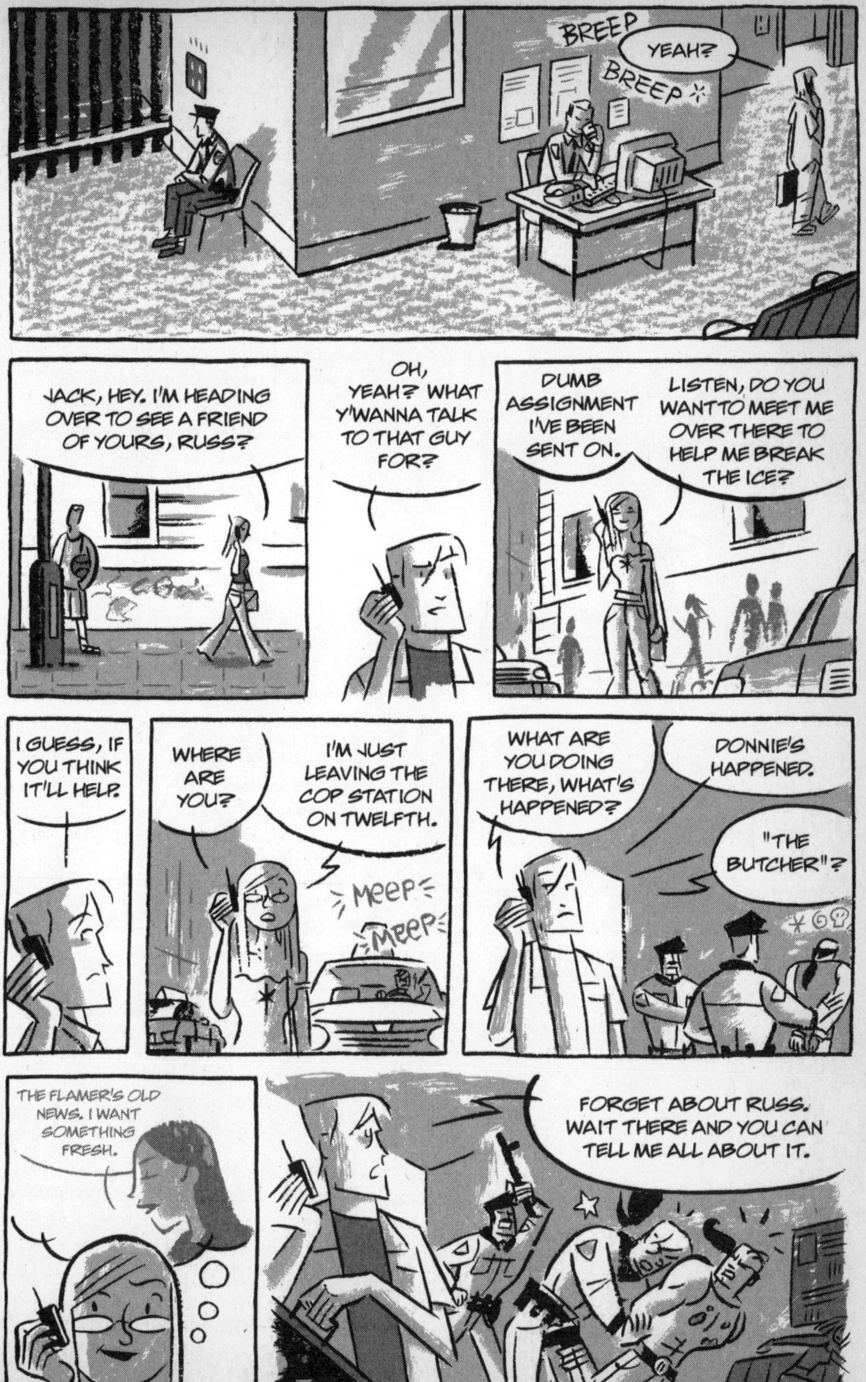
BREEP
YEAH?
BREEP
JACK, HEY. I'M HEADING OVER TO SEE A FRIEND OF YOURS, RUSS?
OH, YEAH? WHAT Y'WANNA TALK TO THAT GUY FOR?
DUMB ASSIGNMENT I'VE BEEN SENT ON.
LISTEN, DO YOU WANT TO MEET ME OVER THERE TO HELP ME BREAK THE ICE?
I GUESS, IF YOU THINK IT'LL HELP.
WHERE ARE YOU?
I'M JUST LEAVING THE COP STATION ON TWELFTH.
MEEP
MEEP
WHAT ARE YOU DOING THERE, WHAT'S HAPPENED?
DONNIE'S HAPPENED.
"THE BUTCHER"?
THE FLAMER'S OLD NEWS. I WANT SOMETHING FRESH.
FORGET ABOUT RUSS. WAIT THERE AND YOU CAN TELL ME ALL ABOUT IT.

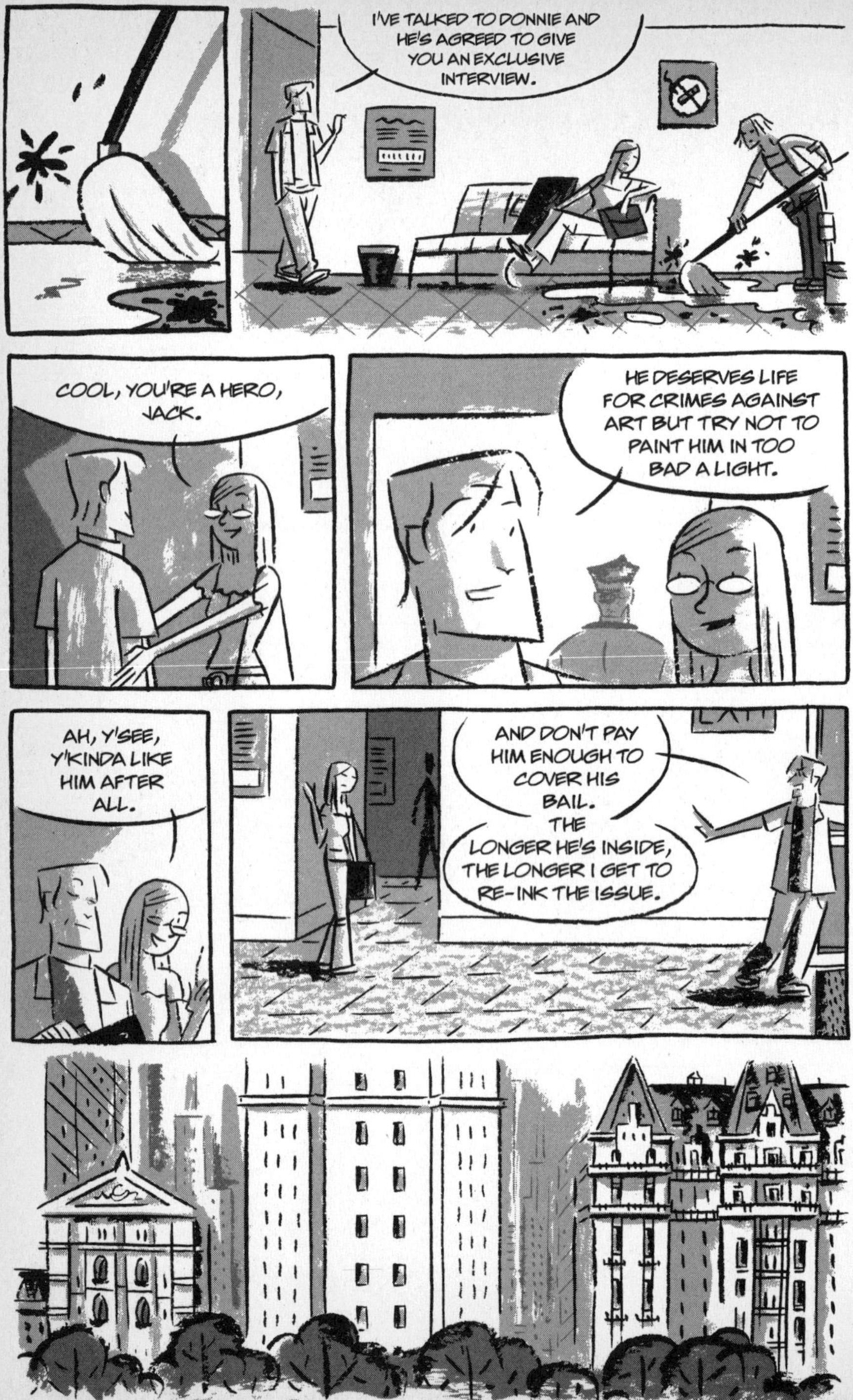
I'VE TALKED TO DONNIE AND HE'S AGREED TO GIVE YOU AN EXCLUSIVE INTERVIEW.
COOL, YOU'RE A HERO, JACK.
HE DESERVES LIFE FOR CRIMES AGAINST ART BUT TRY NOT TO PAINT HIM IN TOO BAD A LIGHT.
AH, Y'SEE, Y'KINDA LIKE HIM AFTER ALL.
AND DON'T PAY HIM ENOUGH TO COVER HIS BAIL.
THE LONGER HE'S INSIDE, THE LONGER I GET TO RE-INK THE ISSUE.

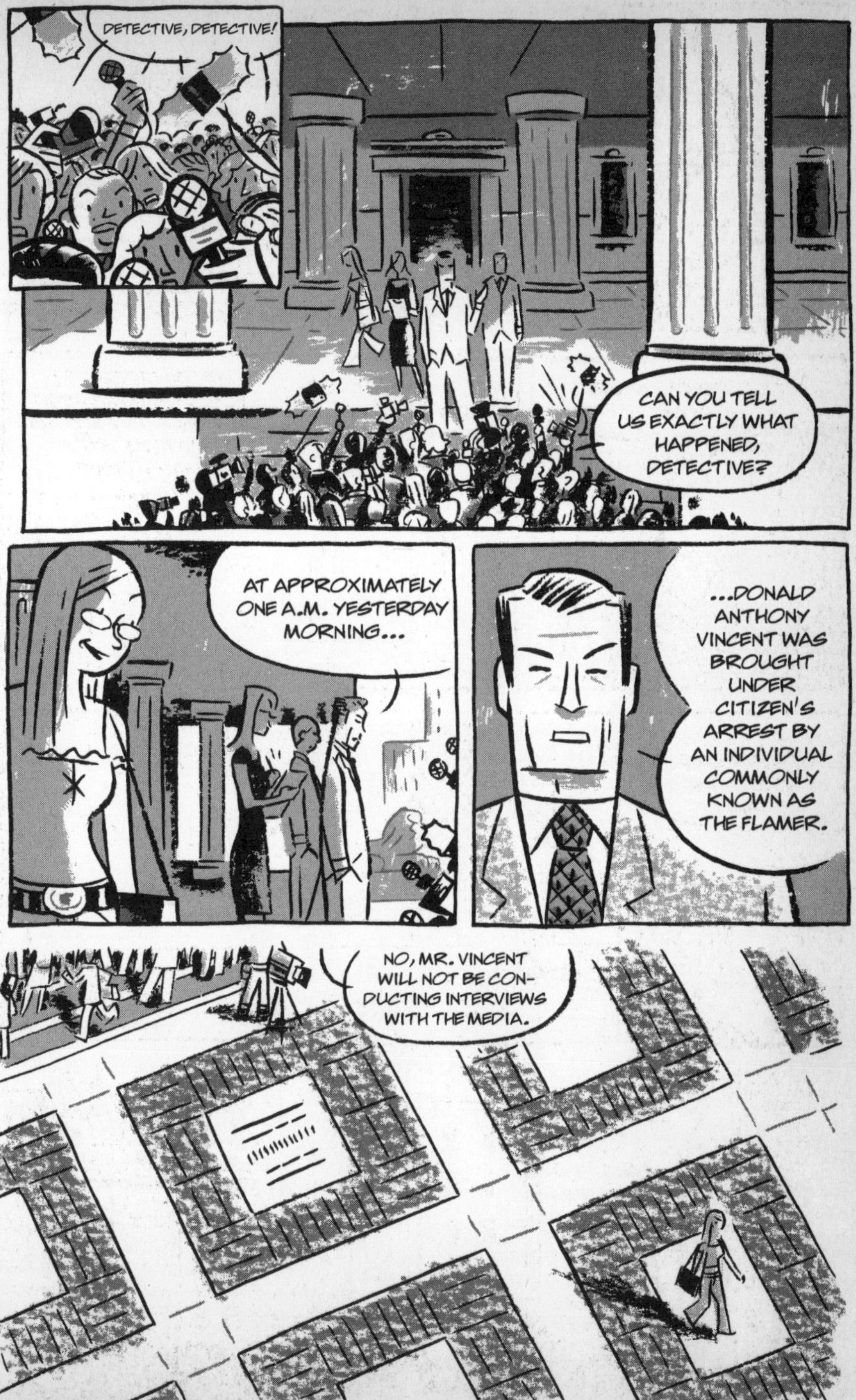

DETECTIVE, DETECTIVE!
CAN YOU TELL US EXACTLY WHAT HAPPENED, DETECTIVE?
AT APPROXIMATELY ONE A.M. YESTERDAY MORNING...
...DONALD ANTHONY VINCENT WAS BROUGHT UNDER CITIZEN'S ARREST BY AN INDIVIDUAL COMMONLY KNOWN AS THE FLAMER.
NO, MR. VINCENT WILL NOT BE CONDUCTING INTERVIEWS WITH THE MEDIA.

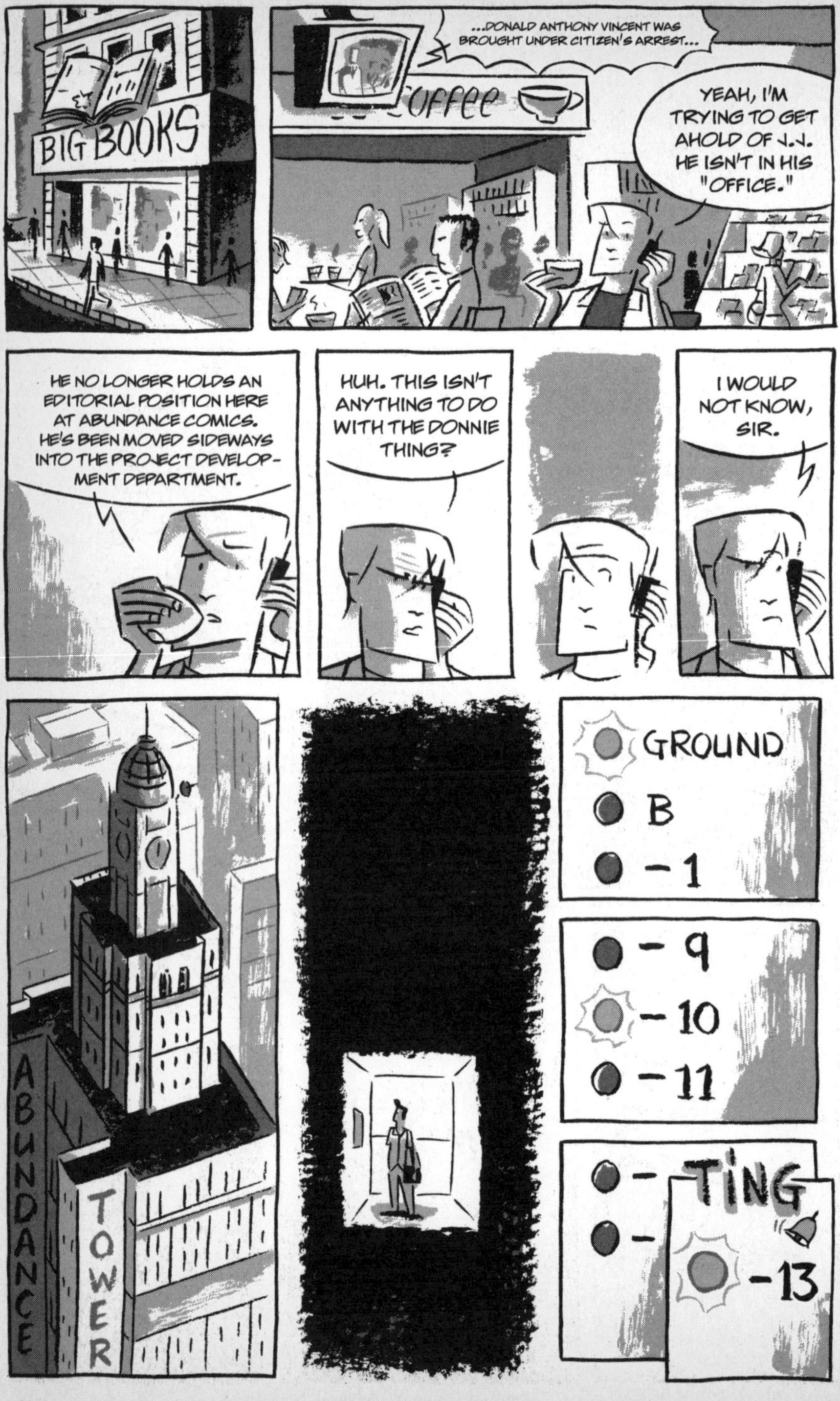

BIG BOOKS
...DONALD ANTHONY VINCENT WAS BROUGHT UNDER CITIZEN'S ARREST...
COFFEE
YEAH, I'M TRYING TO GET AHOLD OF J.J. HE ISN'T IN HIS "OFFICE."
HE NO LONGER HOLDS AN EDITORIAL POSITION HERE AT ABUNDANCE COMICS. HE'S BEEN MOVED SIDEWAYS INTO THE PROJECT DEVELOPMENT DEPARTMENT.
HUH. THIS ISN'T ANYTHING TO DO WITH THE DONNIE THING?
I WOULD NOT KNOW, SIR.
ABUNDANCE TOWER
GROUND
B
-1
-9
-10
-11
TING
-13

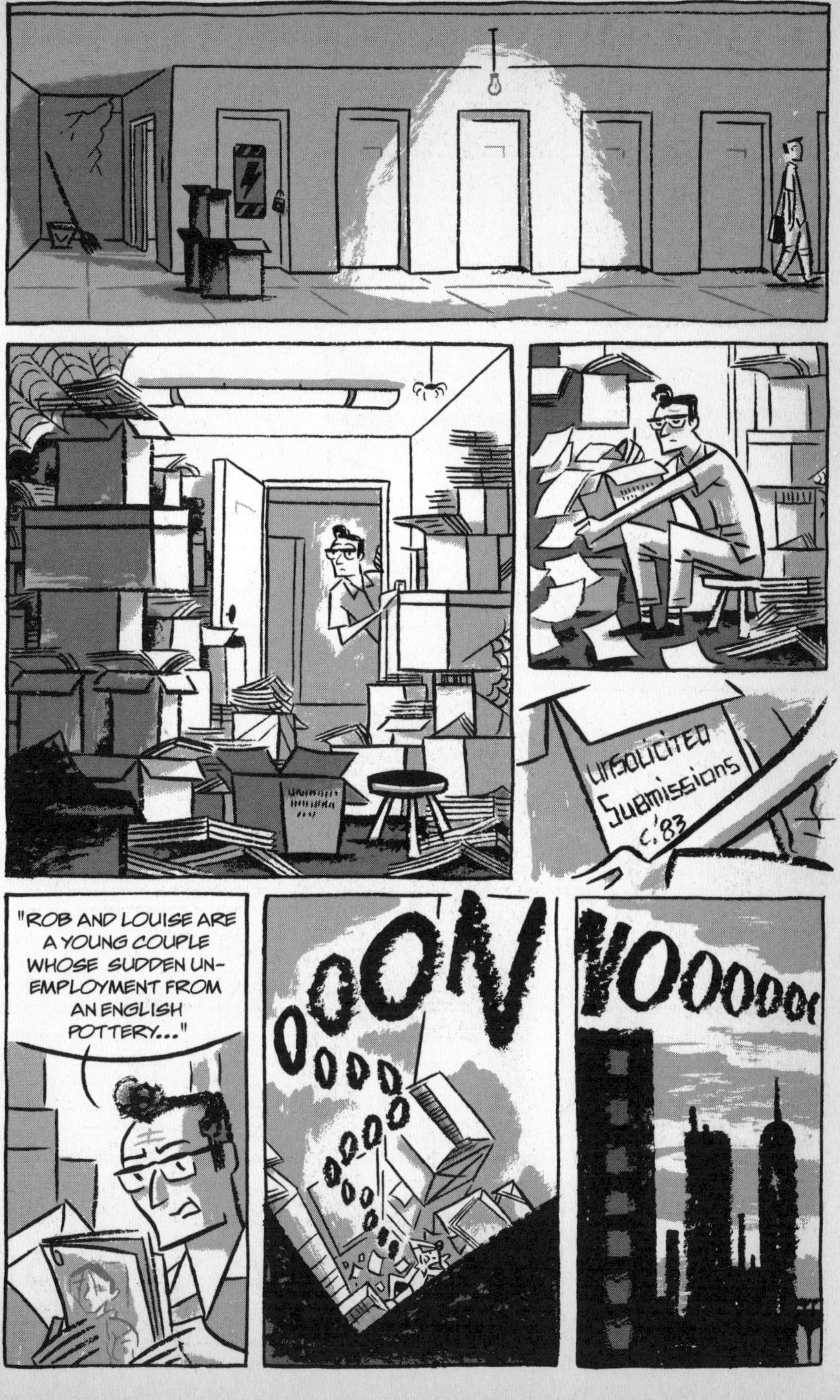
UNSOLICITED
Submissions
c.'83
"ROB AND LOUISE ARE A YOUNG COUPLE WHOSE SUDDEN UN-EMPLOYMENT FROM AN ENGLISH POTTERY..."
OOOON
VOOOOOO

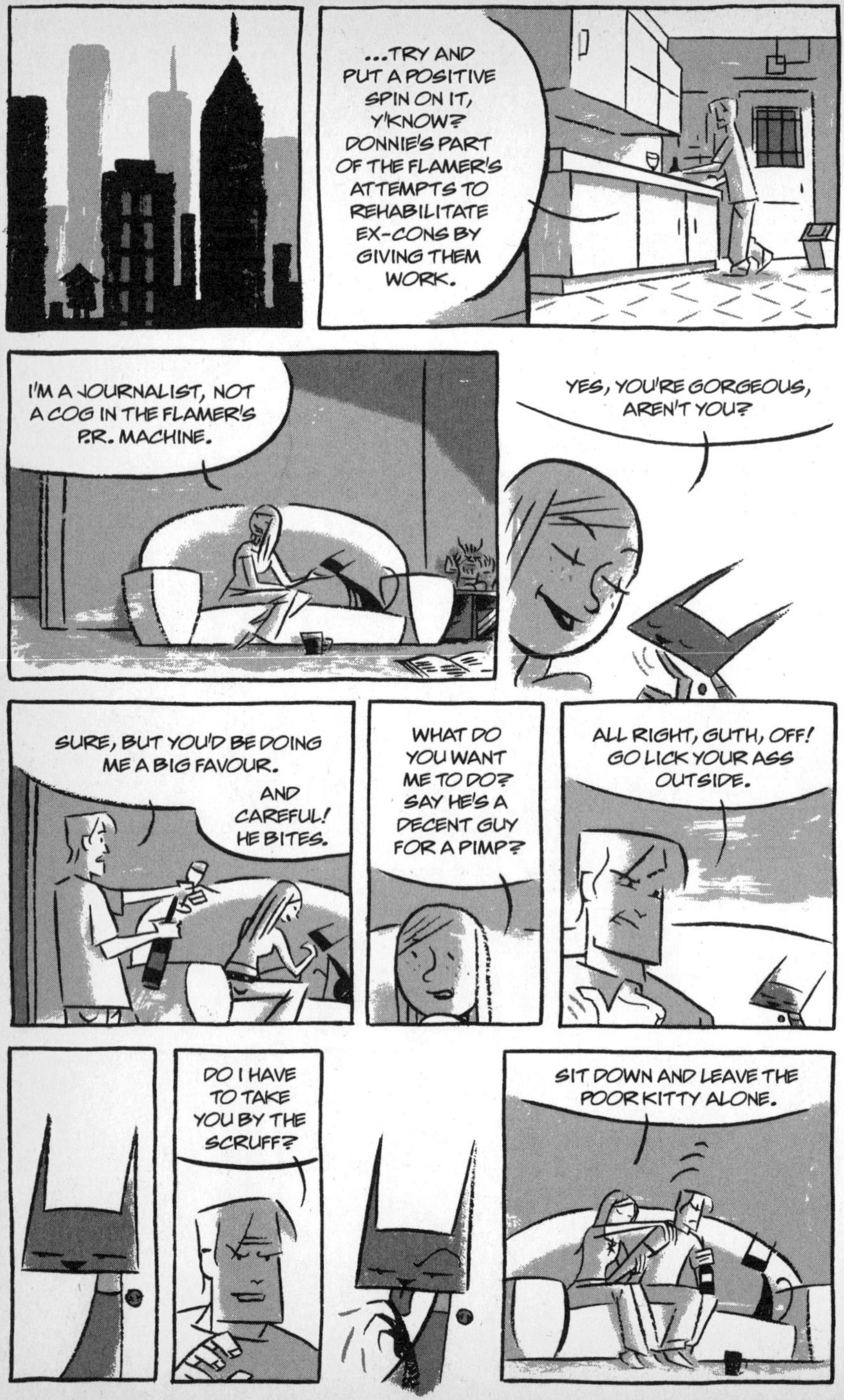
...TRY AND PUT A POSITIVE SPIN ON IT, Y'KNOW? DONNIE'S PART OF THE FLAMER'S ATTEMPTS TO REHABILITATE EX-CONS BY GIVING THEM WORK.
I'M A JOURNALIST, NOT A COG IN THE FLAMER'S P.R. MACHINE.
YES, YOU'RE GORGEOUS, AREN'T YOU?
SURE, BUT YOU'D BE DOING ME A BIG FAVOUR.
AND CAREFUL! HE BITES.
WHAT DO YOU WANT ME TO DO? SAY HE'S A DECENT GUY FOR A PIMP?
ALL RIGHT, GUTH, OFF! GO LICK YOUR ASS OUTSIDE.
DO I HAVE TO TAKE YOU BY THE SCRUFF?
SIT DOWN AND LEAVE THE POOR KITTY ALONE.

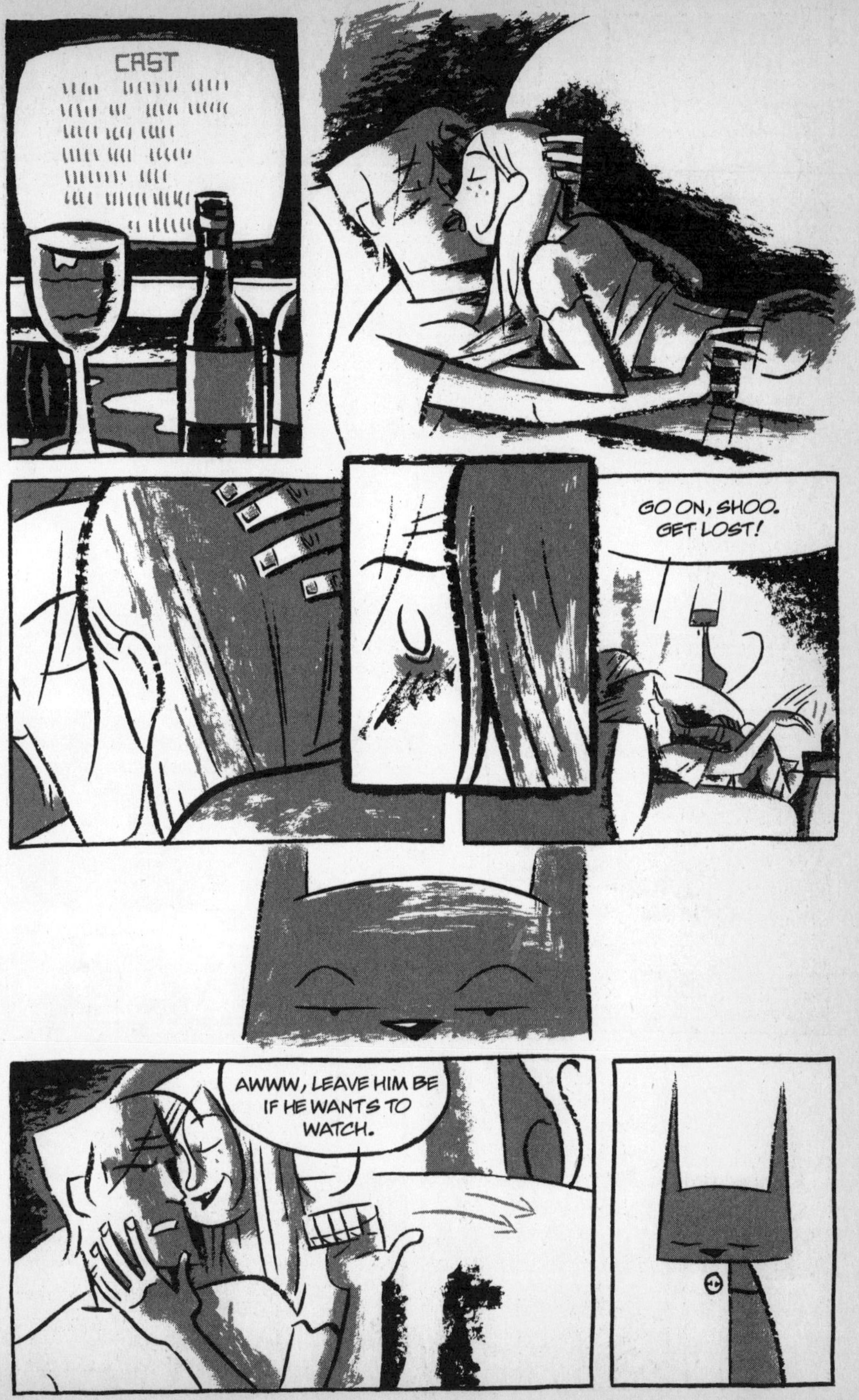
CAST
GO ON, SHOO. GET LOST!
AWWW, LEAVE HIM BE IF HE WANTS TO WATCH.

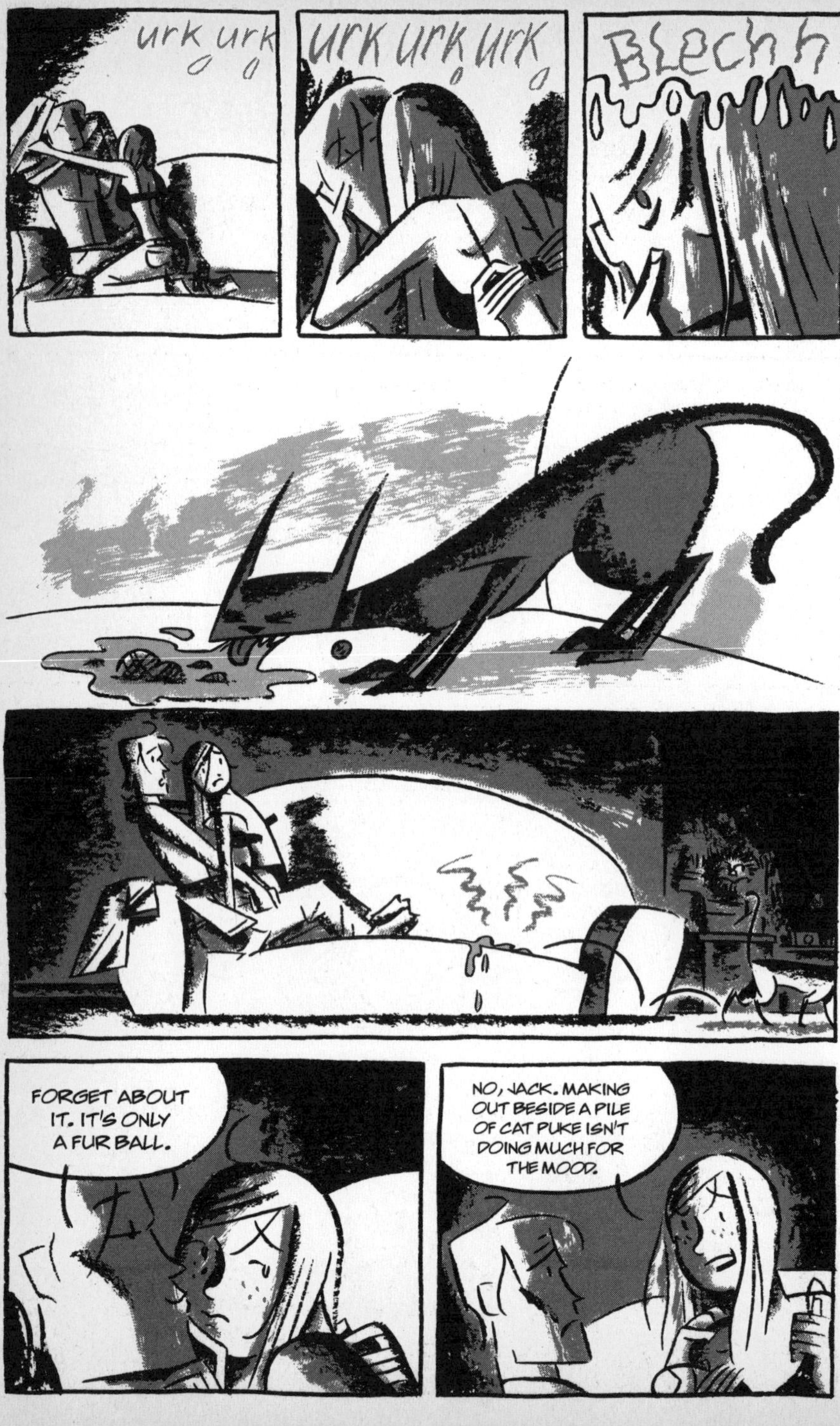
urk urk
urk urk urk
Blechh
FORGET ABOUT IT. IT'S ONLY A FUR BALL.
NO, JACK. MAKING OUT BESIDE A PILE OF CAT PUKE ISN'T DOING MUCH FOR THE MOOD.

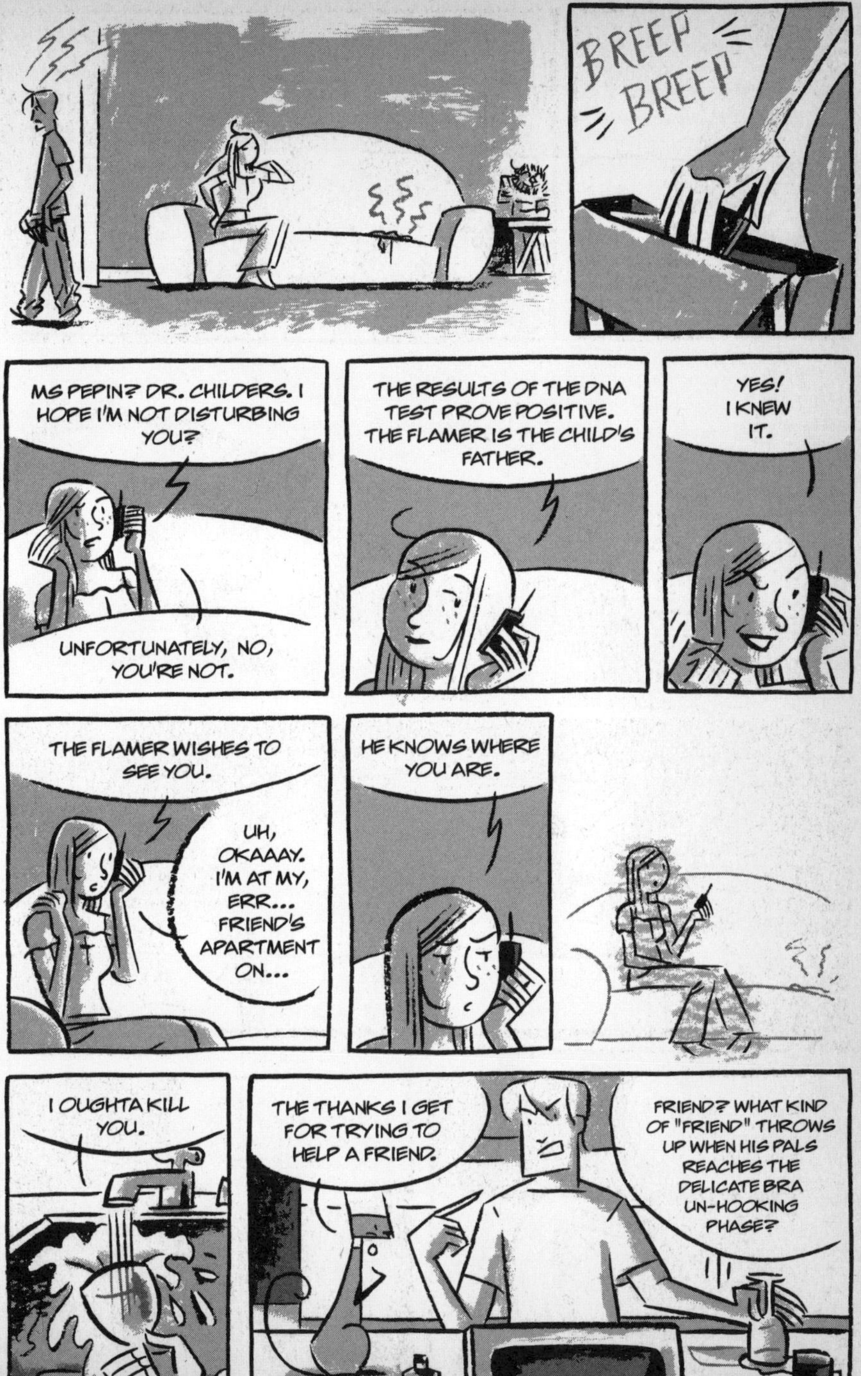
BREEP BREEP
MS PEPIN? DR. CHILDERS. I HOPE I'M NOT DISTURBING YOU?
UNFORTUNATELY, NO, YOU'RE NOT.
THE RESULTS OF THE DNA TEST PROVE POSITIVE. THE FLAMER IS THE CHILD'S FATHER.
YES! I KNEW IT.
THE FLAMER WISHES TO SEE YOU.
UH, OKAAAY. I'M AT MY, ERR... FRIEND'S APARTMENT ON...
HE KNOWS WHERE YOU ARE.
I OUGHTA KILL YOU.
THE THANKS I GET FOR TRYING TO HELP A FRIEND.
FRIEND? WHAT KIND OF "FRIEND" THROWS UP WHEN HIS PALS REACHES THE DELICATE BRA UN-HOOKING PHASE?

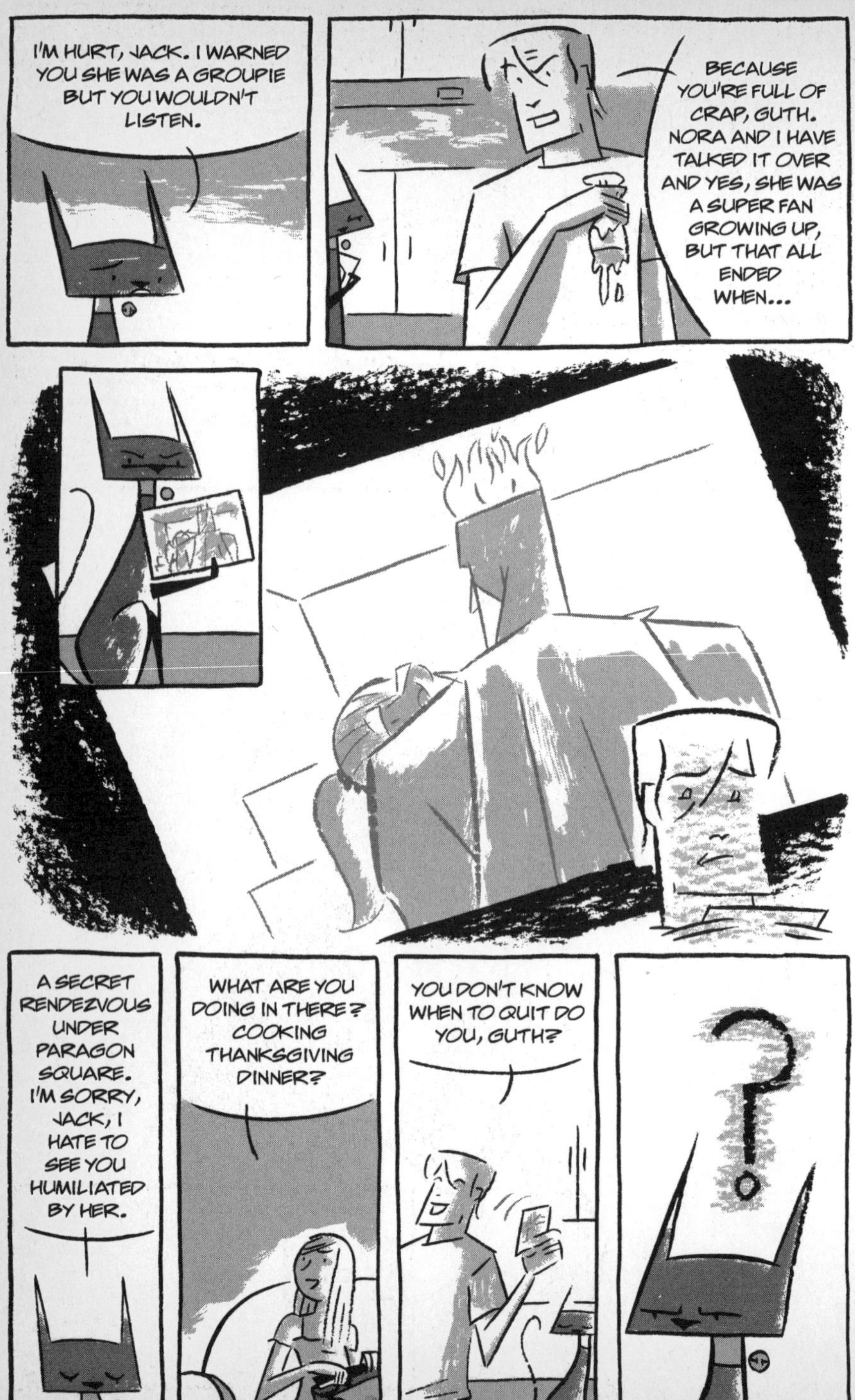
I'M HURT, JACK. I WARNED YOU SHE WAS A GROUPIE BUT YOU WOULDN'T LISTEN.
BECAUSE YOU'RE FULL OF CRAP, GUTH. NORA AND I HAVE TALKED IT OVER AND YES, SHE WAS A SUPER FAN GROWING UP, BUT THAT ALL ENDED WHEN...
A SECRET RENDEZVOUS UNDER PARAGON SQUARE. I'M SORRY, JACK, I HATE TO SEE YOU HUMILIATED BY HER.
WHAT ARE YOU DOING IN THERE? COOKING THANKSGIVING DINNER?
YOU DON'T KNOW WHEN TO QUIT DO YOU, GUTH?
?

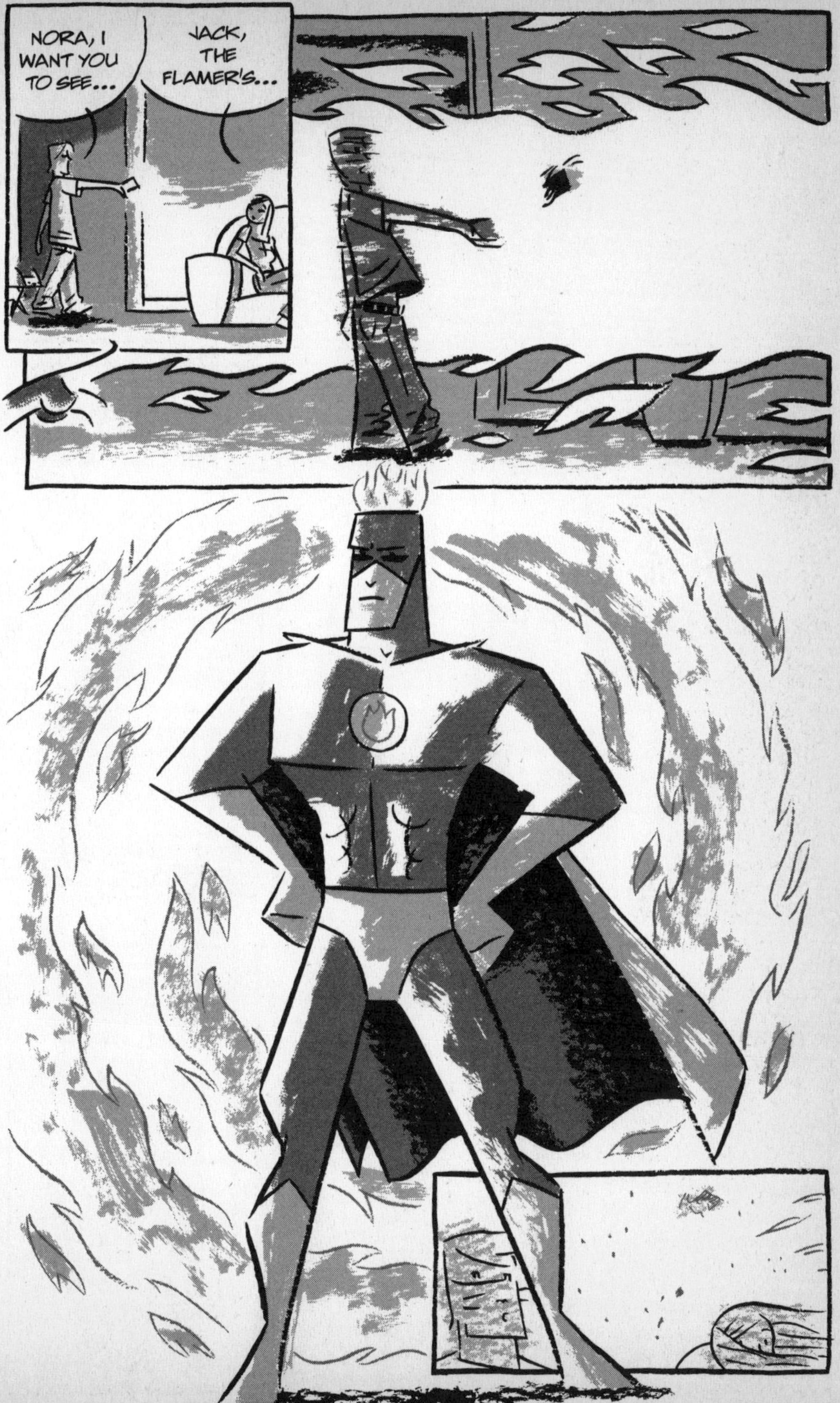
NORA, I WANT YOU TO SEE...
JACK, THE FLAMER'S...

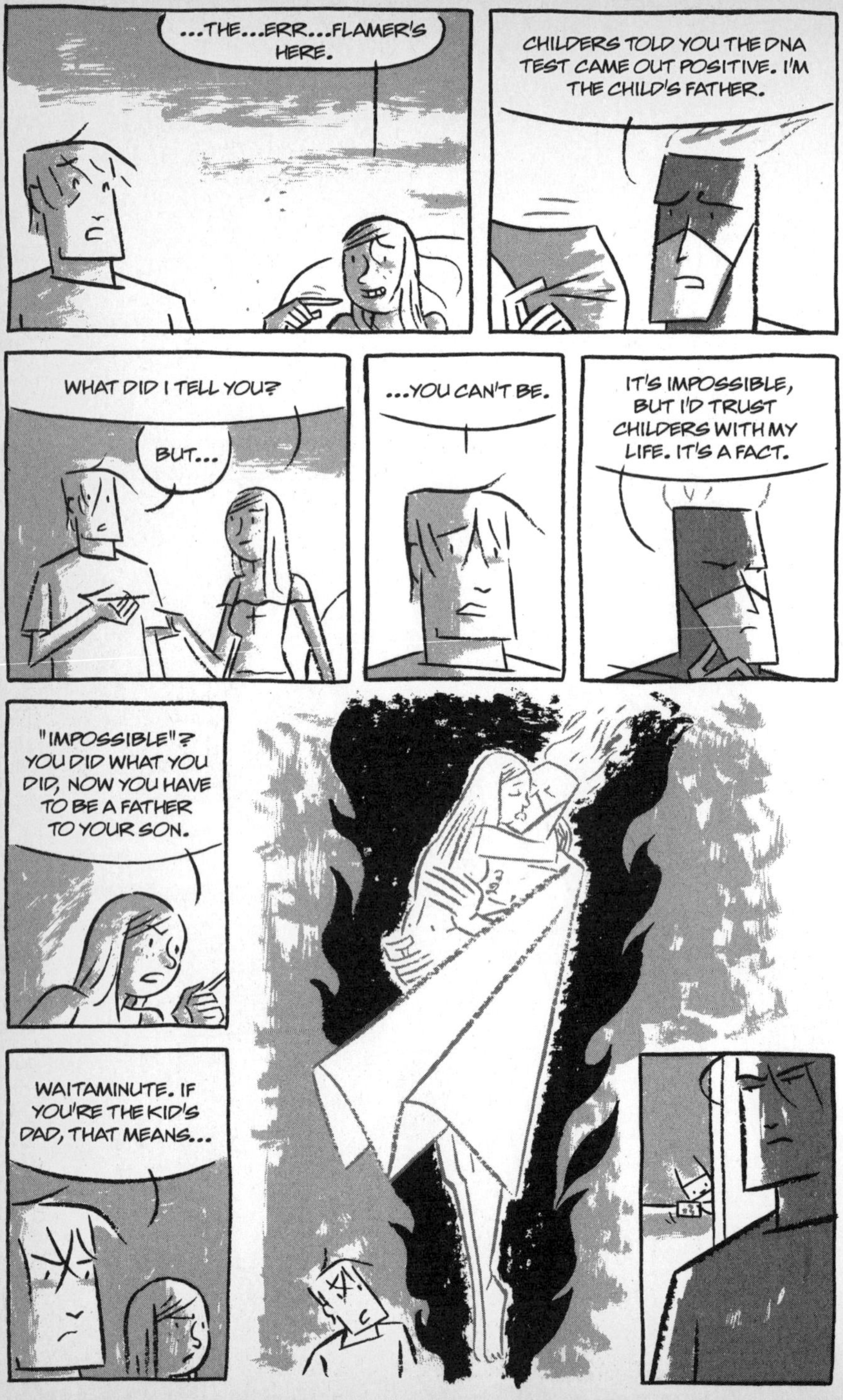
...THE...ERR...FLAMER'S HERE.
CHILDERS TOLD YOU THE DNA TEST CAME OUT POSITIVE. I'M THE CHILD'S FATHER.
WHAT DID I TELL YOU?
BUT...
...YOU CAN'T BE.
IT'S IMPOSSIBLE, BUT I'D TRUST CHILDERS WITH MY LIFE. IT'S A FACT.
"IMPOSSIBLE"? YOU DID WHAT YOU DID, NOW YOU HAVE TO BE A FATHER TO YOUR SON.
WAITAMINUTE. IF YOU'RE THE KID'S DAD, THAT MEANS...

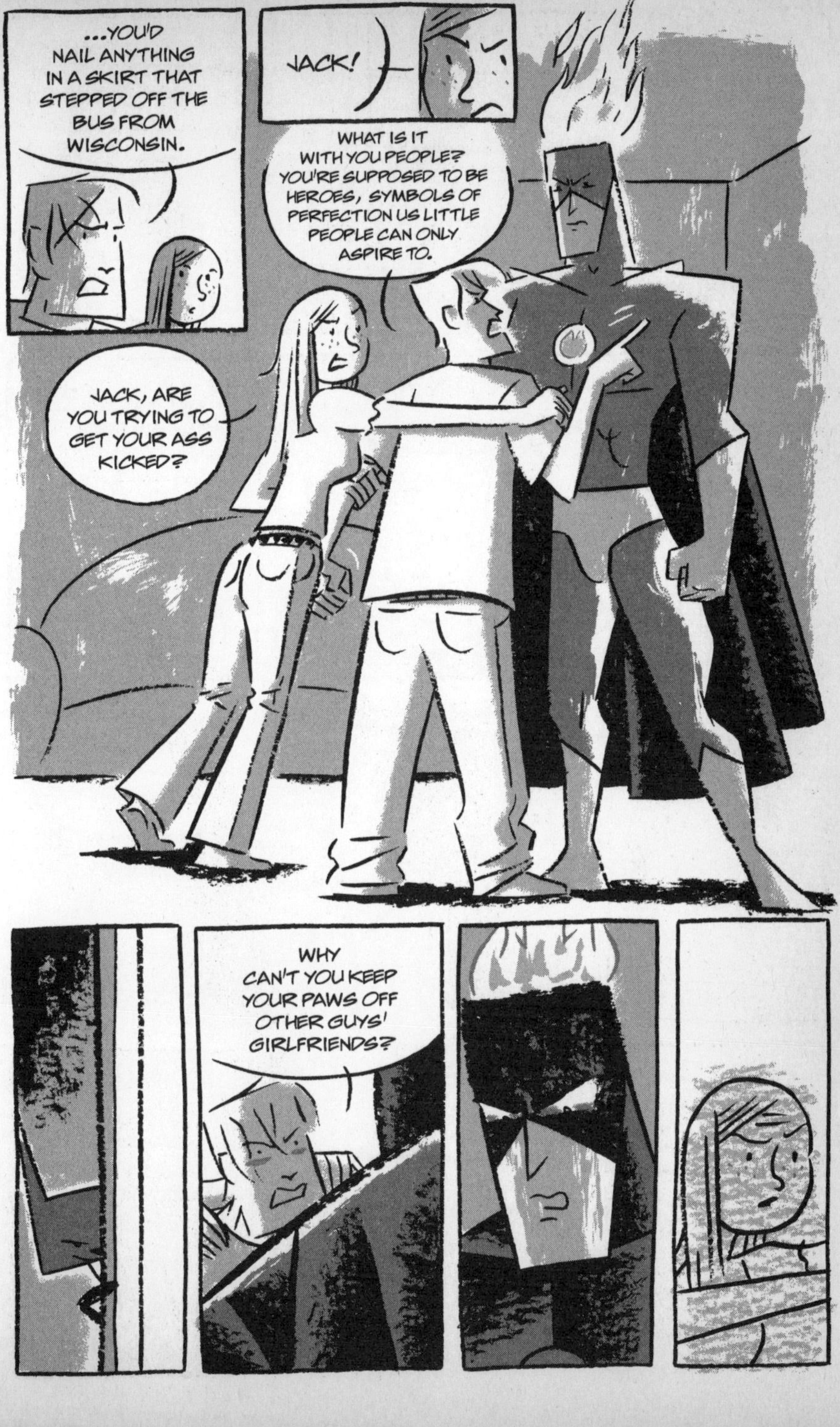
...YOU'D NAIL ANYTHING IN A SKIRT THAT STEPPED OFF THE BUS FROM WISCONSIN.
JACK!
WHAT IS IT WITH YOU PEOPLE? YOU'RE SUPPOSED TO BE HEROES, SYMBOLS OF PERFECTION US LITTLE PEOPLE CAN ONLY ASPIRE TO.
JACK, ARE YOU TRYING TO GET YOUR ASS KICKED?
WHY CAN'T YOU KEEP YOUR PAWS OFF OTHER GUYS' GIRLFRIENDS?

HAVE YOU ANY IDEA WHAT THE HELL YOU'RE TALKING ABOUT, JACK?

YOU THINK I'M STUPID?

ANYTHING I SAY HERE IS OFF THE RECORD, CORRECT?

WHATEVER.

ERR, OKAY.

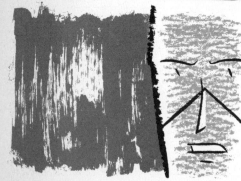

I HAVEN'T SLEPT WITH A WOMAN IN OVER A DECADE.

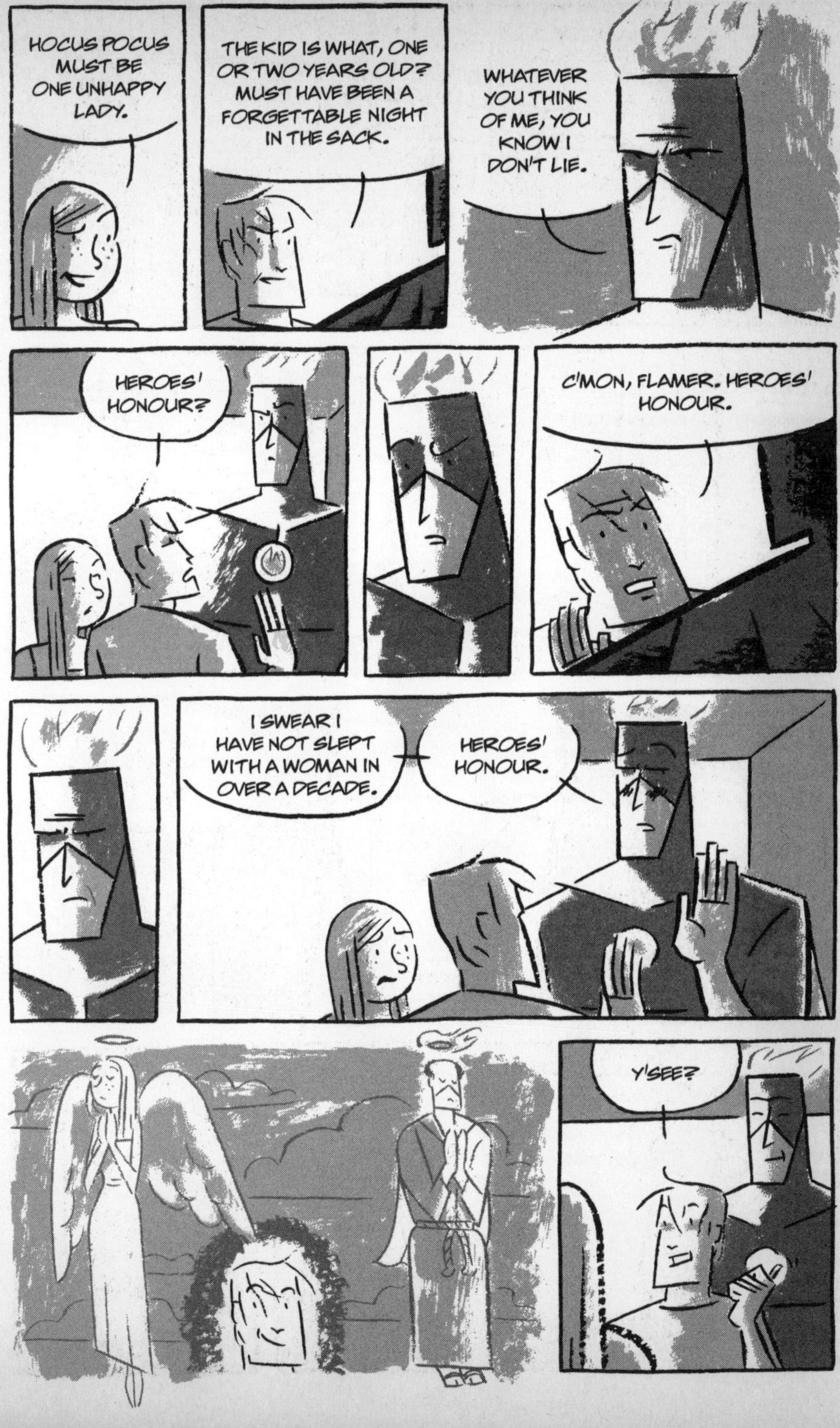
HOCUS POCUS MUST BE ONE UNHAPPY LADY.
THE KID IS WHAT, ONE OR TWO YEARS OLD? MUST HAVE BEEN A FORGETTABLE NIGHT IN THE SACK.
WHATEVER YOU THINK OF ME, YOU KNOW I DON'T LIE.
HEROES' HONOUR?
C'MON, FLAMER. HEROES' HONOUR.
I SWEAR I HAVE NOT SLEPT WITH A WOMAN IN OVER A DECADE.
HEROES' HONOUR.
Y'SEE?

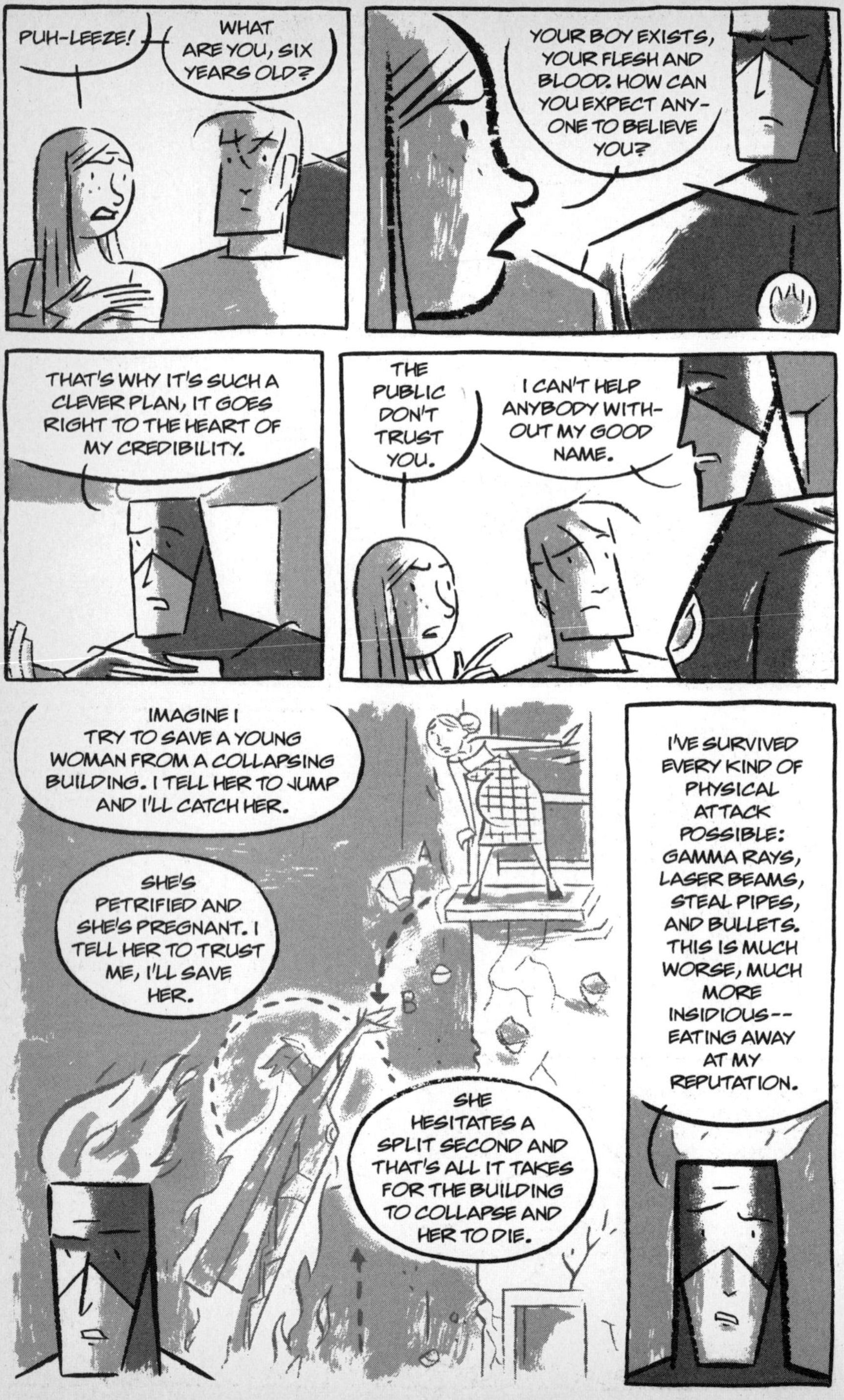
PUH-LEEZE!
WHAT ARE YOU, SIX YEARS OLD?
YOUR BOY EXISTS, YOUR FLESH AND BLOOD. HOW CAN YOU EXPECT ANY-ONE TO BELIEVE YOU?
THAT'S WHY IT'S SUCH A CLEVER PLAN, IT GOES RIGHT TO THE HEART OF MY CREDIBILITY.
THE PUBLIC DON'T TRUST YOU.
I CAN'T HELP ANYBODY WITH-OUT MY GOOD NAME.
IMAGINE I TRY TO SAVE A YOUNG WOMAN FROM A COLLAPSING BUILDING. I TELL HER TO JUMP AND I'LL CATCH HER.
SHE'S PETRIFIED AND SHE'S PREGNANT. I TELL HER TO TRUST ME, I'LL SAVE HER.
A
B
SHE HESITATES A SPLIT SECOND AND THAT'S ALL IT TAKES FOR THE BUILDING TO COLLAPSE AND HER TO DIE.
I'VE SURVIVED EVERY KIND OF PHYSICAL ATTACK POSSIBLE: GAMMA RAYS, LASER BEAMS, STEAL PIPES, AND BULLETS. THIS IS MUCH WORSE, MUCH MORE INSIDIOUS-- EATING AWAY AT MY REPUTATION.

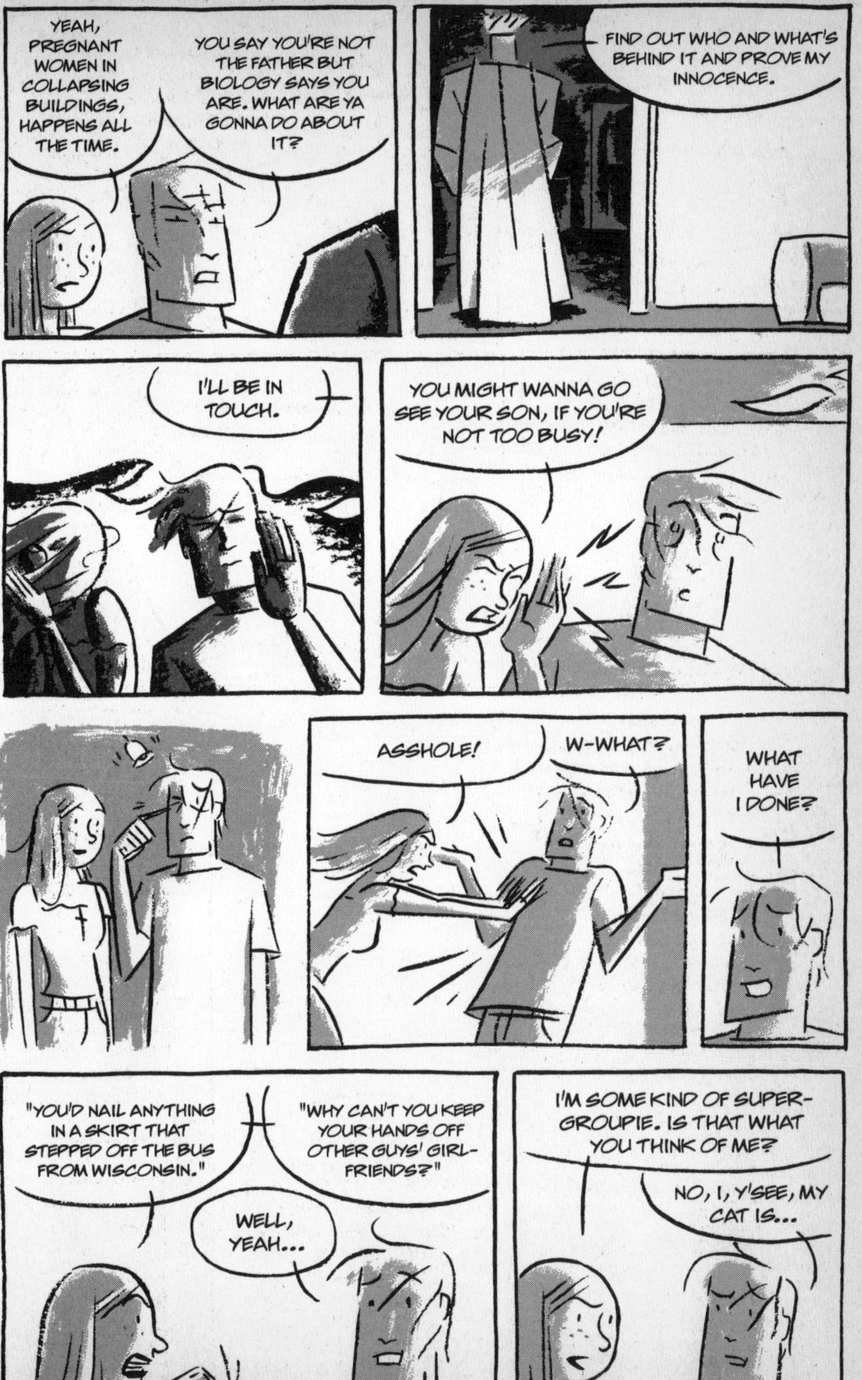
YEAH, PREGNANT WOMEN IN COLLAPSING BUILDINGS, HAPPENS ALL THE TIME.
YOU SAY YOU'RE NOT THE FATHER BUT BIOLOGY SAYS YOU ARE. WHAT ARE YA GONNA DO ABOUT IT?
FIND OUT WHO AND WHAT'S BEHIND IT AND PROVE MY INNOCENCE.
I'LL BE IN TOUCH.
YOU MIGHT WANNA GO SEE YOUR SON, IF YOU'RE NOT TOO BUSY!
ASSHOLE!
W-WHAT?
WHAT HAVE I DONE?
"YOU'D NAIL ANYTHING IN A SKIRT THAT STEPPED OFF THE BUS FROM WISCONSIN."
"WHY CAN'T YOU KEEP YOUR HANDS OFF OTHER GUYS' GIRLFRIENDS?"
WELL, YEAH...
I'M SOME KIND OF SUPER-GROUPIE. IS THAT WHAT YOU THINK OF ME?
NO, I, Y'SEE, MY CAT IS...

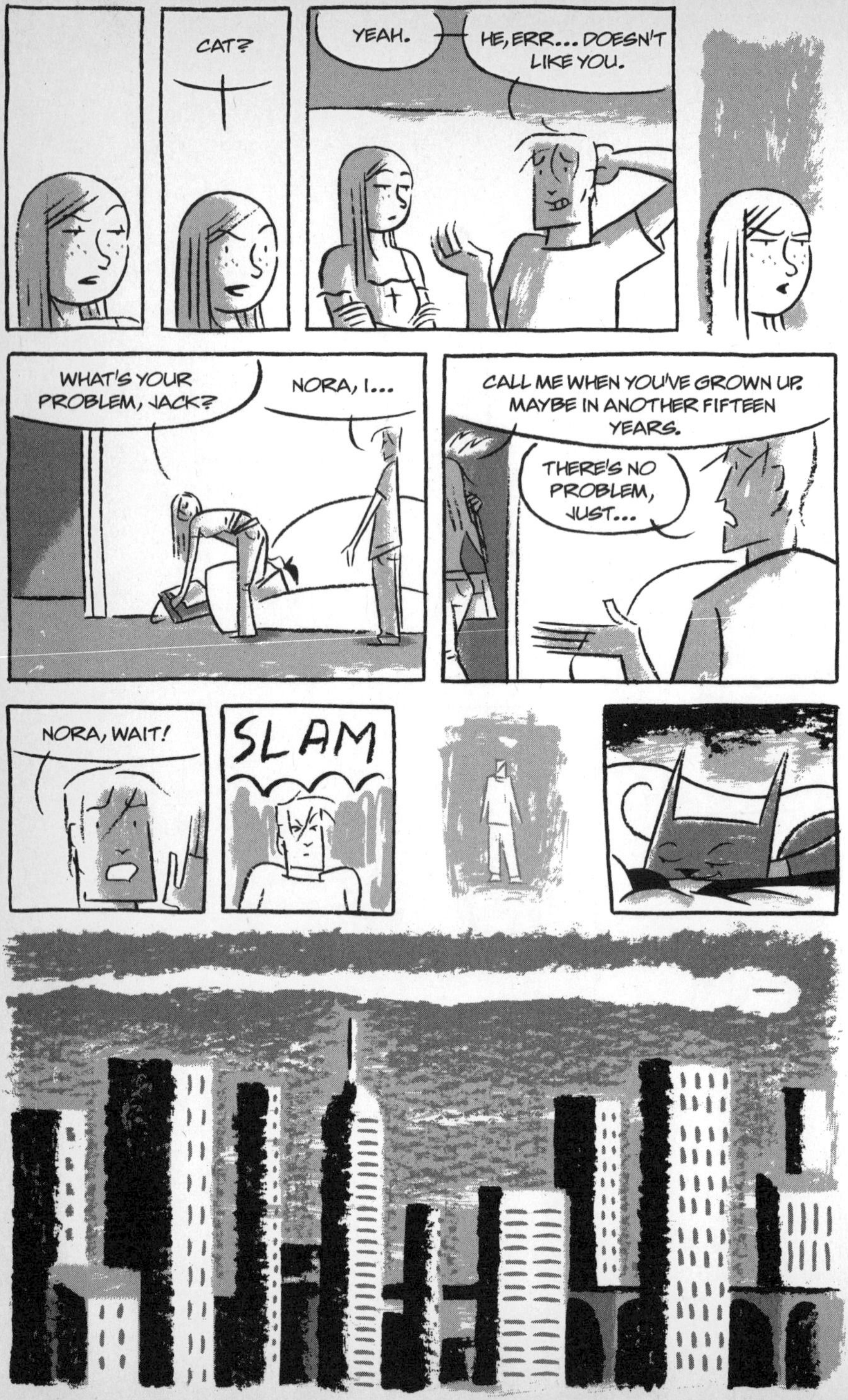
CAT?
YEAH.
HE, ERR... DOESN'T LIKE YOU.
WHAT'S YOUR PROBLEM, JACK?
NORA, I...
CALL ME WHEN YOU'VE GROWN UP. MAYBE IN ANOTHER FIFTEEN YEARS.
THERE'S NO PROBLEM, JUST...
NORA, WAIT!
SLAM

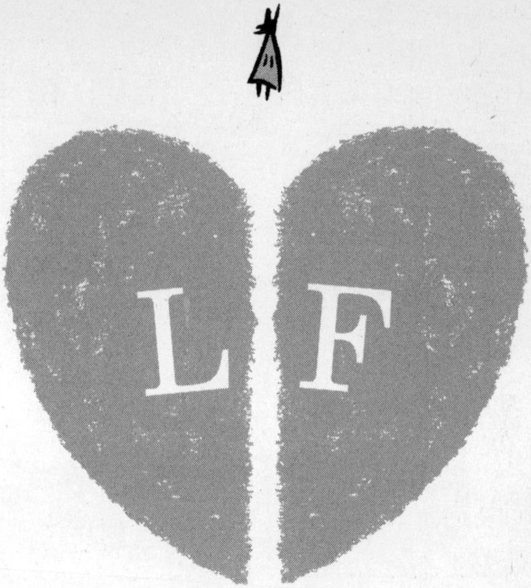
L F

FIGHTING LOVE IN TIGHTS
– An Afterword

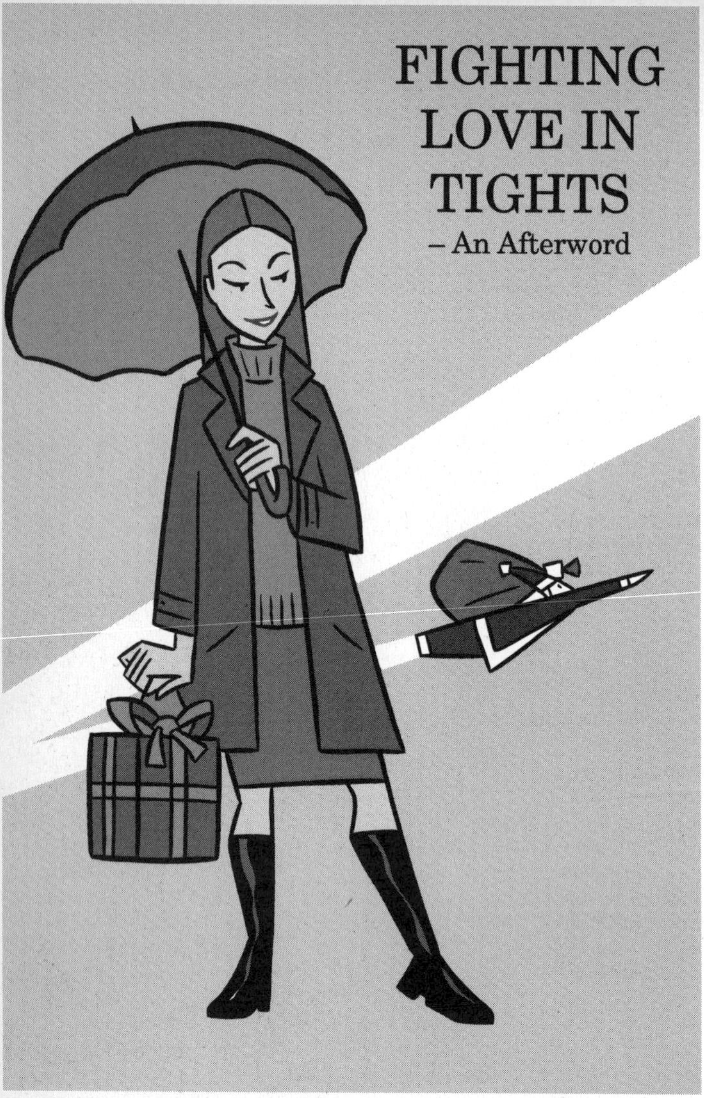

(The following exchange took place one Sunday afternoon via an internet chat.)

BCM: B. Clay Moore (writer and co-creator of *Hawaiian Dick*, *Clean Living*, and *Battle Hymn*, all for Image Comics)

JT: J. Torres (writer and co-creator of many fine Oni books, including The *Copybook Tales*, *Sidekicks*, *Days Like This*, and the forthcoming *Scandalous* and *Love as a Second Language*)

BCM: So. *Love in Tights* and Andi Watson.

JT: I think we should sue Andi. "Love Fights" sure sounds a lot like "Love in Tights."

BCM: And what was *Love in Tights*, J?

JT: You know, the book that made Watson's career. Published by Slave Labor Graphics.

BCM: Right, right. *Love in Tights* was a book you conceived back in the late nineties.

And that I did all the work on.

JT: This isn't about you, Clay.

BCM: Stop me if I'm wrong. *Love in Tights* was an attempt to let creators combine super-hero stories and romance stories, with an emphasis on "independent creators."

JT: Sounds about right. And before taking over the covers, Andi did a story that allowed him to play in the Marvel Universe even before he became Bill Jemas' bitch.

BCM: True. Sort of a fun take on the notion of the family of heroes, a la the Fantastic Four. And then he turned out some fantastic covers for the book.

JT: Yes, and in the process provided some of the best covers I've ever seen on a book that no one's ever seen.

BCM: True that. Andi's covers were hidden gems.

JT: My favorite was the one with a fall theme. I think we were on a kind of quarterly schedule so the seasons kinda fit.

BCM: I agree. I loved that one. For the historians in the audience, I'll mention that *Love in Tights* debuted in 1998 and was published sporadically for a couple of years after that. We managed six issues of heroic hormones and muscle-bound mashing

Jamie [S. Rich, this book's editor] wants us to talk about romance comics in general, too. Being the bigger geek of the two of us, would you like me to give some brief background?

JT: Who cares what Jamie wants? He's leaving

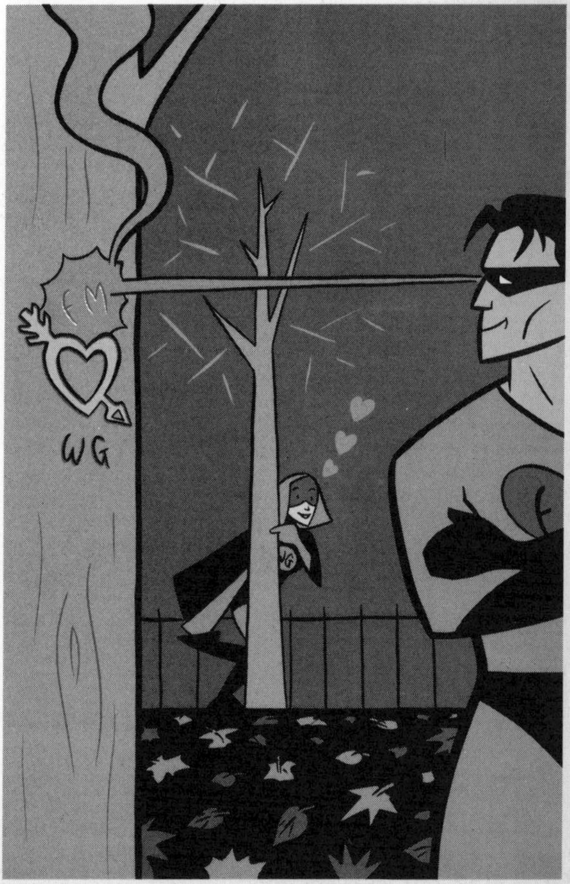
WG

the company. I wanna talk about how we made Andi Watson who he is today.

BCM: I was going to talk about how Joe Simon and Jack Kirby created the romance genre, which people may not know. And how romance comics had a strong foothold in the comics market for decades.

JT: People don't care, Clay. Romance comics don't sell these days. Unless you smoosh them with other elements, like superheroes, or the supernatural, or some cutesy Japanese element like a cherubic magical creature that grants candy wishes or a girl robot whose On-switch is in her no-no place.

BCM: Which explains where you were coming from when you came up with the idea. Of course, as we found out, even "smooshing," and using creators like Andi, romance comics don't sell.

JT: Which brings us back to my lawsuit. *Love in Tights* - the smooshing of romance comics and superheroes. *Love Fights* — the smooshing of romance comics and superheroes. I think I've got a case!

Love Fights is doing well and I want my cut.

BCM: I say we let him off the hook. Maybe we can ride his coattails somewhere.

JT: Fine. But if they ever produce *Love Fights* postcard sets featuring the covers, I wanna be comped.

Andi is such a great designer, which is what brings us here in the first place.

BCM: Yeah. I remember you suggesting we try to trick Andi into doing some covers, and I was amazed he agreed to do it. His sense of design puts him in a unique category. And it's been fascinating to watch his style evolve since then. The way he breaks things down to a more basic level, but still manages to lend a complex feel to his layout and design.

In the case of *Love in Tights*, he immediately

elevated the book with his presence.

JT: Definitely.

Mos def.

You know, someone should also do prints of his *Love in Tights* covers. And cut me in on the action.

But whatever happened to the winter cover?

BCM: Good question. We had a final issue planned, but I was having too much trouble collecting stories from people and finally threw in the towel. I'm pretty sure Andi did a cover for the book.

As it is, three of his covers were published.

JT: Hopefully, Jamie includes it in this book!

BCM: It'll be an exclusive never before seen bonus!

JT: How cool would that be!

BCM: As opposed to the other *LiT* covers, which will be exclusive barely seen bonuses.

JT: Well, whatever bonuses Watson gets from this baby, I want my cut...

BCM: I don't think you mentioned that yet.

JT: At least we can say we knew Andi way back when...

BCM: Let's back up and talk about *Love in Tights* a bit. Since *Love Fights* is being published by Oni, why don't you run through some of the Oni talent who contributed?

JT: No, let's shut up now and let people enjoy the covers and the collected issues, plus whatever Jamie used to pad the book...

BCM: Seriously, let's talk about the book. That's what Jamie asked for!

JT: I honestly don't remember where the idea of

Love in Tights came from. I think it was that I had a few short stories in that vein lying around, wanted them illustrated, and needed somewhere to put 'em. I couldn't fill a whole book so I brought in some friends!

BCM: And me. And how did you know Andi?

JT: Andi and I had met a couple of years earlier at APE [the Alternative Press Expo], I think. He of course got his start doing *Samurai Jam* and *Skeleton Key* at SLG, and my first published work was *The Copybook Tales* for the same company.

BCM: Yeah, I think Andi was doing some knock-out work on *Skeleton Key* around this time.

JT: It was very rainy that weekend so the turnout wasn't the greatest and all there was to do at the SLG booth was talk to Andi about hockey and Canada and what the hell words like "hoover," "spanner," and "lorry" meant.

BCM: I think, even though it didn't set any sales records, it's worth noting that people like Takeshi Miyazawa, J. Bone, Arthur Dela Cruz, Francis Manipul, and Kalman Andrasofszky did some of their earliest work in *Love in Tights*. Hell, even GI Joe Josh Blaylock did a story for the book. Takeshi's story (in *Love in Tights* #1) was actually a forerunner for *Sidekicks*, a series that you and he have since published through Oni.

JT: Are we done now?

BCM: I think so.

JT: Good. I have to go order - I mean, cook dinner now.

BCM: Tip well.

JT: Yes, I'll recommend that they read *Love Fights!*

BCM: bon apetit!

Issues of Love In Tights *are still available from Slave Labor Graphics. Visit them at www.slavelabor.com.*

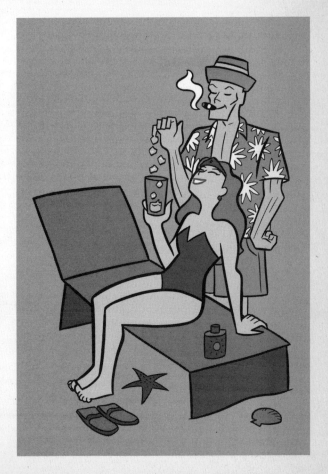

Other books from Andi Watson and Oni Press...

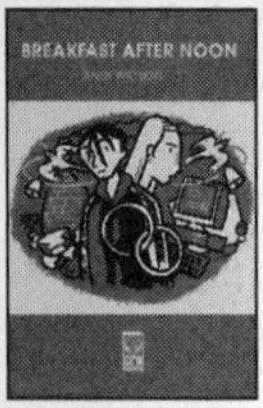
BREAKFAST AFTER NOON

BREAKFAST AFTER NOON™
208 pages,
black-and-white interiors
$19.95 US
ISBN: 1-929998-14-7

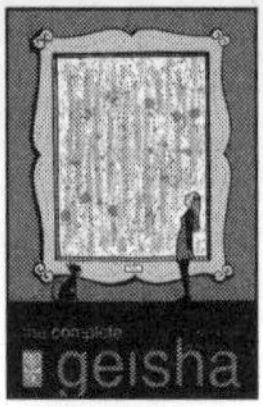
the complete
geisha

THE COMPLETE GEISHA™
152 pages,
black-and-white interiors
$15.95 US
ISBN: 1-929998-51-1

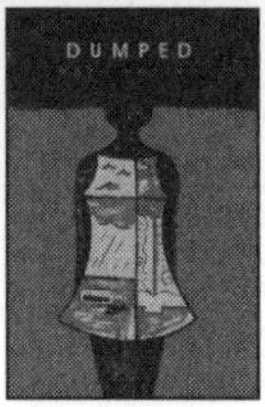
DUMPED

DUMPED™
56 pages,
black-and-white interiors
$5.95 US
ISBN: 1-929998-41-4

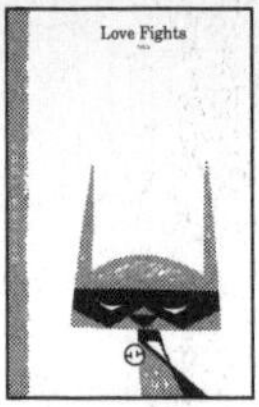
Love Fights

LOVE FIGHTS™ vol. 2
168 pages,
black-and-white interiors
$14.95 US
ISBN: 1-929998-87-2
Available December 2004!

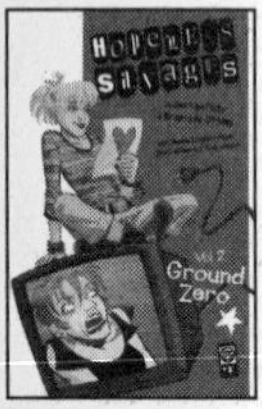
Ground
Zero

HOPELESS SAVAGES, vol. 2: GROUND ZERO™
By Jen Van Meter &
Bryan O'Malley
w/ Chynna Clugston-Major,
Christine Norrie, & Andi Watson
128 pages, black-and-white interiors
$11.95 US
ISBN: 1-929998-99-6

CUT MY HAIR™
by Jamie S. Rich
w/ Chynna Clugston-Major,
Scott Morse, Andi Watson, &
Judd Winick
236 pages, black-and-white text
with illustrations
$15.95 US
ISBN: 0-9700387-0-4

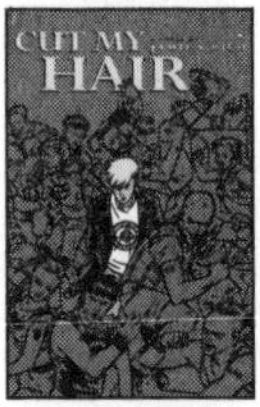
CUT MY
HAIR

For more information, visit www.onipress.com.

Also from Andi Watson...

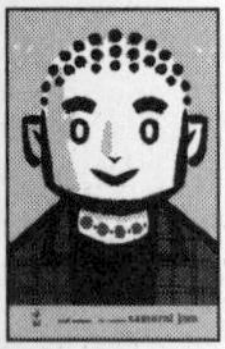

SAMURAI JAM™
144 pages, black-and-white
interiors
$14.95 US
ISBN: 0-943151-74-0

SLOW NEWS DAY™
160 pages, black-and-white
interiors
$16.95 US
ISBN: 0-943151-59-7

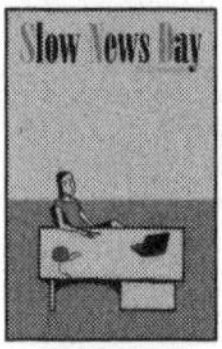

SKELETON KEY™

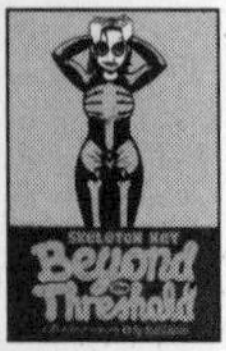
Beyond
Threshold

BEYOND THE THRESHOLD
96 pages, b/w interiors
$11.95 US
ISBN: 0-943151-12-0

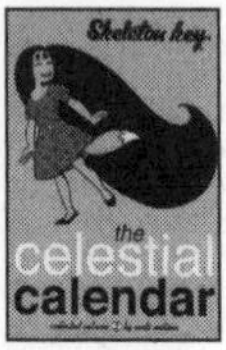
Skeleton key
the
celestial
calendar

THE CELESTIAL CALENDAR
168 pages, b/w interiors
$19.95 US
ISBN: 0-943151-15-5

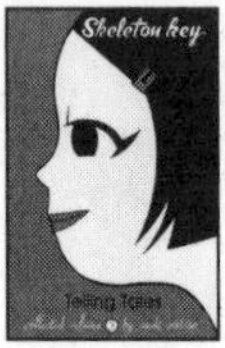
Skeleton key

TELLING TALES
104 pages,
b/w interiors
$12.95 US
ISBN: 0-943151-13-9

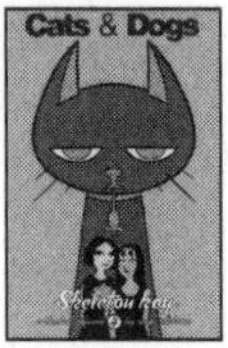
Cats & Dogs

CATS & DOGS
104 pages,
b/w interiors
$12.95 US
ISBN: 0-943151-19-8

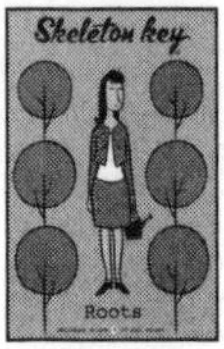
Skeleton key
Roots

ROOTS
112 pages,
b/w interiors
$12.95 US
ISBN: 0-943151-26-0

Slow News Day, *Samurai Jam* and all *Skeleton Key* books are available from Slave Labor Graphics.
For more information visit www.slavelabor.com or call 1-800-866-8929 for a free catalogue.

Andi Watson's graphic novels are available at finer comics shops everywhere.
For a comics store near you, call 1-888-COMIC-BOOK, or visit www.the-master-list.com.